ANCIENT CHRISTIANS

An Introduction for Latter-day Saints

EDITED BY

Jason R. Combs, Mark D. Ellison,
Catherine Gines Taylor, & Kristian S. Heal

Permissions. No portion of this book may be reproduced by any means or process without the formal written consent of the publisher. Direct all permissions requests to: MIpermissions@byu.edu

The views expressed in this book are solely those of the authors and do not necessarily represent those of the editors, The Neal A. Maxwell Institute for Religious Scholarship, Brigham Young University or any of its affiliates, or the Church of Jesus Christ of Latter-day Saints.

∞ The paper used in this publication meets the minimum requirements of the American National Standards for Information Sciences—Permanence of Paper for Printed Library Materials. ANSI Z39.48-19

ISBN: 978-0-8425-0092-0

Library of Congress Control Number: 2022942540
(CIP data on file)

Cover image of apse mosaic at the Church of Saint Pudenziana in Rome, courtesy of Alamy. Used with permission.

Cover design: Andrew Heiss
Book design: Andrew Heiss

Printed in the United States of America

http://maxwellinstitute.byu.edu

CONTENTS

✳ PREFACE ✳

Every contributor to this volume could tell a story of how each was led to the study of the New Testament and early Christianity through a series of spiritual promptings. They all felt called to the work. As the editors of this volume, we also heard the call, and in large part, this book is a natural outgrowth of our desire to respond to that call. In it we have gathered many of the treasures that we have found hidden in the fields of history or buried in arcane volumes on the library shelves. We have journeyed, as what Elder Dieter F. Uchtdorf has called "light gatherers," through the worlds of the earliest believers in Christ, trying to feel across centuries and millennia for their hand of fellowship. The chapters in this volume are filled with our encounters. Above all, and shining through the interstices of every chapter, is the glorious testimony of Jesus that we have found in the hearts, words, and images left behind by our earliest Christian sisters and brothers.

Images were as much a part of early Christian life as the words they wrote and read. Often the visual and material images demonstrate their convictions, their worship, and their beliefs beyond what is retained in text. The visual experience of devotion was deeply impactful for Christians; they lived in a world where what they saw was as concrete and effective as words on a page. This is especially true for ordinary Christians who may not have been able to read and write. In this book, we have thoughtfully curated images directly from the world of late ancient Christians. We have aligned the material world with the contributions of our authors so that, as a viewer, you too may gain deeper insights as the beauty of the art selected resonates with your own aesthetic sensibilities. Our desire is that you will generously enter this world of art with our kindred Christian saints and that it helps you more fully turn your hearts to our believing mothers and fathers.

The goal of this book is to give you a chance to meet, empathize with, and understand better our ancient Christian sisters and brothers, to feel their love for one another and for Jesus Christ. We hope you will finish each chapter with a deeper sense of appreciation for our ancient Christian ancestors, a clearer understanding of the ways in which the restored Church today is both similar to and different from the Church in antiquity, and, therefore, a clearer understanding of how The Church of Jesus Christ of Latter-day Saints relates to contemporary Christianity as a whole. Inasmuch as ancient Christians have expansive, even redemptive, vantage points to offer us, we hope you will also gain new insights and appreciation for our own beliefs and practices as members of the Church of Jesus Christ today.

—The Editors

ACKNOWLEDGMENTS

From the beginning, this project was an act of devotion. It was born of a longing to understand our ancient spiritual ancestors, those who devotedly followed Jesus Christ in the centuries after his mortal ministry. In turning our hearts to our spiritual fathers and mothers, each of us gained new insights into our own religious lives and a better understanding of our relationship with other Christians today. It is fitting, therefore, that we begin this volume by acknowledging our appreciation for those ancient Christians as well as for those today who have encouraged us and labored with us to bring this project to fruition.

First, we thank J. Spencer Fluhman, Director of the Neal A. Maxwell Institute for Religious Scholarship, for believing in this project and for his encouragement and support to make it a signature contribution of the Maxwell Institute in 2023. Maxwell Institute staff have provided support at various stages of this project, including Jeremy King, Anna Krzymowski, Camille Messick, Joseph Stuart, and others. Tessa Hauglid, at the Maxwell Institute, as well as Heather Randall and other editors at the BYU Faculty Publishing Service helped with copy-editing the manuscript. We appreciate their attention to detail and their efficiency. We owe a special debt of gratitude to the anonymous peer-viewers of our chapters, each a specialist in the topics we address, who took time away from their own research to carefully review and provide valuable feedback on our work.

We thank Andrew Heiss for his stunning design and careful attention to our text and images in producing this volume. A subvention grant from BYU's Religious Studies Center allowed us to publish this volume in color. We are grateful to them for believing in this project and helping our vision become a reality. Some early art and design work was completed by Maxwell Institute student employees, Ashley Pun Eveson and Holly Graff; and Reagan Graff assisted with image permissions and procurement. We express heartfelt thanks to all the image providers, who are identified in the figure captions throughout this book. We also appreciate BYU's ThinkSpatial, especially David Busath and Dr. Brandon Plewe, for producing some of our maps. Nicholas Shrum created the index for this volume, and we are indebted to him for his thorough and helpful work. A host of students at BYU contributed of their time and talents to assisting individual authors with research on their chapters as well as offering their insights as reviewers and interested readers of the manuscript. These include Lettie Burton, Alexandra Butterfield, Anne Dallon, Katharine Davidson, Abby Ellis, Allison Foster, Emma Franklin, Kaeli Glissmeyer Cook, Holly Graff, Reagan Graff, Allyson Huffmire, Miriam Johnson, Gerardo Andres Juarez, Brooke Leany, Sol Lee, Charlie Masino, and Annie Ogden. To all of those who had a hand in making this book what it is, we thank you.

Finally, and most importantly, we are profoundly grateful for the inspiration and insights we were blessed with as we read the words and admired the art and artifacts that ancient Christians left behind as an enduring testament to their faith in Jesus Christ.

This ancient Christian symbol combines three key elements. First, at the center is the Christogram, signifying Jesus Christ. It is comprised of the superimposed Greek letters X (chi) and P (rho), the first two letters of the word "Christ" in Greek. Second, to the left and right of the Christogram are the A (uppercase alpha) and ω (lowercase omega), the first and the last letters of the Greek alphabet—the Lord identifies himself as "the Alpha and the Omega" in Revelation 1:8 and 22:13. Third, the wreath that encircles these letters was a widespread symbol of honor and victory in ancient Greek and Roman cultures. Here, it represents Christ's victory for us; truly he has overcome the world (John 16:33).

* 1 *

INTRODUCTION

Understanding Ancient Christians, Apostasy, and Restoration

Jason R. Combs

The [Latter-day Saint] historical consciousness impels
one to step outside the comfortable confines of the
present, develop empathy to understand the past,
and in turn, lay the spiritual groundwork for future
generations.

—Press Release, Dedication of
the Church History Library[1]

I n 1997, I convinced a friend to join me on a road trip to the sacred sites of the Restoration. We arrived at Winter Quarters just after the Visitors' Center of The Church of Jesus Christ of Latter-day Saints had closed. The missionaries were leading a family to the adjacent Mormon Pioneer Cemetery, so we followed. We visited briefly with the missionaries and the family and silently reflected on the sacrifices of our pioneer ancestors. Then, as the family was leaving, one of the children—a young child of no more than seven or eight years—turned back to us. "Goodbye, brothers," she said. We commonly refer to each other as brothers and sisters in church, but never had that term struck me as it did in that moment, standing on that holy ground. Not one of the pioneers buried at that site is my biological ancestor. I am a convert to the Church. Yet every one of them is my spiritual ancestor, and I am indebted to them for their sacrifices and faith.

Since that time, I have encountered other spiritual ancestors. We (the editors and authors of this book) all have. In our studies, we have explored the world of ancient Christians who, like the pioneers, devoted their lives to serving our Lord and Savior Jesus Christ. In the centuries after Jesus's mortal ministry, these Christians wrote and worshiped, faced persecution and plagues, struggled with divisions and the threat of death, but remained devoted followers of Jesus Christ. The legacy they left for us in their stories, theological treatises, art, architecture, and traditions of worship form a foundation for Christianity today, including for The Church of Jesus Christ of Latter-day Saints. There are different ways we could tell this history. There are different ways we could introduce you to these ancient

Christians. To understand why we choose to tell their story in the way we do, it is necessary first to tell you something about past attempts to write about ancient Christian history.

Writing about Ancient Christians

The history of ancient Christianity is complex. Over the past two thousand years, Christian history has been told in different ways. For the sake of simplicity, I will categorize these different narratives as follows: (1) the triumph of Christianity, (2) the decline of Christianity, and (3) the varieties of Christianity.

The triumph of Christianity: Ancient Christian histories

The earliest histories of Christianity were tales of triumph. The Acts of the Apostles, found today in the New Testament, tells how Jesus's disciples inherit his mantle through the endowment of the Holy Spirit at Pentecost (see Acts 1:8; 2:1–4). Then they fulfilled Christ's prophetic proclamation from Acts 1:8 that the gospel should be preached "in Jerusalem, and in all Judaea, and in Samaria, and unto the uttermost part of the earth." The author crafts the narrative to emphasize a very systematic fulfillment of Jesus's words. In Acts, the gospel is literally preached first in Jerusalem and Judea (see Acts 2–7), then in Samaria (see Acts 8), and then to the uttermost part of the earth (see Acts 9–28).[2] Despite persecution and martyrdom, famine and shipwreck, the gospel message proceeds triumphant, and the Church continues to grow.

This triumphalist narrative continued to be told centuries later in the work of Eusebius of Caesarea (circa AD 324). Eusebius has been called the first great historian of Christianity. His written history covers Christianity's origins up to Eusebius's own time, the early fourth century. It narrates how the Church triumphed over heretics, apostates, and persecutors. In Eusebius's narrative, no unhallowed hand can stop the work of the Lord from progressing.[3] For instance, Eusebius narrates how one Christian was led astray by the misguided belief that Jesus was merely human and not divine.[4] That Christian became the bishop of a heretical sect but then experienced a dream in which he was chastised by an angel throughout the night. The next day he repented and returned to the true Church, recanting his misguided views.[5] Triumphalist narratives such as this are found in the writings of other ancient Christian historians who came after Eusebius.[6] For the next thousand years, historians and theologians told the story of Christianity in this way. They focused on the triumph of God through his Church in the history of the world.

The decline of Christianity:
A Renaissance and Reformation narrative

The 1400s gave rise to a new historical narrative. As European humanists revived classical styles of art and literature, they claimed that they were restoring civilization from a millennium of cultural darkness. They depicted people who lived in the medieval "Dark Ages" as barbaric and superstitious.[7] With such claims, they invented a new model of time that divided history into three distinct periods: (1) ancient/classical era, (2) Middle Ages/"Dark Ages," and (3) the Renaissance and modern periods. By the 1500s, Protestant Reformers adapted this periodization of history for their own critique of the Roman Catholic Church.[8] They argued that the Church itself had fallen into a period of darkness and needed restoration. For some, the original purity of the Church had endured until the time of the Roman Emperor Constantine (circa AD 300); for others, it lasted until just after the Christianization of England (circa AD 600–700).[9] But, the Reformers argued, eventually essential aspects of Christianity were lost.

In Eusebius's history, individual and small-group apostasies occurred when heretics promoted misguided views and attempted to draw people away from the Church, but God's true Church continued, unimpeded and triumphant. Now, the writers of this combined humanist and Reformation narrative cast the so-called Middle Ages as a dissident time, a period of apostasy, and upheld their own period as a time for the restoration of biblical teachings and practices.[10] Soon Catholics responded in kind, casting the Protestant Reformers as the origin of a great apostasy.[11] Eusebius's model of the triumphant history

▲ FIGURE 1.1   Eusebius of Caesarea, Rabbula Gospels, folio 2a, sixth century. Eusebius (ca. 260–339), the father of early Church history, is portrayed holding a scroll and making a blessing gesture toward the reader in the canon tables of the Syriac Rabbula Gospels. Photo: Alamy

of the Church was adapted to emphasize not only triumph over apostate people but also over apostate periods of time.

In the centuries that followed the Protestant and Catholic Reformations, religious defenders (apologists) turned to the Bible for evidence to support their new historical narratives. For instance, some turned to a passage in 2 Thessalonians to argue that a great fall or "apostasy" (Greek *apostasia*) within the Church was foreseen by the Apostle Paul: "Let no man deceive you by any means: for *that day shall not come*, except there come a falling away [Greek *apostasia*] first, and that man of sin be revealed, the son of perdition" (2 Thessalonians 2:3). A Presbyterian pastor named Albert Barnes, born in 1830, summarized the history of Catholic and Protestant interpretations of this passage as follows: "Of the Papists [Roman Catholics], a part affirm that the apostasy is the falling away from Rome in the time of the Reformation. . . . Most Protestant commentators have referred it to the great apostasy under the Papacy, and by the 'man of sin,' they suppose there is allusion to the Roman Pontiff, the Pope."[12] These narratives of a "great apostasy" were told and retold by Protestant and Catholic apologists throughout the nineteenth century and even, in some instances, to today.[13]

The varieties of Christianity: Theologians and historians today

The methods that scholars use today to study ancient Christianity took time to develop. Eighteenth- and nineteenth-century historians, sometimes intentionally but often unintentionally, perpetuated an apostasy narrative.[14] One common argument for the Church's decline was the idea that Greek and Roman culture crept into an originally pure Church and corrupted it. Some argued, for example, that Greek philosophy corrupted the Christian notion of God or that pagan religious practices replaced original biblical practices.[15] Historians today have come to realize that this narrative of philosophical and pagan corruption is far too simplistic to be an accurate representation of historical events.[16] The early Christian church was not *corrupted* by Greek and Roman culture. In fact, already by the time of Jesus, Jews had been

BOX 1.1   "Unto [Our] Understanding"

Latter-day Saints affirm that God speaks to people "according to their language, unto their understanding" (2 Nephi 31:3; see also Doctrine and Covenants 1:24). A Christian's use of philosophy or the similarity of Christian teaching to philosophy is, therefore, not sufficient to prove any particular teaching right or wrong. There is nothing inherently bad about ancient Greek philosophy.[17] In 1978, the First Presidency stated: "Philosophers including Socrates, Plato, and others, received a portion of God's light. Moral truths were given to them by God to enlighten whole nations and to bring a higher level of understanding to individuals."[18] Christian teachings should be studied on their own terms and not immediately dismissed when they appear similar to something non-Christian. Latter-day Saints would not want our sacred temple ordinances dismissed because they bear some similarity to Masonic rites.[19]

engaging with Greek thought and culture for hundreds of years—longer than the United States of America has existed as a country! To suggest that the authors of the New Testament texts were uninfluenced by Greek and Roman thought because they were Jewish would be similar to suggesting that modern-day authors such as N. Scott Momaday or Sherman Alexie are not influenced by Western European and US culture because they are Native Americans. Influence and engagement are not corruption, and Greco-Roman culture was part of Christianity from the beginning (see box 1.1).[20]

Historians today recognize that the synthesized humanist/Reformation narrative of a dark age of apostasy, born in the fifteenth and sixteenth centuries, is not supported by historical evidence. Time cannot be easily divided into distinct chronological epochs, and we cannot pretend that the events of one period contributed nothing to the next.

▲ **FIGURE 1.2** Portraits of a woman, "Dionysas, [may you rest] in peace," and a man named Nemesius, wall painting from the Catacomb (underground cemetery) of Callistus, Rome, late third century. Some of the earliest portraits of early Christian mothers and fathers are pictured in Roman catacombs. The damage we see to the plaster on the walls happened later as visitors wanted to collect bones of early believers as relics. We see this faithful woman and man with their arms lifted in the posture of prayer (see chapter 6 for more detail). Photo: Josef Wilpert, *Die Malereien der Katakomben Roms* (Freiburg: Herder, 1903), Taf. 111 (public domain)

For instance, the humanist/Reformation apostasy narrative ignores Christian teachings, art, and practices that arose in the medieval period and remain influential on Christianity today—including on Latter-day Saints.[21] Similarly, the narrative of widespread apostasy ignores evidence that good Christians continually served each other and worshiped God throughout the history of Christianity (see chapter 14 in this volume).

Today, scholars approach the study of ancient Christians in a more positive way. Rather than dismissing entire epochs as corrupt or identifying which forms of ancient Christianity are most true, today we work to understand ancient Christians on their own terms. Some scholars describe this study as "Patristics" (from the Latin *patres*, or "fathers") because it focuses on the writings of the so-called Church Fathers—influential ancient Christian writers, especially from the second through sixth centuries AD. Traditionally, Patristics scholars have studied the Church Fathers to understand what ancient Christians believed; they have also engaged with the Church Fathers to help them think about what contemporary Christians believe and how they should worship. Other scholars today prefer to describe their discipline as "early Christian studies," in part to suggest the importance of sources beyond the Church Fathers. These scholars also devote time to Church Mothers, to art and other material culture, and to forms of Christianity that have been displaced or forgotten. Unlike traditional Patristics, most scholars of early Christian studies tend not to approach ancient Christians from a confessional perspective (whatever their own personal religious commitments may be); rather they focus on situating early Christians in their ancient social and cultural contexts.[22] These modern approaches allow for greater collaboration between Christians of varying denominations—and with those who are not Christian—in exploring our shared history.

Latter-day Saint Narratives of Ancient Christianity

Early Latter-day Saints inherited from Protestants a great apostasy narrative.[23] Some even repeated the early Protestant claim that the pope of the Roman Catholic Church was the "man of sin" from 2 Thessalonians.[24] In the second half of the twentieth century, however, General Authorities of The Church of Jesus Christ of Latter-day Saints have made it clear that our scriptures do not support an anti-Catholic interpretation. For instance, Elder Bruce R. McConkie, beginning in the second edition of *Mormon Doctrine*, wrote: "[The] titles 'Church of the Devil' and 'Great and Abominable Church' are used to identify all churches or organizations of whatever name or nature—whether political, philosophical, educational, economic, social, fraternal, civic, or religious—which are designed to take men on a course that leads away from God."[25] Elder Dallin H. Oaks further clarified that the "church of the devil" (1 Nephi 14:10) is not "a single 'church,' as we understand that term today"; rather, "it must be any philosophy or organization that opposes belief in God."[26] In support of these more recent statements, we acknowledge the need for greater care in discussing a *great apostasy*—a term that does not appear in our standard works.

We unitedly affirm the need for the Restoration, and at the same time, we must be clear in stating precisely what that means. For instance, the Doctrine and Covenants never speaks explicitly of a *restored church*, a fact confirmed by Patrick Mason in his book, *Restoration: God's Call to the 21st-Century World*.[27] When Latter-day Saints use that unscriptural phrase, *restored church*, it should be understood as shorthand for the *restorations* the Doctrine and Covenants does address—namely, the bestowal of priesthood power, authority, and keys associated with making sacred covenants, establishing Zion (Moses 7:18), gathering scattered Israel on both sides of the veil (that is, in this life and beyond), and binding up all dispensations in preparation for the Second Coming of Jesus Christ.[28] These special purposes to which God has called us and for which God has established The Church of Jesus Christ of Latter-day Saints do not require us to spend our time trying to prove other churches and religions wrong or apostate. Likewise, the blessings of restored and new scripture—including the Bible, the Book of Mormon, the Doctrine and Covenants, and the Pearl of Great Price, as well as the revelations and words of modern prophets and apostles—do not require us to dismiss the inspired insights of ancient Christians or even other modern Christians.

Too often, rather than rejoicing in the blessings and purposes of the Restoration, we members of the Church rejoice that we are not like others (see Luke 18:11; Alma 31:28). We might imagine a scenario in which other churches are lacking God's guidance—part of a great apostasy—and The Church of Jesus Christ of Latter-day Saints is a mere replacement of what was lost. Latter-day Saints could imagine such a scenario when we read what God told Joseph Smith in the Sacred Grove, namely, "All their creeds were an abomination . . . [and] those professors were all corrupt" (Joseph Smith—History 1:19), or when we read a quotation by Joseph Smith such as "I believe the Bible as it read when it came from the pen of the original writers. Ignorant translators, careless transcribers, or designing and corrupt priests have committed many errors."[29] Yet neither of these statements implies mass corruption in the ancient Church or a complete loss of everything that was good. For instance, Joseph mentioned "designing and corrupt priests" as one out of three possible explanations for "errors" or changes in the biblical texts.[30] And the statement from Joseph Smith—History regarding those corrupt "professors" of creeds could be understood in a very limited way as "referring to those ministers . . . with which Joseph Smith was involved," as Professor Robert Millet and Elder William Grant Bangerter of the Seventy have explained.[31] Moreover, the Lord could also say very positive things about ministers from other Christian churches (see Doctrine and Covenants 35:3–4; 39:7–8), and the Lord could speak of his "church" already existing at the time that The Church of Jesus Christ of Latter-day Saints was being established (see Doctrine and Covenants 5:14; 10:52–56, 67–69). Rather than imagine ancient (and modern) Christians as duplicitous in their efforts to write about, understand, and practice their faith, it is more accurate to view them as earnest, believing Christians—our ancient spiritual ancestors and modern brothers and sisters (see box 1.2).[32]

When we imagine The Church of Jesus Christ of Latter-day Saints as merely a reinstitution of something that already existed two

BOX 1.2 "Only True . . . Church"

Some Latter-day Saints might assume that Doctrine and Covenants 1:30 "the only true and living church upon the face of the whole earth, with which I, the Lord, am well pleased"—means that God does not care for or inspire any other Christian churches. Yet, when Joseph Smith wrote to Emma that he was her "one true and living friend on Earth," we do not assume that Emma had no other friends.[33] Elder Ezra Taft Benson taught, "God, the Father of us all, uses the [people] of the earth, especially good [people], to accomplish his purposes. It has been true in the past, it is true today, it will be true in the future. 'Perhaps the Lord needs such [people] on the outside of His Church to help it along,' said the late Elder Orson F. Whitney of the Quorum of the Twelve. . . . 'God is using more than one people for the accomplishment of His great and marvelous work. The Latter-day Saints cannot do it all. It is too vast, too arduous for any one people'"[34] (see also Alma 29:8).

thousand years ago, we unnecessarily limit the power, scope, and purposes of God's work for us in this final dispensation. The Doctrine and Covenants is clear: The Church of Jesus Christ of Latter-day Saints is not merely version 2.0 of the Church established in the days of Jesus Christ's ancient apostles. It was not sufficient for John the Baptist alone (see Doctrine and Covenants 27:8), or even Peter, James, and John (see Doctrine and Covenants 27:12), to grant priesthood power and authority to Joseph Smith. Prophets and powerful figures from all dispensations past appeared to Joseph to teach him or to grant him keys and authority.[35] Adam and Abraham (see Doctrine and Covenants 137:5), Moses, Elijah, and an Elias (see Doctrine and Covenants 110:11–16), Moroni (see Doctrine and Covenants 128:20), and others (see Doctrine and Covenants 128:21) also came to Joseph Smith in order to bestow blessings, keys, and authority for this great

▲ **FIGURE 1.3** Mosaic of the Transfiguration depicting Christ, Elijah, Moses, Peter, James, and John, St. Catherine's Monastery, Sinai, sixth century. Against an otherworldly gold background, this mosaic depicts the moment when the disciples fall to the ground and are overcome with the rays of light emanating from the countenance of the transfigured Christ. Attendant figures of Elijah and Moses are pictured to the left and right of Christ, respectively (see Mark 9:2–8; Matthew 17:1–8). Photo: Wikimedia Commons

work. And yet, even that was not sufficient. God the Father and Jesus Christ appeared to the Prophet (see Joseph Smith—History 1:17; Doctrine and Covenants 76:22–24; 110:1–10). The purpose of The Church of Jesus Christ of Latter-day Saints goes beyond the work of dispensations past. For that reason, it necessarily includes "those things which *never have been revealed* from the foundation of the world but . . . shall be revealed . . . in this, the dispensation of the fulness of times" (Doctrine and Covenants 128:18; emphasis added).

A New Latter-day Saint Approach to Ancient Christians

What does this careful reading of our Latter-day Saint teachings regarding the Restoration mean for this volume about ancient Christians? First, it means that we cannot assume that something found in The Church of Jesus Christ of Latter-day Saints today necessarily existed in the ancient Church (see Doctrine and Covenants 124:38, 41). We cannot assume that today's Church is a template for what the first-century Church must have been, or vice versa. For that reason, in this book, our authors acknowledge the differences between ancient Christians and Latter-day Saints without automatically assuming such differences to be evidence of apostasy. When our authors encounter these differences, they work to explain how and why ancient Christians developed beliefs and practices that contrast with our own—working toward understanding them from a position of respect and even "holy envy."[36]

Second, we believe that the truth regarding the power and purposes of The Church of Jesus Christ of Latter-day Saints is not dependent

▶ **FIGURES 1.4 & 1.5** Mosaics of processions of female and male saints, Sant'Apollinare Nuovo, Ravenna, Italy, sixth century. The processional figures on opposite sides of the nave wall depict both female and male saints, mothers and fathers of the Church. They are each haloed and carry a crown representing their martyrdom or eternal reward as they progress toward images of Christ and Mary, the mother of God. The Byzantine-style gold background shows us that they occupy a heavenly space; they are enjoying the fruits of their faithfulness in a paradisiacal setting. Photos: Courtesy of José Luis via Wikimedia Commons

CA VINCENTIA † SCA · VALERIA † SCA CRISPINA † SCA LVCI

The Gathering of Truths

President Brigham Young stated, "It is our duty and calling, as ministers of the same salvation and Gospel, to gather every item of truth and reject every error. Whether a truth be found with professed infidels, or with the Universalists, or the Church of Rome, or the Methodists, the Church of England, the Presbyterians, the Baptists, the Quakers, the Shakers, or any other of the various and numerous different sects and parties, all of whom have more or less truth, it is the business of the Elders of this Church (Jesus, their Elder Brother, being at their head) to gather up all the truths in the world pertaining to life and salvation, to the Gospel we preach . . . wherever it may be found in every nation, kindred, tongue, and people and bring it to Zion."[37]

on proving that other Christian churches are deficient, not guided by God, or worse. In fact, the message of The Church of Jesus Christ of Latter-day Saints regarding other Christian churches is quite the opposite. Joseph Smith warned that "the character of the old churches have [*sic*] always been slandered by all apostates since the world began."[38] In response to similar slander, the Prophet insisted: "The old Catholic church traditions are worth more than all you have said."[39] According to President Brigham Young, Latter-day Saints should be learning and gathering truths about "the Gospel we preach" from other churches (see box 1.3). Certainly, this practice should also include gathering truths from ancient Christians.

This book, therefore, is an act of devotion. This book is a new Latter-day Saint approach to ancient Christianity.[40] It is an act of turning our hearts to our spiritual fathers and mothers (see Malachi 4:5–6; Joseph Smith—History 1:38–39; Doctrine and Covenants 2:1–3; 27:9; 110:13–16; 128:17) so that we can learn to love and appreciate them. And by understanding ancient Christians better, we can simultaneously understand better our fellow Christians today, who do not share all our beliefs and practices. Additionally, we can gain insights from the words, art, and practices of ancient Christians that will deepen our own devotion as Latter-day Saints. We, as authors of this volume, hope that each chapter will bless you with greater Christ-like love for other Christians and for the work of God throughout time. Welcome to the world of ancient Christians!

Notes

1. "'A Record Kept': Constructing Collective Memory," Newsroom, The Church of Jesus Christ of Latter-day Saints, June 11, 2009, https://newsroom.churchofjesuschrist.org/article/a-record-kept-constructing-collective-memory; cited in Miranda Wilcox, "Narrating Religious Heritage: Apostasy and Restoration," *BYU Studies Quarterly* 60, no. 3 (2021): 213–28; see 215.

2. In order for the author of Acts to make his message clear, he occasionally avoids or omits details that his Christian readers would have been interested to know. For instance, Luke and Acts say nothing about the disciples meeting Jesus on a mountain in Galilee after his Resurrection (see Matthew 28). A trip to Galilee (outside of Judea) would have interrupted the flow of the narrative in Luke-Acts: Jerusalem and Judea, then Samaria, and then the ends of the earth. And what happens with Simon Peter after Acts 15? He disappears entirely from the narrative. The author does this to emphasize his point about Christianity's triumph: Paul is the Apostle to the Gentiles (Galatians 2:9), so the gospel is borne by Paul to the ends of the earth (Acts 16–28). For more on how the narrative of Acts fulfills Jesus's words in Acts 1:8 and presents the Church of God as triumphant, see C. Kavin Rowe, *World Upside Down: Reading Acts in the Graeco-Roman Age* (New York: Oxford University Press, 2009).

3. For a general introduction to Eusebius's history intended for nonspecialists, see Bart D. Ehrman, *Lost Christianities: The Battles for Scripture and the*

Faiths We Never Knew (New York: Oxford University Press, 2003), 164–79. For a recent academic study, see Michael J. Hollerich, *Making Christian History: Eusebius of Caesarea and His Readers*, vol. 11 of the Christianity in Late Antiquity Series (Oakland: University of California Press, 2021), 32–40.

4. For more on the nature of Christ, see chapter 8.

5. See Eusebius, *Ecclesiastical History* 5.28.1–12.

6. For instance, the ecclesiastical histories of Socrates of Constantinople, Sozomen, and Theodoret of Cyrrhus (fifth century), as well as Evagrius Scholasticus (sixth century). See Glenn F. Chesnut, *The First Christian Histories: Eusebius, Socrates, Sozomen, Theodoret, and Evagrius* (Macon, GA: Mercer University Press, 1986), 175–230; Hollerich, *Making Christian History*, 59–87.

7. See Carter Lindberg, *The European Reformations* (Malden, MA: Wiley-Blackwell, 2010), 5–6; Hollerich, *Making Christian History*, 197–202.

8. Protestants elided the tripartite historical periodization of classical antiquity, Middle Ages, and Renaissance with the ecclesial paradigm of a great apostasy. Lindberg, *European Reformations*, 1–22; Ernst Breisach, *Historiography: Ancient, Medieval, and Modern* (Chicago: University of Chicago, 2007), 166–170; Hollerich, *Making Christian History*, 197–202; Euan Cameron, "Primitivism, Patristics, and Polemic in Protestant Visions of Early Christianity," in *Sacred History: Uses of the Christian Past in the Renaissance World*, ed. Katherine van Liere, Simon Ditchfield, and Howard Louthan (Oxford: Oxford University Press, 2012), 27–51.

9. See Lindberg, *European Reformations*, 6; Breisach, *Historiography*, 168. For early Latter-day Saints who argued that priesthood authority continued on the earth into the fifth century, see Christopher C. Jones and Stephen J. Fleming, "'Except among that Portion of Mankind': Early Mormon Conceptions of the Apostasy," in *Standing Apart: Mormon Historical Consciousness and the Concept of Apostasy*, ed. Miranda Wilcox and John D. Young (New York: Oxford University Press, 2014), 60–61.

10. For the Lutheran author of the so-called Magdeburg Centuries, the fall of the Church was due to the expansion of the power of the papacy; see Lindberg, *European Reformations*, 6–7; Breisach, *Historiography*, 167; Hollerich, *Making Christian History*, 206–10.

11. See Lindberg, *European Reformations*, 14–15; Hollerich, *Making Christian History*, 211–17; Giuseppe Antonio Guazzelli, "Cesare Baronio and the Roman Catholic Vision of the Early Church," in *Sacred History: Uses of the Christian Past in the Renaissance World*, ed. Katherine van Liere, Simon Ditchfield, and Howard Louthan (Oxford: Oxford University Press, 2012),

52–71.

12. Albert Barnes, *Notes, Explanatory and Practical on the Epistles of Paul to the Thessalonians, to Timothy, to Titus, and to Philemon* (New York: Harper & Brothers, 1849), 91.

13. See William M. Shea, *The Lion and the Lamb: Evangelicals and Catholics in America* (Oxford: Oxford University Press, 2004); see also Mark A. Noll and Carolyn Nystrom, *Is the Reformation Over? An Evangelical Assessment of Contemporary Roman Catholicism* (Grand Rapids, MI: Baker Academic; Bletchley, UK: Paternoster, 2005).

14. For a summary of the development of Patristics and early Christian studies as academic disciplines, including the influence of anti-Catholicism in their development, see Elizabeth A. Clark, "From Patristics to Early Christian Studies," in *The Oxford Handbook of Early Christian Studies*, ed. Susan Ashbrook Harvey and David G. Hunter (Oxford: Oxford University Press, 2008), 7–41. For a more detailed discussion, see Elizabeth A. Clark, *Founding the Fathers: Early Church History and Protestant Professors in Nineteenth-Century America* (Philadelphia: University of Pennsylvania Press, 2011). For a specific example of how anti-Catholicism influenced one prominent scholar's understanding of the influence of Hellenism in Christianity, see William V. Rowe, "Adolf von Harnack and the Concept of Hellenization," in *Hellenization Revisited: Shaping a Christian Response within the Greco-Roman World*, ed. Wendy E. Helleman (Lanham, MD: University Press of America, 1994), 69–98.

15. For instance, see Edwin Hatch, *The Influence of Greek Ideas and Usage upon the Christian Church*, ed. A. M. Fairbairn (London: Williams & Norgate, 1890); reprinted as *The Influence of Greek Ideas on Christianity* (Gloucester, MA: Peter Smith, 1970). See the early response to Hatch's work in William Sanday, "Greek Influence on Christianity," *The Contemporary Review* 59 (1891): 678–90; republished in William Sanday, *Essays on Biblical Criticism and Exegesis*, ed. Craig A. Evans and Stanley E. Porter, Journal for the Study of the New Testament Supplement Series 225 (Sheffield: Sheffield Academic Press, 2001), 108–22. Some Latter-day Saint scholars uncritically adopted these early academic ideas that Greco-Roman culture corrupted an original, culturally pure Christianity. For instance, see Richard R. Hopkins, *How Greek Philosophy Corrupted the Christian Concept of God*, 2nd ed. (1988; repr., Springville, UT: Horizon Publishers, 2009). Stephen E. Robinson, in his otherwise excellent analysis of 1 Nephi 13–14, offered a concluding opinion that the great and abominable church from Nephi's vision must be "Hellenized Christianity"; see Robinson, "Early Christianity and 1 Nephi 13–14," in *First Nephi, The Doctrinal Foundation*, ed. Monte

S. Nyman and Charles D. Tate Jr. (Provo, UT: Religious Studies Center, Brigham Young University, 1988), 177–91. See also the more nuanced view in Noel B. Reynolds, "What Went Wrong for the Early Christians?," in *Early Christians in Disarray: Contemporary LDS Perspectives on the Christian Apostasy*, ed. Noel B. Reynolds (Provo, UT: BYU Press, 2005), 14.

16. For a description of this new approach to early Christians' use of philosophy, see Mark Edwards, "Introduction," in *The Routledge Handbook of Early Christian Philosophy*, ed. Mark Edwards (New York, NY: Routledge, 2021), 1–12; for a description of this new approach to early Christian art, see Robin Margaret Jensen, *Understanding Early Christian Art* (New York: Routledge, 2000); for the development of ritual in early Christianity, see Andrew Mc-Gowan, *Ancient Christian Worship: Early Church Practices in Social, Historical, and Theological Perspective* (Grand Rapids, MI: Baker, 2016).

17. In Colossians 2:8 we read, "Beware lest any man spoil you through philosophy and vain deceit." This passage is not a critique of philosophy in general. If the word philosophy were replaced with religion, one would not assume that it was a critique of all religion. Rather it would be a critique of anyone who would use religion to lead someone away captive—to "spoil," or better, "despoil" them. Of note, Judaism and Christianity were both understood to be philosophies in the ancient world; see Josephus, *Antiquities* 18.1.2–6; Justin Martyr, *Dialogue with Trypho* 8.

18. "Statement of the First Presidency Regarding God's Love for All Mankind," quoted in Wilcox and Young, *Standing Apart*, 343.

19. See Church History Topics, s.v. "Masonry," accessed September 20, 2021, https://www.churchofjesuschrist.org/study/history/topics/masonry; Steven C. Harper, "Freemasonry and the Latter-day Saint Temple Endowment Ceremony," in *A Reason for Faith: Navigating LDS Doctrine and Church History*, ed. Laura Harris Hales (Provo, UT: Religious Studies Center, Brigham Young University, 2016), 143–57.

20. Greco-Roman influence can readily be seen in the first-century Christian texts now found in the New Testament; see, for instance, David E. Aune, *The New Testament in Its Literary Environment*, Library of Early Christianity Series (Philadelphia: Westminster, 1987); Troels Engberg-Pedersen, *Paul and the Stoics* (Louisville, KY: Westminster John Knox Press, 2000); Robyn Faith Walsh, *The Origins of Early Christian Literature: Contextualizing the New Testament Within Greco-Roman Literary Culture* (Cambridge: Cambridge University Press, 2021).

21. For instance, the teachings of Anselm of Canterbury (eleventh century) and Thomas Aquinas (thirteenth century) regarding the Atonement of Jesus Christ (satisfaction theory) paved the way for the penal substitution

theory that remains influential on Latter-day Saints today—even though Latter-day Saints derive our understanding of the Atonement of Jesus Christ primarily from the Book of Mormon and the Doctrine and Covenants. See Terry L. Givens, *Wrestling the Angel: The Foundations of Mormon Thought: Cosmos, God, Humanity* (Oxford: Oxford University Press, 2015), 220–240; Charles R. Harrell, *"This Is My Doctrine": The Development of Mormon Theology* (Sandy, UT: Greg Kofford Books, 2011), 282–286. For more on ancient understandings of the Atonement of Jesus Christ, see chapter 9 in this volume.

22. See Clark, "From Patristics to Early Christian Studies," 7–41.

23. The history of Latter-day Saint conceptions of a great apostasy is complex. For a summary of Latter-day Saint writings about other forms of Christianity past and present, see Wilcox, "Narrating Religious Heritage," 213–228. For a more detailed analysis, see the collection of articles in Wilcox and Young, *Standing Apart.*

24. See the prior section titled, "The decline of Christianity: A Renaissance and Reformation narrative."

25. Bruce R. McConkie, *Mormon Doctrine* (Salt Lake City, UT: Bookcraft, 1966), 137–38. The original edition of *Mormon Doctrine* (1958) identified the Roman Catholic Church as the church of the devil.

26. Elder Dallin H. Oaks, "Witnesses of God," address delivered at Brigham Young University–Idaho on February 25, 2014, https://www.byui.edu/devotionals/elder-dallin-h-oaks.

27. See Patrick Q. Mason, *Restoration: God's Call to the 21st-Century World* (Meridian, ID: Faith Matters, 2020), 11–37.

28. See Doctrine and Covenants 27:6; 45:17; 77:15; 84:2; 86:10; 103:13, 29; 128:17. For more on Joseph Smith's understanding of *restoration*, see Philip L. Barlow, "To Mend a Fractured Reality: Joseph Smith's Project," *Journal of Mormon History* 38, no. 3 (2012): 28–50.

29. *Documentary History of the Church* 6:57; "History, 1838–1856, volume E-1 [1 July 1843–30 April 1844]," p. 1755, The Joseph Smith Papers, accessed September 20, 2021, https://www.josephsmithpapers.org/paper-summary/history-1838-1856-volume-e-1-1-july-1843-30-april-1844/127.

30. The Book of Mormon affirms, despite changes that occurred within the text of the Bible (1 Nephi 13:28), that the Bible remains the word of God and is true (1 Nephi 13:39–41). The Book of Mormon itself functions to confirm the truthfulness of the Bible (see 2 Nephi 29). In an important recent study on the Book of Mormon's representation of apostasy in early Christianity, Nicholas J. Frederick and Joseph M. Spencer argued that 1

Nephi 11–14 depicts supersessionism and the rejection of God's original covenant people, the Jews, as the primary problem; see Nicholas J. Frederick and Joseph M. Spencer, "Remnant or Replacement? Outlining a Possible Apostasy Narrative," *BYU Studies Quarterly* 60, no. 1 (2021): 105–27. For an introduction to the history of changes in the text of the New Testament intended for a nonspecialist reader, see Bart D. Ehrman, *Misquoting Jesus: The Story Behind Who Changed the Bible and Why* (New York, NY: HarperOne, 2005); for an academic introduction to the history and discipline of New Testament textual criticism, see Bruce M. Metzger and Bart D. Ehrman, *The Text of the New Testament: Its Transmission, Corruption, and Restoration*, 4th ed. (New York: Oxford University Press, 2005); D. C. Parker, *An Introduction to the New Testament Manuscripts and Their Texts* (Cambridge: Cambridge University Press, 2008).

31.   Robert Millet, professor emeritus of ancient scripture at Brigham Young University, quoted Elder William Grant Bangerter, a member of the Seventy from 1976–1989; Robert Millet, "It's a Two-Way Street," address delivered on August 4, 1985, in *1984–85 BYU Speeches of the Year* (Provo, UT: Brigham Young University Publications, 1985), 161. See Robert L. Millet, "Joseph Smith and 'The Only True and Living Church,'" in *A Witness for the Restoration: Essays in Honor of Robert J. Matthews*, ed. Kent P. Jackson and Andrew C. Skinner (Provo, UT: Religious Studies Center, Brigham Young University, 2007), 201–31.

32.   While it is possible that there were some Christians who were corrupt or who wrote with ulterior motives, the idea of mass corruption and a unified effort, intentional or unintentional, to reshape the earliest teachings of Christianity into something foreign and false is not supported by the extant ancient records—heresiological discourse notwithstanding.

33.   See Philip Barlow, "The Only True and Living Church?," Faith Matters, April 12, 2020, https://faithmatters.org/the-only-true-and-living-church/; citing "Letter to Emma Smith, 13 October 1832," p. [2], The Joseph Smith Papers, accessed May 27, 2019, https://www.josephsmithpapers.org/paper-summary/letter-to-emma-smith-13-october-1832/2. See also Mason, *Restoration*, 40.

34.   Ezra Taft Benson, "Civic Standards for the Faithful Saints," *Ensign*, July 1972, 59; quoting Orson F. Whitney, in *Conference Report*, April 1928, 59.

35.   See Michael Hubbard MacKay, "Event or Process? How 'the Chamber of Old Father Whitmer' Helps Us Understand Priesthood Restoration," *BYU Studies Quarterly* 60, no. 1 (2021): 73–101; Richard Lyman Bushman, *Joseph Smith: Rough Stone Rolling: A Cultural Biography of Mormonism's Founder* (New York: Knopf, 2005), 133–137.

36. The term *holy envy* was coined by Krister Stendahl, Lutheran bishop and biblical scholar, and used to convince the people of Stockholm, Sweden, that they should allow The Church of Jesus Christ of Latter-day Saints to build a temple there; see Barbara Brown Taylor, *Holy Envy: Finding God in the Faith of Others* (New York, NY: HarperOne, 2019), 64–66.

37. John A. Widtsoe, ed., *Discourses of Brigham Young* (Salt Lake City, UT: Deseret Book Company, 1925), 382; quoted in *Teachings of Presidents of the Church: Brigham Young* (Salt Lake City, UT: The Church of Jesus Christ of Latter-day Saints, 1997), 17. For more on Latter-day Saints discovering religious truth among other religions, see Mauro Properzi, "Learning about Other Religions: False Obstacles and Rich Opportunities," *Religious Educator* 16, no.1 (2015): 129–49.

38. *History of the Church* 6:478; "Discourse, 16 June 1844–A, as Reported by Thomas Bullock," p. [5], *The Joseph Smith Papers*, accessed September 20, 2021, https://www.josephsmithpapers.org/paper-summary/discourse-16-june-1844-a-as-reported-by-thomas-bullock/5.

39. *History of the Church* 6:478; see note 38. Although the quotations are affirming, they bracket an analogy seeming to imply that any Protestant churches that have "branched" off from the Catholic Church must be corrupt if the Catholic Church is corrupt. Joseph's point in this sermon, however, is not to denounce Catholics or Protestants but to denounce William Law—a member of the First Presidency who had apostatized and criticized Joseph Smith for his teachings on the plurality of gods. This sermon is not, therefore, a treatise on religious history but a response to the immediate concerns caused by William Law's apostasy. (Thanks to Gerrit J. Dirkmaat for this helpful context.) For more on this sermon in the context of early Latter-day Saint apostasy narratives, see Jones and Fleming, "'Except among that Portion of Mankind,'" 55–76. For the current position of The Church of Jesus Christ of Latter-day Saints on anti-Catholicism, see above, notes 25 and 26.

40. Other Latter-day Saint scholars have been calling for a new approach to studying ancient Christianity; see Wilcox and Young, *Standing Apart*; Daniel Becerra, "Beginning of What? A Reflection on Hugh Nibley's Legacy and LDS Scholarship on Late Antique Christianity," *Studies in the Bible and Antiquity* 7 (2015): 59–65.

✳ 2 ✳

PREACHING
CHRIST

Scripture, Sermons,
and Practical Exegesis

Kristian S. Heal

For Christ did not send me to baptize but to preach
the gospel, and not with eloquent wisdom, lest the
cross of Christ be emptied of its power.
—1 Corinthians 1:17
Revised Standard Version

P reaching punctuated the religious experience of early Christians. They heard sermons at their conversion (missionary sermons), during their preparation for baptism (catechetical sermons), each week as they worshiped with their fellow believers (Sunday and weekday sermons), and even as part of death (funerary sermons). These sermons often retold, explained, and expounded the stories and teachings of Jesus, making these stories relevant to the lives of Christians through exhortation. Several thousand sermons survive from early Christianity, written in Armenian, Coptic, Greek, Latin, and Syriac. Within this vast collection is the surest guide to what the earliest Christians were taught and believed.[1] Importantly, sermons also show how early Christian preachers ministered to their congregations, offering comfort, encouragement, guidance, and drawing them back repeatedly to Jesus Christ (see box 2.1).

In the first part of this chapter, we will explore some aspects of preaching in the early Church, examine its origins, consider some early descriptions of preaching from eyewitnesses, look more closely at the sermons given to candidates for baptism, and read some advice to a young preacher. In the second part of the chapter, we will turn our attention to sermons about the life of Jesus Christ and hear the voices of preachers from around the ancient Roman Empire. At the end of this chapter, you will know more about how early Christians preached and will have a clearer sense of the centrality of the person and message of Christ in early Christian preaching.

Faith in the gospel comes from hearing it proclaimed (see Romans 10:17). Preaching is therefore foundational not only to the spreading of the Christian message but to the ongoing project of teaching, inspiring, guiding, chastening, and caring for the souls of those who turn to Christ. Early Christian preaching was a heady practice, a high-wire act in which preachers often balanced rhetorical gifts and pure love to reach and teach the congregation before them. The desire to tend to the wounded, to teach and edify, and above all to preach the message of Jesus is perhaps no more evident in all early Christian literature than it is in the preacher's sermon.

Preaching in the Early Church

John preached in the wilderness (see Mark 1:4; Luke 3:3). Jesus preached "the gospel of the kingdom of God" in the countryside (Mark 1:14 RSV) and in the synagogues (see Luke 4:16–22). After the ascension, the apostles continued to "teach and preach Jesus Christ" in public and private spaces (Acts 5:42 RSV). Paul also refers to his preaching in his letters (see 1 Corinthians 15:1). And it was not just the apostles who preached. As the earliest believers were scattered by their enemies, they "went about preaching the word" (Acts 8:4 RSV).[2] The Epistle to the Hebrews is also thought by many to have started as a sermon (see Hebrews 13:22).[3] As one scholar observed, "Christianity from its earliest beginnings was a preaching religion. At the center of its worship was the reading and preaching of scripture."[4]

The combination of (1) reading and (2) preaching the scriptures finds its origins in the Jewish synagogue.[5] Notice the interplay of these two elements in Luke's account of Jesus at the synagogue in Nazareth:[6]

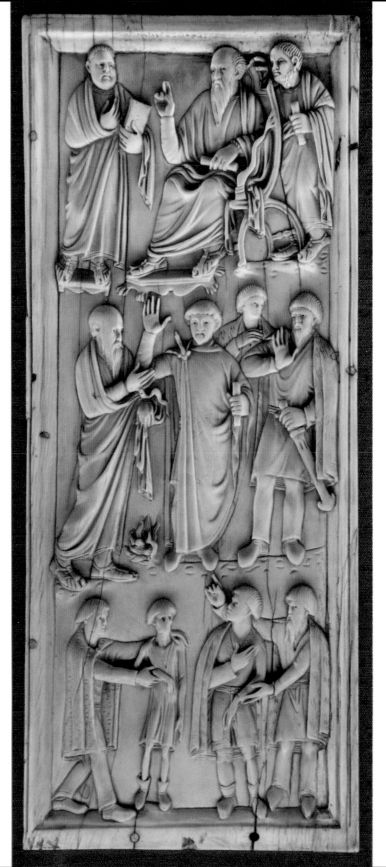

And [Jesus] came to Nazareth, where he had been brought up; and he went to the synagogue, as his custom was, on the sabbath day. And he stood up to read; and there was given to him the book of the prophet Isaiah. He opened the book and found the place where it was written, "The Spirit of the Lord is upon me, because he has anointed me to preach good news to the poor. He has sent me to proclaim release to the captives and recovering of sight to the blind, to set at liberty those who are oppressed, to proclaim the acceptable year of the Lord." And he closed the book, and gave it back to the attendant, and sat down; and the eyes of all in the synagogue were fixed on him. And he began to say to them, "Today this scripture has been fulfilled in your hearing." And all spoke well of him, and wondered at the gracious words which proceeded out of his mouth. (Luke 4:16–22)

A careful reading of this passage reveals three important features, which appear to have been influential in shaping the sermon in the Christian tradition. Firstly, notice that these particular "gracious words" are spoken in a liturgical setting, where Jesus is speaking as part of a formal and structured religious worship occurring in a building dedicated to the worship of and teaching about God. To be sure,

Jesus and his followers preached in many settings. But here we see the usual practice of preaching in the context of a worship service, a practice that became normative within both early Judaism and Christianity. Secondly, the sermon is preceded by and based on a reading of scripture. It is not clear whether this reading was part of a regular cycle[7] or whether Jesus turned to this passage in order to give a specific message. Nonetheless, in both Judaism and early Christianity, the pattern of reading the scriptures as part of the weekly worship service quickly became established. Thirdly, Jesus applies the scripture to his setting, in this case by proclaiming the fulfillment of a prophecy in the moment of the sermon. The scriptures, in the course of the sermon, cease to be embers from the past and instead become the living fire of prophecy speaking directly within the presence of the congregation. The sermon fans this fire of prophecy, spreading the message of Christ among the congregation to instruct and inspire them in their discipleship. The early Christian homily (another name for a sermon) continued to follow this threefold pattern seen in the preaching of Jesus, and it embodied "an urgent engagement on the pastor's side and a release of spiritual energy among the people he addressed."[8]

Witnesses to preaching

The earliest surviving description of a Christian worship service comes from Justin Martyr (died before AD 167), a Palestinian Christian who lived not much more than one hundred years after Jesus preached in Nazareth. In Justin's time there appears to be an order to the weekly worship, as well as a hierarchy, with a presiding authority and other offices, including readers and deacons:

> On the day which is called Sunday we have a common assembly of all who live in the cities or in the outlying districts, and the memoirs of the Apostles or the writings of the Prophets are read, as long as there is time. Then, when the reader has finished, the one presiding over the assembly verbally admonishes and invites all to imitate such examples of virtue.[9]

Note that the worship service begins with the reading of the scriptures, and then the presiding authority gives the sermon. In Justin's description, the sermon is a robust admonition, intended to inspire the congregation to imitate the examples of virtue that they have found in the scriptures. The life of the righteous, as recorded in the scriptures, is thus the target toward which Christian disciples aim in their pursuit of a virtuous life.[10] Early Christian preaching was rooted in scripture but related directly to the spiritual life of the congregation. It was intentional and invitational.

What kind of a sermon would have been heard in such a worship service? Fortunately, one sermon has survived that was written very near to the time that Justin described this Christian Sunday service (circa AD 140). Though a sermon, this work was transmitted to posterity as a letter and is known as *The Second Epistle of Clement to the Corinthians*.[11] In the sermon, the preacher immediately focuses on Christ, encouraging the congregation to recognize the divinity of Christ, to "think about (or esteem) Jesus Christ as we think about God," and to remember their indebtedness to him for saving them from their pagan worship of idols.[12] "We were maimed in our understanding," says the preacher, "worshipping stones and pieces of wood and gold and silver and copper—all of them made by humans."[13] The theme of humanity's indebtedness to Christ is worked out more fully in the preacher's interpretation of Isaiah 54:1, which he seems to base his sermon on.[14] The preacher explains how this passage "is referring to us."[15] Thus, like Jesus in Nazareth did when he taught, the preacher summons the scriptures from some distant historical past and places them firmly within his congregation's present day. In this way, the scriptures become prophecy that is fulfilled this very day. This homily preaches devotion to Christ, a humble devotion that recognizes our complete indebtedness to him for our salvation and that is tied intimately to the admonition to an ethical life of obedience,[16] to "conduct ourselves in a holy and upright way" on the right path,[17] to repent,[18] and to pursue virtue.[19] Those who heed such an admonition become the upright, who eschew the competitions and prizes of the world and instead choose to compete in the contest of the living God in this life that they might "be crowned in the one to come."[20]

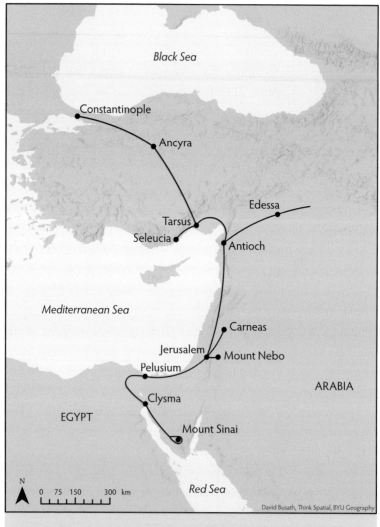

▲ **FIGURE 2.2** Map of Egeria's travels in the eastern provinces of the Roman Empire.

Just over two centuries later, a noble woman from the western part of the Roman Empire, what is today Spain or southern France, took a three-thousand-mile pilgrimage through the greatest sites of the Christian East during the years AD 381–84.[21] Her name was Egeria, and the account of her pilgrimage is one of the most engaging books

The Lectionary

The lectionary was a collection of scriptural readings that formed part of the liturgy, or worship service, for Sundays and holy days. Readings were taken from the Old and New Testaments, especially the Psalms and the Gospels. The lectionary may have begun as a continuous reading of the scriptures in worship services, but it soon developed into a cycle of readings appropriate for Sunday services and holy days. For example, in the early Syriac lectionary lists, the story of the binding of Isaac (see Genesis 22) and the story of Joseph were read as Old Testament readings for Easter.

from the early Christian world.[22] In the first part of her account, she describes her journey from Sinai to Jerusalem, then to Mount Nebo, Antioch, Edessa, Harran, and then to Constantinople via the pilgrimage shrines set up to Thecla and Euphemia (see fig. 2.2). In the second part of her account, Egeria brings the reader back to Jerusalem to describe her experiences with the worship services she encountered there.[23]

The first thing Egeria noticed in Jerusalem was a greater abundance of preaching on Sunday, the Lord's Day, than she was used to. Rather than the bishop (the presiding authority) being the only one to preach, Egeria says: "You should note that here it is usual for any presbyter who has taken his seat to preach, if he so wishes, and when they have finished there is a sermon from the bishop."[24] Presbyters were ordained members of the clergy who preached alongside bishops in many places in the early Christian world. It is interesting that Egeria notes that the presbyter preaches "if he so wishes." Perhaps in the church in Jerusalem there was still a memory of the ancient order in which people preached as they were moved upon by the Spirit (see 1 Corinthians 14:26–31).[25] Egeria also noted that the readings and preaching for festivals such as Holy Week or Epiphany "is appropriate to the day."[26] This remark refers to the lectionary readings, a collection of biblical readings that relate to the yearly cycle of sacred religious festivals and Sunday worship (see box 2.2).

What is the purpose of all this preaching? It is clear to Egeria: "The object of having this preaching every Sunday is to make sure that the people will continually be learning about the Bible and the love of God" and "will continue to learn God's Law."[27] The sermon was a compelling means of instruction and edification. With the scriptures at its heart, the sermon lifted and inspired the congregation, turning their hearts to God with greater love and a greater commitment to obedience.

Preaching to candidates for baptism

The instructional aspect of preaching is even more present in the catechetical sermons that were preached to those who were preparing for baptism on the eve of Easter Sunday (see box 2.3). Egeria describes this intensive course of scriptural and doctrinal instruction in some detail:

> During the forty days [the bishop] goes through the whole Bible, beginning with Genesis, and first relating the literal meaning of each passage, then interpreting its spiritual meaning. He also teaches

---

BOX 2.3   Catechumen

A catechumen is a disciple or student of the Christian gospel who has yet to be baptized. The formal teaching of such disciples is called catechesis, with the adjectival form, catechetical, applied to sermons preached to the candidates prior to baptism. These terms derive from the Greek verb *katechein*, which means "to instruct orally."

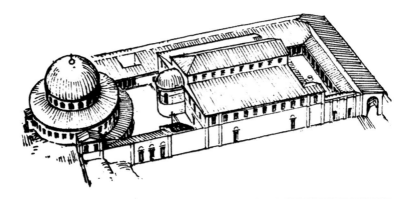

▲ **FIGURE 2.3**　Church of Holy Sepulcher, early fourth century (ca. 326). This line drawing depicts the church built over an early rock-cut tomb, a popular site of Christ's burial. Pilgrims visited this site as commemorated by Constantine's mother, Helena, from the early fourth century with veneration and ritual memory dating back even further. Image: Wikimedia Commons (public domain)

them at this time all about the resurrection and the faith. And this is called *catechesis*. After five weeks' teaching they receive the Creed, whose content he explains article by article in the same way as he explained the Scriptures, first literally and then spiritually. Thus all the people in these parts are able to follow the Scriptures when they are read in church, since there has been teaching on all the Scriptures from six to nine in the morning all through Lent, three hours' catechesis a day.[28]

In these sermons, the boundaries between preaching and teaching are blurred, and it may not be inappropriate to call these sermons lectures. Catechetical sermons are systematic, focused on scripture and the core doctrines of Christianity. And by them, candidates for baptism are reoriented to their new lives as Christians and prepared to continue their instruction each week through the Sunday sermons.

Baptismal candidates are not, however, taught about the mystery of
baptism until after they have experienced that ordinance on Easter
Sunday. After that, the bishop spends eight days teaching them the
deep mysteries of baptism.[29]

It is quite possible that the lectures Egeria heard in Jerusalem
were the same or similar to those that were first delivered some thirty
years earlier in AD 348 by Cyril, who was then the newly ordained
bishop of Jerusalem. Some sense of the seriousness and profound
spiritual occasion of Christian baptism is found in the prologue of
Cyril's catechetical sermons:

> Already, my dear candidates for Enlightenment
> (i.e. Baptism), scents of paradise are wafted to-
> wards you; already you are culling mystic blossoms
> for the weaving of heavenly garlands; already the
> fragrance of the Holy Spirit has blown about you.
> Already you have arrived at the outer court of the
> palace (i.e. at the threshold of Baptism): may the
> King lead you in! Now the blossom has appeared
> on the trees; God grant the fruit be duly harvested!
> Now you have enlisted; you have been called to the
> Colors (i.e. as part of Christ's army against Satan).
> You have walked in procession with the tapers of
> brides in your hands and the desire of heavenly citi-
> zenship in your hearts; with a holy resolve also, and
> the confident hope which that brings in its train. For
> He is no liar who said: "For those who love Him,
> God makes all things conspire to good" (Romans
> 8:28). Yes, God is generous and kind; nevertheless
> He requires in every man a resolve that is true. That
> is why the Apostle adds: "For those who are called
> in accordance with a resolve" (Romans 8:28). It
> is the sincerity of your resolution that makes you
> "called." It is of no use your body being here if your
> thoughts and heart are elsewhere.[30]

The imagery is luxurious, the language elevated, the repetition fore-shadowing what one scholar called "the awe-inspiring rites" of initiation that these candidates are preparing to receive.[31] Notice, too, the carefully chosen scriptural language about being called, and the way that each candidate's attention is drawn back to the love of God as the beginning of discipleship. These candidates are preparing to leave the humdrum world of the late Roman Empire and enter the Heavenly Kingdom to sit down with the King in the royal courts on high. They are joining the army of God, taking upon them his name and resolving to follow him in righteousness. Imagine this kind of teaching for three hours each day, over an eight-week period. Imagine also emerging on the other side of baptism, partaking of the Eucharist for the first time in the company of the believers, and then hearing another set of sermons revealing the mysteries of this holy ordinance. Such an act of imagination can bring us somewhere close to feeling what Egeria felt as she witnessed this scene, or what these candidates felt as they began their journey toward baptism by immersion and anointing with oil, preparatory to receiving the Eucharist.[32]

As Egeria's pilgrimage was drawing to an end, Augustine of Hippo (AD 354–430), perhaps the most famous of early Christians, first heard the sermons of Ambrose in Milan (AD 384). Augustine colorfully described this encounter in his *Confessions*. At the time he heard the sermons, Augustine was not yet a Christian. He made his living as a professor of rhetoric, and this training clearly colored his first impression of Ambrose's preaching: "I used enthusiastically to listen to him preaching to the people, not with the intention which I ought to have had, but as if testing out his oratorical skill to see whether it merited the reputation it enjoyed or whether his fluency was better or inferior than it was reported to be. I hung on his diction in rapt attention, but remained bored and contemptuous of the subject-matter. My pleasure was in the charm of his language."[33] No amount of ornamentation could make the Christian message appealing to the young Augustine at this time. What moved him was not Ambrose's preaching but his person. "That 'man of God' (2 Kings 1:9) received me like a father," reports Augustine, "and expressed pleasure in my

▲ **FIGURE 2.4** Octagonal baptismal font, Milan, Italy, fourth century. This is the site where Ambrose baptized Augustine during the Easter vigil, from 24–25 April 387. Photo: Mark D. Ellison

coming with kindness most fitting in a bishop. I began to like him, at first indeed not as a teacher of the truth, . . . but as a human being who was kind to me."[34] This episode from Augustine's *Confessions* suggests that at least two things were at work in the early Christian sermon: the preacher's language and the preacher's goodness. The late ancient world of Augustine was a great age of rhetoric. It was a noble pursuit to study language and the reading of texts. Learning how to read and interpret a text and how to deploy elegant and persuasive language to persuade another of its meaning were the equivalent of elite graduate school training in our day. But rhetoric can be used for good or ill, which is why the Christian preacher sought for holiness as well as eloquence.

Guidance for preaching

Christian teachers and leaders of the fourth and early fifth centuries realized both the potential and the dangers of Christian preaching fueled by contemporary rhetoric, and examples of their counsel to other preachers survive. We will consider just one example of this counsel, from Jerome (circa AD 347–419), an ascetic and one of the greatest Christian scholars of late antiquity. Jerome is best known to posterity as the translator of the Bible into Latin from the original Hebrew and Greek, which work became known as the Vulgate. But he is also the author of other works, including important biblical commentaries, sermons, and lively letters. Regarding his letters, one scholar notes, "Jerome's gifts made him a brilliant letter writer, rich in biblical erudition and the spiritual treasures of the East, delicate with friends, caustic with enemies, fascinating, given to extremes, brilliant in his versatility."[35] In Jerome's *Letter 52 to Nepotian*, written in AD 393, we see many of these gifts on display as he gives his correspondent advice about preaching:

> When you preach in church, let not applause . . . be elicited; let the tears of your listeners be your accolades. Let the presbyter's sermon be seasoned by his reading of Scripture. I do not want you to be a declaimer, a ranter, or a windbag, but an exceptionally well-trained expert on the deep things and mysteries of your God's Scripture. Reeling off words and speaking briskly to win admiration from the unwashed masses are the ploys of ignorant men. The shameless man often explains what he does not know, and after convincing others he asserts for himself a possession of knowledge. When I asked my former teacher, Gregory of Nazianzus, to elucidate the meaning of the phrase "δευτερόπρωτον ([*deutero-prōton*] or 'second-first') sabbath" in Luke's Gospel (Luke 6:1), he craftily quipped: "I will tell you in church what it means. There, as the entire congregation applauds me, either you will be forced against your will to know what you do not know, or at any rate if you alone remain quiet, you alone will be put down by everyone as a fool." There is nothing as easy

as deceiving the illiterate rabble with a slick style of
speaking, for whatever they do not understand they
admire all the more.[36]

Jerome is responding in this letter to a destructive culture of
persuasive rhetoric that aims to win the applause of the congregation for the speaker rather than the hearts of the congregation for
God.[37] Jerome is scathing as he mocks the "ranter" or the "windbag"
who speaks without knowledge and claims that truth is whatever he
can get a credulous congregation to believe. Instead of rhetorical ele-
gance, Jerome advises his friend to let his sermons be "seasoned by
his reading of Scripture." Jerome is not advising a perfunctory reading
of scripture, however, but the kind of reading that leads the reader
to become "an exceptionally well-trained expert on the deep things
and mysteries of your God's Scripture." Nor should such knowledge
be seen as sufficient qualification for the young preacher. Rather,
Jerome believed that deep personal righteousness acquired through
Christian discipleship and diligent right-living should be the defining
feature of the Christian preacher.[38] It seems that Jerome imagined
that more seekers, like Augustine, would be drawn to the Christian
message through the goodness and kindness of the preacher than by
his profound eloquence alone.

Preaching Christ in the Early Church

Just as Egeria once visited the places where God's power was man-
ifested in the early history of Christianity, we will now embark on
our own pilgrimage. We will visit some of the most compelling moments in the life of Christ as described by early Christian preachers.
Like Egeria, who stopped first at Sinai, we too must recognize that
the story of Jesus begins in the lives and words encountered in the
Old Testament. We will continue from there to the birth of Jesus, his
preaching (particularly of the parables), and finally to the events of
Holy Week, culminating in the glorious Resurrection of Jesus Christ.
Also, like Egeria, we will learn more about early Christian preaching
by hearing the words of the preachers themselves. In these sermons

we learn how early Christians talked of Christ, rejoiced in Christ, and preached of Christ.[39]

Preaching Christ through the Old Testament

When Jesus walked with his disciples on the road to Emmaus (see Luke 27:13–35), he found them dazed and confused, unaware of the full shape of the Messiah's redeeming mission. In response to their ignorance, "beginning with Moses and all the prophets, he interpreted to them in all the scriptures the things concerning himself" (Luke 24:27 RSV). It seemed that because they could not recognize Jesus in the scriptures, they also could not recognize him then, as he spoke to them. This eye-opening, informal sermon, given on a dusty first-century road to a deflated group of disciples opened their minds and caused them to exclaim: "Did not our hearts burn within us?" (Luke 24:32 RSV). It is here that we find the foundation of the Christian reading of the scriptures (then only comprising what we today call the Old Testament). The good news of Jesus Christ—his birth, life, ministry, suffering, death, and Resurrection—became the interpretative key to understanding scripture and the basis of Christian preaching of the Old Testament.[40]

For early Christians, the Old Testament became a treasury of prophetic words and types.[41] This perspective is especially true for the fifth-century preacher Jacob of Serugh. Jacob preached in Syriac, an Aramaic dialect similar to the one spoken by Jesus. He was educated in Edessa (modern Urfa in southeast Turkey) almost a century after Egeria visited that famous city on her grand pilgrimage. Jacob was one of the most prolific preachers in the early Christian world, and over four hundred of his sermons survive, many on the Old Testament.[42]

The Old Testament was so important to Jacob because, as one scholar notes: "For Jacob of Sarug, there is not even one line in the Old Testament that does not proclaim the way of the Son."[43] Jacob's conviction that Jesus shines through the pages of the Old Testament is seen clearly in his sermon *The Veil on Moses' Face* (see Exodus 34:29–35).[44] In this scene, Moses comes down from Mount Sinai

▲ **FIGURE 2.5** Moses parting the Red Sea, Via Latina catacomb fresco, Rome, fourth century. This early Christian catacomb painting depicts Moses leading the children of Israel toward Sinai as the tumbling Egyptian soldiers are about to be drowned. A large and beardless Moses looks back over his shoulder and wields the rod of Aaron in a gesture that resembles images of Christ elsewhere in the catacomb. Moses's physical appearance could be read as a type for Christ as a "new Moses" and this event as a foreshadowing of Christian baptism (see 1 Corinthians 10:1–2). Photo: Scala/Art Resource NY

and has to cover his face with a veil because it shone so brightly. In his sermon, Jacob responds to a question about why Moses veiled his face.[45] He answers that the veil of Moses symbolizes that "the words of prophecy are veiled," meaning the words of the Old Testament.[46] Jacob's answer explains why the disciples did not fully understand the nature of Christ's messianic ministry. The veil had yet to be rent (see Mark 15:38). Instead, the Old Testament "hides its content in parables so that they might not be recognized . . . so that the world might not become openly aware of the Son of God."[47] In the Old Testament, "through the Spirit, . . . the prophets brought news to the entire world of the Son in secret, and the veil which was on Moses' face was spread over their words whenever they spoke of the Only-Begotten."[48] In fact, without the key to understand it, "the whole Old Testament is veiled after the fashion of Moses." Nonetheless, "within the veil which lies over scripture there sits resplendent Christ as judge."[49] In other words, "the radiance of Moses was in fact Christ shining in him."[50]

Jacob taught that only in the life and ministry of Christ did the entire Old Testament become comprehensible. The veil over it was removed with the coming of Christ "in whom all mysteries were explained to the entire world."[51] When Christ came, "he uncovered Moses' face" and let the light of Christ shine out over the whole earth, thereby explaining the "symbols and figures and parables" of the Old Testament.[52] This example of the veil of Moses both explains and exemplifies Jacob's understanding of the Old Testament as a work bursting with types of the life of Christ. For Jacob, "certain happenings and objects are presented in the Old Testament in a particular manner only because they serve as types of Christ."[53]

The birth of Christ

Part of the preacher's art was "appealing to the imagination of his hearers in descriptive pictures."[54] For example, when the fifth-century Isaac the Teacher preaches a sermon on the Magi who come to worship Jesus, he imagines the scenes described and evoked by the biblical text (see Matthew 2:1–12). This imagining includes a vivid word picture of the moment when the Magi, or wise men, arrive in the Holy Land:

They reached the land of Judah, and they passed within the border of the Hebrews, thinking that they would see crowds entering the place as well. They entered and saw that the place was silent—a people not in a state of rejoicing! A great number of sentient beings were in the land, but they were asleep in the sleep of the unrighteous. They saw that the villages were quiet and the towns were silent. And they were worried that the sight that they saw was not real. However, they were not deceived about the sight, nor were they deprived of their truth. They blamed the land and its lords, for not being worthy to recognize its God. "What is this quiet?" the Magi intoned to one another. "Did God only let us know the day of his appearance? Within Persia there is a great deal of excitement, but here, a great stillness. In our country there is a huge festival, but in Judah a silent respite. God is in this land, but its inhabitants are still sleeping! The Lord of All is among the earthly inhabitants, but the Hebrews are unaware of Him!"[55]

The preacher captures so well the contrast between what is expected by those who believe, and what is enacted by those who do not believe. "God is in this land!" That truth known to those who believe resounds at the end of this passage like a trumpet that should wake the drowsiest soul. And yet it does not. What it does instead is allow the believer to live into this story through their imagination, to walk into this country with the Magi and be amazed that no one knows what has happened while they do.

Preachers also utilized the rhetorical use of contrast when they wanted to convey to their congregations the marvel of the Incarnation, God's coming into flesh. Early Christian preachers delighted in imagining the implications and contrasts involved in this act of condescension by God himself. Augustine, for example, in his sermon

▲ **FIGURE 2.6**   Sarcophagus relief with the Adoration of the Magi, Vatican Museum, from the cemetery of St. Agnes, fourth century. The Magi ("wise men," see Matthew 2:1–12) were a popular subject in early Christian art, often depicted as three men approaching Mary and the Christ child in adoration and recognition of the new-born king. They are dressed in short tunics, trousers, and Phrygian caps as was typical for showing figures from the East. The charming addition of the camels in the background accentuates the eager figures who have followed the star, to which one of the Magi points, as they come bearing gifts. Photo: Scala/Art Resource NY

for Christmas Day AD 411 or 412, evokes the contrasts inherent in the Incarnation. In doing so, he demonstrates his capacity to preach lyrically and symbolically about the nativity of Christ:

> The maker of man, he was made man, so that the director of the stars might be a babe at the breast; that bread might be hungry, and the fountain thirsty; that

the light might sleep, and the way be weary from a journey; that the truth might be accused by false witnesses, and the judge of the living and the dead be judged by a mortal judge; that justice might be convicted by the unjust, and discipline be scourged with whips; that the cluster of grapes might be crowned with thorns, and the foundation be hung up on a tree; that strength might grow weak, eternal health be wounded, life die.[56]

Here Augustine "rises from the simple exposition to a rapturous artistry which transcends the boundary between poetry and prose."[57] The contrasting images are poignant, drawing from both the acts of God in the Old Testament and the titles of Christ in the New Testament. These kinds of evocative rhetorical flourishes reeducated the Christian mind to see the world around them in sacramental and symbolic terms. Such flourishes reinforced the reality of God's action in the world by reimagining it and restaging it Sunday after Sunday in Christian churches around the Roman Empire and beyond.

Preaching the parables

Scores of sermons survive that are devoted to preaching the life and teachings of Jesus Christ. These range from long series of sermons to individual sermons that expound and reflect on particular scenes or stories. Augustine (AD 354–430) and John Chrysostom (died AD 407) taught daily sermons that worked through entire Gospels.[58] There are beautiful sermons in the Syriac tradition that reimagine and retell Jesus's encounter with the sinful woman (see Luke 7:36–50).[59] John tells us concerning the ministry and deeds of Jesus that "were every one of them to be written, I suppose that the world itself could not contain the books that would be written" (John 21:25 RSV). The early Christians, it seems, believed that the four gospels themselves were similarly inexhaustible.

To take one example from this cloud of witnesses, a homily by Origen of Alexandria (circa AD 185–254) reveals the possibilities in interpreting the parables. Origen is perhaps the greatest scriptural

BOX 2.4   The Fourfold Sense of Scripture

John Cassian (circa AD 360–435) describes the fourfold sense of scripture:

- **Literal/historical**: Scripture gives us "knowledge of past and visible things."
- **Allegorical**: Scripture is a metaphor, or a type that is prefiguring a mystery.
- **Anagogical**: Scripture reads as prophecy about "what lies in the future" (i.e., in the afterlife).
- **Tropological**: Scripture offers a "moral explanation pertaining to correction of life and practical instruction."

Example: "Jerusalem can be understood in a fourfold manner. According to history it is the city of the Jews. According to allegory it is the Church of Christ. According to anagogy it is the heavenly city of God 'which is the mother of us all' (Galatians 4:26). According to tropology it is the soul of the human being, which under this name is frequently either reproached or praised by the Lord."[60]

interpreter in the early Church. Importantly, "it was through [Origen] that exegesis and preaching were so firmly united that throughout the history of the ancient church and long afterwards they remained intertwined."[61] In other words, Origen's concern to correctly interpret the meaning of the scriptural text (exegesis) was intimately connected with his desire to make scripture come alive in the everyday life of Christians (preaching). Although his works were later condemned, his influence reverberated throughout the early Christian world for centuries.[62] One especially striking sermon by Origen is his homily on the good Samaritan (see Luke 10:25–37), which he delivered in AD 233–34 as part of a series on the Gospel of Luke.[63] Origen begins his sermon with a summary of the parable and its immediate context, clarifies the meaning of the text, cites the relevant intertexts that Jesus alludes to, and articulates the purpose of the parable. The parable of the good Samaritan teaches that this man beaten on the road to Jericho was only considered a neighbor by the one "who willed to keep the commandments and prepare himself to be a neighbor to everyone who needs help."[64] So far, Origen focuses on the plain meaning of the New Testament text (see box 2.4).

Origen then tells his congregation about a traditional interpretation for this parable coming from "one of the elders" in the Church:

> The man who was going down is Adam. Jerusalem is paradise, and Jericho is the world. The robbers are hostile powers. The priest is the Law, the Levite is the prophets, and the Samaritan is Christ. The wounds are disobedience, the beast is the Lord's body, the *pandochium* (that is, the stable), which accepts all who wish to enter, is the Church. And further, the two *denarii* mean the Father and the Son. The manager of the stable is the head of the Church, to whom its care has been entrusted. And the fact that the Samaritan promises he will return represents the Savior's second coming.[65]

We notice immediately that this anonymous elder has a novel way of approaching scripture, which is to interpret the text allegorically. In fact, this approach had been used in the schools of Alexandria for some time and was actively used by Origen. "For Origen, allegory was doubtless the means by which he presented the message of the gospel as he understood it. It was his method of prophesying."[66] That is to say, an allegorical reading was a way to apply the scripture to the audience. In this instance, an allegorical reading suggests that though the text may say one thing (a parable about a good Samaritan), it is really saying something else (a description of the entire divine economy from the Fall to the Second Coming). Frances Young gives us a more detailed definition: "The word *allegoria* is derived from a Greek verb meaning 'to speak in public' compounded with the adjective

▶ **FIGURE 2.7** Parable of the Good Samaritan, Rossano Gospels, sixth century. This page from a sumptuous Gospels book is illuminated with the continuous narrative of the parable of the Good Samaritan. Top, from left to right: the city of Jerusalem; Christ as the Good Samaritan who finds the wounded man; the man on a donkey as Christ/the Samaritan pays the innkeeper to care for the man until his return. Early Christians read this parable allegorically as a salvific typology of Christ. Below the parable scenes are figures from the Septuagint (Greek translation of the Old Testament), from left to right: David, Micah, David, and Sirach. As they point upward to Christ, their words support the allegorical interpretation of the parable (the quotations are from Psalm 94:17; Micah 7:19; Psalm 118:7; and Sirach 18:12). The title of the parable, "Concerning the One who Fell among Thieves" (seen in Greek above the parable scenes), guides the reader to identify with the wounded man and remember that we are all in need of Christ's succor and redemption. Photo: Wikimedia Commons

allos, meaning 'other.' Ancient definitions all ring the changes on the same theme: allegory is 'to mean something other than what one says.' It is discussed in the rhetorical textbooks on style as a *trope,* a 'turn' or figure of speech, and lies on a spectrum with metaphor and irony."[67] Allegory is, then, one way of reading a text. There are allegorical readings of Homer and allegorical readings of the Bible, both using the same rhetorical techniques. Allegorical readings are seen, however, to be a special feature of Alexandrian scriptural interpretation, or exegesis. That is to say, texts in Alexandria tended to be read in this way. In other places, for example, in Antioch, texts tended to be read with concern for "the narrative logic of particular stories."[68]

What does this all mean for Origen's sermon? Firstly, it means that Origen's reading, and that of the unnamed elder, are readings that belong to a particular time and place, informed by the broader culture of reading texts. Texts are read in communities, and the rhetorical and exegetical approaches of the community tend to inform how the text is read. If you take the text out of one community and place it in another, the reading will invariably change, even if that text is scripture. Secondly, it means that Origen gives us a very interesting reading of the parable of the good Samaritan, which extends the important ethical message accessible to every reader, especially the reader concerned only with the story's narrative logic. He takes the traditional reading and expands on it using his interpretative gifts and resources to examine the text more closely. As he does so, he notices, for example, that it is not just fitting to see the Samaritan allegorically as Christ, but the parable tells us more about Christ in the way it describes the Samaritan:

> The Samaritan is that man whose care and help all who are badly off need. The man who was going down from Jerusalem and fell among thieves, who was wounded and left by them half-alive, needed the help of this Samaritan most of all. You should know that, according to God's providence, this Samaritan

was going down to care for the man who had fallen
among thieves. You learn that clearly from the fact
that he had bandages, oil, and wine with him. I do
not think that the Samaritan carried these things
with him only on behalf of that one, half-dead man,
but also on behalf of others who, for various reasons, had been wounded and needed bandages, oil,
and wine.[69]

For Origen, this wounded man is not just Adam, but all humankind, each of us who is wounded by vices and sins, pains and sorrows,
and needs binding up and taking care of. Notice, too, how Origen
understands the Samaritan's action to be a deliberate act of kindness,
rather than a random act. He came prepared. He was going out looking for the wounded and the suffering, for all those "who, for various
reasons, had been wounded and needed bandages, oil, and wine."
Origen thereby succeeds in not only recognizing that the traditional
interpretation "has been said reasonably and beautifully"[70] but extends that interpretation by making it relevant to his congregation.
He applies this interpretation not only to all who feel the wounds of
mortality and come to the Church for relief but to those disciples of
Jesus Christ who wish to "go and do likewise" (Luke 10:37 RSV):

According to the passage that says, "Be imitators of
me, as I too am of Christ," (1 Corinthians 4:16) it
is possible for us to imitate Christ and to pity those
who "have fallen among thieves." We can go to them,
bind their wounds, pour in oil and wine, put them
on our own beasts, and bear their burdens. The Son
of God encourages us to do things like this. He is
speaking not so much to the teacher of the Law as
to us and to all men when he says, "Go and do likewise" (Luke 10:37). If we do, we shall obtain eternal
life in Christ Jesus, to whom is glory and power for
ages of ages. Amen.[71]

Preaching the Holy Week

Melito of Sardis was, by all accounts, one of the most important Christian voices of the second century.[72] Ancient sources say that "he always lived his life in the Holy Spirit."[73] During Holy Week, the week commemorating the last week of the life of Jesus Christ, Melito preached a homily titled "On the Pasch," taken from the Aramaic word meaning "Passover."[74] As the title indicates, from the earliest period of Christian history, the death of Christ was understood in terms of the Passover lamb and the Exodus story. Unfortunately, other than his homily "On the Pasch," only a few fragments of his works survive from antiquity, and even this homily was only discovered and published in the last century.[75]

Melito's homily "On the Pasch" is a rhetorically and typologically rich exploration of the meaning of the suffering and death of Christ, with special reference to the Old Testament and Israel.[76] The sermon reflects the desire to follow the pattern of Jesus who, "beginning with Moses and all the prophets, . . . interpreted to [his disciples] in all the scriptures the things concerning himself" (Luke 24:27 RSV). While Melito was preaching this homily, local Jews were also celebrating Passover and telling the Exodus story. Melito retells the same story, often with poignant images. For example, listen to how Melito captures the terrible moment when death seizes the firstborn Egyptian children:

> In the darkness that could be grasped lurked death that could not be grasped, and the wretched Egyptians were grasping at the darkness, while death was seeking out and grasping the firstborn of the Egyptians at the angel's bidding. If therefore one was grasping at the darkness, he was led to execution by death. And one firstborn, as he clasped dark body in his hand, terrified in soul let out a piteous and dreadful cry: "Whom does my hand hold? Whom does my soul dread? Who is this dark one enveloping my whole body? If it is father, help; if mother, comfort; if brother, speak; if friend, support; if

enemy, go away, for I am a firstborn." But before the firstborn grew silent, the long silence of death caught him and addressed him: "You are my first-born; I am your destiny, the silence of death."[77]

Despite his ability to evoke this terrible moment so brilliantly, Melito believed the Passover story to be only a type, an impression, a sketch of the true story, which is the story of Jesus's redemption of the world from Satan's power at Easter.[78] And it may be that the vividness of his description of this moment is meant to remind his Christian audience of the awful woundedness of those who do not reach out for Jesus.

Importantly, Israel is saved from this awful fate by slaughtering a sheep and placing its blood on their door posts (see Exodus 12). Or, as Melito phrases it, "The death of the sheep became a wall for the people."[79] Melito is struck by this fact and by the mystery contained in this act. There must have been more to Israel's protection than the blood of a sheep. So, rhetorically he asks the angel why he really passed by Israel's bloodied doors:

> O strange and inexpressible mystery! The slaughter of the sheep was found to be Israel's salvation, and the death of the sheep became the people's life, and the blood won the angel's respect. Tell me, angel, what did you respect? The slaughter of the sheep or the life of the Lord? The death of the sheep or the model of the Lord? The blood of the sheep or the Spirit of the Lord? It is clear that your respect was won when you saw the mystery of the Lord occur-ring in the sheep, the life of the Lord in the slaughter of the lamb, the model of the Lord in the death of the sheep; that is why you did not strike Israel, but made only Egypt childless.[80]

Melito tells the great story of Holy Week, the triumph of Jesus over death and hell, through a reframing of the Passover story in Ex-odus. The ancient reality of the Passover, its central place in Israel's

▲ FIGURE 2.8   The Maskell Passion Ivory, Resurrection panel, British Museum, London, ca. 420–430. The resurrected Jesus features prominently at the center of this ivory panel. Jesus's bodily reality is highlighted by the probing touch of Thomas's finger at the wound-space revealed at Jesus's left side. Three other apostles look on in wonder at Christ, now haloed and standing on a dais (raised platform) to indicate his resurrected state of being. Photo: Scala/Art Resource NY

identity and claim to heavenly protection, is recast as a foreshadowing of an even greater moment of redemption. In this recasting, the
power of these great moments of Israel's past, the meaning of the
greatest stories, the most potent prophecies, is all actually found in
Christ. In fact, for Melito, it always had been Christ and always would
be. At the end of his poetic sermon, Melito gives voice to Jesus, who
invites all to come to him for salvation: "Come then, all you families
of men who are compounded with sins, and *receive forgiveness of sins.*
For I am your forgiveness, I am the Passover of salvation, I am the
lamb slain for you; I am your ransom, *I am* your *life, I am* your *light,* I
am your salvation, *I am* your *resurrection,* I am your king. I will raise
you up by my right hand; I am leading you up to the heights of heav-
en; there I will show you the Father from ages past."[81]

Conclusion

Melito's invitation, placed in the mouth of Jesus Christ, epitomizes
the message and intent of early Christian preaching. The concern was
pastoral—the care of souls—and the intent was to invite and entice
the audience to come unto Jesus. Whether the sermon was simple,
as is the case with *2 Clement*, or highly artistic, as is the case with the
sermons of John Chrysostom, the intention is evident. Early Christian preaching was a ministry to the wounded: like the good Samaritan, preachers went out weekly, or daily, into the world of beaten and
weary souls to comfort them with a message of hope and salvation in
Christ. The foundation of the message was the scriptures. Not only
were the sermons often based on the regular cycle of scriptural reading in the worship services, but the scriptures were ever-present in the
sermons. One scripture supported another or interpreted another,
giving power to a message or simply perfuming the oil that bound
up the wounded soul. Early Christians learned the scriptures through
sermons, not just as catechumens preparing for baptism. The sermon

retold the scriptural stories, remapping their meaning on the everyday life of the Christian believer. The sermon reoriented all scripture towards Christ and constantly demonstrated how the life and ministry of Jesus was the key to scriptural understanding.

Notes

1. Learned engagement with scripture is represented in the early Christian commentary tradition. For an introduction to this literature for a Latter-day Saint audience, see Carl W. Griffin and Kristian S. Heal, "Early Christian Biblical Interpretation," in *The Bible and the Latter-day Saint Tradition*, ed. Taylor G. Petrey, Cory Crawford, and Eric A. Eliason (Salt Lake City, UT: University of Utah Press, 2022), 297–309.
2. See also Acts 2:14–16; 3:12–26; 13:16–41; 17:22–31.
3. See Raymond E. Brown, *An Introduction to the New Testament* (New Haven: Yale University Press, 1997), 690.
4. Hughes Oliphant Old, *The Reading and Preaching of the Scriptures in the Worship of the Christian Church* (Grand Rapids, MI: Eerdmans, 1998), 1:111. Useful surveys of the history of early Christian preaching are found in Yngve Brilioth, *A Brief History of Preaching* (Philadelphia: Fortress Press, 1965), and more effusively, in the first three volumes of Hughes Oliphant Old, *The Reading and Preaching of the Scriptures in the Worship of the Christian Church*, 7 vols. (Grand Rapids, MI: Eerdmans, 1998–2010). More detailed studies of Greek sermons are found in Mary Cunningham and Pauline Allen, eds., *Preacher and Audience: Studies in Early Christian and Byzantine Homiletics*, vol. 1 of A New History of the Sermon series (Leiden: Brill, 1998). Of Latin sermons, see Anthony Dupont et al., eds., *Preaching in the Patristic Era: Sermons, Preachers, and Audiences in the Latin West*, vol. 6 of A New History of the Sermon series (Leiden: Brill, 2018). The most thorough treatment is still Alexandre Olivar, *La predicación Cristiana Antigua* (Barcelona: Editorial Herder, 1991). A valuable, and brief, introduction to the interpretation of scripture, with a very nice selection of sources, can be found in Karlfried Froehlich, ed. and trans., *Biblical*

Interpretation in the Early Church, vol. 4 in the Sources of Early Christian Thought series (Philadelphia: Fortress Press, 1984). For a deeper engagement, the best place to start is Frances M. Young, *Biblical Exegesis and the Formation of Christian Culture* (Peabody, MA: Hendrickson, 2002). For anyone wishing to read more early Christian sermons, there is a splendid collection in M. F. Toal, *The Sunday Sermons of the Great Fathers*, 4 vols. (San Francisco: Ignatius Press, 2000). Modern translation of the sermons of individual early Christian preachers can be easily found among The Fathers of the Church series (Catholic University of America Press), the Ancient Christian Writers series (Paulist Press), and the Popular Patristics series (Saint Vladimir's Seminary Press).

5. See Alistair Stewart-Sykes, *From Prophecy to Preaching: A Search for the Origins of the Christian Homily* (Leiden: Brill, 2001), 39.

6. See Brilioth, *Brief History of Preaching*, 8–10.

7. See, for example, Michael Goulder, *The Evangelists' Calendar: A Lectionary Explanation of the Development of Scripture* (London: SPCK Publishing, 1978).

8. Philip Rousseau, "Homily and Exegesis in the Patristic Age: Comparisons of Purpose and Effect," in *The Purpose of Rhetoric in Late Antiquity*, ed. Alberto J. Quiroga Puertas (Tübingen: Mohr Siebeck, 2013), 11.

9. *1 Apology* 67. Translation from Justin Martyr, *The First Apology, The Second Apology, Dialogue with Trypho, Exhortation to the Greeks, Discourse to the Greeks, The Monarchy; Or the Rule of God*, trans. Thomas B. Falls, vol. 6 in The Fathers of the Church: A New Translation series (Washington, DC: The Catholic University of America Press, 1948), 106–107; adapted.

10. Examples of this process from the fifth century can be found in Kristian S. Heal, "Narsai and the Scriptural Self," in *Narsai: Rethinking His Work and His World*, ed. Aaron M. Butts, Kristian S. Heal, and Robert A. Kitchen (Tübingen: Mohr Siebeck, 2020), 133–43.

11. See Brilioth, *Brief History of Preaching*, 20. The sermon is introduced and translated in Bart D. Ehrman, ed. and trans., *The Apostolic Fathers*, vol. 1, *I Clement. II Clement. Ignatius. Polycarp. Didache*, Loeb Classical Library (Cambridge: Harvard University Press, 2003), 154–99. As noted above, the New Testament Epistle to the Hebrews is also considered by most scholars to be a sermon rather than a letter (see Hebrews 13:22).

12. *2 Clement* 1.1.

13. *2 Clement* 1.6.

14. See *2 Clement* 2.

15. *2 Clement* 2.2.

16. See *2 Clement* 17.3.

17. *2 Clement* 5.6.

18. See *2 Clement* 8.1, 13.2, 17.1.

19. See *2 Clement* 10.1.

20. *2 Clement* 20.2.

21. See Paul Devos, "La date du voyage d'Egérie," *Analecta Bollandiana* 85 (1967): 165–94.

22. I cite *Egeria's Travels* in the translation from John Wilkinson, *Egeria's Travels: Newly Translated with Supporting Documents and Notes* (Warminster, UK: Aris & Phillips, 1999). See also Anne McGowan and Paul F. Bradshaw, *The Pilgrimage of Egeria: A New Translation of the* Itinerarium Egeriae *with Introduction and Commentary* (Collegeville, MN: Liturgical Press, 2018).

23. See Old, *Reading and Preaching of the Scriptures*, 2:136–43. See also chapter 6 in this volume.

24. Egeria, *Egeria's Travels* 25.1; 26. Wilkinson suggests that Egeria's emphasis on this point indicates that she was used to less preaching in the Sunday service; see Wilkinson, *Egeria's Travels*, 58. On the preaching being done seated, see Brilioth, *Brief History of Preaching*, 26.

25. See Brilioth, *Brief History of Preaching*, 19.

26. Egeria, *Egeria's Travels* 25.10; 42.

27. Egeria, *Egeria's Travels* 25.1; 27.6.

28. Egeria, *Egeria's Travels* 46.2–3.

29. See Egeria, *Egeria's Travels* 46.5–6.

30. Cyril of Jerusalem, *Works, Volume 1: Procatechesis and Catechesis 1–12*, trans. Leo P. McCauley and Anthony A. Stephenson, vol. 61 in The Fathers of the Church: A New Translation series (Washington, DC: The Catholic University of America Press, 1969), 69–70.

31. Edward Yarnold, S. J., *The Awe-Inspiring Rites of Initiation: The Origins of the RCIA* (Collegeville: Liturgical Press, 1994).

32. See chapter 6 for an explanation of the Eucharist.

33. Augustine, *Confessions*, 5.23; translation from Henry Chadwick, *Saint Augustine: Confessions*, Oxford World Classics series (Oxford: Oxford University Press, 2008), 88.

34. Augustine, *Confessions*, 5.23; Chadwick, *Saint Augustine*, 88.

35. J. Gribomont, "Jerome," in *Encyclopedia of Ancient Christianity, Volume 2: F-O*, ed. Angelo Di Berardino (Downers Grove, IL: IVP Academic, 2014), 400. For more on Jerome's letters, see Andrew Cain, *The Letters of Jerome: Asceticism, Biblical Exegesis, and the Construction of Christian Authority in Late Antiquity* (Oxford: Oxford University Press, 2009).

36. Jerome, *Letter 52 to Nepotian* 8; translation from Andrew Cain, *Jerome and*

the Monastic Clergy: A Commentary on Letter 52 to Nepotian with an Intro-duction, Text, and Translation (Leiden: Brill, 2013), 47; adapted. Transla-tion also in *Nicene and Post-Nicene Fathers* 1/6:93. Discussed in Rousseau, "Homily and Exegesis," 16.

37. The variety of congregational responses is discussed in Cain, *Jerome and the Monastic Clergy*, 190, with further references.

38. See Andrew Cain, *The Letters of Jerome: Asceticism, Biblical Exegesis, and the Construction of Christian Authority in Late Antiquity* (Oxford: Oxford University Press, 2009), 147.

39. Borrowing language from 2 Nephi 25:26.

40. See Frances Young, "Typology," in *Crossing the Boundaries: Essays in Bib-lical Interpretation in Honour of Michael D. Goulder*, ed. Stanley E. Porter, Paul M. Joyce, and David E. Orton (Leiden: Brill, 1994), 29–48, with ref-erence to 40.

41. See, for example, Kristian S. Heal, "Joseph as a Type of Christ in the Syriac Tradition," *BYU Studies Quarterly* 41, no. 1 (2002): 29–49.

42. See Roger-Youssef Akhrass, "A List of Homilies of Mar Jacob of Serugh," *Syriac Orthodox Patriarchal Journal* 53 (2015): 87–161.

43. Armando Elkhoury, "Jesus Christ, the Eye of Prophecy," in *Les exégètes syriaques, Patrimoine Syriaque. Actes du colloque XIII. Mgr. Paul Féghali* (Antélias, Lebanon: Editions du CERO, 2015), 63–84, citing from 67.

44. I cite this beautiful homily by line number from Sebastian P. Brock, *Jacob of Sarug's Homily on the Veil on Moses' Face*, vol. 20 in the Texts from Christian Late Antiquity series (Piscataway, NJ: Gorgias Press, 2009).

45. See Jacob, *Veil on Moses' Face*, lines 1–2.

46. Jacob, *Veil on Moses' Face*, lines 21–22.

47. Jacob, *Veil on Moses' Face*, lines 36–38.

48. Jacob, *Veil on Moses' Face*, lines 47–50.

49. Jacob, *Veil on Moses' Face*, lines 59–62.

50. Jacob, *Veil on Moses' Face*, line 51. Compare, for example, 2 Corinthians 4:6.

51. Jacob, *Veil on Moses' Face*, lines 76.

52. Jacob, *Veil on Moses' Face*, lines 77–84.

53. Johns Abraham Konat, "Typological Exegesis in the Metrical Homilies of Jacob of Serugh," *Parole de l'Orient* 31 (2006): 121.

54. Brilioth, *Brief History of Preaching*, 65, referring specifically to Caesarius of Arles (circa AD 470–543).

55. Translated by the author from Vatican Syriac 120 folio 198 a–b. The text unfortunately exhibits anti-Judaism that was, as Adam Becker has noted, "foundational to Syriac Christianity." Adam H. Becker, "Syriac

Anti-Judaism: Polemic and Internal Critique," in *Jews and Syriac Christians: Intersections across the First Millennium*, ed. Aaron Michael Butts and Simcha Gross (Tübingen: Mohr Siebeck, 2020), 47.

56. Augustine, *Sermon 191*, in *Sermons (184–229)*, ed. John E. Rotelle, trans. Edmund Hill, part 3, vol. 6 of The Works of Saint Augustine: A Translation for the 21st Century series (New York: New York City Press, 1993), 42.

57. Brilioth, *Brief History of Preaching*, 52.

58. For example, Chrysostom's eighty-eight sermons on the Gospel of John (Sister Thomas Aquinas Goggin, trans., *Saint John Chrysostom: Commentary on Saint John the Apostle and Evangelist*, vol. 33 [*Homilies 1–47*] and vol. 41 [*Homilies 48–88*] in The Fathers of the Church: A New Translation series [Washington, DC: The Catholic University of America Press, 1957, 1959]) and Augustine's 124 sermons on the Gospel of John (Augustine, *Homilies on the Gospel of John*, part 3, vol. 12 [*1–40*] and vol. 13 [*41–124*], ed. Allan D. Fitzgerald, trans. Edmund Hill, in the The Works of Saint Augustine: A Translation for the 21st Century series [New York: New City Press, 2009]). On Augustine preaching daily, see J. Patout Burns Jr. and Robin M. Jensen, *Christianity in Roman Africa: The Development of Its Practices and Beliefs* (Grand Rapids, MI: Eerdmans, 2014), 271; for Chrysostom, see Brilioth, *Brief History of Preaching*, 37.

59. As discussed in Susan Ashbrook Harvey, "Why the Perfume Mattered: The Sinful Woman in Syriac Exegetical Tradition," in *In Dominico Eloquio/In Lordly Eloquence: Essays on Patristic Exegesis in Honor of Robert Louis Wilken*, ed. Paul M. Blowers, Angela Russell Christman, David G. Hunter, and Robin A. Darling Young (Grand Rapids, MI: Eerdmans, 2002), 69–89.

60. John Cassian, *Conferences* 14.8.4. Translation from Boniface Ramsey, *John Cassian: The Conferences* (Ancient Christian Writers 57; New York: Newman Press, 1997), 510.

61. Brilioth, *Brief History of Preaching*, 22.

62. See Elizabeth A. Clark, *The Origenist Controversy: The Cultural Construction of an Early Christian Debate* (Princeton, NJ: Princeton University Press, 1992).

63. I cite the homily according to Henri Crouzel, François Fournier, and Pierre Périchon, *Origène: Homélies sur S. Luc.*, vol. 87 in the Source Chrétiennes series (Paris: Les Éditions du Cerf, 1962) and the translation of Origen, *Homilies on Luke, Fragments on Luke*, trans. Joseph T. Lienhard, vol. 94 in The Fathers of the Church: A New Translation series (Washington, DC: The Catholic University of America Press, 1996), 137–41. For this parable in early Christian sources, see Riemer Roukema, "The Good Samaritan in Ancient Christianity," *Vigiliae Christianae* 58 (2004): 56–74. For a

Latter-day Saint reading of this parable that draws on the early Christian tradition, see John W. Welch, "The Good Samaritan: A Type and Shadow of the Plan of Salvation," *BYU Studies Quarterly* 38, no. 2 (1999): 51–115.

64. Origen, *Homilies on Luke* 34.3.

65. Origen, *Homilies on Luke* 34.3.

66. Brilioth, *Brief History of Preaching*, 24–25.

67. Frances M. Young, *Biblical Exegesis and the Formation of Christian Culture* (Cambridge: Cambridge University Press, 1997; repr., Peabody, MA: Hendrickson, 2002), 176.

68. Frances M. Young, "Interpretation of Scripture," in *The Oxford Handbook of Early Christian Studies*, ed. Susan Ashbrook Harvey and David G. Hunter (Oxford: Oxford University Press, 2008), 854.

69. Origen, *Homilies on Luke* 34.6.

70. Origen, *Homilies on Luke* 34.4.

71. Origen, *Homilies on Luke* 34.9.

72. His life and works are outlined in Eusebius, *Ecclesiastical History* 4.26; translated in Jeremy M. Schott, *Eusebius of Caesarea. The History of the Church: A New Translation* (Oakland: University of California Press, 2019), 211–14. See also Stuart G. Hall, *Melito of Sardis, On Pascha and Fragments* (Oxford: Clarendon Press, 1979), xi–xvii.

73. Eusebius, *Ecclesiastical History* 5.24, citing a letter from the second-century Bishop Polycrates of Ephesus; Schott, *Eusebius of Caesarea*, 265.

74. "Pascha has no English equivalent. It is the Greek form of the Aramaic *pasḥā*. It can denote the Passover festival, the Passover meal, the Passover lamb, or the Christian feast (Holy Week and Easter) which continues and replaces Passover." Hall, *Melito of Sardis, On Pascha*, 3n1.

75. Cited as Melito, *On Pascha*, together with the line number(s) from the edition and translation found in Hall, *Melito of Sardis, On Pascha*.

76. The style is not to everyone's taste: "The massing of forced antitheses and typological applications of Old Testament subjects makes the sermon difficult and unpalatable." Brilioth, *Brief History of Preaching*, line 21.

77. Melito, *On Pascha*, lines 145–64.

78. See Melito, *On Pascha*, lines 213–55.

79. Melito, *On Pascha*, line 198.

80. Melito, *On Pascha*, lines 199–212.

81. Melito, *On Pascha*, lines 766–80.

✳ 3 ✳

CREATING CANON

Authority, New Prophecy, and Sacred Texts

Thomas A. Wayment

But for you, continue in what you have learned and believed, knowing from whom you learned and that from infancy you have known the sacred writings, which provide wisdom for salvation through faith in Christ Jesus.

—2 Timothy 3:14–15[1]

Modern religions, like many institutions, rely on published texts to guide them in decision-making, community building, and day-to-day practice. In industry, these texts take the form of manuals, codes, bylaws, contracts, and published governing procedures. In religious life, these texts are often referred to as scripture. Each religion further defines which books they accept as scripture and which ones they reject. For example, Latter-day Saints accept an enormous canon, when compared to other Christians, with nearly a thousand pages of additional texts accepted as authoritative. Closed canons, or canons that are no longer added to, are the standard for most religions today. Open canons, while promising new revelation or the reappraisal of old documents that may come to light, are exceptional because they run the risk of destabilizing the existing institution with new religious ideas.

Textual canons—lists of authoritative books—are important because they identify power and authority structures within a faith community. Additionally, they shape the way scripture is interpreted because they define which texts are authoritative and which texts are not. A tertiary effect, or perhaps an unintended effect, is that they function to emphasize texts in hierarchical ways because no two books within a canon are precisely equal in importance. Canons also function to exclude books from certain spheres, such as reading them in church or for use in ordinances, and at times they also forbid the use of certain books absolutely. In one sense, canons have fuzzy borders. For example, a canon may permit believers to use some books

▲ **FIGURE 3.1**　Eusebian canon tables, sixth century Ethiopian Garima Gospels, showing lists of scriptural passages (developed by Eusebius of Caesarea in the early fourth century) within an architectural design. Photo: Wikimedia Commons

ΕΝ CΑΡΓΑΝΗ ΕΧΑΛΑCΘΗΝ ΔΙΑ ΤΟΥ ΤΕΙΧΟΥC
ΚΑΙ ΕΞΕΦΥΓΟΝ ΤΑC ΧΕΙΡΑC ΑΥΤΟΥ ΚΑΥΧΑC
ΘΑΙ ΔΕΙ ΟΥ CΥΜΦΕΡΟΝ ΜΕΝ ΕΛΕΥCΟΜΑΙ ΔΕ
ΕΙC ΟΠΤΑCΙΑC ΚΑΙ ΑΠΟΚΑΛΥΨΕΙC ΚΥ ΟΙΔΑ
ΑΝΘΡΩΠΟΝ ΕΝ ΧΩ ΠΡΟ ΕΤΩΝ ΔΕΚΑΤΕCCΑΡΩΝ
ΕΙΤΕ ΕΝ CΩΜΑΤΙ ΟΥΚ ΟΙΔΑ ΕΙΤΕ ΕΚΤΟC ΤΟΥ CΩ
ΜΑΤΟC ΟΥΚ ΟΙΔΑ Ο ΘC ΟΙΔΕΝ ΑΡΠΑΓΕΝΤΑ ΤΟΝ
ΤΟΙΟΥΤΟΝ ΕΩC ΤΡΙΤΟΥ ΟΥΡΑΝΟΥ ΚΑΙ ΟΙΔΑ ΤΟΝ
ΤΟΙΟΥΤΟΝ ΑΝΘΡΩΠΟΝ ΕΙΤΕ ΕΝ CΩΜΑΤΙ ΕΙΤΕ
ΧΩΡΙC ΤΟΥ CΩΜΑΤΟC ΟΥΚ ΟΙΔΑ Ο ΘC ΟΙΔΕΝ ΟΤΙ
ΗΡΠΑΓΗ ΕΙC ΤΟΝ ΠΑΡΑΔΕΙCΟΝ ΚΑΙ ΗΚΟΥCΕΝ
ΑΡΡΗΤΑ ΡΗΜΑΤΑ Α ΟΥΚ ΕΞΟΝ ΑΝΘΡΩΠΩ ΛΑ
ΛΗCΑΙ ΥΠΕΡ ΤΟΥ ΤΟΙΟΥΤΟΥ ΚΑΥΧΗCΟΜΑΙ ΥΠΕΡ
ΔΕ ΕΜΑΥΤΟΥ ΟΥΔΕΝ ΚΑΥΧΗCΟΜΑΙ ΕΙ ΜΗ ΕΝ ΤΑΙC
ΑCΘΕΝΑΙΑΙC ΕΑΝ ΓΑΡ ΘΕΛΩ ΚΑΥΧΗCΟΜΑΙ
ΟΥΚ ΕCΟΜΑΙ ΑΦΤΩΝ ΑΛΗΘΕΙΑΝ ΓΑΡ ΕΡΩ
ΦΕΙΔΟΜΑΙ ΔΕ ΜΗ ΤΙC ΕΙC ΕΜΕ ΛΟΓΙCΗΤΑΙ ΥΠΕΡ
Ο ΒΛΕΠΕΙ ΜΕ Η ΑΚΟΥΕΙ ΤΙ ΕΞ ΕΜΟΥ ΚΑΙ ΤΗ
ΥΠΕΡΒΟΛΗ ΤΩΝ ΑΠΟΚΑΛΥΨΕΩΝ ΙΝΑ ΜΗ
ΥΠΕΡΑΙΡΩΜΑΙ ΕΔΟΘΗ ΜΟΙ CΚΟΛΟΨ ΤΗ CΑΡΚΙ
ΑΓΓΕΛΟC CΑΤΑΝΑ ΙΝΑ ΜΕ ΚΟΛΑΦΙΖΗ ΙΝΑ
ΥΠΕΡΑΙΡΩΜΑΙ ΥΠΕΡ ΤΟΥΤΟΥ ΤΡΙC
ΠΑΡΕΚΑΛΕCΑ ΙΝΑ ΑΠΟCΤΗ ΑΠ
ΕΜΟΥ ΚΑΙ ΕΙΡΗΚΕΝ ΜΟΙ ΑΡΚΕΙ CΟΙ Η ΧΑ
ΔΥΝΑΜΙC

outside the canon, but it may also restrict usage in specific contexts. Thus, canonical and noncanonical texts can coexist while not allowing the noncanonical to supplant the canonical.

Whether religious or otherwise, canon has always been a fairly fluid concept, even within a canonical context that is considered closed or formally decided. For example, believers who accept a closed canon of scriptural texts regularly read all sorts of additional religious texts and, in turn, allow those other texts to inform their opinions about canonical texts. Early Christians were no different, and during the second to sixth centuries AD, Christians read noncanonical gospels, acts of apostles, Christian romances (adventure tales), Gnostic treatises, and a host of other types of literature of Christian interest. Those same Christians accepted canonical texts as a voice of authority while also drawing meaning, if only personal, from the noncanonical texts at their disposal.

In this chapter, I will document the process by which the canon came to be an expression of localized Christian authority and power structures. In turn, I will also problematize the notion that canonization was an attempt to squash or erase a type of true or authentic form of early Christianity and, thereby, to suppress Christian texts.[2] In order to explore this issue, I will first need to discuss revelation briefly, because the closing of the canon had implications for what could be revealed. I will also engage the topic from the perspective of an open canon that includes ongoing revelatory statements, which is quite familiar to Latter-day Saints (see box 3.1). This latter section of the chapter will grapple with the potential that an open canon may function as an unending, an indeed unbounded, source of authority within the community.

The topic of the canon might seem far removed from today's concerns. The canon, however, represents a signifier of a shared belief and commitment to God. Nearly all Christian churches share the same scriptural books, and while Christians may interpret these books differently, they accept a canon of God's words. We Latter-day Saints, who accept a much larger canon, stand outside of that shared tradition, and so it is important for us to understand how the canon was formed and how an extended canon functions for our own faith.

Canon as an Expression of Power and Authority[3]

The beginnings of a canonical conversation can be traced to a passage in Paul's letters where he states:

> But we will not boast beyond limit, and we will observe the limits [Greek *canon*] God has appointed to us which reaches as far as you. For we were not overextending ourselves when we reached you, because we were the first to come to you with the gospel of Christ. We did not boast beyond limit with regard to the labor of others, but we have hope that as your faith grows, our work among you may be greatly enlarged so that we may proclaim the gospel in regions beyond, without boasting of work already done in another person's area [Greek *canon*]."
> (2 Corinthians 10:13–16)

As was common at the time, Paul used the Greek noun *canon* (κανών) to define a place that is measured and bordered and, thus, in one sense, a canonical space. But in seeing the boundaries of his own missionary labor, both physical and spiritual because he did not want to intrude on the work of previous missionaries, Paul laid out an argument for regional authority—"we will observe the limits"—that had been established by himself or other ecclesiastical leaders. This idea of a limit or boundary is similar to how the textual canon was initially and later conceived.

Among the earliest texts to imply the existence of a canon that guided Christian action and belief, or more accurately a *regula fidei* (a guiding rule of the faith), is found in a late first-century text. Written by a Roman Christian whom scholars and tradition have identified simply as Clement, *The First Epistle of Clement to the Corinthians* (written circa AD 95–96) counsels early Christians about various matters of belief. This ancient epistle offers counsel from the vantage point of a spiritual leader and outlines how a canon or rule of faith, not necessarily written, functioned in this early period: "Beloved, we inform you by letter about these things, not only admonishing you but also reminding ourselves. . . . Wherefore let us leave behind empty and vain thoughts and let us walk in the famous and revered canon [Greek *canon*] that has been handed down to us."[4] Notably, Clement conceives of a "famous and revered canon" that has been "handed down," thus establishing two guidelines for the development of a canonical consciousness or mindset. First, the canon was famous, well known, or even glorious (all possible meanings of the passage), and therefore it was the one recognized by the widest possible body of believers or the most recognizable. Second, the canon had been handed down, thus establishing a genealogy of authority going back to earlier Christians of reputation. One can use this canon, or rule of faith, to leave behind old ways of thinking and repent, which is precisely how Clement interpreted the meaning of the rule of faith for his reader. Furthermore, he noted that prophets had often called people to repentance and that those calls resulted in a change of heart. These early calls to repentance were now supplanted by the rule of faith that functioned in the same way—namely, to call people to repentance and change. The early tenets of belief were derived from scriptural books, but they were not limited to the books themselves. In other

▲ **FIGURE 3.3** Relief sculpture depicting Christ presenting an unfurled scroll to the apostle Peter (right) accompanied by the apostle Paul, who holds a rolled scroll (left). Sarcophagus, ca. 366– 400, Musée départemental Arles Antique. Scrolls in early Christian art alluded to knowledge, learning, authority, and scripture. This image of Christ handing over the law (*traditio legis*) emerged in fourth-century Christian art, conveying the idea that the rule of faith and authority (symbolized by scrolls) were passed down from Christ to the apostles and thence to the church. Photo: Mark D. Ellison

words, belief derived from authoritative teaching was more important than a list of authoritative books.

Tertullian of Carthage, an early third-century Christian author, also argued for a canon that would regulate Christian faith. His writings inform us about a growing Christian awareness of the need for a defined or agreed upon canon.[5] Because of his association with the New Prophecy (later called Montanism), a movement that accepted both female and male prophets, some have argued that his views may not necessarily represent more mainstream Christians. Despite these limitations, his views are useful for establishing how the early canon functioned in regulating the faith.[6] Tertullian noted, "In the following resides the defense of our opinions: according to scripture, nature, and discipline. Scripture establishes the law, nature bears witness, and discipline brings it to an end. . . . Scripture is of God, nature is of God, and discipline is of God."[7] This threefold hierarchy of authority and doctrine—scripture, nature, and discipline—is built on the sequential relationship of teachings (scripture) that lead to action (discipline) and the presupposition that Christian doctrine is, by definition, obvious, thus projecting it into the realm of indisputable and, therefore, required beliefs.

For Tertullian, the rule of faith had been handed down in the Church, thus keeping it safe and establishing lines of authority for the Christian community: "If they have these things [the teachings] for themselves, and the truth is judged by us, everyone of us walks in this rule, which the church handed down from the apostles, the apostles from Christ, and Christ from God, the contract that we proposed stands firm."[8] In this way, Tertullian makes it clear that apostolic writings through oral tradition, and including authoritative texts, ought to be prioritized in the canonical conversation, thus subtly moving away from governance through spiritual manifestations and toward governance through consistent application of scriptural principle. This outline provides an additional insight: not all canonical texts are of equal authority. According to early Christian tradition, some New Testament texts were not written by apostles. Luke, for instance, was believed to be a disciple of the Apostle Paul but not an apostle himself, and Mark makes no claim to apostolic authority although later tradition connected his gospel to Peter. From Tertullian's writings, we can conclude that these canonical principles create demarcated boundaries that placed his church on one side and its enemies, those who relied on different formulations of their Christian beliefs, on the opposite side.

Irenaeus (circa AD 130–202) also reports something important about the canonical process at the beginning of the third century.

As a Christian author in Lugdunum (Lyon in France), Irenaeus was a relatively minor figure within the wider ecclesiastical structure of the third-century Christian church, but nonetheless, he established the concept that the Church is a vehicle of preserving and handing down the true teachings that, in turn, laid the foundation for the rule of faith. He leaned heavily into the belief that the Church taught the same doctrine everywhere, *and* the Church protected that same doctrine.[9] It may seem questionable that the Church "protected the same doctrine" and did so evenly in all its churches, but Irenaeus noted, "While scattered throughout the whole world, the Church has received this message and this faith and still—as if living in only one house—carefully preserves it. She believes these points of doctrine as if she had only one soul."[10]

From the foregoing, it is clear that the Church—the one that spanned the whole world, to use Irenaeus's words—had the authority and ability to protect and pass down the traditions that could be traced back to the apostles (so Tertullian). These safeguarded teachings were fortunately under the control of an institution that viewed the teachings' preservation and transmission as a matter of utmost concern. That same institution also emphasized the need to keep the teaching of those truths consistent and in harmony with what had been passed on from the earlier generations. Additionally, the Church began shifting its focus to canonical texts, in part because the churches had the means to produce copies of the scriptures. In other words, the institutional church had an outsized role in producing the texts that supported canonical teachings. As is apparent from these early statements, one of the earliest points of emphasis in the growing sense of canon was the acknowledgement that the Church needed a centralized authority to maintain consistency and to distribute globally the teachings about Jesus. The emerging power structure—the Church—was viewed favorably by these early commentators, who recognized the need for something greater than a localized approach to canon and authority in an environment with a functionally open canon.

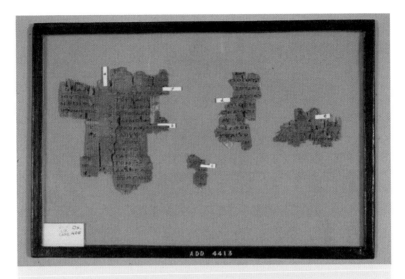

▲ **FIGURE 3.4**   Cambridge University library manuscript 4113, Papyrus Oxyrhynchus 405, containing some of the writings of Irenaeus (ca. 130–202). Photo: Wikimedia Commons

What Was Actually Canonized

From the foregoing examples, it is clear that in the second and third centuries the idea of canonical teachings developed before an actual list of books was compiled.[11] This is an important distinction because it helps draw attention to what was potentially excluded in the later canon lists—namely, those teachings, books, and writings that did not support the canonical teachings and beliefs that the Church and its various authorities had endorsed. Returning to the writings of the second and third centuries will help draw out what was being taught that needed careful safeguarding and that could in turn become a reason to exclude books from the canon.

Irenaeus, in a work entitled *The Demonstration of the Apostolic Preaching*, records what had been passed on to him and what he accepted as the canonical teaching of the late second-century church. The wording of the rule of faith that he passed down to his readers is punctuated by formulaic statements of belief about God the Father,

BOX 3.2   Irenaeus's Articles of Our Faith

At the end of the second century, Irenaeus summarized the core teachings of Christianity as follows:

> "And this is the order of our faith, the foundation of [the] edifice and the support of [our] conduct: God, the Father, uncreated, uncontainable, invisible, one God, the Creator of all: this is the first article (κεφάλαιον) of our faith. And the second article: the Word of God, the Son of God, Christ Jesus our Lord, who was revealed by the prophets according to the character of their prophecy and according to the nature of the economies of the Father, by whom all things were made, and who, in the last times, to recapitulate all things, became a man amongst men, visible and palpable, in order to abolish death, to demonstrate life, and to effect communion between God and man. And the third article: the Holy Spirit, through whom the prophets prophesied and the patriarchs learnt the things of God and the righteous were led in the path of righteousness, and who, in the last times, was poured out in a new fashion upon the human race renewing man, throughout the world, to God."[12]

the Son, and the Holy Spirit, and he affirms separate categories for each: the Creator, the Word of God through whom creation was carried out, and the Holy Spirit who inspired the prophets to speak (see box 3.2). A noticeably similar version of the rule of faith was set forth by Tertullian, who wrote at the turn of the third century (see box 3.3). He too was familiar with a standard, or rule of faith, that established something of a minimum set of beliefs for Christians.

Both authors affirm that the earliest authoritative teaching consisted of a declaration about the Father, Son, and Holy Spirit, including

BOX 3.3   **Tertullian's Rule of Faith**

At the beginning of the third century, Tertullian summarized the core teachings of Christianity as follows:

> "However, the rule of faith is this, that from this point we may defend what we confess, that it is obvious what is believed: 'There is one God only, none other than the creator of the world, who fashioned the universe from nothing through his own Word, the first of all sent forth; that word is called his Son, in the name of God and was seen in various manifestations by the patriarchs, always heard by the prophets, at last carried down by the Spirit and power of God the Father into the Virgin Mary, who was made flesh in her womb, and from her was born and went forth as Jesus Christ; after that he taught a new law and the promise of a new kingdom of heaven, he performed miracles, and having been crucified he rose the third day; and having ascended into heaven he sat on the right of the Father, and he sent in his place the power of the Holy Spirit to lead the believing; he will come in splendor taking up the saints into the enjoyment of eternal life and the heavenly promises, and condemning the evil to perpetual fire, after the resurrection of these have occurred with the restoration of their flesh.' This is the rule instituted by Christ."[13]

teachings on their work and their nature. Although not officially a creed at that point in time, one can easily draw direct lines from it to the fourth-century Apostles' Creed that is accepted broadly by modern Christian denominations.[14] These early creed-like statements were part of the canonical process, a process that reflected the Christian belief in God, his Son, and the Holy Spirit. Such statements do not exclude the teaching of other truths or other ideas, or even reading a

✠ SANCTVS IRENÆVS ✠

wide collection of Christian texts, but they do establish a minimum of belief, a type of baseline that Christians had to accept in order to be considered as standing in solidarity with the early Christian church. Its power was two-fold: (1) to establish boundaries for those who wished to stand *with* the church and (2) to create an argument for excluding those who could not accept these creed-like statements.

From this point, it is fairly easy to chart the path toward formal canonization of texts and books of scripture—what might be termed in this environment inspired writings, or writings that helped bolster the early creed-like rules of faith. In his now famous letter establishing the celebration of Easter, Athanasius of Alexandria (died AD 373) put into writing what had become the officially recognized, although not clearly voted upon, canon of the church. The letter written in AD 367 listed the twenty-seven books of the New Testament in their current order and with an "Old Testament" of twenty-two books.[15] Although Athanasius was not the first to consider or even write about canon-ical books, he represents a turning point in the process in which the Church shifted its interests from establishing a rule of faith to creating a fixed collection of books that supported the rule of faith. Moving forward in time, the lists of canonical books reflect the Athanasian imprint. For the modern reader, Athanasius was a Christian leader who found the canon to be a productive tool to regulate unity within the churches.

In an earlier written summary of events that took place at the Council of Nicaea (AD 325), Athanasius had already used the lan-guage of exclusion to reject certain texts as not belonging to the canon. Historically speaking, his denunciation of particular Chris-tian texts was challenging because at least one text he rejected was

▲ **FIGURE 3.6**　Codex Sinaiticus, written in the mid-fourth century. It contained the earliest complete collection of the books of the New Testament, as well as the books of the Old Testament in their Greek translation (the Septuagint, or LXX). It also included the *Shepherd of Hermas*. Photo: codexsinaiticus.org

accepted by some Christians and rejected by others, and in his summary of the text, he quoted its teachings to support his own views even though he openly acknowledged that the text was not part of the Christian canon.[16] The text in question—the *Shepherd of Hermas*—taught the important truth that God was the creator of all things, a truth established and passed on in the rule of faith that the Church had safeguarded. To prove his opponents wrong in their rejection of the eternal sonship of the Son of God, Athanasius wrote: "In the *Shepherd* it is written, since they accept this book, even though it is not of the Canon, 'First of all believe that God is one, who created all things, and arranged them, and brought all things from not being into being.'"[17] Athanasius stood with some of his second- and third-century colleagues when he denounced the *Shepherd of Hermas*, a book that had already been rejected as either spurious or apocryphal. However, he was clearly aware of its contents in the fourth century, indicating he had read it, and he marshalled that text in the defense of his own faith.[18]

What was at stake in the discussion of faith at the Council of Nicaea was not a list of books that could be read in the liturgy and worship services but rather a defense of the Church's rule of faith. When a noncanonical, to use an anachronistic term in this period, text supported the rule of faith, Athanasius was happy to cite it in defense of his own beliefs. This usage of noncanonical texts demonstrates a key tenet of this chapter—namely, that in the second, third, and early fourth centuries, canon debates functioned as a means of maintaining the purity and truth of the Church's teachings, which, in turn, resulted in a focus on which books supported those teachings (see box 3.4). Such considerations may have played a part in Athanasius's

---

BOX 3.4 **Doctrine and Canon among the Latter-day Saints**

The influence of doctrine on the shape of canon can also be seen in the history of The Church of Jesus Christ of Latter-day Saints. Some of Joseph Smith's earliest revelations were published in 1833 as the Book of Commandments. Two years later, when this book was published again, new revelations and a series of theological lectures (today called the *Lectures on Faith*) were added. The Book of Commandments was then renamed the Doctrine and Covenants. In 1921, however, the *Lectures on Faith* were removed from the Doctrine and Covenants because, it was argued, they conflicted with revelations received by Joseph Smith after the lectures were first added to the Doctrine and Covenants. For instance, the *Lectures on Faith* describe God the Father as a "personage of Spirit." Yet a revelation received by Joseph Smith in 1843 states: "The Father has a body of flesh and bones as tangible as man's" (Doctrine and Covenants 130:22). The prioritization of this doctrine in 1921, in part, led to the decanonization of the *Lectures on Faith*.[19]

twenty-two-book canon of the Old Testament, thus causing him to reject seventeen books that are canonized by Christians today.

A turning point in the discussion about canon appears to have taken place at the Council of Laodicea that convened in Asia Minor (AD 363–64). That council issued a statement in the form of a decree that forbade the reading of certain books in the Christian liturgy. The fifty-ninth decree uses the terms *canonical* and *noncanonical* to designate the books that were then under consideration and in general circulation. The sixtieth decree specifically lists the books that were noncanonical or not to be read in the liturgy. Interestingly, the decree failed to include the Book of Revelation in the New Testament, and it set forth a twenty-two-book Old Testament that differed slightly from Athanasius's. The sixtieth decree or canon is, however, disputed because it does not appear in many of the early copies of the council's proceedings; therefore, it may have been added later to reflect canonical disputes from a later period, but the designations of canonical and noncanonical belong to the fifty-ninth canon and are, therefore, relatively secure, historically speaking.

So, what was actually canonized? In this section, I laid out some of the evidence for the concept that emerging canonical conversations began already in the second century and took full shape in the fourth century in the form of excluding books and designating them as existing outside the canon.[20] Those conversations about canon were initially conceived as a way to establish, support, and bolster the rule of faith that was accepted in the churches, and while it initially had little to do with excluding books, it later evolved to such a discussion. The conversation about canon, from what remains of the historical record, took place first in the writings of the Church's educated elites—Tertullian, Irenaeus, and certainly others—and later became an agenda item for the Church's ecumenical councils. These conversations took place among the Church's bishops and trained clergy. Eventually, their decrees were circulated among the churches to attempt a Churchwide policy on the rule of faith and which books could productively be read as supportive of that rule of faith.

▲ **FIGURE 3.7** Christ seated and holding an open book inscribed DOMINVS LEGEM DAT (Latin, "The Lord gives the Law"), surrounded by apostles and Gospel authors who also hold codex-style books or scrolls; the apostle at left is identified as Matthew on his scroll. Relief from the sarcophagus of Concordius, Musée départemental Arles Antique, late fourth century. This is the earliest sarcophagus known to be made for a Christian bishop, and with its numerous reliefs depicting men with codices, scrolls, and bundles of scrolls, it seems to represent a bishop's particular interest in the authority of the church as represented by the canon, which was passed from Christ to apostles to the church. Photo: Mark D. Ellison

▲ **FIGURE 3.8**   Illumination of Origen of Alexandria, Bayerische Staatsbibliothek, Clm 17092, f. 130v, twelfth century. This author portrait page features Origen as an ambidextrous writer at his unique lectern held up by a dragon's tail. Writing with both hands may indicate Origen's adept learning in both Alexandrian Christian theology and Neoplatonic philosophy. Photo: Used with permission, Bayerische Staatbibliothek

Canon Formation as a Product of a Power Struggle

By focusing the discussion of the canon on the dynamics of exclusion and the people who managed that discussion, it is tempting to ascribe motives to those who established the arguments for the exclusion of texts. Such motives are hazy at best and warrant further attention and consideration. One context for the setting of the early canon debate was the power struggle between North African Christian charismatic teachers, those who placed spiritual manifestation at the forefront, and those who supported broad and powerful church governance. This section of the chapter will describe the final moments of canon formalization in the fourth century. Those who came out victorious, Athanasius and his allies, were able to control the canon and thereby limit the availability and authority of some Christian texts used by their antagonists.

In the third and fourth centuries, charismatic Christian teachers found their liberal views on scripture to be the object of intense scrutiny. A particularly strong example of this scrutiny is Epiphanius's condemnation of the Christian liberal thinker Origen of Alexandria, who had used analytical and allegorical methods to interpret scripture—approaches to scripture that were later deemed to be unreliable and that yielded interpretations that fell outside of the rule of faith.[21] The liberal Alexandrian teachers accepted a broad canon that included both religious texts and books by pagan philosophers, and they favored allegorical interpretation of scripture.[22]

Particularly important was the role of charismatic teachers, who promoted personal visions and contacts with the divine mind. These teachers existed in a robust intellectual environment that favored new thinking and reinterpretation of Christian literature as well as the potential to emend or shape the interpretation of even the most authoritative Christian texts.[23] Some of the most notable Christian charismatic figures of this type are Clement of Rome (died circa AD 98/99), Valentinus (died circa AD 150), Pantaenus (died circa AD 200), Ptolemy (died late second century), Origen (circa AD 185–254), and Arius (died AD 336). Some of these figures created a thriving Christian school environment where the teacher attracted pupils who would support allegorical interpretation of scripture. These teachers had followers and pupils, all of whom appear to have felt dedicated to the Christian gospel, albeit flavored by their Alexandrian training.

Athanasius and other bishops in the fourth century who stood against Arius (anti-Arian), however, were of a different bent, and they advocated a more liturgically oriented approach. By controlling the liturgy—the way that church services were conducted and what was taught—they were able to control what the masses heard in church. They thereby sought strict oversight of Christian practice and greater consistency in the presentation of the gospel. The turning point in the debate between the charismatics and those who wanted greater ecclesiastical oversight took place "when Arius's teachings appeared to Alexander [Athanasius's predecessor] to transgress the limits of acceptable diversity."[24] This point was important in the conversation at the Council of Nicaea, although not its main purpose. The Council ultimately denounced Arius formally and bolstered Athanasius and his church-minded allies. Moving forward after Nicaea, Athanasius continued to strengthen his position—with several setbacks in the form of personal exiles—through ecclesiastical letters to the churches. In his second festal letter, purportedly written in AD 330, although possibly in AD 342, Athanasius made his position quite clear: Christian disciples should be reading the words of New Testament authors rather than listening to charismatic teachers from their own time. "Of these [New Testament authors] the Word would have us disciples, and these should of right be our teachers, *and to them only is it necessary to give heed*, for of them only is 'the word faithful and worthy of all acceptation'; these not being disciples because they heard from others, but being eye-witnesses and ministers of the Word, that which they had heard from Him have they handed down."[25] Returning to the larger interest of canonization, this type of thinking about the canon is important because it positions the word of God and its appropriate interpretation as the unique authority in the Church, while false teachers are also positioned as outsiders and different from the true Nicene faith.

▲ **FIGURE 3.9** Mosaic depicting an open cabinet containing the four New Testament Gospels: MARCVUS, LVCAS, MATTEVS, and IO-ANNES; Mausoleum of Galla Placidia, Ravenna, Italy, 425–450. The mosaic represents furnishings and books typical of what fifth-century Christians would have seen in the churches, oratories, and other spaces where they worshiped. The four separate Gospel books reflect a time when books or collections of books circulated as individual codices but were not always bound together in a single Bible. They also represent a time when the majority of Christians had come to accept the four canonical Gospels as authoritative and appropriate for reading aloud in worship services. Photo: Mark D. Ellison

Ultimately, the fourth century saw the proposal for and endorsement of a Churchwide canon of books. That canon was produced in the environment of inner-church debates about who should hold authority over the minds and hearts of Christian disciples: the charismatic teachers or the bishops with their perspectives on maintaining church governance. In the end, the need for harmony and unity of message prevailed over the charismatic interests of the members, and the canon reflects a message of stability, consistency, and authority.

Canon as a Means of Balancing Revelation and Scripture

Situated within the larger developments of the Church's early statements about the canon was a conversation about revelation and the function of the Holy Spirit. As any religious tradition with brick-and-mortar edifices has confronted, the proper place of revelation in the Church's declaration of faith and belief is something that requires attention and care (see box 3.5). With too many people offering revelations, the message of the faith quickly spirals out of control and loses its unique identity, and with too strict control over revelation, the institution suppresses the voice of the Holy Spirit. This balance is as true of early Christianity as it is true today.

Regulation of prophecy, prophets, and revelation took place within an environment wherein Christians sought to declare the end of prophecy among Jews as a sign that the Holy Spirit had abandoned them. These early anti-Jewish arguments were part of the Christian message to establish its own unique claims to spirit-informed belief. The regulation of prophecy was used against Jews and also other Christians, and was used in the context of Christians who broke away from the Western Church because those Christians rejected the Western view of controlled or regulated revelation. An example of the types of statements Christians made to explain the end of the ministration of the Holy Spirit among Jews is found in the writings of Justin Martyr. Writing in the late second century, Justin authored what is likely a fictional dialogue with a Jewish interlocutor named Trypho.

BOX 3.5 Revelation and Authority among the Latter-day Saints

Joseph Smith Jr. was not the only person to experience visions and receive revelations in the early days of The Church of Jesus Christ of Latter-day Saints. Early openness to the power of divine revelation, however, created a potential crisis of authority in the growing Church. For instance, in August 1830, Joseph Smith learned that Hiram Page, one of the eight witnesses to the Book of Mormon, had written and circulated revelations for the Church that he (Hiram) had said he received through a seer-stone. In response, in September 1830, Joseph Smith delivered to Oliver Cowdery the following revelation regarding Hiram Page: "But, behold, verily, verily, I [the Lord] say unto thee, no one shall be appointed to receive commandments and revelations in this church excepting my servant Joseph Smith, Jun., for he receiveth them even as Moses. . . . And again, thou shalt take thy brother, Hiram Page, between him and thee alone, and tell him that those things which he hath written from that stone are not of me and that Satan deceiveth him" (Doctrine and Covenants 28:2, 11). Hiram Page denounced his own writings and submitted to the authority of Joseph Smith.

In the dialogue, Justin expressed what has come to be seen as a type of early Christian belief in supersessionism—the belief that God had ended his covenant relationship with Jews and initiated a new covenant relationship with Christians (by contrast, see Romans 11:26). Justin argued that the cessation of God's special relationship with Jews was signaled by the withdrawal of the Holy Spirit and, hence, the removal of the prophetic voice: "The Scriptures state that these gifts of the Holy Spirit were bestowed upon [Christ], not as though he were in need of them, but as though they were about to rest upon him, that is, to come to an end with him, so that there would be no more prophets among your people as of old, as is plainly evident to you, for after him there has not been a prophet among you."[26]

Some Christians also attempted to define types of inspiration and prophecy that stood outside of acceptable norms. Hippolytus of Rome, writing near the beginning of the third century, attempted to discount certain expressions of inspiration in an attempt to normalize Christian worship practices. What is important in Hippolytus's critique of certain manifestations of prophecy is his reliance on scripture as a way of determining what was improper and unacceptable. For Hippolytus, scripture and inspiration needed to be received in measure and ought to be subject to one another as a means of defining what was good and acceptable for the faith. As he relates in the story of a prophet from Pontus, those who advocate a life guided by prophecy are subject to misunderstanding and misinterpretation of the promptings they receive. Furthermore, they are subject to having their prophecies proven wrong when they attempt to foretell events that will come to pass (see box 3.6).

What This Means for Latter-day Saints

The canon debates may seem distant to the modern reader, who has received an agreed upon canon that forms a foundation for modern practice and belief. Despite the temporal distance that exists between our own day and that of the age of canonization, the process by which the canon came to be established contains several important concepts that are still relevant.

1. The period of an open canon was productive for charismatics who drew on visionary experiences and revelation in their presentation of the gospel. There was a newness about the message, and it resulted in the production of new Christian texts, some of which have been called Gnostic by modern scholars. The period of open canon mirrors certain prophetic moments in the history of The Church of Jesus Christ of Latter-day Saints.

Testing a Visionary Man

At the beginning of the third century, Hippolytus of Rome warned against so-called new revelations exceeding the bounds of canon:

"But a certain other man was similarly in Pontus, and he himself governed the church, being a reverent and humble man, though not applying himself unfailingly to the Scriptures but rather believing dreams which he saw. For when a first and second and a third dream happened to him, he began to foretell the future to the brothers as a prophet, 'This I saw and this is about to be.' And once, having been led astray he said, 'Brothers, know that after one year the judgment is about to be.'

"They who heard him who predicted, 'The day of the Lord is imminent,' with weeping and lamenting they begged the Lord night and day holding before their eyes the approaching day of judgment and he led the brothers to such fear and terror so to allow their lands and fields to be desolate, and the wealthy to destroy their possessions. But he said to them, 'If it does not happen just as I said, do not believe the Scriptures anymore but do whatever each of you wishes.'

"But they waited for the result and after a year nothing was fulfilled of what that man said happened, and he himself was shamed as a deceiver, but the Scriptures were shown as true, but the brothers were found scandalized so that henceforth their virgins were married and their men dwelt in fields. They, who sold their possessions without plan, were found later begging."[27]

2. Closing the canon was the result of a struggle for authority, and while the open canon promised newness, it was also associated with the authority of charismatic Christian teachers. In other words, both the open and closed canons were part of larger structures of authority in the Church. For some, the closed canon functioned as a weapon to push other Christians out of the Church. For others, an open canon functioned similarly to declare that other Christians were closed off from the Holy Spirit.

3. Canonization, whether closed or open, resulted in struggles for maintaining or extending religious authority. In reopening the canon, Latter-day Saints have shifted authority away from those who support the traditional canon and relocated that authority in modern Latter-day Saint apostles and prophets.

4. Given that a canon is a function of ecclesiastical authority, an open canon allows for boundless or unlimited ecclesiastical authority. This authority may be seen in new revelations and statements of belief that allow the institutional church to maintain an absolute position of authority to reveal the word of God, similar to Roman Catholicism and other forms of Christianity with a strong hierarchal system of governance.

Notes

1. All translations of the New Testament are taken from Thomas A. Wayment, *The New Testament: A Translation for Latter-day Saints: A Study Bible* (Salt Lake City: Deseret Book; Provo, UT: Religious Studies Center, Brigham Young University, 2018).

2. For an example of an early Latter-day Saint view of canon and authority, see James E. Talmage, *The Great Apostasy in the Light of Scriptural and Secular History* (Salt Lake City: Deseret News, 1907), chapter 3.

3. For readers interested in the topic and for how Christians generally approach the issue, I have included below some of the most recent and important studies. Latter-day Saint scholars have continued to wrestle with the concept of an open canon; therefore, I have also included several of the most important studies on that topic as well. See Lee Martin McDonald, *Formation of the Bible: The Study of the Church's Canon* (Peabody, MA: Hendrickson, 2012); Bruce M. Metzger, *The Canon of the New Testament: Its Origin, Development, and Significance* (New York: Oxford University Press, 1997). The most recent work on the canon by Latter-day Saint authors tends to be descriptive; see Daniel Becerra, "The Canonization of the New Testament," in *New Testament History, Culture, and Society: A Background to the Texts of the New Testament*, ed. Lincoln H. Blumell (Provo, UT: Religious Studies Center, Brigham Young University; Salt Lake City: Deseret Book, 2019), 772–85. Targeting the concept of an open or expanded canon, a conference—organized by Brian Birch, Boyd Petersen, and Blair Van Dyke—brought to the fore the subtle power dynamics of Latter-day Saint claims to having extracanonical texts and the possible production of new religious texts in the future. The introduction to the aforementioned conference collection carefully lays out the challenges and problems of an intentionally expanding canon. See Blair G. Van Dyke, Brian D. Birch, and Boyd J. Peterson, eds., *The Expanded Canon: Perspectives on Mormonism and Sacred Texts* (Salt Lake City: Greg Kofford Books, 2018). Finally, an important collection of essays grapples with tracing a Latter-day Saint narrative within early Christian history by attempting to build bridges to existing scholarly approaches to the canonization period; see Miranda Wilcox and John Young, eds., *Standing Apart: Mormon Historical Consciousness and the Concept of Apostasy* (New York: Oxford University Press, 2014). For representative studies on the topic of the canon by academics, see Harry Gamble, *The New Testament Canon: Its Making and Meaning* (Philadelphia: Fortress Press, 1985).

4. *1 Clement* 7.1–2. Translation by author.

5. See John F. Jansen, "Tertullian and the New Testament," in "Tertullian," ed. Everett Ferguson, special issue, *The Second Century: A Journal of Early Christian Studies* 2, no. 4 (Winter 1982): 191–207.

6. See J. N. D. Kelly, *Early Christian Creeds*, 3rd ed. (London: Routledge, 2014), 87; David L. Eastman, *Early North African Christianity: Turning Points in the Development of the Church* (Grand Rapids, MI: Baker, 2021), 42–44.

7. *The Veiling of Virgins* 16.1. Translation by author. Latin text from Vincent Bulhart, *Tertullian-Studien* (Cambridge: Cambridge University Press, 2009).

8. *Prescription against Heretics* 37.1. Compare the similar, and earlier, rule of faith in Irenaeus, *Against Heresies* 1.2: "The church...which accepts this belief: one God, Father, Almighty, who made the heaven and the earth and the seas and all things in them, and one Christ Jesus, the Son of God, who was made flesh for our salvation, and one Holy Spirit, who declared through the prophets the plan of salvation and his coming, and the virgin birth, and the suffering, and the resurrection from the dead, and the bodily ascension into heaven of our beloved Christ Jesus, our Lord."

9. See Denis Minns, *Irenaeus: An Introduction* (London: T&T Clark, 2010), 2.

10. Irenaeus, *Against Heresies* 1.10.1. Translation from James R. Payton, *Irenaeus on the Christian Faith: A Condensation of 'Against Heresies'* (London: Lutterworth, 2012), 32. The translation favors the Greek wording and word order, although as with much of the remainder of *Against Heresies*, a Latin translation is the most substantive witness to Irenaeus.

11. Compare Gamble, *The New Testament Canon*, 17, who discusses the purpose of the early statements about the rule of faith. Compare also C. Rebecca Rine, "Canon Lists Are Not Just Lists," *Journal of Biblical Literature* 139, no. 4 (2020): 809–31.

12. Irenaeus, *On the Apostolic Preaching*, trans. John Behr, vol. 17 in the Popular Patristics Series (Crestwood, NY: St. Vladimir's Seminary Press, 1997), 43–44.

13. Tertullian, *Prescription against Heretics* 13.1–5. Author's translation based on the Latin from Tertullian, *On the Prescription of Heretics* (Frankfurt: Minerva, 1968).

14. See Kelly, *Early Christian Creeds*, 398–434.

15. For Origen's list of canonical books, which was delivered nearly a century before Athanasius's list, see Michael Kruger, "Origen's List of New Testament Books in *Homiliae on Josuam* 7.1: A Fresh Look," in *Mark, Manuscripts, and Monotheism: Essays in Honor of Larry W. Hurtado*, ed. Chris Keith and Dieter Roth (London: Bloomsbury, T&T Clark, 2014), 99–117. The twenty-two-book canon of the Hebrew Bible may be the result of Christians finding a symbolic meaning behind the twenty-two letters of the Hebrew alphabet. A translation of Athanasius's letter can be found in "From Letter XXXIX," in *Nicene and Post-Nicene Fathers*, series 2, ed. Philip Schaff, vol. 4, *Athanasius: Select Works and Letters*, Christian Classicals Ethereal Library, https://www.ccel.org/ccel/schaff/npnf204. xxv.iii.iii.xxv.html. For Athanasius's epistle, festal letter 39, see D. Brakke,

Athanasius and the Politics of Asceticism, Oxford Early Christian Studies series (Oxford: Oxford University Press, 1995), 326–332. Athanasius's canon list may have been descriptive or proscriptive. For an exploration of this matter, see Bart D. Ehrman, "The New Testament Canon of Didymus the Blind," *Vigiliae Christianae* 37, no. 1 (1983): 1–2.

16. To read about Athanasius fighting against Melitians and charismatic teachers and, thus, attempting to push for a distinctly Athanasian view of the canon, see David Brakke, "Canon Formation and Social Conflict in Fourth Century Egypt: Athanasius of Alexandria's Thirty-Ninth 'Festal Letter,'" *The Harvard Theological Review* 87, no. 4 (1994): 399.

17. Athanasius, *Defense of the Nicene Definition* 18, quoting Hermas, *Mandates* 1.1.

18. See Athanasius, *Defense of the Nicene Definition* 18. See also Tertullian, *On Modesty* 10.6, and Irenaeus, *Against Heresies* 1.20.1, who condemn the *Shepherd* as extracanonical.

19. See Church History Topics, s.v. "Lectures on Theology ('Lectures on Faith')," accessed December 14, 2021, https://www.churchofjesuschrist.org/study/history/topics/lectures-on-faith.

20. I have intentionally avoided discussing the influence of Marcion (circa AD 85–160), who was one of the early forces to initiate a conversation about the early Christian canon, because his influence, while important, was of a different type. Marcion forced Christians to come to terms with the writings passed on in the Hebrew Bible and to consider whether some New Testament writings should be rejected because they were supportive of Jewish ideas about God and the Creator.

21. Origen, who had died in the mid-third century (circa AD 254), was later condemned by Epiphanius (died AD 403) in several works, including the *Panarion*. The later effort to condemn Origen led to his posthumous excommunication at the Second Council of Constantinople (AD 553).

22. This acceptance of a broad canon is evidenced in the eclectic nature of the Nag Hammadi tractates, which include, among other things, copies of some of Plato's dialogues. See Brakke, "Canon Formation," 401.

23. See Brakke, "Canon Formation," 402.

24. Brakke, "Canon Formation," 404.

25. Athanasius, *Festal Letters* 2.7, in *Nicene and Post-Nicene Fathers*, series 2, trans. Philip Schaff, vol. 4, *Saint Athanasius: Select Writings and Letters* (New York: Charles Scribner's Sons, 1907), 512; emphasis added. On the topic of dating of the second epistle, see Brian Brennan, "Athanasius' 'Vita Antonii': A Sociological Interpretation," *Vigiliae Christianae* 39, no. 3 (1985): 221; Brakke, "Canon Formation," 405; G. Christopher Stead, "Athanasius' Earliest Written Work," *The Journal of Theological Studies* 39

(1988): 76–91. On events surrounding Athanasius's first exile (AD 335), see H. A. Drake, "Athanasius' First Exile," *Greek, Roman, and Byzantine Studies* 27 (1986): 193–204.

26. Justin Martyr, *Dialogue with Trypho* 87, in Justin Martyr, *Dialogue with Trypho*, ed. Michael Slusser, trans. Thomas B. Falls, vol. 3 in Selections from the Fathers of the Church series (Washington, DC: Catholic University of America, 2003), 136. Although Justin Martyr insists prophecy ended among the Jews after Jesus, Jewish authors describe prophecy continuing in various forms. For instance, more than thirty years after Jesus's death and resurrection, a Jewish prophet foretold the destruction of the Jerusalem temple (AD 70) according to Josephus, *Jewish War* 6.300–309.

27. Hippolytus, *Commentary on Daniel* 4.19. Translation from Thomas C. Schmidt, *Hippolytus of Rome: Commentary on Daniel and 'Chronicon'* (Piscataway, NJ: Gorgias Press, 2017).

✳ 4 ✳

CHURCH ORGANIZATION

Priesthood Offices and Women's Leadership Roles

Ariel Bybee Laughton

I commend to you our sister Phoebe, a deacon of the church at Cenchreae. . . . Greet Prisca and Aquila who work with me in Christ Jesus, and who risked their necks for my life, to whom I not only give thanks, but also all the churches of the Gentiles. Greet also the church in their house. Greet my beloved Epaenerus, who was the first convert in Asia, for Christ. Greet Mary, who has worked very hard among you. Greet Andronicus and Junia, my relatives, who were in prison with me; they are prominent among the apostles, and they were in Christ before I was.

—Romans 16:1, 3–7,
New Revised Standard Version

T he sixteenth chapter of Paul's letter to the Romans is an extended
greeting to numerous members
of the Christian church at Rome. Often including praise for the works
of various individuals, Paul's salutations give the impression of a busy,
vibrant body of Saints of different statuses—men and women alike—
who were working together side by side to preach the gospel, to teach
and witness of Christ, and to serve and support other members of their
community. For Latter-day Saint readers, this passage of scripture is
particularly striking because of the prominence of women and the association of some of these women with the terms "apostle" and "deacon."
In the structure of the Church of Jesus Christ today, these terms are
titles for specific offices of the priesthood and are limited to men. But
in Paul's time, these titles and the organizational structures that would
come to define priesthood offices of the Church in coming centuries
were new, still largely undefined, and much more fluid than they are
today.

Evidence for organized hierarchies of leadership in the New Testament is fragmentary and vague at best. The Gospels record that
Jesus called and set apart the Twelve Apostles and sent them out to
preach the gospel (see Mark 6:7; Matthew 10:1; Luke 9:1–2), and

▶ FIGURE 4.1   Funerary inscription from the fifth-century basilica
at Philippi, Greece, memorializing the female deacon Agathē and
a man named John (likely her husband). It reads: "Grave belonging
to the deaconess Agathe and to John the cashier and linen-weaver."
Photo: Used with permission, © bilwander / https://www.flickr.com/
photos/bilwander

that seventy were called later on and sent to preach in a similar manner (see Luke 10.1). James, the brother of Jesus, seems to have exercised a particular leadership office over the Church in Jerusalem (see Acts 15:13; 21:18; Galatians 1:19; 2:9, 12) along with a group of elders (see Acts 11:30; 15:22; 1 Timothy 5:17; James 5:14), and Peter held a commission from Jesus to be the founding rock (Greek *petra*) upon which Christ would build his Church (see Matthew 16:18). But the primary calling and office of Christian leaders during the first century was to "go into all the world, and preach the gospel to every creature" (Mark 16:15 NRSV; see also Matthew 28:19; Luke 24:47; Acts 1:8), and the missionary-focused Christian community had not yet defined many of its leadership positions beyond the apostolic calling to spread the gospel to all the world.[1] Thus, we can see Paul using terms like *apostle, elder,* and *deacon* broadly and in various ways throughout his writings and in reference to both men and women.[2] This loosely defined leadership structure of the early Christian community opened up a number of possibilities for Christian women. The New Testament clearly shows that women actively led and participated in the early Church as missionaries, prophets, teachers, and patrons. As the Church grew, however, and became more focused on the management of the Church as an institution, its offices became more well-defined, and opportunities for women to participate in worship and hold leadership roles became more limited. In the centuries that followed Christianity's birth, common cultural attitudes about women and proper gender roles increasingly determined the ways in which women were viewed by Church leaders and how they were allowed to contribute (see box 4.1).

Women's Participation in the First-Century Church

In the Greco-Roman world, women were considered to be inferior to men, as they were in most cultures of the first century. During this time, all women, apart from some priestesses of various pagan cults, were expected to marry and bear children in order to secure the family line.[3] Greco-Roman women were expected to embody traditional

BOX 4.1   Why It Matters

As Latter-day Saints, we believe in "the same organization that existed in the Primitive Church" (Articles of Faith 1:6). Studying the development of Church offices in early Christianity helps us understand the ways in which the restored Church today both reflects and diverges from early Christian churches. It also highlights the critical role of women in the early Christian movement and sensitizes us to some of the ways in which women's opportunities to lead and participate in church, then and now, have been minimized over time by social and cultural factors. We also gain greater appreciation for living prophets whose teachings are opening greater opportunities for women's leadership and participation today.

female virtues such as modesty, silence, chastity, and piety.[4] However, in Roman society, social class was always a more important indicator of power and prestige than gender, and thus a woman's real-life experience was determined not only by her sex but also by other factors such as her wealth, marital status, citizenship, family of origin, and whether she was a slave, freed slave, or free-born person.[5] Therefore, it is not surprising to see women throughout the first-century Roman Empire, especially those of status and wealth, holding and managing property, running businesses, and serving as leaders and patrons of people, organizations, and projects. By the first century, Roman laws allowed women greater freedom to manage more of their own property and affairs, including initiating divorce or remarriage, without male supervision.[6]

The rights and privileges women enjoyed in Roman society, in conjunction with the loose and undefined nature of early Christian leadership structures, translated into opportunities to participate and exercise leadership in the early Christian community.[7] For example,

▲ **FIGURE 4.2** An early Christian woman named Cerula, portrayed veiled and in the posture of prayer beneath a staurogram (symbol of Christ with the letters alpha and omega), surrounded by gospel books, and accompanied by the inscription "Cerula [rests] in peace." From the San Gennaro Catacomb, Naples, Italy, fifth–sixth centuries. Photo: Courtesy of Dominik Matus via Wikimedia Commons (public domain)

women were active and prominent missionaries who taught the gospel and brought many of the first converts to the Church. Following the pattern that Christ had set when he sent the Twelve out to preach the gospel two by two (see Mark 6:7), early Christian missionaries generally traveled in pairs as they worked to spread the gospel message. Some women also worked in missionary pairs with brothers or sons, such as Nereas and his sister (see Romans 16:15) and Rufus and his mother (see Romans 16:13). Elsewhere, Paul names two women of Philippi, Euodia and Syntyche, who have "struggled beside me in the work of the gospel, together with Clement and the rest of my co-workers," and urges them to be "of the same mind in the Lord," perhaps suggesting that these women worked together in a missionary companionship (Philippians 4:2–3 NRSV). But most pairs Paul mentions that include women are male-female missionary couples who worked together teaching men and women the gospel by bearing Spirit-filled testimony of Jesus Christ. In his letter to the Romans, Paul greets companionships such as Prisca (or Priscilla) and Aquila, "who work with me in Christ Jesus" (Romans 16:3 NRSV), Philologus and Julia (see Romans 16:15), and Andronicus and Junia, who had suffered persecution for their missionary efforts and had been in jail with Paul (see Romans 16:7). Prisca and her husband Aquila were teachers and spiritual mentors to Apollos, a well-educated and eloquent Jew from Alexandria who became a powerful and effective Christian missionary in his own right (see Acts 18:24–26).[8]

Paul describes the missionary couple Andronicus and Junia as being "prominent among the apostles" and as earlier converts to Christianity than Paul himself (Romans 16:7 NRSV). The term "apostle" (Greek *apostolos*) is striking here because modern readers connect the title with the twelve male apostles who had been authorized by Jesus to preside in proclaiming the gospel, but here Paul applies the title to a woman. Paul understood and used this title more broadly than Christians of later centuries would use it (see box 4.2). He applied it not only to the Twelve whom Jesus set apart (see 1 Corinthians 15:5) but also to Apollos (see 1 Corinthians 4:6, 9), Barnabas (see Acts 14:4, 14; 1 Corinthians 9:5–6), Titus (see 2 Corinthians 8:23), Epaphroditus (see Philippians 2:25), and Silvanus and Timothy (see 1 Thessalonians 1:1; 2:7). In general, Paul considered an apostle to be one who had encountered the risen Christ (see 1 Corinthians 9:1; Galatians 1:1, 15–17) and received from him a commission to preach the gospel (see Romans 1:1–5; 1 Corinthians 1:1; Galatians 1:1, 15–17).[9] However, Paul also recognized the special power particular to the apostolic office of the Twelve, citing the "signs and wonders and

The title "apostle" is an English translation of the Greek word *aposto-los*, which means "one who is sent forth." The term was used as early as the fifth century BC to designate someone who was a messenger or diplomat. In the Greco-Roman world, the word *apostolos* was often used to indicate a commissioned agent, or someone who was authorized to transact business or take political action on behalf of someone else. Early Christians adopted this title from their society to designate those who were commissioned agents working on behalf of Jesus Christ.

mighty works" (2 Corinthians 12:12 NRSV) that he had performed before the Corinthians as evidence that he was not "at all inferior to these super-apostles, even though I am nothing" (2 Corinthians 12:11 NRSV). When he called Junia and Andronicus "prominent among the apostles," it may indicate that they too had manifest the "signs, wonders, and mighty works" Paul considered the markers of his own apostolic office, indicating that Junia, along with her spouse Andronicus, were commissioned agents of Jesus Christ who held a special calling of leadership and authority among the disciples.[10]

Many other early Christian missionaries and teachers of the gospel were also women. In his first letter to the Corinthians, Paul asks if he does not have the same right "to be accompanied by a believing wife, as do the other apostles and the brothers of the Lord and Cephas," suggesting that at least some of the Apostles and leaders of the Church were married, including Peter (Cephas), and that they traveled with their wives (1 Corinthians 9:5 NRSV). Similarly, Clement of Alexandria, a second-century Christian writer, reported that several Apostles were married, including Paul, and that their wives worked alongside them to spread the gospel.[11] Recent scholarship has

Deacons

The Greek word for "deacon," *diakonos*, was used from the fifth century BC onward by Greek-speaking people to mean "messenger," "mediator," or "servant." While some interpreters of the Bible have understood a *diakonos* to be a humble household servant, other scholars have argued that in ancient society, *diakonos* was a position of responsibility and honor in higher circles in settings such as at court. Adopting this title into a religious context, early Christians like Paul and John the Evangelist used this term to describe a special position of honor, service, and responsibility held by certain members of the earliest churches.

highlighted the likely presence of female missionary companions to Apostles and other male missionaries of Jesus in early Christian missionary work, beyond the companionships named in Paul's letters.[12]

Christian women also taught, preached, and led in other capacities beyond missionary work. In his letter to the Romans, Paul praises a woman named Phoebe, a "deacon [Greek *diakonos*] of the church at Cenchreae" (Romans 16:1 NRSV). *Diakonos* is a title Paul uses elsewhere to describe his own ministry (see 1 Corinthians 3:5; 2 Corinthians 3:6; 6:4; 11:23; Ephesians 3:7; Colossians 1:23, 25) as well as to describe other men such as Apollos (see 1 Corinthians 3:5), Tychicus (see Ephesians 6:21), Timothy (see Philemon 1:1), and Epaphrus (see Colossians 1:7). The structure of Paul's Greek and Phoebe's specific designation as a deacon of a particular church suggests that she held a recognized position of honor and responsibility within the Christian church at Cenchreae.[13] She was likely the bearer of Paul's letter and perhaps also was acting as an official delegate from her congregation when she brought it to Rome.[14] Paul also credits Phoebe with being his benefactor as well as the patron or protector of

▲ **FIGURE 4.3** Raising of Tabitha, marble bas-relief, Arles, Musée départemental Arles Antique, fourth century. This sarcophagus fragment depicts Peter raising the disciple Tabitha (Dorcas) from the dead with the weeping widows depicted behind her. Tabitha was known for her generous philanthropy toward the poor, also shown in diminutive form at the side of her bed. This topic is thematically appropriate for display on a sarcophagus, a large stone tomb that was meant to house the dead until they too were called forth in resurrection. Photo: Catherine Gines Taylor

many others (see Romans 16:2), suggesting that she was a woman of means who used her money or connections to support his missionary work as well as the work of other Christians (see box 4.3).[15]

Female patronage represented an important type of female leadership in the Roman world because "a person of higher social status and access to power could function as mediator and dispenser of favor regardless of sex, with the same expectations of reciprocity, in terms of honor, praise, and loyalty, on the part of clients."[16] As within Greco-Roman society at large, women patrons exercised leadership in the early Church through acts of patronage. In Romans 16, Paul publicly shows deference and expresses a debt of gratitude to Phoebe, his patron, by providing her with a letter of acquaintance to the Roman Christians she did not yet know. In the letter, he tells them of her position of responsibility in the Church at Cenchreae, perhaps at her request. As an example of more modest patronage, Acts 9 gives an account of Tabitha, a "disciple" known for her good works and charity, who takes ill and dies. Peter is summoned to her house in Joppa, where he finds "all the widows" weeping around her body, who eagerly show him the tunics and other clothing that Tabitha had made for them (Acts 9:36–39 NRSV). Tabitha, likely a widow herself, acted as a patron to these widows by providing clothing and probably other means for them, earning their gratitude, respect, and the care of her body when she died (see Acts 9:37). The Greek terminology suggests that she may have had a personal association with Jesus and Peter and was a leader of this community of Christian widows at Joppa.[17]

Christian women patrons feature prominently in New Testament texts as hosts of the earliest Christian gatherings, which were held in private homes (see box 4.4). These include Mary the mother of John Mark in Jerusalem (see Acts 12:12), Lydia (see Acts 16:14–15, 40), Nympha (see Colossians 4:15), and Prisca, who hosted a church along with her husband (see Romans 16:3–5). These early Christian women of property and means acted as patrons to their communities by opening their homes for meetings, meals, and missionary work. In addition, they provided hospitality and preaching venues to traveling Apostles and other male and female disciples.

> ### BOX 4.4　Women Patrons
>
> In addition to acting as benefactors of missionary work, the first Christian women also acted as benefactors of other Christians. Women from all levels of society participated in the distinct system of patronage that characterized many of the relationships of Roman society. Women of the elite upper class often acted as patrons of other women and men by levying their wealth, property, and family connections to exert legal and political pressure in the public forum. Women of more modest means used their influence to further the business and personal interests of their working-class clients in exchange for loyalty and gratitude. Even poor women of the lowest classes and slaves might act as patrons through acts of charity and making donations. In this system, female patrons exercised significant influence in their communities.

In Greco-Roman society, the house was largely a woman's domain. Traditional gender roles dictated that a woman's proper place of work was in the private sphere—the home (*domus*) and the spaces adjacent to it where she would perform work appropriate for women. She was expected to be a good household manager, supervising the work of servants and slaves, as well as perform labor herself. While her husband, the lord (*dominus*) of the house, was considered the head of the household, his attentions were to be turned to public life, deemed by society to be the proper domain of males. Thus, the private house could be a place of great authority and autonomy for women, especially if the husband was absent or had died.[18] When Lydia and many of her household are converted and baptized, she insists that Paul and Silas accept her hospitality in Philippi (see Acts 16:14–15), effectively electing them to preside over the Church in her house for a time. After Paul and Silas are imprisoned and miraculously liberated, they immediately return to her house where they

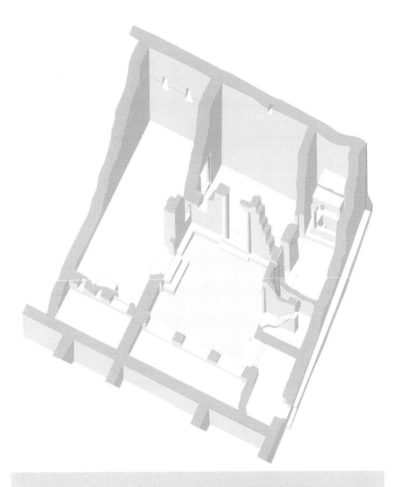

▲ **FIGURE 4.4** Isometric drawing of the house-church at Dura-Eu-ropos, Syria, ca. 240, where a house was converted into a building used by the local Christian community for Sunday worship, instruc-tion, and baptismal rituals. Women served in important roles in house-churches from the first century forward. Drawing by Marsyas, after Kraeling 1967 (Wikimedia Commons)

meet and worship with other Christians before they leave the city (see Acts 16:40). In her roles as prominent merchant, patron of a house church, and household manager, Lydia would have been hard for Paul and Silas to refuse. She likely presided at many of the Church meetings and meals that took place in her home when the Apostles were not in residence, as she would have as patron and household manager of any other person or organization in her home. We can assume from Paul's statement in 1 Corinthians 11:5—"every woman that prayeth or prophesieth with her head uncovered dishonoureth her head"—that women like Lydia actively prophesied and prayed in first-century Christian house churches. While staying in Philip's home in Caesarea, Paul and his traveling companions encountered Philip's four daughters who had the gift of prophecy and perhaps heard them pray and prophesy in worship meetings during the several days that the travelers resided there (see Acts 21:8–10).

In summary, the first-century Christian texts record that women exercised significant leadership in the early Christian church as missionaries, teachers of the gospel, and patrons and leaders of house churches. Some women—such as Junia, Phoebe, Tabitha—seem to have held special callings of office, status, or leadership in the early Church. Others, like Prisca, actively sought out and taught male converts in companionships. Some women with means and property, like Lydia, led as patrons of churches and hosts to Church leaders and prophesied and prayed in the churches.

The Church and Greco-Roman Gender Roles

In 1 Corinthians 11, Paul commends the righteousness of the Corinthian Christians but asks them to remember that "the head of every man is Christ; and the head of the woman is the man.... Every woman that prayeth or prophesieth with her head uncovered dishonoureth her head.... For a man indeed ought not to cover his head, forasmuch as he is the image and glory of God: but the woman is the glory of the man" (1 Corinthians 11:3, 5, 7). Even as Paul shows approval for women's active participation in church worship, he also shows continuing concern for maintaining traditional Greco-Roman customs and ideas about women's roles. While praying and prophesying, women must continue to show proper modesty and deference to men by wearing the head covering in accordance with cultural norms.[19]

Paul seems to advocate female deference to a more extreme level later in the same letter: "Let your women keep silence in the churches: for it is not permitted unto them to speak; but they are commanded to be under obedience. . . . If they will learn any thing, let them ask their husbands at home: for it is a shame for women to speak in the church" (1 Corinthians 14:34–35). Many scholars have argued that this passage is a later non-Pauline addition to the text for various reasons, especially because it is inconsistent with Paul's earlier permission of women's praying and prophesying.[20] Understanding this passage as a later addition to Paul's letter also makes sense in light of the concern for women's obedience and subordination that emerges in some of the later epistles in the New Testament whose authorship is uncertain.[21] Both letters to the Ephesians and Colossians teach that wives are to be subject to their husbands in all things as in the same manner as they are to the Lord (see Ephesians 5:22–23; Colossians 3:18). Additionally, 1 Timothy develops these themes and the thrust of 1 Corinthians 14:34–35 to a greater extent: women are to "learn in silence with all subjection" and are not allowed to teach in church "nor to usurp authority over the man" (1 Timothy 2:11–12).

In the late first-century and early second-century period, when these later works were written, early offices of the clergy were becoming more visible and well-defined. The author of 1 Timothy gives instructions to many groups of early Christians as to how to make God's Church a house of order, including an extensive explanation of the qualifications for church offices. For example, bishops are to be good managers of their household with good reputations, display proper virtues and good behaviors for their communities, be married only once, and keep their children submissive and respectful (see 1 Timothy 3:2–5). Deacons must also be serious, well-mannered, faithful, married only once, and able to prove their worthiness for their office (see 1 Timothy 3:8–10). Their women must also be well behaved, temperate, and faithful (see 1 Timothy 3:11 and box 4.5). The author of 1 Timothy establishes bishops and deacons as men who manage their wives and children as well as the household of the Church. The elders (Greek *presbyteros*) who rule well are to be honored for their

While a common interpretation of the "women" (Greek *gynaikas*) referred to in 1 Timothy 3:11 is that they were wives of the deacons discussed in verses 8–10, some scholars have also suggested that verse 11 may be addressed to an order of female deacons. The literal translation of the word indicates that these women were wives of the deacons mentioned, but the parallel structure of the Greek with the previous verses suggests that these women in fact may have been female deacons.[22]

preaching and teaching and must be given benefit of the doubt when any accusations are made against them (see 1 Timothy 5:17, 9).

While establishing correct behavior and operations for these offices, the author of 1 Timothy seeks to bring order to some of the unruly single women of the Church. Only widows who have had children, show duty to their families, and spend their time in faith-filled prayer are considered worthy of honor (see 1 Timothy 3:3–6). If they are over the age of sixty, have married only once, and have shown good works in the community, these widows qualify to be put on the list to receive assistance from the Church (see 1 Timothy 3:9–10). On the other hand, widows under the age of sixty or who have been married more than once may not receive assistance from the Church because they are idle as well as gossips and busybodies whose sensual desires tempt them to remarry and come under condemnation for breaking their pledge not to (1 Timothy 3:11–13). The young widows should instead marry again, have children, and take up their proper role as household managers so that no one can reproach the Christian community on their account (see 1 Timothy 5:14).[23] In this passage, the author uses stereotypes common to Roman culture about single women behaving badly to reinforce that a woman's proper place was married and managing a household. They serve as a strong contrast to the male bishops, deacons, and elders who rule in the Church and their households with decorum, solemnity, and righteousness, further solidifying the status and authority of these newly emerging clerical offices.

Church Offices and Other Early Christian Writers

Other early Christians were eager to affirm and expand the authority of church offices laid out by the author of 1 Timothy. One of the oldest Christian writings outside of the New Testament texts, attributed to Clement bishop of Rome (AD 88–97), is the earliest to record that bishops had been appointed by the Apostles to be their successors.[24] Ignatius, bishop of Antioch (died circa AD 110), elevated an order of bishops, deacons, and elders to a divine, mystical relationship between the Father, Son, Apostles, and commandments. He was the first Christian author in known history to assert the presiding authority of the bishop over rituals such as baptism and the Eucharist (or sacrament).[25]

Over the course of the second and third centuries, bishop, elder (see box 4.6), and deacon emerged as the three central leadership offices in the Church. This evolution coincided with a number of other changes in the Church that impacted women's participation and leadership. As the gospel message spread throughout the Roman Empire, more male members of the upper-class ruling elite became Christians and began to fill the leadership roles of the Church. These men brought with them notions of organization, leadership, and order that stemmed from Roman public life. While the earliest Christians had understood Church leadership as defined by a special commission to preach the gospel as missionaries, this concept was gradually replaced by the idea that Christian leaders were called to govern the established body of the Church.[26]

Tertullian (active circa AD 200), a highly-educated Christian writer who lived in the Roman city of Carthage in North Africa, was one of the first of these elite, well-educated Roman men to explain the Church in terms of Roman law and government. Tertullian

Elders

The Greek word for elder (*presbyteros*) literally means "old man" and is often translated as "presbyter" or "priest" in other Christian denominations today. While the term *presbyteros* appears often in the Gospels to designate members of the community who sat on the Sanhedrin (or great council) of the Jews, evidence suggests that individual synagogues of Jesus's day were also led by groups of male elders. Christians adopted this style of Church leadership from Jewish culture early on, as we can see in the early Church at Jerusalem where James and a council of elders presided.

understood the proper order of the Church to reflect Roman society, with different classes and ranks of people. For him, the clergy (or the organization of bishops, elders, and deacons in the Church) represented the senatorial or elite ruling class of Rome, while the laity (or people without church office) represented the plebian or lower classes (see box 4.7).[27] Tertullian defined the clerical offices of the Church not by special commissions to preach the gospel but rather by the special rights and privileges these offices held: the right to baptize, the right to teach, the right to restore fellowship after repentance of sins, and the right to offer the Eucharist. A male citizen of Rome would have understood his own status in terms of rights in a similar legalistic manner.[28] Furthermore, this new idea of Christian leadership marginalized women's participation in proselytizing and teaching the gospel. As earlier discussed, women had been some of the earliest, most active and most effective missionaries in the Church, traveling and teaching at the side of male missionaries like Paul, and received honor and recognition from him for their efforts as well as authority in the Christian community. However, when the qualifications for Church leadership shifted from a missionary to a

BOX 4.7 The Rise of the "Priesthood"

In the third century, writers like Tertullian began to understand Christian bishops, elders, and deacons as holders of "priesthood" offices (Latin *sacerdotium*) by connecting their special callings in the Church to the Hebrew priesthood offices of the Old Testament. Tertullian made this connection to argue that, like the ancient Levitical priests, Christian office holders, or "priests," must also be men who have only been married one time (see Tertullian, *Exhortation to Chastity* 7.1–2; see also *On Monogamy* 12.2).

Roman imperial government model, women lost this avenue to visible participation and influence in the Church.

The new Christian governing elite also magnified the influence of Greco-Roman ideas of gender on the Church's culture. As previously mentioned, Roman society imagined the proper place of a woman to be in the private sphere of the household, whereas the ideal man was devoted to the public sphere and spent his day in public activities, leaving the management of the household to his wife. Being managers of the household had opened possibilities for women to lead and actively participate in the earliest Christian house churches.[29] The teaching that a bishop must preside over common religious practices, as first asserted by Ignatius and later by many others, would have had a significant impact on woman's leadership and participation in the house church, even if a woman had been a patron and leader of the Church.

But Tertullian's definition of the clerical order based on the rights it held, in Roman legalistic language, had a lasting detrimental effect on women's status and participation in the Church. In the third and fourth centuries, the gradual physical relocation of Church meetings from private houses to basilicas and other public buildings, as well as the idea that Church organization was a shadow of the Roman government, moved churches from private to public space. In Roman society, public space was understood to be the proper domain of the Roman man, the place where he exercised his rights of citizenship and participated in government and civic events. Women, on the other hand, were generally expected to adhere to traditional Roman female virtues such as modesty and silence when in public space and were not permitted to hold public office or participate in public debate or functions. Thus, it was easy for Tertullian and other later Roman Christian writers to conclude that women had no rights to speak or act in the "public" of the Church and were barred from baptizing, teaching, offering the Eucharist, and holding any church office.[30] These offices were now positions of public leadership with public functions. Respectable women who adhered to the traditional values of modesty and silence could not appear with their heads unveiled or speak in a public setting without shaming themselves and their families.[31] The new model of worship advanced by Tertullian, in which the clergy was reimagined as a governing institution in the public sphere, stands in stark contrast to the private household gatherings of early Christianity where women had been leading, prophesying, teaching, and officiating.

As highly structured hierarchies of church offices became more well-developed in the third century, bishops began to restructure the Roman patronage system to their advantage in ways that decreased women's visibility and leadership. While some wealthy and elite Christian women had acted as patrons of house churches, missionary endeavors, religious feasts, and other charitable works, bishops began to reorder the patronage system around their own office. For example, Cyprian of Carthage, a bishop in North Africa in the first half of the third century, used his significant resources and personal social connections to establish the episcopacy (or office of the bishop) as the primary benefactor of the community (see box 4.8). The bishop personally oversaw the disbursement of the Church's funds to care for the poor of the community and to pay the clergy. He further enhanced the prestige of the bishopric in his community

BOX 4.8 Bishops

The Greek term *episkopos*, which is commonly translated today as "bishop," literally means "overseer" or "guardian." In the ancient world, this title was held by government officials in Greek cities. Later on, Greco-Roman voluntary associations (or private interest groups that met in people's homes) adopted the title to designate the overseer or guardian of their group. The earliest Christian house churches, modeled after these voluntary associations, adopted the practice of appointing an *episkopos*, or guardian, to oversee their congregations.

by urging wealthy Christians to make all charitable donations to the Church, which he would then distribute to the poor, thus establishing himself as the primary patron of the Christian community at Carthage.[32] Invoking the language and imagery of patronage, Cyprian promised great honor and blessings to wealthy Christians who donated money to the Church on behalf of the poor: "What sort of gift is it, beloved brethren, whose giving is celebrated in the sight of God? If it seems a great and a glorious thing to have proconsuls and emperors present when a gift of the Gentiles is given . . . how much more illustrious and great is the glory of having God and Christ as the spectator of the gift?"[33] Wealthy Christians are portrayed as patrons who earn honor before God by supporting the poor through donations to the Church.

By encouraging wealthy Christians to give their donations to the Church and then redistributing those donations in public as gifts to the poor from the bishop, the influence of the community's wealthy donors was weakened and the power and prestige of patronage was consolidated in the office of bishop. Over the coming centuries, this "consolidation of charity" became the standard way for Christians throughout the Church to exercise generosity. By the fourth century, this new order of patronage replaced the networks of personal patronage through which some women of means and status had been able to exercise power and influence in their Christian communities in earlier centuries.[34] Women who had acted as patrons and leaders in the early house churches were now replaced by the bishops who served as both leader and patron of their congregations.

New Orders: Women Deacons, Widows, and Virgins

While most of women's early leadership roles were erased or absorbed by the clergy by the fourth century, we can trace the development of new offices for women in the Church during this time. In the second through fourth centuries, "orders" of female deacons, widows, and virgins emerge as part of the Church's leadership hierarchy. These orders brought potentially troublesome single women—especially widows and virgins—under the patriarchal authority of the bishop. The evidence that exists from this period suggests that the role of a female deacon was largely limited to working with other women and performing tasks that male clergymen could not perform while maintaining propriety.[35] Widows and virgins mostly served as symbols and examples of virtue and holiness to other Christians.

The *Teachings of the Apostles* (*Didascalia Apostolorum*), an early third-century church order text (a handbook of ecclesiastical instructions) from Syria, provides evidence of women's active participation in the clergy as deacons in the East. Surpassing Tertullian's comparison that Christian priests are similar to the Levitical priests of ancient Israel, the *Teachings* lays out a well-defined, highly-structured clerical order explained in relation to the priestly offices of ancient Israel, with the bishop likened to the high priest, the elder to the Israelite priest, and the Levites seen in the deacons, lectors, cantors, porters, female deacons, widows, virgins, and orphans, "but the high priest is above all of these."[36] It also depicts male deacons standing next to the bishop as the Son stands next to the Father, while female deacons are to be "honored by you as the type of the Holy Spirit, doing or saying nothing apart from the deacon," thus carefully preserving the subordinance of the female deacon to both the bishop and the male deacon.[37]

In the *Teachings of the Apostles*, female deacons are part of the clerical order of the Church, but their role is largely limited to performing those functions that maintain the Greco-Roman norms of modesty and propriety for women. For example, no woman was allowed to approach a male deacon or the bishop unless she was chaperoned by a female deacon.[38] Female deacons were tasked with standing at the women's entrances to church buildings and helping females find seats.[39] They were to attend to women living in houses where, for concerns about propriety, male deacons were not able to go.[40] Since, during this time period, people were fully naked at baptism, and the body was anointed with oil before the ordinance was performed, female deacons held the responsibility for anointing the bodies of women after the male deacon had anointed their heads and before the bishop performed the baptism so that the baptism was performed with "sobriety."[41] As in Tertullian's writings, women are explicitly forbidden from baptizing and teaching in the Church. They are allowed "only to pray and hear the teachers," suggesting that the office of female deacon is best understood as a concession to maintaining modesty rather than as an authoritative position.[42] In the public space of the Church, the women seem to have played largely passive and silent roles, only permitted to act and speak when social mores forbid the male clergy from doing so.[43]

Along with information regarding female deacons, the *Teachings of the Apostles* included women's orders of widows and virgins in its ordering of the Church. As discussed earlier, independent women, many of whom were probably widows, had a visible and active presence in the Church from its earliest times and were important missionaries, patrons, teachers, and leaders of house churches.[44] A few inscriptions from Rome indicate that women belonged to an order of widows in the Western Church as early as the second century.[45] However, most evidence pertaining to Rome and the Western Church suggests that the functions of the widow's office were rather limited and became a position of honor, more than one of action or leadership, in the Church during this period. The *Apostolic Tradition*, a church handbook possibly authored by Hippolytus of Rome in the third century, refers to widows being appointed to a special office in the Church but specifies that they are not to be ordained by the laying on of hands because a widow does not offer the Eucharist nor does she have a "sacred ministry," as members of the clergy do. The appointed widow's only duty is to pray and intercede as all other members are commanded. [46]

In the Eastern Roman Empire, there is little evidence for an office of widows before the third century.[47] Widows are clearly a recognized order in *Teachings of the Apostles*, but the only duty specifically assigned to them is prayer. On the other hand, *Teachings* contains a strikingly long list of accusations directed toward widows: gossip, greed, embezzlement, usury, complaining, being distracted during prayer, and a myriad of other transgressions. Widows are admonished to be meek, gentle, and quiet and to stay at home instead of moving about in the community. They are specifically prohibited from answering religious questions, baptizing, fasting or eating or drinking with others, praying over or laying hands upon anyone, or accepting gifts from anyone, unless the bishop or the (male) deacon has permitted them to do so. They must show proper meekness and be prepared to obey whatever they are ordered by their superiors, which include the bishops, elders, male deacons, and female deacons, and especially to "obey the teachings of the bishop as if to God."[48] This condemnation, however, suggests that even in the third century, women in some churches were actively engaged in teaching the gospel, ministering, visiting the sick, sharing meals with other Christians, blessing and healing, baptizing, and receiving and dispersing charitable donations, as well as engaging in economic pursuits in the community. As we have previously discussed, many of these actions were in the traditional domain of female discipleship since New Testament times. But the *Teachings* attempts to marginalize competitors for leadership and authority in the community by disparaging the behavior of widows and limiting their roles in order to reallocate these functions to the clergy and to the bishop in particular.[49]

BOX 4.9   Asceticism

Renouncing a second marriage or taking a vow of perpetual virginity are two ways in which some early Christians engaged in asceticism, or the practice of self-denial for religious reasons. In addition to maintaining widowhood or virginity, some early Christian ascetic practices included fasting, giving away money and property, dressing in rough clothing, making a vow of silence, and leaving family life to live alone or with other ascetics. Through these actions, early Christians hoped to gain greater spiritual power, a closer communion with God, and salvation after death. In the modern Church, Latter-day Saints practice acts of self-denial such as fasting, paying tithes and offerings, and performing missionary service with similar hopes of gaining greater spiritual strength, answers to prayer, and increased blessings in this life and the life to come.

Christian Women and Sexual Renunciation

The author of 1 Timothy insisted that not only enrolled, or officially recognized, widows be married only once but also bishops (see 1 Timothy 3:2–7). Spurred on by Paul's admonition that the unmarried and widows should stay unmarried as he is (see 1 Corinthians 7:8), renunciation of second marriages and of marriage and sexuality in general quickly became the marker of priestly masculinity and authority (see box 4.9).[50] While clerical celibacy was not universally required until well after the fourth century, those who had renounced second marriages, who had pledged to renounce marital relations with their living spouses, or who had retained perpetual virginity were considered to have a higher degree of spiritual authority and greater qualifications for leadership.[51] Christian women who assumed the life of virginity were thought to have chosen a holier way of life in comparison to other Christians, and thus they were often thought to enjoy special divine protection and spiritual power. Because female virgins renounced to some extent their "femaleness" by rejecting marriage and childbearing—the hallmarks of most women's lives in the ancient world—some ancient Christian writers extolled the "manliness" of these women and praised them for exercising privileges and authority usually reserved for male clerics.[52]

For example, in the second-century text *Acts of Paul and Thecla,* the virgin Thecla pledges herself to perpetual chastity when she hears Paul preach about the blessedness of virginity and then rejects the man her family wants her to marry. She is denounced by her mother before the governor and is thrown into the gladiatorial arena twice. But rather than dying, she displays multiple times in the arena the miraculous divine protection given to those who pledge themselves to perpetual virginity. On one occasion, Thecla is saved from being burned alive when God suddenly sends a storm to put out the flames. On another, a fierce lioness fights off other wild beasts who are sent in to kill Thecla. Later in the narrative, Thecla is stripped naked to be humiliated, but God provides a cloud of fire to cover her and protect her modesty. Time and again in the narrative, Thecla enjoys divine favor and protection because she has dedicated herself to God through a vow of perpetual virginity.

As a virgin of God, Thecla is also empowered to exercise religious authority not usually permitted to women. In the arena, she baptizes herself in a pool of ferocious seals without being harmed, and later in the narrative, Paul accepts this baptism as legitimate. When released, Thecla dresses as a man and travels as a missionary, teaching and converting others to Christianity. The special power and authority given to her by God on account of her virginity allow her to perform a number of miracles, including healing the sick, casting out evil spirits, and interceding on behalf of the dead for their salvation.[53] In short, Thecla's virginity grants her divine favor and the ability to assume the "masculine" virtues of courage and self-control, saving her from a martyr's death but also giving her authority to baptize herself, teach, travel independently, and perform miracles.

The rise of the order of virginity in the church hierarchy was an

▲ **FIGURE 4.5** Fifth-century limestone roundel depicting Saint Thecla between two beasts at her feet and surrounded by two angels.
Her hands are bound behind her back, indicating her captivity in
the arena, while the nimbus or halo indicates holy protection for this
early follower of Paul, the heroine of the second-century *Acts of Paul
and Thecla*. Photo: Courtesy of Daderot via Wikimedia Commons
(public domain)

▲ **FIGURE 4.6**   Mosaic, San Zeno Chapel, Church of Santa Prassede, Rome, depicting the widow Theodora (far left), titled "Episcopa" for her piety and position as mother of Pope Paschal I, accompanied by Saint Praxedes (Santa Prassede), Mary the Mother of Jesus, and Saint Pudenziana. Though these mosaics date to the ninth century, they illustrate the lasting veneration of early Christian women. Photo: Courtesy of Livioandronico2013 via Wikimedia Commons

answer to the story of Thecla and other charismatic women of the second and third centuries who were claiming power and authority to lead, teach, and baptize based on sexual renunciation. Early Church writers like Tertullian denounced Thecla's account as fiction and forgery, reasoning that it was not credible that Paul "would give a female the power to teach and baptize who has not even allowed a woman to learn by right" and reminding readers of that curious passage in 1 Corinthians that insisted that women keep silent in the churches and ask their husbands any questions at home (see 1 Corinthians 14:34–35).[54] On a smaller scale, Tertullian sought regulation of the virgins of his home church at Carthage. These virgins, who sat in a place at the front of the congregation with their heads unveiled, were urged to cover their heads as other women had to, a reminder to them that they were still women and still in a subordinate position to the clergy and the men present.[55]

In spite of Tertullian's scorn for Thecla and his dressing down of the virgins of Carthage, the office of female virgins continued to rise in number and prestige over the coming centuries. Christian writers of the fourth century lavishly extolled female virginity as able to transcend the lowly state of regular women. Jerome of Stridon, a fourth-century theologian, asserted that once a woman prefers Jesus Christ over marriage and babies that she "will cease to be a woman and will be called a man."[56] Ambrose, bishop of Milan, claimed that virgins transcend the bonds of female flesh and become superior to not only their sex but to married men as well.[57] While man is the head of the woman, he reasoned, only Christ is the head of the virgin.[58] At the same time, these Christian writers reaffirmed the femaleness and subordination of virgins by speaking of them as "brides of Christ."[59] Fourth-century writers like Athanasius of Alexandria, Gregory of Nyssa, and Ambrose of Milan used scripture from the Song of Solomon to explain that virgins enjoy a special "marital" relationship with the Bridegroom, Jesus Christ, while at the same time affirming that female virgins were still women whose ultimate destiny was marriage and that they were still subordinate to a heavenly husband.[60]

While the *Teachings of the Apostles* refers to the existence of an order of virgins in the church hierarchy, no teaching is given concerning their function or status within the Church. The later *Apostolic Constitutions*, a compilation of church orders from fourth-century Syria, reflects the growing influence of asceticism in the Church. For example, female deacons must now be virgins, or at least widows who have only been married once.[61] The ordination of virgins is forbidden, as they do not perform ministerial duties.[62] The *Apostolic Constitutions* specifically forbids any deaconess (virgin or widow) to do any kind of blessing at the altar or perform anything that the ordained clergy does. Her only roles are to watch the doors and help the priests in the baptism of women "for the sake of decency."[63]

Whatever limits were placed on orders of virgins and widows in the Church, a good deal of evidence suggests that women who renounced married life—both widows and virgins—enjoyed influence and opportunities in the Christian community beyond what other women of the day enjoyed. Removed from the constraints of common gender roles, these ascetic women of means and status were able to dedicate themselves to scholarly pursuits, travel, engage in public debates, and form close and lasting friendships with well-educated and influential men.[64] The virgin Macrina (AD 330–379) managed her family's vast estates, founded a monastery for women on her property, devoted herself to reading and the study of scripture, and converted her brother Basil, later bishop of Caesarea, to the ascetic life.[65] Melania the Elder (circa AD 350–410) was widowed at a young age, and after becoming a Christian, she committed herself to stay unmarried. She traveled to Egypt to learn from the monks in the deserts outside of Alexandria before traveling to Jerusalem and founding a convent and a monastery on the Mount of Olives. Melania acted as patron and spiritual mentor to some important clergymen of the day, including Rufinus of Aquileia and Evagrius Ponticus. Marcella of Rome (AD 325–410) was a Roman aristocrat and Christian ascetic who Jerome of Stridon later praised for her scriptural scholarship and abilities in theological debate. She publicly refuted heretics, including priests and monks.[66] Marcella acted as patron for a group of ascetic women in Rome, providing her home as a meeting place for worship and retirement, and trained other young ascetics in her home.[67] Olympias, widow and deaconess in the Church at Constantinople (circa AD 361–408), was a close friend of John Chrysostom, archbishop of Constantinople, and a great patron of several charitable foundations and works, including a hospital, orphanage, and the first monastery for women in Constantinople.[68] While most of these female ascetics were aristocratic women of great wealth who would have enjoyed a number of rights and privileges based on their societal status, sexual renunciation enhanced their prestige in the Christian community and opened up opportunities for their engagement in teaching, learning, proselytizing, traveling, mentoring, and serving as patrons and leaders of early monastic communities.

Conclusion

In this chapter, I have highlighted some of the ways in which women exercised leadership and participated in the earliest Christian churches as missionaries, teachers, and patrons. Then I traced the diminishment of women's leadership roles as the clerical offices of bishop, priest, and deacon became more defined in the second and third centuries and traditional Greco-Roman ideas about gender became increasingly integrated into the teachings and culture of the Church. As older models of women's participation and leadership were absorbed by the male clergy, orders of female deacons, widows, and virgins were established to organize potentially troublesome women under the authority of the bishop.

This chapter could be read as a narrative of loss but it is also one of grace. Some Latter-day Saint readers may be tempted to see the rise of the clerical orders in the third century and the simultaneous suppression of women as part of a decline and fall into apostasy. However, we may gain some perspective on the restored Church of Jesus Christ as we take into consideration the sixth article of faith, written by Joseph Smith in 1842: "We believe in the same organization that existed in the Primitive Church, namely, apostles, prophets, pastors, teachers, evangelists, and so forth." We believe in this organization of a "primitive" church of traveling missionary prophets and teachers, but we must also acknowledge that the Church of Jesus Christ today does not much resemble this organization of traveling missionary leaders and teachers, of people gathering in homes to teach and prophesy to each other and share a religious feast, that Joseph Smith found in the New Testament. Offices of leadership in the restored Church of Jesus Christ have far more in common with the church hierarchy of bishops, elders, and deacons established in the third century and beyond. The institutions and offices of the Church of Jesus Christ are constantly being born, dying, and evolving—as they did anciently—both in response to prophetic revelation and the cultural and social needs of the community of Saints.

But here is where we see grace: women's participation and leadership roles in the restored Church of Jesus Christ are circling back toward those they held in the ancient Church as they become increasingly visible and take on more leadership roles in missionary work, preaching, prophesying, teaching, and management and organization on all levels of administration. In 2014, Elder Dallin H. Oaks inquired: "We are not accustomed to speaking of women having the authority of the priesthood in their Church callings, but what other authority can it be?" Elder Oaks explained that women receive priesthood authority to perform priesthood functions as full-time missionaries or when set apart as leaders or teachers in a Church organization by someone who holds priesthood keys.[69] This statement confirms the authority and leadership that ancient Christian women exercised as missionaries, teachers, deacons, and apostles (in Paul's broad sense) and opens up further possibilities for the authorized engagement of women's authority and leadership in the restored Church of Jesus Christ.

In addition, the Church's recent move toward home-centered, church-supported models of learning and worship is a return in many respects to the house church model of ancient Christianity and presents new possibilities for women's leadership and participation. In 2018, Elder Oaks explained that "the principle that priesthood authority can be exercised only under the direction of the one who holds the keys for that function is fundamental in the Church but does not apply to the exercise of priesthood authority in the family."[70] Elder Oaks specifies the family as an organization in which priesthood offices and keys are not needed in order to authorize the exercise of priesthood power, presenting opportunities for women to claim authority to receive revelation, teach, bless, and exercise leadership as they did anciently in the house church. In addition, President Nelson has taught that women whose husbands die preside in the priesthood in their homes.[71] These teachings confirm the authority of women like Lydia, Nympha, and the mother of John Mark, who were the host and leaders of churches in their home. While we continue to pray for additional prophetic revelation to validate and increase women's leadership and participation in The Church of Jesus Christ of Latter-day Saints, we can rejoice today that God has restored these ancient models of women's leadership and authority once again.

Notes

1. Scholars like Elizabeth Schüssler Fiorenza see the Gospel writers as promoting a "discipleship of equals" based on their understanding of Jesus's teachings. See Schüssler Fiorenza, *In Memory of Her: A Feminist Theological Reconstruction of Christian Origins* (New York: Crossroad, 1983), xxiv.

2. The Greek term for "bishop" (*episcopos*) and the word for "elder" (*presbyteros*) are used interchangeably in much of the New Testament (for example, see Acts 20:17; Titus 1:5–7; 1 Peter 5:1). For the influence of Jewish offices of organization on the earliest Christian churches, see James Tunstead Burchaell, *From Synagogue to Church: Public Services and Offices in the Earliest Christian Communities* (Cambridge, UK: Cambridge University Press, 1992), 272–338.

3. For a good summary of women's roles in the first century, see Christine Schenk, *Crispina and Her Sisters: Women and Authority in Early Christianity*

(Philadelphia: Fortress Press, 2017), 15–28.

4. Susan B. Hylen discusses how these virtues functioned in society at large but also suggests that they opened the way for women's greater leadership and participation in ancient house churches. See Hylen, *Women in the New Testament World* (New York: Oxford, 2019), 42–64.

5. See Carolyn Osiek, "Family Matters," in *Christian Origins*, ed. Richard A. Horsley (Minneapolis, MN: Fortress Press, 2005), 212.

6. For a thorough review of women's legal and social positions in Greco-Roman society, see Hylen, *Women in the New Testament World*, 65–130.

7. Scholar and theologian Paul Bradshaw has suggested three important ways in which early Christians, male and female, exercised leadership in the Church during the first three centuries of Christianity: (1) leadership was exercised by those in the community who had been blessed with Spirit-inspired gifts, such as the gift to prophesy and to teach by the Spirit; (2) leadership was exercised by the patron or host of a household in which Christians gathered for worship and learning; and (3) leadership was exercised through some structured way of authorizing leadership for the community. See Paul Bradshaw, *Rites of Ordination: Their History and Theology* (Collegeville, MN: Liturgical Press, 2013), 17–38. These general categories are useful for considering some of the ways in which women actively participated and led in the early Christian community. Many New Testament women actively exercised leadership through missionary work and teaching the gospel by the Spirit, and some acted as patrons and leaders of the earliest Christian churches. The third type of leadership, based upon the ability to authorize leaders for the community, was exercised infrequently by women but would come to be the dominant form of male leadership in the second and third centuries with the rise of clerical offices in the Church.

8. Prisca is called by a common nickname, Priscilla, in some passages of the New Testament. Prisca and Aquila are mentioned six times in Paul's letters, and Prisca's name precedes that of her husband four of those times, including when they teach Apollos. Some scholars have argued that this arrangement may suggest that she was the principal teacher of Apollos and, thus, a woman of "excellent didactic qualities and missionary skills as well as outstanding education." See Dominika A. Kurek-Chomycz, "Is There an Anti-Priscan Tendency in the Manuscripts?: Some Textual Problems with Prisca and Aquila," *Journal of Biblical Literature* 125, no. 1 (2006): 125–26.

9. Paul refers to the Twelve as apostles (see 1 Corinthians 1:1; 2 Corinthians 1:1; Colossians 1:1), but he also refers to himself as an apostle (see 1 Thessalonians 2:7; Galatians 1:17–19) although his calling to preach the gospel

had not come in the same way the original Twelve or their successors had been designated, nor was he an official part of an organized quorum of Apostles, as Latter-day Saint readers might expect in light of Church organization today. For accounts of Paul's conversion and apostolic calling, see Acts 9:1–19; 22:6–21; 1 Corinthians 15:3–8; 2 Corinthians 12:1–7; Galatians 1:11–16. On the origins and usage of the word *apostolos* outside of the Christian community, see F. Agnew, "On the Origin of the Term *Apostolos*," *Catholic Biblical Quarterly* 38, no. 1 (1976): 49–53.

10. Paul uses the Greek term *epistemos* to describe Andronicus's and Junia's "prominent" position among the apostles. As Robert K. Jewett has noted, this adjective "lifts up a person or thing as distinguished or marked in comparison with other representatives of the same class, in this instance with the other apostles." See Jewett, *Romans: A Commentary on the Book of Romans*, ed. Eldon Jay Epp, Hermeneia series (Minneapolis, MN: Fortress Press, 2007), 963.

     In many translations of the New Testament, Junia has been mistakenly translated as Junius, simply on the assumption that she could not have been a woman if she was called "apostle" by Paul. Hope Stephenson reviews ancient and modern evidence and arguments about this issue in her article "Junia, Woman and Apostle," in *Women in the Biblical World: A Survey of Old and New Testament Perspectives*, ed. Elizabeth A. McCabe (Lanham, MD: University Press of America, 2009).

11. See Clement of Alexandria, *Stromata* 3.6.53, in *Patrologiae cursus completus*, Series graeca, ed. Jacques-Paul Migne (Paris, 1857–86), 8:152. Clement, eager to downplay the marital relationships of the Apostles, claims that they only bring wives along so that they might teach women in their houses without causing a scandal and argues that the married Apostles traveled with these women not as wives but as sisters, probably reflecting his desire to stress the goodness of sexual continence.

12. For example, New Testament scholar Joan Taylor has suggested that Mark's description of the Twelve being sent to preach "two by two" (Mark 6:7 NRSV) as well as Jesus's dispatch of seventy in the same manner (see Luke 10:1) refer to male-female companionships rather than to male-male ones in the ancient Aramaic language that Jesus and his disciples spoke. Taylor connects the Greek for "two by two" (*duo duo*) as an Aramaic idiom that refers to the language of Noah bringing male and female pairs of all living animals onto the ark (see Genesis 6:19–20; 7:2–3). This connection further illuminates the important role women played in spreading the gospel message from the very beginning of Christianity. See Taylor, "Two by Two: The Ark-etypal Language of Mark's Apostolic Pairings," in *The Body*

in Biblical, Christian, and Jewish Texts, ed. Joan E. Taylor (Bloomsbury: T&T Clark, 2014), 58–82.

Similarly, Ilaria Ramelli has argued New Testament use of the Greek term *suzygos* (yokefellow, partner, colleague, or wife) suggests that early Christian missionary pairings could be male-male, male-female, or female-female. See Ramelli, "Colleagues of Apostles, Presbyters, and Bishops: Women *Syzygoi* in Ancient Christian Communities," in *Patterns of Women's Leadership in Early Christianity*, ed. Joan E. Taylor and Ilaria L. E. Ramelli (Oxford University Press, 2021), 26–58.

13. Of the thirty-one occurrences of the term *diakonos* in the KJV New Testament, it is most often translated as "minister" (twenty times), sometimes as "servant" (eight times), and occasionally as "deacon" (three times), a demonstration of how translators' personal biases might inform their choice of words and, in turn, influence the scriptural understandings of readers for generations to come.

On the Greek sentence structure indicating that Phoebe was an established office holder in the Church, see Franz J. Leenhardt, *The Epistle to the Romans: A Commentary* (London: Lutterworth, 1957), 379.

Other translations of the Bible, such as the International Standard Version, translate *diakonos* in Romans 16:1 as "deaconess." However, the direct proper translation of the word as it is used in the New Testament is always masculine, not feminine. The word *diakonissa* (deaconess) does not appear in Christian writings before the fourth century. See Ute E. Eisen, *Women Officeholders in Early Christianity: Epigraphic and Literary Studies* (Collegeville, MN: Liturgical Press, 2000), 13–14.

14. On the argument that *diakonos* is an emissary or position of honor in high circles, see Bart J. Koet, *The Go-Between: Augustine on Deacons* (Leiden: Brill, 2018), 7–8. Koet reviews the use of the term *diakonos* in the ancient world in pages 7–25.

15. See Elizabeth A. McCabe, "A Reevaluation of Phoebe in Romans 16.1–2 as a *Diakonos* and *Prostatis*: Exposing the Inaccuracies of English Translations," in *Women in the Biblical World: A Survey of Old and New Testament Perspectives*, ed. Elizabeth A. McCabe (Lanham, MD: University Press of America, 2009). See also Hylen, *Women in the New Testament World*, 110–11.

16. Carolyn Osiek and Margaret Y. MacDonald with Janet Tulloch, *A Woman's Place: House Churches in Early Christianity* (Minneapolis, MN: Fortress, 2006), 209. Much of Roman social life was organized around a distinctive system of patronage. People sought the help of patrons, or persons of greater wealth, power, and influence, in society, to further their own interests.

For example, a patron might intercede on behalf of his "client" by helping further their business interests, arranging an advantageous marriage, securing a loan, or helping him obtain a political office. In return, the patron might gain the social prestige that came with having numerous clients as well as the deference and loyalty of his dependents. See Osiek and MacDonald with Tulloch, *A Woman's Place*, 194–203; Hylen, *Women in the New Testament World,* 100–107 on women's participation in the patronage system.

17. While the masculine word for "disciple" in Greek (*mathētēs*) is commonly applied to followers of Jesus throughout the New Testament, Tabitha is the only person called a *mathētria,* the feminine form. For this reason, some scholars have suggested that she was one of the women who knew and followed Jesus in Galilee and may have known Peter well before he raised her from the dead. See Bonnie Thurston, *Women in the New Testament: Questions and Commentary* (New York: Crossroad, 1998), 120–21.

18. See Osiek and MacDonald with Tulloch, *A Woman's Place*, 147–48. In pages 144–52, Osiek and MacDonald provide a good survey of ideas throughout antiquity about woman's connection to the household. While such gender ideals pervaded Greco-Roman society, they were largely only realized in upper-class households. Women of lower social and economic statuses often worked alongside their husbands, in the house as well as in the marketplace, at the family industry.

19. On the custom of female head veiling in the ancient world, see Tahmina Tariq, "Let Modesty Be Her Raiment: The Classical Context of Ancient Christian Veiling," *Implicit Religion* 16, no. 4 (2013): 493–506.

20. For a summary of scholars and arguments made supporting this position, see Raymond Collins, *First Corinthians* (Collegeville, MN: Liturgical Press, 1999), 515. New Testament scholar Richard Hays has argued that the best reason to reject that this passage was Paul's original work is because it stands "in glaring contradiction" to the evidence that Paul included women in all aspects of his mission. Hays, *First Corinthians* (Louisville, KY: John Knox, 1997), 246.

21. Of the epistles in the New Testament, modern scholars almost universally agree that Romans, 1 and 2 Corinthians, Galatians, Philippians, 1 Thessalonians, and Philemon were definitely written by Paul. Others, including Ephesians, Colossians, 1 and 2 Timothy, and Titus are of "disputed" or inconclusive authorship. On the disputed authorship of 1 Timothy, 2 Timothy, and Titus, see I. Howard Marshall, *A Critical and Exegetical Commentary on the Pastoral Epistles*, International Critical Commentary series (London: T&T Clark, 1999) 58, 79. On the disputed authorship of

Ephesians, see Raymond E. Brown, *An Introduction to the New Testament* (New Haven: Yale University Press, 1997), 626–30. On the disputed authorship of Colossians, see Bart Ehrman, *The New Testament: A Historical Introduction to the Early Christian Writings* (New York: Oxford University Press, 2004), 378–81. Because the authorship of these texts is uncertain (and to varying degrees, unlikely), I do not refer to the author(s) of these epistles as "Paul" in this chapter.

22. For the argument that the "women" (*gynaikas*) in 1 Timothy 3:11 may indicate an order of female deacons, see Margaret Y. MacDonald, "Reading Real Women through the Undisputed Letters of Paul," in *Women and Christian Origins*, ed. Ross Shepard Kraemer and Mary Rose D'Angelo (Oxford: Oxford University Press, 1999), 208.

23. See Gail P. C. Streete, "Bad Girls or Good Ascetics? The *Gynaikaria* of the Pastoral Epistles," in *Women in the Biblical World: A Survey of Old and New Testament Perspectives*, ed. Elizabeth A. McCabe (Lanham, MD: University Press of America, 2009). Streete argues that the author of 1 Timothy is seeking to push back on groups of women who are practicing a kind of asceticism, or self-denial for religious purposes. Harry O. Maier understands the widows who are exhorted to remarry as women who were exercising independence and leadership as patrons based on their successful entrepreneurship in ways that fell outside of the traditional gender roles prescribed to them as wives and mothers. Thus, the author of 1 Timothy attempts to bring order again to the Church and society by bringing these women once again under the authority of husbands. See Maier, "The Entrepreneurial Widows of 1 Timothy," in *Patterns of Women's Leadership in Early Christianity*, ed. Joan E. Taylor and Ilaria L. E. Ramelli (Oxford University Press, 2021), 59–73.

24. See *The First Epistle of Clement to the Corinthians* 42.4–5; 44.1–2, in *The Apostolic Fathers*, vol. 1, *I Clement. II Clement. Ignatius. Polycarp. Didache.*, ed. and trans. Bart D. Ehrman, Loeb Classical Library (Cambridge: Harvard University Press, 2003), 111, 113.

   On the Greco-Roman origins of the title *episkopos*, see Korinna Zamfir, "Once More About the Origins and Background of the New Testament Episcopos," *Sacra Scriptura* 10, no. 2 (2012): 202–22.

25. See Ignatius, *Letter to the Smyrneans* 8.1, in *The Apostolic Fathers*, vol. 1, *I Clement. II Clement. Ignatius. Polycarp. Didache.*, ed. and trans. Bart D. Ehrman, Loeb Classical Library (Cambridge: Harvard University Press, 2003), 304–5.

26. See Karen Jo Torjesen, *When Women Were Priests* (San Francisco, CA: HarperSanFrancisco, 1995), 155–56.

27. See Tertullian, *On Exhortation to Chastity* 7, in *Patrologiae cursus completus*, Series latina, ed. Jacques-Paul Migne (Paris, 1844–64) 2:922–23. In this chapter, the series will be abbreviated to PL and cited by volume and column number.

28. See Torjesen, *When Women Were Priests*, 163–64. Torjesen points out that Tertullian uses the same word for "right" (*ius*) to describe clerical privileges as was commonly used in the Roman legal system to describe a citizen's rights.

29. See Torjesen, *When Women Were Priests*, 62–65, 76–82. Torjesen asserts that "so long as church leadership continued to model itself on the familiar role of household manager, there was no cultural barrier to women assuming leadership roles. First- and second-century Christians, familiar with the authority and leadership role of the female head of household, would have perceived women's leadership within the church as not only acceptable but natural" (Torjesen, 82).

30. See Tertullian, *On the Veiling of Virgins* 9.1 (PL 2:902).

31. Tertullian reads 1 Corinthians 14:34–35 to support his claim that women cannot possibly have the right to teach or baptize since Paul has forbidden women from even *learning* in church and must wait to ask their husbands to teach them in private if they have questions. See Tertullian, *On Baptism* 17.4 (PL 1:1218).

32. See Charles Arnold Bobertz, "Cyprian of Carthage as Patron: A Social-Historical Study of the Role of Bishop in the Ancient Christian Community of North Africa," (PhD. diss., Yale University, 1988), 65, 70.

33. Cyprian of Carthage, *De opera et eleemosynis* 21 (PL 4:617–18); my own translation of the Latin. While Church leaders had collected money for the poor since the New Testament period, Cyprian may have been the first to insist that it is superior for an individual to donate to the Church rather than directly to the poor and needy.

34. See Osiek and MacDonald with Tulloch, *A Woman's Place*, 213, 218–19.

35. The *Apostolic Teachings* includes a fifth-century prayer of ordination for female deacons. This prayer is the first evidence for the ordination of women to a priesthood office. See Kevin Madigan and Carolyn Osiek, ed. and trans., *Ordained Women in the Early Church: A Documentary History* (Baltimore: Johns Hopkins University Press, 2005), 112. English translations of *Teachings of the Apostles* and *Apostolic Constitutions* are taken from this edition translated by Madigan and Osiek.

36. *Teachings of the Apostles* 9.3.

37. *Teachings of the Apostles* 9.5–6. In the Greek, the masculine word for deacon (*diakonos*) is still being used for male and female deacons, but the

text clearly indicates that these deacons are female here by the use of the feminine article with *diakonos*. The Greek word for deaconess (*diakonissa*) is not in use until the fourth century. See Madigan and Osiek, *Ordained Women*, 107, 111.

38. See *Teachings of the Apostles* 9.6.

39. See *Teachings of the Apostles* 12.

40. See *Teachings of the Apostles* 16.1.

41. *Teachings of the Apostles* 16.2, 4.

42. See *Teachings of the Apostles* 15. Later church orders in the fourth-century *Apostolic Constitutions* incorporated the *Teachings of the Apostles* and added more instructions and constraints for female deacons, further limiting their roles and influence.

    The office of female deacons is widely attested in the Eastern Church through the sixth century, as is demonstrated by the compilation of evidence made by Madigan and Osiek, *Ordained Women*, 26–130. In contrast, female deacons do not appear in the West until the sixth century, and only a handful of sources attest their existence in the Western Church between the sixth and eleventh centuries. See Madigan and Osiek, *Ordained Women*, 131–48.

43. Teresa Berger makes this point in her article "Women's Liturgical Practices and Leadership Roles in Early Christian Communities," in *Patterns of Women's Leadership in Early Christianity*, ed. Joan E. Taylor and Ilaria L. E. Ramelli (Oxford University Press, 2021), 183.

    In the version of the *Teachings of the Apostles* incorporated into the *Apostolic Teachings* in the fourth century, the stipulation that deaconesses be virgins, or at least widows who have only been married once, is included, excluding most women from being able to hold the office. See Madigan and Osiek, *Ordained Women*, 112.

44. Some early organization of Christian widows may be suggested in 1 Timothy 5:9–10 (KJV) when qualifications are established for a widow to be "taken into the number." Another translation of the original Greek verb in this phrase, *katalegesthō*, is "to be registered" or "to be enrolled," making it difficult to discern whether an order of widows is being established here or widows are being registered on a list as welfare recipients. For a summary of this ongoing debate, see Eisen, *Women Officeholders in Early Christianity*, 14.

    The widow who had only been married once, the *univira*, was a station of honor in Roman society before Christianity, and 1 Timothy's preference for both women and men officeholders that had only been married once suggests that early Christians also saw it as a badge of virtue to remain loyal to a deceased spouse. See Hylen, *Women in the New Testament World*, 54.

45. See Eisen, *Women Officeholders in Early Christianity*, 143–45.

46. *Apostolic Tradition* 1.11; 3.25, in Burton Scott Easton, trans., *The Apostolic Tradition of Hippolytus* (Cambridge: Cambridge University Press, 1934), 40, 50.

47. Polycarp, bishop of Smyrna (AD 69–155), reminded widows that they were "God's altar" and would be inspected for blemish, implying that widows played an important intercessory role in the community, but it is not clear that they yet constituted an organized group with status in the Church. On the image of a widow as an altar, see Margaret L. Butterfield, "Sacred Intercessors: Widows as Altar in Polycarp, *Philippians*," in *Patterns of Women's Leadership in Early Christianity*, ed. Joan E. Taylor and Ilaria L. E. Ramelli (Oxford University Press, 2021), 74–95.

48. *Teachings of the Apostles* 15.

49. Eisen, *Women Officeholders in Early Christianity*, 150–51. Eisen argues that the overarching objective of the *Teachings* is to strengthen the authority of the bishop's office at the expense of the other church offices.

50. See David G. Hunter, "'A Man of One Wife': Patristic Interpretations of 1 Timothy 3:2, 3:12, and Titus 1:6 and the Making of Christian Priesthood," *Annali di Storia dell'Esegesi* 32, no. 2 (2015): 337–41; Berger, "Women's Liturgical Practices," 187.

51. Canon 33 from the Council of Elvira (AD 305–306) is the first Church proclamation forbidding all clergy from marrying.

52. Elizabeth A. Clark has noted that perpetual virginity allowed women to overcome the negative qualities associated with femaleness in the ancient world: vanity, lightmindedness, lack of intelligence, frivolity, and so forth. Perpetual viriginity gave women a new angelic or "manly" status that transcended being a woman. See Clark, "Devil's Gateway and Bride of Christ: Women in the Early Christian World," in *Ascetic Piety and Women's Faith: Essays on Late Ancient Christianity* (Lewiston, NY: Edwin Mellen Press, 1986), 43–45.

53. For an in-depth summary and analysis of Thecla's story, see Lynn H. Cohick and Amy Brown Hughes, *Christian Women in the Patristic World: Their Influence, Authority, and Legacy in the Second through Fifth Centuries* (Ada, MI: Baker Academic, 2017), 1–25.

54. Tertullian, *On Baptism* 17.4 (PL 1:1218); my own translation of the Latin.

55. See Tertullian, *On the Veiling of Virgins* 9 (PL 2:902).

56. Jerome, *Commentary on Ephesians* 3, Ephesians 5:28 (PL 26:512); my own translation of the Latin.

57. See Ambrose of Milan, *Concerning Virgins* 2.5.35, in *Verginità et vedovanza: Tutte le opera di Sant' Ambrogio*, ed. and trans. Franco Gori (Milan: Biblioteca

Ambrosiana, 1989), 196.

58. See Ambrose of Milan, *Concerning Virgins* 2.3.29, in *Verginità et vedovanza*, 190.

59. This phrase first appears in Tertullian's writings *On the Resurrection of the Flesh* 61 (PL 2:883–84) and *The Veiling of Virgins* 7 (PL 2:898).

60. On the Song of Songs in fourth-century ascetic discourse, see Elizabeth Castelli, "Virginity and Its Meaning for Women's Sexuality in Early Christianity," *Journal of Feminist Studies in Religion* 2 (1986):61–63.

61. See *Apostolic Constitutions* 6.17.4.

62. See *Apostolic Constitutions* 8.24.2.

63. *Apostolic Constitutions* 8.28.6.

64. See Clark, "Devil's Gateway and Bride of Christ," in *Ascetic Piety*, 46–48.

65. See Gregory of Nyssa, *Vita Macrinae* (PL 46:959–99).

66. See Jerome, *Epistle* 127.4, 7, 9–10 (PL 22:1089, 1091–3).

67. See Jerome, *Epistle* 127.5 (PL 22:1090).

68. See *Vie anonyme d'Olympias*, in Sources chrétiennes (Paris: Les Editions du Cerf, 1943–), 13:418–20.

69. See Dallin H. Oaks, "The Keys and Authority of the Priesthood," *Ensign*, May 2014, 51. President Nelson later confirmed this teaching: "When you [women] are set apart to serve in a calling under the direction of one who holds priesthood keys—such as your bishop or stake president—you are given priesthood authority to function in that calling." See Russell M. Nelson, "Spiritual Treasures," *Ensign*, November 2019, 78.

70. Dallin H. Oaks, "The Powers of the Priesthood," *Ensign*, May 2018, 67.

71. See Russell M. Nelson, "Spiritual Treasures," *Ensign*, November 2019, 79.

5

SACRED SPACES
&
PLACES OF WORSHIP

From House Churches
to Monumental Basilicas

Matthew J. Grey

Now, therefore, you are no longer strangers and for-
eigners, but fellow citizens with the saints and members of the household of God . . . [growing] into a
holy temple in the Lord, in whom you also are being
built together for a dwelling place of God.

—Ephesians 2:19–22
New King James Version

According to the New Testament Acts of the Apostles, Jesus's earliest disciples spent the days after his resurrection assembling with other Jews at the Jerusalem temple to worship the God of Israel (see Acts 2:46; 5:42), preaching and debating their message of salvation within local synagogues (see Acts 6:9; 9:20), and privately gathering in the homes of believers to pray, read scripture, share meals, and welcome new converts into their emerging messianic movement (see Acts 1:12–26; 2:1–4, 43–47). These accounts reflect the complex beginnings of early Christianity as a small Jewish sect that fully participated in Judaism's preeminent institutions but that—as an increasingly marginalized group within the Jewish community—also began to find its own places to meet in which its members could explore new Christ-centered interpretations of Old Testament scripture, develop new forms of communal worship and ritual activity, and organize their internal hierarchy separate from the existing social structures that surrounded them. As, over time, their sectarian identity gradually became distanced from its Jewish origins through increasing Gentile conversion, the destruction of the Jerusalem temple, and separation from local synagogue assemblies, the followers of Jesus continued to cultivate their own sacred spaces in which they could carve out a place for themselves within the larger Roman Empire.

During the decades and centuries following their initial gatherings in Jerusalem, early Christians would come to utilize a fascinating variety of venues to facilitate their religious gatherings and to practice their holiest rituals. These included domestic and work spaces of the Roman world that, in the first through third centuries, were adapted and used for Christian assembly (settings often referred to as "house churches"); homes that, in the third and early fourth centuries, were renovated in order to accommodate more formalized worship services (structures often designated as *domus ecclesiae*); and monumental basilicas that, in the fourth century and beyond, came to be identified as the new temples of Christianity—each of which reflected the changing historical circumstances of the young faith and helped shape the ways its members viewed their relationship to God, society, and each other.

In this chapter, I will survey the various forms of sacred space and places of worship used by early Christians, from their modest origins as a religious minority group within the Greco-Roman culture of the first century to their dominant status after the fourth century as the official religion of the Roman-Byzantine Empire. To do so, I will provide a brief description of the different structures in which Christians held their earliest gatherings, attempt to envision the religious experience they would have had in each setting, and consider how each venue both influenced and reflected the ongoing development of Christian self-perception, religious worldviews, and efforts to commune with God. It is my hope that these rough sketches will allow Latter-day Saint readers to appreciate more fully the devotional experiences of their early Christian predecessors and to contemplate more thoughtfully their modern expressions of faith, worship, and community as experienced in their own sacred spaces (see box 5.1).

The New Family and Household of God: House Churches and *Domus Ecclesiae* from the First to the Third Centuries

Early Christianity had its origins in the eastern Mediterranean world of the first-century Roman Empire—a culture that was full of sacred spaces (such as temples and shrines that housed local deities), public buildings (such as basilicas and *bouleteria* that facilitated the deliberations of administrative bodies), and places for group assemblies (such as private associations, *collegia*, trade guilds, and mystery cults), each of which met the various religious, civic, and cultural needs of

BOX 5.1 **Why It Matters**

The practice of gathering in sacred spaces for teaching, worshipping, and performing ceremonial ordinances has long played a prominent role in the religious and community life of The Church of Jesus Christ of Latter-day Saints. Throughout the history of the Restoration, such activities have occurred in a wide variety of physical settings, each of which reflect the spiritual needs, ecclesiastical developments, and historical circumstances of the time. In the early days of the Church, for example, assembly spaces for study, sermons, and sacraments included open-air venues (such as riversides and clearings in wooded groves), as well as repurposed private structures (such as homes and workspaces). However, as the Church's needs for gathering have continued to grow and the nature of its sacred rituals has continued to unfold, the community has utilized more formal and dedicated buildings, such as chapels, assembly halls, and temples.

In several ways, the history of Latter-day Saint places of worship has a fascinating parallel in the development of sacred space among early Christians who, over the span of the movement's first few centuries, used houses, apartment complexes, semipublic spaces, and eventually monumental church structures to facilitate their gatherings and the performance of their holiest ceremonies. Although the precise forms of assemblies and liturgical practices vary between the ancient and modern churches, understanding the ways in which various physical settings housed the communal activities of Jesus's earliest followers can help Latter-day Saints more deeply appreciate the religious experiences of their predecessors in the faith and more thoughtfully reflect on their own uses of sacred space.

the Empire's diverse populations.[1] However, while the first Christians would have come into contact with all of these structures in their hometowns and travels, the earliest movement of Jesus followers primarily emerged from within a Jewish context and, as a result, found its initial footing within Judaism's central institutions: the Jerusalem temple and public synagogues. Both of these settings had a distinct place within the Jewish community—the temple as Judea's national shrine housing the presence of the God of Israel among his people, and synagogues as common spaces for the gathering of Jews at the local level—and both played a formative role in the development of early Christian assemblies, preaching, and worship.[2]

With their gradual separation from the sacred spaces of first-century Judaism and their identity as a Jewish sect, though, early Christians felt the need to begin developing their own social identity and places of gathering—two features of new religious movements that often work together in community formation. In this process of creating new spaces and a sense of belonging for a growing number of believers, New Testament writers and their successors drew upon various social metaphors that would help create purpose, identity, and cohesion among members of the community as they navigated the Jewish and Roman environments that surrounded them. One such metaphor described the movement as being a new "family" or "household of God" to which the faithful belonged as daughters, sons, sisters, and brothers (regardless of their natural familial connections), while another described the church as being a new "temple" in which the spirit of God now dwelled and in which he could now be worshipped with spiritual sacrifices.[3] These community metaphors also came to be reflected in the creation of unique Christian spaces for gathering and worship: the so-called "house churches" and *domus ecclesiae* of the first through third centuries, and the monumental basilicas (viewed by many Christians as successors to the Jerusalem temple) of the fourth century and beyond.

▲ **FIGURE 5.1** A model of first-century Jerusalem at the Israel Museum, which includes a proposed reconstruction of the elite homes of the Upper City (on the upper left) and more modest homes closer to the Lower City (in the center). While aspects of this reconstruction are debated by scholars, it generally reflects the types of domestic settings that have been attested in Jerusalem through archaeological excavations and that could have served as meeting places for Jesus's earliest followers. Photo: Used with permission, Matthew Grey

As seen throughout the writings of the New Testament, long before Christians had resources to build their own structures or had congregation sizes that required large meeting places, the earliest followers of Jesus naturally gathered for their community activities in the houses of local believers. The Acts of the Apostles claims that the first such settings were the homes and "upper rooms" of members scattered throughout the city of Jerusalem, where small groups could meet outside the purview of public authorities and begin to develop the internal workings of their emerging movement (see box 5.2 and fig. 5.1).[4] Acts and other writings also assert that, as Jesus's

BOX 5.2 Early Christian House Gatherings in Jerusalem

Although several ancient domestic structures have been uncovered in the city of Jerusalem, none show clear archaeological evidence of the early Christian gatherings referred to in the Acts of the Apostles. Some of these excavated homes, however, do allow us to envision the types of settings in which such gatherings may have occurred. While most of the first-century houses found in Jerusalem's Upper City are palatial residences of the city's Romanized aristocracy (an unlikely socio-economic setting for meetings of early Jesus followers), more modest homes excavated along the western slope of the Tyropoeon Valley highlight the domestic activities of the city's less affluent families. These homes were terraced houses that were cut into the bedrock and included small open-air courtyards for food preparation, a series of small living rooms on the upper terraces (each with bedrock floors, lightly plastered walls, and beam-supported ceilings), modest dining rooms (with niches that served as cupboards for pottery or stone vessels), and subterranean rooms that housed storage cellars and ritual immersion installations (*miqva'ot*). Given the social status of Jesus's earliest disciples in Jerusalem, it is possible to imagine such homes as providing the gathering places they used to pray, read scripture, and fellowship with one another.

disciples shared their messianic message among Jews and eventually Gentiles throughout the Roman Empire, they continued this practice by meeting in converts' homes and workspaces located in some of the major cities of the eastern Mediterranean, including in Syria, Asia Minor, Greece, and Italy.[5] These types of community gatherings, which Christian writings often referred to as the "household(s) of faith," provided the setting for what many scholars now describe as early Christian house churches.[6]

According to references found in available sources, during the first, second, and third centuries a wide variety of physical spaces from the Greco-Roman world could be used as house churches, as they simply needed to accommodate localized groups of between ten to fifty believers who assembled to read, pray, eat, sing, and converse (the basic activities of earliest Christian worship; see below). Unfortunately, because Christians had not yet developed their own distinct material culture or artistic tradition apart from their Greek, Roman, or Jewish neighbors, no clearly identifiable remains of an early Christian house church have survived to inform our understanding of how these spaces were used. However, the many examples of contemporary domestic and industrial structures that have survived from the region—particularly at locations such as Pompeii, Herculaneum, and Ostia (in Italy),[7] Corinth (in Greece),[8] and Ephesus (in Asia Minor)[9]—can help us imagine what house church gatherings may have been like for Christianity's first two centuries. While the precise forms of these structures could have varied over time and across locations, they tended to share some common characteristics that illustrate the types of Christian gatherings attested in the literary sources.

For example, one of the most prominent settings for an early house church likely would have been the homes of wealthy converts who lived in or near the cities in which the Christian message had been taught and who could support the practical needs of small groups of local believers (see fig. 5.2).[10] Based on examples found in archaeological excavations, such upper-class homes were typically accessed through a doorway (*fauces*) leading from the busy city street into an enclosed atrium that could have been used for members of the household to meet with family, friends, neighbors, or associates. This interior space was typically surrounded by living rooms (*cubicula*); adorned with colorful wall frescoes, tiled flooring, and statuary; and had at its center a shallow pool (*impluvium*) that was filled with rainwater from an opening in the roof above it, which also naturally illuminated the atrium during the daytime (see fig. 5.3). Further into the house would often be a beautiful open-air garden (*hortus*), the surrounding columns of which supported a partial roof to provide

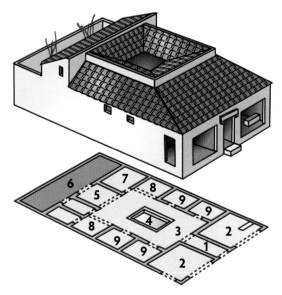

1. *fauces*   4. *impluvium*   7. *triclinium*
2. *tabernæ*   5. *tablinum*   8. *alæ*
3. *atrium*   6. *hortus*   9. *cubiculum*

▲ **FIGURE 5.2**   The top plan of a typical Roman home, with rooms and spaces labeled. Image: Courtesy of Tobias Langhammer via Wikimedia Commons (CC BY-SA 3.0)

shade along the edges (see fig. 5.4). A series of additional rooms often included a richly decorated dining room (*triclinium*) with couches on which family and honored guests could recline while they ate (see fig. 5.5); space for women and children to gather and conduct their routine responsibilities; storage and kitchen facilities for the preparation of daily meals; and modest accommodations toward the back for household slaves. This arrangement (or variations of it) allowed for an entire world of household business and leisure activities to flourish within a space that was easily accessible to, but still partially separated from, the bustle of city life in the nearby streets.

Although it is difficult to know for certain how various spaces in such wealthy houses functioned when they were used for Christian

▲ **FIGURE 5.3**   The remains of an atrium (*impluvium*) and adjacent living rooms in the first-century House of Menander at Pompeii. Photo: Courtesy of Nik893 via Wikimedia Commons (CC BY-SA 4.0)

▼ **FIGURE 5.4**   A reconstruction of a first-century peristyle garden at the House of the Vettii in Pompeii. Photo: Courtesy of sailko via Wikimedia Commons (CC BY-SA 3.0)

▲ **FIGURE 5.5** A reconstruction of a Roman-style *triclinium*, with its couches for reclining, decorative wall frescoes, and floor mosaics, Bavarian State Archaeological Collection, Munich. Photo: Wikimedia Commons (public domain)

gatherings, scattered references in the surviving literature allow for a few general observations, and reasonable guesses based on the physical layout of the homes allow for a modest reconstruction of how weekly worship activities may have occurred within them (see chapter 6). For instance, it seems that the head of the household—whether male or female—would have served as a patron(ess) or "deacon(ess)" (see box 5.3) over a small group of between ten and fifty believers who, on a given day of the week (such as on the Jewish Sabbath or on Sunday as "the Lord's Day"), gathered in the atrium to offer the "kiss of peace" to each other and to members of the household.[11] The group would then proceed to the *triclinium* to share a meal (sometimes referred to as an *agape* feast) provided by the patron(ess) or supplied by others (see fig. 5.6) and would conclude the meal with partaking of bread and wine in remembrance of Jesus's Last Supper (see Mark 14:22–26; see

BOX 5.3   Patrons and Patronesses of Early House Churches

New Testament and early Christian writings name several examples of men and women of means who, by opening their homes to small gatherings of believers, functioned as patrons or patronesses (sometimes as deacons or deaconesses) in house churches around the eastern Mediterranean. These include Lydia, "a dealer of purple cloth" in the Macedonian city of Philippi (Acts 16:14–15, 40 NRSV); Jason in the Macedonian city of Thessalonica (see Acts 17:5–9); the evangelist Philip and his prophecy-filled daughters in the coastal city of Caesarea (see Acts 21:8–14); Phoebe in the Greek city of Cenchreae (see Romans 16:1–2); Prisca/Priscilla and her husband Aquila in the cities of Corinth, Ephesus, and Rome (see Romans 16:3–5; see also 1 Corinthians 16:19); Chloe, Gaius, and Stephanus in the Greek city of Corinth (see 1 Corinthians 1:11, 14–16; see also Romans 16:23); Philemon, Apphia, and Archippus in Asia Minor (see Philemon 1–2); Nympha in the city of Laodicea (see Colossians 4:15–16); Tavia, a woman in Smyrna with a non-Christian husband; and an unnamed widow in the same city (Ignatius, *Letter to the Smyrnaeans* 13.2; *Letter to Polycarp* 8.2).

also 1 Corinthians 10:14–21; 11:17–34)—a practice that became the precedent for the later Christian Eucharist (the Sacrament).[12]

Following the meal, members of the group likely retired to the atrium or peristyle garden, where together they would read and discuss scripture (consisting mostly of Old Testament material supplemented by the limited collection of New Testament writings they may have had in their possession), sing hymns (see Ephesians 5:19), offer prayers, and express whatever charismatic spiritual gifts may have flourished among them (see 1 Corinthians 12–14).[13] Despite some variety in how they were likely conducted over time and from

▲ **FIGURE 5.6**   This third-century or early fourth-century depiction of a Christian banquet scene from the catacomb of Saints Marcellinus and Peter in Rome likely represents a funerary meal held at the graveside, but it may also resemble early Christian shared meals (*agape* feasts) held around a semicircular table or a *triclinium*. Photo: Wikimedia Commons (public domain)

place to place, these activities seem to have formed the core of early house church fellowship, with the domestic setting and relationship dynamics of this arrangement showing a remarkable degree of social equalization among the men, women, children, and slaves of the group (see Galatians 3:28).[14] This latter feature of early Christian gatherings added a tangible reality to the "family" and "household of faith" metaphors being used to forge community cohesion among believers in a sometimes hostile cultural environment (see Galatians 6:10; 1 Thessalonians 2:1–17).[15]

In locations where believers might not have had a wealthy patron(ess) to provide such a comfortable home for gatherings, similar activities likely occurred and a similar sense of group identity could be achieved in a wide variety of other physical settings.[16] For example, there is evidence that, from the earliest days of the Jesus movement, groups of lower working-class members could meet in much smaller living rooms in multistory apartment buildings (*insulae*), which were common above taverns and workshops in the more densely populated areas of a Roman city (see fig. 5.7).[17] These tenement buildings were often cramped, not well ventilated or lit (relying mostly on oil lamps for internal light), and lacked many of the amenities found in wealthy villas, but such apartments could nevertheless provide space for small groups of believers to read, pray, sing, or converse in evening gatherings following the workday (see Acts 20:5–21).[18] Other possible settings for early Christian house churches could include industrial workshops (where members of a trade guild could meet among their work implements to discuss their new faith),[19] taverns or hotels with gardens and sufficient dining space (which could either be rented or owned by believers),[20] the modest residential spaces above markets or eating establishments (where believers may have worked or run businesses),[21] and the barns or stables of villa estates (which could be utilized by believing slaves if their owners were not Christians and would not open their homes to gatherings).[22]

While these various settings sufficiently served the modest Christian community of the first and second centuries, over time congregation sizes began to grow beyond small clusters of local believers. As part of this growth, leadership structures began to develop from a patron(ess) or deacon(ess) presiding over domestic gatherings to a more hierarchical organization of regional bishops and localized elders (see chapter 4). The common liturgy also started to expand around a more regulated baptismal initiation, cyclical scripture readings during specified assembly days, authoritative instruction given to the congregation by ordained clergy, and a Eucharist of consecrated bread and wine (the remnant of fellowship meals after the *agape* feasts had gradually disappeared). Together, these developments necessitated an adjustment to the physical spaces in which Christians were meeting.[23] To accommodate these needs, by the early to mid-third century some larger domestic structures were renovated, sometimes by removing walls between rooms to create

▲ **FIGURE 5.7**   The remains of a second-century apartment complex (*insula*) at Ostia, Italy. Photo: Wikimedia Commons (public domain)

▼ **FIGURE 5.8**   A restored fresco depicting the *Chi-Rho* symbol from the possible *domus ecclesia* in the early fourth-century villa at Lullingstone, Britain. Photo: Courtesy of Udimu via Wikimedia Commons (CC BY-SA 3.0)

larger meeting spaces, installing modest liturgical furnishings (such as baptismal fonts and speaking platforms), and adding wall frescoes with biblical or Christ-centered art (see fig. 5.8). These homes that were renovated primarily to house Christian ritual gatherings were called *domus ecclesiae* ("assembly houses").[24]

Unlike their house church predecessors, a few examples of *domus ecclesiae* are archaeologically attested from the late Roman world, providing a clearer picture of how such spaces were used for Christian worship services.[25] The oldest and most impressive of these structures is at a frontier town in eastern Syria called Dura Europos.[26] There, during the 240s AD, a courtyard home was renovated by converting a room in the west corner into a baptistery that was furnished with a canopy-covered font and adorned with wall frescoes depicting biblical scenes (see room 6 in fig. 5.9);[27] by opening a medium-sized space along the southwest wall where a small group of newly initiated Christians (*neophytes*) could be taught (see room 5 in fig. 5.9); by combining a room and the *triclinium* along the southeast wall to create a large assembly hall with a raised platform on its east side for a congregation of about seventy-five people to be instructed by an ecclesiastical leader (see room 4 in fig. 5.9); and by adding other rooms for storage or library space (see, for example, room 3 in fig. 5.9), all of which surrounded a central courtyard (see room 1 in fig. 5.9).[28] These features allow us to imagine the liturgical activities that occurred within the building, including the giving of introductory teachings (catechism) in the small meeting space in the southwest, the anointing with oil and immersion in water of initiates in the baptistery,[29] and the weekly gathering of baptized members under the supervision of local clergy in the assembly hall for scripture reading, sermons, and the Eucharist.[30]

Although there seems to have been regional variation in the types of architectural modifications and liturgical performances in *domus ecclesiae* of this period, the structure at Dura Europos reflects important developments occurring within Christian worship practices of the third century. For example, the renovations that occurred within domestic church spaces highlighted the growing distinctions

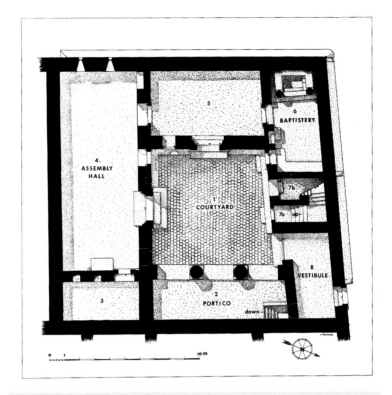

▲ **FIGURE 5.9** The floor plan of the third-century *domus ecclesiae* at Dura-Europos. Image: Courtesy of Yale University Art Gallery, Dura Europos Collection

among congregation members (with catechumens [the unbaptized], baptized laity, and ordained clergy each having designated access to certain parts of the building); the increased prominence of institutional leadership (with bishops and elders becoming more central to the liturgy as they mediated scriptural instruction and community rituals); the accompanying decline in ecclesiastical roles for women (who gradually went from being significantly involved in house church leadership, instruction, and rituals to being restricted in their congregational activities); and the formalization of ritual routine (with more standardized catechistic, baptismal, and Eucharistic practices).[31] (For more on these developments and other forms of sacred activities that emerged in this period—such as vigils held at martyr shrines, funerary meals held at family tombs, and the evolution of sermon culture within congregations—see chapters 2, 4, 6, and 11.)

Throughout the Roman Empire, these various types of domestic structures—the private house churches of the first through early third centuries and the renovated *domus ecclesiae* of the mid-third to early fourth centuries—effectively met the social, religious, and practical needs of early Christians by providing adaptable meeting places. They also fostered a sense of community identity by transforming congregations into the new "family" or "household(s) of God," a need that was still very much felt by Christian minority groups gathering in a sometimes-hostile cultural environment. While these structures were typically viewed by Jesus followers as having only a limited (albeit gradually increasing) degree of sanctity,[32] for the most part, Christians meeting in residential settings kept their eternal hopes focused on the heavenly temple, where Jesus as the "Great High Priest" was before God's throne making intercession on their behalf and preparing a way for the faithful to one day enter the divine presence (concepts that had been developing within the Jesus movement since the first century; see box 5.4).[33] By the early fourth century, however, drastic political and religious transformations in the empire would radically alter the status of Christian communities in the Mediterranean world. These transformations would also have an enormous impact on Christian gatherings as, beginning with the construction of monumental church buildings, believers found themselves worshipping in new state-supported sanctuaries that brought the heavenly temple and earthly church together through liturgies that provided communion with God's throne room.

The New Temples of God: Monumental Basilica Churches from the Fourth to Sixth Centuries

With the turn of Constantine's favor toward Christianity in the early fourth century (a development that provided legalization and a protected status to the previously marginalized movement) and

According to New Testament writings, Jesus's earliest first-century disciples joined with other Jews in seeing the Jerusalem temple as the central location of God's dwelling and as the place where he could be worshipped through the offering of prayers and sacrifices (see Luke 24:52–53; Acts 2:46; 3:1–10; 5:20–25, 42; 21:26–30; 22:17). However, as Jesus followers became increasingly alienated from the temple, and after the temple was destroyed by the Romans in AD 70, Christians began to compensate for its diminishing role in their religious life by seeing Jesus's death as the ultimate fulfillment of the temple's sacrificial system (see John 1:29–34; 19:14–37; Romans 3:23–26; 5:8–11; Hebrews 8–10; Revelation 1:6; 5:6), by seeing the Christian community itself as the new spiritualized temple that housed the divine presence on earth (see 1 Corinthians 3:16–17; 2 Corinthians 6:16–18; Ephesians 2:19 –22; 1 Peter 2:4 –10), and by turning their attention to the heavenly temple where Jesus provided the ultimate intercession for humanity as the Great High Priest (see Hebrews 2–4, 9; Revelation 1, 4–5; see also *1 Clement* 36.1–3; Ignatius, *Epistle of Ignatius to the Philadelphians* 9.1–2; Tertullian, *To the Jews* 14; and Lactantius, *Divine Institutes* 4.14).

These early Christian views of the community as the new temple on earth and of Jesus's death as the ultimate atoning sacrifice continued into the second and third centuries as writers began symbolically referring to the prayers and Eucharistic meals of their house church gatherings as the new spiritual sacrifices that replaced the rituals of the destroyed Jerusalem temple (see, for example, *Didache* 14; Irenaeus, fragment 37; Tertullian, *Against Marcion* 3.7; and *Apostolic Tradition* 4.1–13). During the third century, it also seems that some Christian communities, particularly in Syria, may have begun to see their *domus ecclesiae* as increasingly sacred spaces by referring to them as a "temple [*hayklā*] of the church" (see the Syriac *Edessene Chronicle* for AD 201; see also Porphyry, *Against the Christians* fragment 76) or as "houses of the Lord" (Eusebius, *Ecclesiastical History* 9.10.10–11). While not functioning as proper temples in the ancient or modern (Latter-day Saint) sense, these renovated church spaces seem to have gradually adopted aspects of temple-holiness that added an elevated level of sanctity to Christian liturgy—a process of "templization" that would culminate with the monumental church buildings of the fourth century and beyond.

the imperial edicts issued by Theodosius in the late fourth century (which made Christianity the official religion of the Roman Empire), the community of Jesus followers experienced a massive shift in its social standing. Within two generations, believers went from belonging to a persecuted minority group to being members of a state-supported Church network that granted them empire-wide patronage, privilege, prestige, and position. This remarkable political and religious transition also allowed for an unprecedented shift in views of sacred space and the construction of monumental buildings to house Christian worship. No longer needing to rely as heavily on the metaphor of believers being a separate "family" and "household of faith" within a hostile Roman world, Christians of the fourth century onward would see in their church buildings the creation of new sanctuaries to replace the traditional Greco-Roman shrines of the empire. They would also find new meaning in the New Testament imagery of their community being the dwelling place (or "temple") of God's presence.[34] While this latter metaphor had been loosely applied to believers in a spiritual sense since the first century, during the late Roman and Byzantine periods it would find physical expression in locations throughout the empire in the form of monumental churches, in which the liturgy of the heavenly throne room could be performed for believers on earth by a mediating priesthood of bishops, elders, and deacons (see chapter 4).[35]

To mark the new social reality and political status of Christianity, monumental church construction of the fourth century onward drew

▲ **FIGURE 5.10** The remains of the (non-Christian) Roman basilica at Pompeii (second century BC), with its colonnaded central aisle, side aisles, and elevated *bema* for audiences with government officials. Photo: Courtesy of Rabax63 via Wikimedia Commons (CC BY-SA 4.0)

upon one of the most prominent architectural forms of public civic buildings known throughout the Roman world: the basilica.[36] For hundreds of years, the basilicas built in most Greek and Roman cities were large structures that were typically divided by columns into three aisles with an elevated platform (*bema*) placed at one end of the central aisle (*nave*; see fig. 5.10), and that were designed to facilitate royal audiences, judicial hearings, or other business requiring space for an assembly to appear before state officials.

Believing that this architectural form was ideal for large Christian assemblies—as well as for demonstrating imperial support for Christianity throughout the empire—Constantine, his successors, and other officials commissioned the building of basilical churches at prominent locations in cities throughout the empire.[37] In these churches, the architectural features of traditional basilicas were adapted for Christians to house the presence of God, to accommodate an increasingly formalized

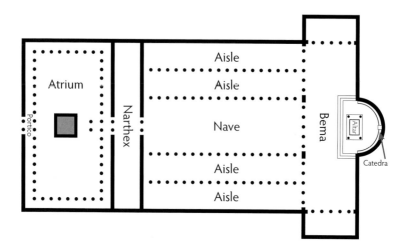

▲ **FIGURE 5.11**　The floor plan of the fourth-century Basilica of St. Peter in Rome with the common architectural features of basilical churches, including the atrium, narthex, nave, side aisles, bema, and sanctuary set within a semicircular apse. Image: Wikimedia Commons (public domain)

▼ **FIGURE 5.12**　The exterior of the nave and semicircular apse of the Church of Saint Sabina (a fifth-century basilica) in Rome. Photo: Mark D. Ellison

▲ **FIGURE 5.13** The interior of the Basilica of Sant'Apollinare in Classe, Ravenna, Italy, showing its nave, side aisles, and semicircular apse. Constructed in the sixth century. Photo: Wikimedia Commons (public domain)

Christian liturgy, and to offer access to the divine realm through the ritual activities of Christian priests. In short, Christian basilicas were to become the new temples of Christianity.[38]

Like their civic predecessors, Christian basilicas would have architectural variation over time and from place to place, but they tended to follow a general template (see figs. 5.11–13). For example, basilical churches were typically rectangular structures oriented on a longitudinal (east-west) axis with a colonnaded (open-air) atrium, a covered entryway (*narthex*) for group gathering in front of the entrance, a roofed interior consisting of a central hall (*nave*), and two or more side aisles (divided by rows of columns supporting the roof) for congregational assembly within the church.[39] The liturgical focus of the building was a raised platform (*bema*) with a semicircular apse (the sanctuary), which was set apart from the congregation by a veiled chancel screen (*templon*), contained the Eucharistic altar,

BOX 5.5 The Use of Veils and Curtains in Monumental Churches

It is not certain when, exactly, veils began to be hung over chancel screens to hide activities in the apse (such as the consecration of the Eucharist) from the view of the congregation. There is evidence that, in some areas such as Syria, Palestine, Jordan, and Egypt, veiled chancel screens appeared with the earliest basilical churches. For example, liturgical texts from the fourth century describe the blessings pronounced over veils in eastern churches (see *Liturgy of Saint James* 2; *Liturgy of the Blessed Apostles* 11), and sixth-century church mosaics in Jordan frequently depict hanging curtains covering doors, shrines, and apses. In other areas such as Constantinople, however, it appears that veiled screens were only added in subsequent centuries. This issue is further complicated by the lack of clarity in some literary sources that describe various curtains, veils, and other coverings used in churches; it is sometimes not clear whether these sources are referring to curtains that hung in baptisteries (to help protect the modesty of initiates being anointed and baptized in the nude), at the doors of the church (to shield the Eucharistic service from the view of uninitiated outsiders), between the columns separating the side aisles from the nave (to demarcate congregational spaces), above the chancel screen (to separate the nave and congregation from the sanctuary and clergy), or on the altar (to cover the Eucharistic bread and wine)—each of which is attested in churches during the Byzantine period. Nevertheless, it seems that, over time, veils, hanging curtains, and other cloth coverings become increasingly used as a way to highlight and guard the sacred nature of the liturgies being performed within churches.

SS. PETER
AND PAUL,
GERASA

▲ **FIGURE 5.14** A drawing of the sanctuary in the sixth-century Church of Saints Peter and Paul at Jerash in Jordan, with its apse, chancel screen, Eucharistic altar, and semicircle of benches (including the *cathedra*) for the clergy. Image: Wikimedia Commons (public domain)

and included a semicircle of benches for the clergy (the central seat being the *cathedra*, or seat of the bishop; see fig. 5.14 and box 5.5).[40]

Architectural variations on this layout could also include the addition of small aisles (a *transept*) running north and south across the nave or bema (creating a cross-shaped [cruciform] church), a centralized platform for the delivery of sermons by the clergy (a feature

◀ **FIGURE 5.15**   The apse mosaic at the Church of Saint Pudenziana in Rome (ca. 400), which depicts Christ (crowned with a divine halo) enthroned in judicial robes as the eschatological judge and surrounded by his disciples, as well as by prominent locations of his earthly ministry and the winged creatures of the heavenly throne room. Photo: Courtesy of Welleschik via Wikimedia Commons (CC BY-SA 3.0)

◀ **FIGURE 5.16**   The modern dome of the Church of the Holy Sepulchre in Jerusalem (in classical Byzantine style), depicting *Christ Pantocrator* ("Christ Almighty") as the heavenly mediator encircled by archangels and disciples. Photo: Courtesy of Diego Delso via Wikimedia Commons (CC BY-SA 4.0)

especially common in Syrian churches),[41] and—particularly in the Byzantine east—a large dome on the roof over the juncture of the nave and sanctuary.[42]

These features of monumental basilicas were imbued with potent symbolism that set apart church space as reflecting Christianity's new political and religious power. For example, since the architectural form of the basilica was inherently associated with civic authority, by dedicating it to Christ, framing its apse with a triumphal arch (traditionally associated with imperial military victory), and adorning it with exquisite art that highlighted Jesus's divinity (such as a depiction of Jesus sitting on a throne in the apse or an image of *Christ Pantocrator* in the center of the dome; see figs. 5.15–16), monumental churches declared to the Roman-Byzantine world that Jesus (divine patron of the emperor) was the cosmic ruler, earthly victor, eschatological judge, and ultimate mediator between heaven and earth.[43]

This latter image was particularly meaningful to worshippers who saw the church building itself as the meeting place of the heavenly and earthly realms, with the nave (the space of the congregation) representing the earth, the sanctuary (the space of the priestly clergy) representing the heavenly throne room of God, and the chancel screen or a domed roof (in eastern Byzantine churches) representing the merging of the two.[44]

This symbolism was also powerfully conveyed by the liturgy (or ritual worship) that was performed within the building (see box 5.6).[45] While, as with architectural features of the church, there were often liturgical variations that developed regionally and over time, the common worship services of the Constantinian and Byzantine periods typically had two parts, or "entrances": The First Entrance, or "liturgy of the word," was a procession of the bishop, priests, and deacons dressed in their liturgical vestments and bearing the Gospels (the "Word of God") followed by the congregation (consisting of both catechumens and baptized Christians), all of whom had assembled in the narthex and entered the nave with singing, incense,

BOX 5.6   Sources on the Eucharistic Liturgy after the Fourth Century

Although regional variations and limited sources do not allow for a comprehensive reconstruction of early Christian worship practices within late Roman- and Byzantine-era church buildings, there are several surviving texts that provide valuable insights into the ritual activities, significance, and development of Eucharistic services from the fourth century and beyond. These texts include the writings of Cyril of Jerusalem (circa AD 313–86), whose lectures on the Christian sacraments (the *Protocatechesis* and the five *Mystagogical Catecheses*) prepared initiates to participate in the Eucharist mysteries; the sermons of John Chrysostom (died AD 407), who often described aspects of the weekly services (and after whom the traditional eastern liturgy would later be named); the Apostolic Constitutions, a late fourth-century Church Order that collated and expanded upon previous liturgical works; and the Mystagogia of Maximus the Confessor (circa AD 628–30), which contains the earliest complete text of the Byzantine rite.

▲ **FIGURE 5.17** A sixth-century mosaic from the Basilica of Saint Vitale in Ravenna, Italy, depicting the First Entrance, with the imperial court (at left) and the Emperor Justinian (center) joining the clergy (at right), who are dressed in their liturgical vestments and holding ritual items (such as the Gospels and an incense burner) for the "liturgy of the word." Photo: Courtesy of Roger Culos via Wikimedia Commons (CC BY-SA 3.0)

prayers, and offerings (see figs. 5.17–18). As the clergy moved past the chancel screen into the sanctuary to take their seats in the apse, the Gospels were placed on the altar and read (along with other biblical texts) to the congregation standing in the nave.[46] Following the scriptural reading, additional incense-borne prayers, and the singing of accompanying psalms, the bishop would then deliver the sermon from his seat (cathedra) in the apse (or, on occasion, from a position closer to the nave).

SCS·MARTINVS·SCS·CLEMES·SCSVS

MOR·SCSFELIX·SCSAPOLLINARS·SCSEBSTIANV·SCSDEMITER·SCSPOLICARPVS·SCSVINCENTIVS·SCSBRIGRATIVS·SCRIGONIVS·SCSPROTVS·SCS

▲ **FIGURE 5.18** *(PREVIOUS PAGES; PANORAMIC IMAGE SPLIT IN HALF)* A sixth-century mosaic from the Basilica of Sant'Apollinare Nuovo in Ravenna, Italy, of saints and martyrs processing to offer their crowns to Jesus, who sits enthroned surrounded by angels (see Revelation 4:2–11). This image likely models the liturgical processions of clergy and worshippers that would occur through the nave toward the apse during church services, thus allowing worshippers to see themselves as participating in the liturgy of the heavenly throne-room. The disembodied hands, visible on some palace columns (lower right), are the remnants of images that were erased during the confiscation of Arian churches (mid-sixth century). Some Latter-day Saints have misinterpreted this mosaic as reflecting our modern temple practices and clothing; see boxes 5.8 and 6.12. Photo: Courtesy of Chester M. Wood via Wikimedia Commons (CC BY-SA 4.0)

For the Second Entrance, or Entrance of the Mysteries, the uninitiated catechumens were dismissed, the doors of the church were closed or veiled, and the "liturgy of the faithful" would commence (see fig. 15.9).[47] It began with a procession of the Eucharistic bread and wine, which was placed on the altar in the (now veiled) sanctuary (see fig. 5.20).[48] The initiated members of the congregation (those who had been washed and anointed at baptism) would then cite a creedal profession of faith and participate in the *anaphora*—a Eucharistic prayer led by priests in the sanctuary that included the *trisagion* (the chants of "Holy, Holy, Holy is the Lord God Almighty" sung by the angelic beings in God's throne room; see Isaiah 6:1–4; Revelation 4:2–8), which liturgically represented the merging of the earthly church with the heavenly temple.[49]

After the bishop consecrated the bread and wine (imbuing them with the divine presence), the congregation would form a line at the chancel screen, where the bishop standing on the opposite side of the barrier—the meeting place between earth (the nave) and heaven (the sanctuary)[50]—would offer the sacramental emblems through the parted veil, allowing initiated worshippers to experience fellowship with the divine presence and heavenly realm.[51] After the Eucharistic mysteries were administered at the chancel screen, a priest offered

▲ **FIGURE 5.19**   A fifth-century mosaic of a basilical church (displayed in the Louvre), showing the church's entryways covered with hanging curtains or veils, which were opened during the "liturgy of the word" but closed during the "liturgy of the faithful." Photo: Courtesy of Bas-tienM via Wikimedia Commons (CC BY-SA 3.0)

a final prayer of thanksgiving and pronounced a blessing upon the congregation (based on the priestly blessing of Numbers 6:22–27), the congregation was dismissed, and the clergy led an exit-procession out of the building.

This liturgical arrangement had multiple layers of meaning and served a multiplicity of purposes in the late Roman and Byzantine world. As a demonstration of Christianity's newfound political pow-er, the Eucharistic service—particularly when attended by imperi-al officials (see, for example, fig. 5.17)—forged a close connection

▲ **FIGURE 5.20**　A sixth-century mosaic from the Basilica of Sant'Apollinare, Classe, Ravenna, Italy, depicting the Eucharistic bread and wine placed on an altar, with curtains on either side pulled back to reveal the consecration of the Eucharist by the biblical priest-king, Melchizedek, who is flanked by Abel offering his sacrifice and Abraham offering Isaac. This scene likely reflects the practice and symbolism of the Eucharistic liturgy performed by the bishop in the apse of the church. Photo: Courtesy of José Luiz Bernardes Ribeiro via Wikimedia Commons (CC BY-SA 4.0)

between the ecclesiastical authority of the Christian priesthood and the civic authority of the imperial court. As a demonstration of Christian social hierarchy, it provided a clear demarcation of roles, with members of the clergy (who ministered within the veiled apse) mediating the divine realm, the baptized members of the congregation (who were restricted to the nave) receiving communion from them, and the uninitiated being excluded from full fellowship in the community.[52] And, as a demonstration of Christianity's spiritual power, this liturgy both asserted a supersessionist triumph over Judaism— representing Christians as the new chosen people with their churches being the heir of the earthly temple in Jerusalem—and an ability to join the congregation of believers with the presence of God in the throne room of the heavenly temple.

For example, from the earliest construction of monumental churches in the fourth century, Christian writers celebrated the ways in which their new buildings and liturgy evoked, replicated, replaced, or superseded the features and function of the Jerusalem temple from biblical times (see box 5.7).[53] The Jewish temple in Jerusalem had been a tripartite structure (divided by partition walls and veils into

---

BOX 5.7 The Christian Legacy of the Jerusalem Temple in the Fourth to Sixth Centuries

The first Christian writer to identify the associations between monumental church architecture of the fourth century and the sacred space of the first-century Jerusalem temple may have been Eusebius. In his dedicatory sermon for the newly built church at Tyre (circa AD 315-317), Eusebius referred to the nave of the church as the *naos* (the Greek term for the inner court of the Jerusalem temple), the area of the church apse as the Holy of Holies (the name of the temple's innermost sanctuary), and the church's presiding bishop as a new Solomon and Zerubbabel (the builders of Jerusalem's biblical temples; see Eusebius, *Ecclesiastical History* 10.4). This pattern of seeing basilical churches as the heirs of the Jerusalem temple—with their ecclesiastical offices as the heirs to the temple priesthood and their Eucharistic liturgy as the heir to the temple's sacrificial system—eventually spread throughout the Byzantine world. Such connections were particularly pronounced in churches built in Jerusalem, the location of the original temple and of Jesus's sacrificial death.

There, the fourth-century Church of the Holy Sepulchre was considered by many to be a new temple designed to supplant the biblical sanctuary, with its eastward orientation facing the ruined temple mount, its shrine at Golgotha as the new altar of sacrifice, its shrine at the tomb of Christ as the new Holy of Holies, its liturgical services replacing the rituals of the temple, and its dedication believed to have been on the same date as the dedication of Solomon's temple (see Eusebius, *Life of Constantine* 3.33.1–2; see also Egeria, *Egeria's Travels* 48.1). Similarly, the Nea Church built in the city by Justinian during the sixth century was viewed as yet another symbolic successor to the Jerusalem temple by the displaying of treasures from Herod's temple within the massive basilica.

Although connections made between churches and the Jerusalem temple were often metaphorical or rhetorical, some churches were constructed to have close architectural similarities with the biblical temple as well. A fascinating example of this is the early sixth-century Church of Saint Polytheuktos in Constantinople, which attempted to physically resemble the layout, proportions, dimensions, and décor of Solomon's temple as recorded in the Old Testament.

the outer court, inner court, and Holy of Holies) that housed God's presence among his covenant people;[54] that brought heaven and earth together by symbolizing the layers of the cosmos (the earthly realm, the heavenly dome, and the throne room of God);[55] and that, through its priestly mediators, provided the routine rituals (sacrifice, prayer, incense, and blessing) necessary for atonement and divine communion.[56] According to Christian writers, monumental churches now fulfilled each of these functions through designating and dedicating

▲ **FIGURE 5.21** The apse of the sixth-century Chapel of the Theotokos on Mount Nebo (in Jordan), with a mosaic depiction of the
Jerusalem temple, its altar, and its sacrifices (two bulls; see Psalm
51:19) at the access point of the chancel screen in front of the church
altar. This scene presumably illustrated the function of the Christian
Eucharist as the new (bloodless) sacrifice of Christ's body, replacing
the former animal sacrifices of the Jerusalem temple. Photo: Courtesy
of DuiMDog via Wikimedia Commons (CC BY-SA 4.0)

them as "temples,"[57] as well as through their architectural layout, with
the atrium of the church being seen as the new outer court for all, the
nave as the new inner court for the initiated, the chancel screen as
the new veil covering the presence of God, and the apse as the new
Holy of Holies only accessed by the priesthood.[58] Christian writers
also saw churches as replicating Jerusalem temple features through
their cosmic symbolism (which often attached earthly and heavenly significance to architectural features),[59] their ritual performances
(with the priests burning incense, uttering prayers, pronouncing
blessings, and offering a bloodless Eucharistic sacrifice on behalf

of the congregation; see fig. 5.21),[60] and the rhetoric that attended church construction (which often referred to church builders as a "new Solomon" or "new Zerubbabel"—builders of the biblical temples).[61] All of these images forged a strong connection between the previous Jerusalem temple and the new churches being constructed throughout the empire.

Related to the claim that churches served as the new temple is the notion that Christian churches reflected the heavenly temple and that their liturgies facilitated communion with the worship of God that occurred in the heavenly throne room. As alluded to previously (see box 5.4), since the first century, Jesus followers (along with other Jews) envisioned that God's true temple existed in heaven, whereas the Jerusalem temple was simply an earthly reflection of it.[62] With their conviction that Jesus was the mediating High Priest of the heavenly temple, early Christians naturally looked forward to the day when Christ's priestly intercession would allow them access to the true Holy of Holies in heaven. Monumental churches, however, brought earthly and heavenly worship together in the same space by replicating features of the heavenly temple, particularly as described in the biblical book of Revelation (see chapter 13).[63] For example, just as in Revelation's description of the heavenly sanctuary, monumental churches placed the altar in the apse (the Holy of Holies), rather than in the outer court where it was located in the earthly temple (see Revelation 8:3–4); placed crypts or relics of the martyrs under the altar (see Revelation 6:9); designed the seating of the clergy in a semicircle around the throne or cathedra (see Revelation 4:2–4); depicted scenes of Jesus on his throne surrounded by angelic beings (see Isaiah 6; Revelation 4–5) within or near church apses (see figs. 5.14–15, 18); and had the congregation join in the hymns of praise sung by angelic attendants around God's throne in biblical visions (see Isaiah 6:3; Revelation 4:8).[64] Together, such architectural and liturgical features mystically fused earthly and heavenly worship in ways that were palpable and that reflected the salvific power of Christianity.

To some extent, therefore, Christian worship and sacred space of the late Roman and Byzantine periods had come full circle with the movement's first-century roots. Once again Christians viewed God's presence as being housed in temples, access to that presence as being offered through the rituals mediated by an ordained priesthood, and the heavenly realm as being brought to earth through a sacred liturgy experienced by participants. By the fourth century onward, these aspects of sacred space and worship would be overtly infused with the Christological symbolism that the earliest followers of Jesus had seen in them centuries before—with Christ's death serving as the ultimate sacrificial atonement (as reflected in the Eucharist) and his ongoing work of priestly intercession bringing believers into God's presence, both on earth and in heaven. Such architectural, liturgical, and symbolic developments would lay the foundations of Christian churches and ritual into modern times as later Catholic, eastern Orthodox, and (high church) Protestant traditions would continue to draw upon their powers of facilitating divine communion for the faithful.[65]

Conclusion

The development of sacred space and liturgy in early Christianity provides profound insight into the unfolding history, theology, self-perception, religious experience, and social dynamics of the movement's first several centuries. Through surveying its places of worship ranging from the first to sixth centuries, this chapter has highlighted the origins of Christianity as a small Jewish sect that was fully involved in the institutions of early Judaism (the Jerusalem temple and public synagogues), its gradual marginalization and separation from these institutions, the creation of unique Christian spaces in private settings (including house churches and *domus ecclesiae*), and ultimately the construction of monumental basilicas that stood as public proclamations of Christianity and that allowed believers to experience their own Christ-centered temple space.

Each of these developments reflect in significant ways the early creation of Christian social identity (ranging from the movement forging a new "family" and "household" in a hostile Roman world to building the new "temples" of the Christianized empire), Christian

BOX 5.8 **Ancient Christian Worship and Modern Latter-day Saint Temples**

As discussed by Mark Ellison (chapter 6) and Catherine Taylor (chapter 11), Latter-day Saints often expect to find close parallels between ancient church liturgy and our own modern temple ceremonies. It is true that early Christians did have ceremonies that resemble aspects of modern Latter-day Saint temple worship (such as a washing and anointing at baptism, prayer with uplifted hands, and intercessory rites on behalf of the deceased), and a comparison between these ritual practices can be mutually informing; however, efforts to understand the connections between the two must be approached in ways that are methodologically responsible. This includes avoiding an overly enthusiastic "parallelomania" (attempting to find correlations where they may not exist), being informed as to the similarities and differences of the rituals being compared (both as to their performances and their intended meanings), and being respectful of the different socio-historical contexts of each community. In addition, while the impulse to seek connections between the former-day and latter-day ritual practices is understandable and can serve to turn the hearts of the children to their spiritual ancestors, it is also helpful for Latter-day Saints to remember the teachings of Restoration scripture that God works with people of different times and locations according their own language and cultural understanding (see 2 Nephi 31:1; Doctrine and Covenants 1:24) and that many practices and teachings of the modern temple endowment were only revealed in this last dispensation (see Doctrine and Covenants 121:26–32; 124:38–41).

As Latter-day Saints, we can expect to be inspired, informed, and enlightened as we learn about the fascinating rituals of early Christianity, but we should not always expect to see an exact parallel between those rituals and our own sacred activities. Rather than seeking for potentially artificial "one-to-one" comparisons between ancient and modern practices, Latter-day Saints might be more enriched by coming to appreciate the shared conceptual vocabulary of the two and by allowing ancient rituals to provide valuable per-spectives on similar practices found in modern ceremonies.

This observation also applies to possible comparisons between ancient Christian church architecture and modern Latter-day Saint temples. Even though there is no evidence that early Christians built "temples" separate from their churches where they performed vi-carious baptism, endowment, or sealing ordinances, early churches contained several features that can help Latter-day Saints more ful-ly appreciate aspects of our own temple experience. For example, early churches demarcated zones of sacred space through the use of doors, veils, and chancel screens that facilitated ritual movement within the building; they used altars and apses to represent the di-vine presence within the sanctuary; they relied on priestly personnel (wearing sacred liturgical clothing) to perform a liturgy that provid-ed communion between the earthly congregation and the heaven-ly throne room; and they often employed artistic and architectural symbolism that pointed to the building as being the meeting place between heaven and earth. Each of these features found within an-cient churches, despite not facilitating an "endowment" per se, offers profound conceptual vocabulary that can greatly inform, enrich, and inspire the temple experience of modern Latter-day Saints as we "learn the language" of ritual and symbolism from our early Christian forebears.

leadership and religious hierarchy (beginning with more localized household patronage and gradually forming around a more clearly defined ecclesiastical priesthood structure), Christian ritual (includ-ing the origins of communal prayer, scripture reading, and the Eucha-rist), and Christian efforts to commune with deity through accessing God's presence in both earthly and heavenly spheres. By providing these rough sketches of the various settings in which early Christians met over time, I hope that we Latter-day Saints can more fully appreciate the religious experience of our predecessors in the faith and be able to reflect more thoughtfully on our own approaches to the sacred spaces, rituals, and worship that help facilitate the journey of Christian discipleship (see box 5.8).

Notes

1. For helpful overviews of sacred spaces, religious gatherings, and meeting places within the Roman Empire, see John Stambaugh, *The Ancient Roman City* (Baltimore: The Johns Hopkins University Press, 1988), 106–22, 209–24; Philip A. Harland, *Associations, Synagogues, and Congregations: Claiming a Place in Ancient Mediterranean Society* (Minneapolis, MN: Fortress Press, 2003). For the relationship between these settings and the emergence of early Christianity in particular, see David W. J. Gill and Bruce W. Winter, "Acts and Roman Religion," in *The Book of Acts in Its Graeco-Roman Setting*, ed. David W. J. Gill and Conrad Gempf, vol. 2 in The Book of Acts in Its First Century Setting series (Grand Rapids, MI: Eerdmans, 1994), 79–118.

2. Helpful overviews of these institutions and the roles they played in the formation of the Christian movement can be found in Timothy Wardle, *The Jerusalem Temple and Early Christian Identity* (Tübingen: Mohr Siebeck, 2010); Eyal Regev, *The Temple in Early Christianity: Experiencing the Sacred* (New Haven: Yale University Press, 2019); Jordan J. Ryan, *The Role of the Synagogue in the Aims of Jesus* (Minneapolis, MN: Fortress Press, 2017).

3. For more on the process of forming community and social identity within the early Jesus movement, particularly within the context of its Jewish and Roman cultural setting, see Philip A. Harland, *Dynamics of Identity in the World of the Early Christians: Associations, Judeans, and Cultural Minorities* (London: T&T Clark, 2009), esp. 61–96.

4. Acts 1:13, 15–26; 2:1–4, 46; 5:42; 12:12–17; 21:16; see also John 20:19–20. For examples of first-century residential structures that have been excavated in Jerusalem, see Nahman Avigad, *The Herodian Quarter*

in Jerusalem (Jerusalem: Keter Publishing House, 1989); Zvi Greenhut, "A Domestic Quarter from the Second Temple Period on the Lower Slopes of the Central Valley (Tyropoeon)," in *Unearthing Jerusalem: 150 Years of Archaeological Research in the Holy City*, ed. Katharina Galor and Gideon Avni (Winona Lake, IN: Eisenbrauns, 2011), 257–93; Bradley Blue, "Acts and the House Church," in *The Book of Acts in Its Graeco-Roman Setting*, ed. David W. J. Gill and Conrad Gempf, vol. 2 in The Book of Acts in Its First Century Setting series (Grand Rapids, MI: Eerdmans, 1994), 130–38, 140–44.

5.   New Testament and early Christian references to believers meeting in houses from the first to early third centuries include Acts 8:3; 10:24–48; 11:12; 16:14–15, 25–34, 40; 17:5–9; 20:18–35; 21:4–14; Romans 16:3–5; 1 Corinthians 16:19; Philemon 1:1–2; 2 John 1:10; *Shepherd of Hermas, Similitudes* 8.10.3; 9.27.2; Ignatius, *Epistle to the Ephesians* 16.1; *Epistle to the Smyrnaeans* 13.1–2; *Epistle to Polycarp* 8.2; *Acts of Paul* 3.5, 7; 9–10; *Acts of Peter* 13; *Acts of John* 46, 62, 106–110; *Acts of Andrew* 3, 22, 6–10; *Acts of Thomas* 105, 131–33, 155–58; Pseudo-Clementina, *Recognitions* 4.2, 6–7; 6.15; 8.36–38; 10.71.

6.   For overviews of early Christian house churches, including their architectural features, ritual uses, and social contexts, see L. Michael White, *Building God's House in the Roman World: Architectural Adaptation among Pagans, Jews, and Christians* (Baltimore: The Johns Hopkins University Press, 1990), 11–25, 102–10; Blue, "Acts and the House Church," 119–222; Carolyn Osiek and David L. Balch, *Families in the New Testament World: Households and House Churches* (Louisville, KY: Westminster John Knox Press, 1997), 5–35. Jeanne Halgren Kilde, *Sacred Power, Sacred Space: An Introduction to Christian Architecture and Worship* (Oxford: Oxford University Press, 2008), 3–23, also considers the various religious and hierarchical dynamics of these settings.

7.   See Andrew Wallace-Hadrill, *Houses and Society in Pompeii and Herculaneum* (Princeton, NJ: Princeton University Press, 1994); Janet DeLaine, "Housing Roman Ostia," in *Contested Spaces: Houses and Temples in Roman Antiquity and the New Testament*, ed. David L. Balch and Annette Weissenrieder (Tübingen: Mohr Siebeck, 2012), 327–51.

8.   See Jerome Murphy-O'Connor, *St. Paul's Corinth: Texts and Archaeology*, 3rd ed. (Collegeville, MN: Liturgical Press, 2002), 178–85.

9.   See Director and Researchers of the Ephesus Museum, ed., *The Terrace Houses in Ephesus* (Istanbul: Hitit Color, 1985); Hilke Thür, "Art and Architecture in Terrace House 2 in Ephesos: An Example of Domestic Architecture in the Roman Imperial Period," in *Contested Spaces: Houses and*

Temples in Roman Antiquity and the New Testament, ed. David L. Balch and Annette Weissenrieder (Tübingen: Mohr Siebeck, 2012), 237–59.

10. For the possible uses of wealthy houses for early Christian meetings, see Osiek and Balch, *Families in the New Testament World,* 5–11, 14–17; Murphy-O'Connor, *St. Paul's Corinth,* 178–85.

11. For more on the experience of women in these household settings and the activities that occurred within them, see Carolyn Osiek and Margaret Y. MacDonald with Janet H. Tulloch, *A Woman's Place: House Churches in Earliest Christianity* (Minneapolis, MN: Fortress Press, 2006), 144–63, 194–219.

12. For more on the *agape* feast—including the centrality of communal meals in Christian fellowship, their role in the development of the Eucharist, their possible similarities to Roman *symposia,* and the economic disparity that occasionally accompanied such gatherings among upper- and lower-class members (see 1 Corinthians 11:33–34)—see Osiek and Balch, *Families in the New Testament World,* 193–214. Brief descriptions of *agape* feasts and Eucharistic practices from the late first, second, and early third centuries can be found in *Didache* 9–10, 14; Ignatius, *Epistle to the Ephesians* 5.2–3; *Epistle to the Smyrnaeans* 8.1; Justin Martyr, *1 Apology* 61–67; Tertullian, *Apology* 39; *Apostolic Tradition* 4, 22, 26–29, 36–38. See L. Michael White, *The Social Origins of Christian Architecture,* vol. 2, *Texts and Monuments for the Christian Domus Ecclesiae in its Environment* (Valley Forge, PA: Trinity Press International, 1997), 36–43, 54–59.

13. See Wayne A. Meeks, *The First Urban Christians: The Social World of the Apostle Paul,* 2nd ed. (New Haven: Yale University Press, 2003), 140–63.

14. For more on the complex social dynamics of women, children, and slaves within early Christian house churches, see Osiek and Balch, *Families in the New Testament World,* 27–35, 103–55, 174–92; Osiek and MacDonald with Tulloch, *A Woman's Place.*

15. For further reflection on the connection between house church settings and "household" theology of early Christian communities (particularly in Pauline circles), see Vincent P. Branick, *The House Church in the Writings of Paul* (Wilmington, DE: Michael Glazier, 1989).

16. Studies on the complexities of meeting in wealthy homes and the wide variety of alternative meeting spaces include David L. Balch, "Rich Pompeiian Houses, Shops for Rent, and the Huge Apartment Building in Herculaneum as Typical Spaces for Pauline Churches," *Journal for the Study of the New Testament* 27, no. 1 (2004): 27–46; Edward Adams, *The Earliest Christian Meeting Places: Almost Exclusively Houses?* (London: T&T Clark/ Bloomsbury, 2013).

17. See Robert Jewett, "Tenement Churches and Communal Meals in the Early Church: The Implications of a Form-Critical Analysis of 2 Thessalonians 3:10," *Biblical Research* 38 (1993): 23–43; Osiek and Balch, *Families in the New Testament World*, 17–24.

18. Additional references to tenement housing possibly being used for Christian gatherings include Acts 28:7–31 (Paul using his rental lodgings as teaching space) and *Martyrdom of Justin* 2 (Justin Martyr using his home above a Roman bath for meetings and the bath itself for baptisms); see Adams, *Earliest Christian Meeting Places*, 72–74.

19. See Peter Oakes, *Reading Romans in Pompeii: Paul's Letter at Ground Level* (Minneapolis, MI: Fortress Press, 2009), 94–95; Adams, *Earliest Christian Meeting Places*, 137–56. For a mid-third-century description of Christians meeting in "women's apartments, leather shops, or fullers' shops" to teach their message, see Origen, *Contra Celsum* 3.55. More on the spread of Christianity among the trade guilds and occupational networks of Roman cities can be found in Harland, *Dynamics of Identity*, 29–36.

20. See David L. Balch, "The Church Sitting in a Garden (1 Corinthians 14:30; Romans 16:23; Mark 6:39–40; 8:6; John 6:3, 10; Acts 1:15; 2:1–2)," in *Contested Spaces: Houses and Temples in Roman Antiquity and the New Testament*, ed. David L. Balch and Annette Weissenrieder (Tübingen: Mohr Siebeck, 2012), 201–35; Adams, *Earliest Christian Meeting Places*, 157–71; Thomas A. Wayment and Matthew J. Grey, "Jesus Followers in Pompeii: The *Christianos* Graffito and 'Hotel of the Christians' Reconsidered," *Journal of the Jesus Movement in Its Jewish Setting* 2 (2015): 102–46.

21. David G. Horrell argues that such housing above the butcher shops in Corinth is the social setting for the debate over believers eating sacrificial meat in 1 Corinthians 8–10; see Horrell, "Domestic Space and Christian Meetings at Corinth: Imagining New Contexts and the Buildings East of the Theater," *New Testament Studies* 50 (2004): 349–69.

22. See Peter Oakes, "Nine Types of Church in Nine Types of Space in the Insula of the Menander," in *Early Christianity in Pompeian Light: People, Texts, Situations*, ed. Bruce W. Longenecker (Minneapolis, MN: Fortress Press, 2016), 23–58; Adams, *Earliest Christian Meeting Places*, 181–92.

23. For liturgical handbooks of the third century that reflect these and other developments, see the *Apostolic Tradition* (from Rome?), the *Didascalia Apostolorum* (from Syria), and the early layers of the *Eucharistic Prayer of Addai and Mari* (also from Syria). For other brief accounts of Christian liturgical services from this period, see Origen, *Oration* 31.5–6; Cyprian, *Epistle* 39.4.1, 5.2; Gregory Thaumaturgus, *Epistle* 11; see also White, *Social Origins*, 67–70, 84.

24. For detailed overviews of the architectural features of known *domus ecclesiae*, as well as the liturgical developments that necessitated their renovations, see White, *Building God's House*, 111–26; Robert G. Ousterhout, *Eastern Medieval Architecture: The Building Traditions of Byzantium and Neighboring Lands* (New York: Oxford University Press, 2019), 3–19.

25. Possible examples of *domus ecclesiae* to survive from this period include a renovated prayer hall at Megiddo, the renovated "house of Peter" in Capernaum, some altered domestic structures at Il-Medjdel and Umm idj-Djimal in Syria, the Christianized Roman villa at Lullingstone in Britannia, and a series of so-called *tituli* churches in Rome that may have served as early sites of Christian worship but were later transformed into public churches. See Blue, "Acts and the House Church," 144–71; Adams, *Earliest Christian Meeting Places*, 96–107. For architectural variations on *domus ecclesiae* from this period (including hall-centered structures called *aula ecclesiae*), see White, *Building God's House*, 127–39.

26. See Michael Peppard, *The World's Oldest Church: Bible, Art, and Ritual at Dura-Europos, Syria* (New Haven: Yale University Press, 2016).

27. These scenes include Jesus healing the paralytic, Jesus walking on the water, women at a tomb or at a wedding banquet in a tent, the Samaritan woman or Mary at a well, the Good Shepherd with a flock, Adam and Eve in a paradise scene, David slaying Goliath, and a procession of women.

28. For more detail on the renovations and uses of these rooms, along with artistic reconstructions of the building, see Peppard, *World's Oldest Church*, 16–20.

29. For sources on the third-century Syrian baptismal rites of anointing and washing, see *Didascalia* 9, 16; *Gospel of Philip* 22, 41, 47, 59, 60, 67, 72, 80, 83, 84, 86, 90, 106–7; *Odes of Solomon* 11, 19, 42; see also E. C. Whitaker, *Documents of the Baptismal Liturgy*, rev. ed. Maxwell E. Johnson (Collegeville, MN: Liturgical Press, 2003), 23–62.

30. In light of the surviving biblical art and liturgical features in the building (such as a niche for anointing oil, a veiled baptismal font, and assembly spaces), Michael Peppard imagines the ways in which the initiation rituals, processional movement, and congregational liturgy might have occurred within the various rooms of the Dura Europos *domus ecclesia*; see Peppard, *World's Oldest Church*, 22–85.

31. See Osiek and Balch, *Families in the New Testament World*, 116–17; Paul Bradshaw, *Liturgical Presidency in the Early Church* (Bramcote, England: Grove Books, 1983), 9–28. For Christian literary sources from the third century that describe certain spatial features (such as platforms, segregated areas, and other ritual furnishings) designed to accompany the liturgical

developments in this period, see Cyprian, *Epistle* 38.2; 59.81.1; *Didascalia* 12.44–46.

32. Jenn Cianca considers the ways in which some Christians during the first and second centuries may have seen their domestic meeting places as sacred within the context of Roman household religion; see Cianca, *Sacred Ritual, Profane Space: The Roman House as Early Christian Meeting Place* (Montreal: McGill-Queen's University Press, 2018).

33. See Wardle, *Jerusalem Temple and Early Christian Identity*; Regev, *The Temple in Early Christianity*; G. K. Beale, *The Temple and the Church's Mission: A Biblical Theology of the Dwelling Place of God* (Downers Grove, IL: InterVarsity Press, 2004).

34. See Wardle, *Jerusalem Temple and Early Christian Identity*; Regev, *The Temple in Early Christianity*; G. K. Beale, *The Temple and the Church's Mission*.

35. For brief theoretical reflections on the shift in the fourth century from churches being seen as merely housing the congregation to housing the presence of God, see Lizette Larson-Miller, "Does God Live Here? Lessons from History on *domus ecclesiae* and *domus dei*," in *Architektur und Liturgie: Akten des Kolloquims vom 25. bis 27. Juli 2003 in Greifswald*, ed. Michael Altrip and Claudia Nauerth (Wiesbaden, Germany: Reichert Verlag, 2006), 15–23.

36. For detailed overviews of Constantinian and Byzantine churches—including their architectural precedents, main features, regional variations, and development from the fourth century onward—see Thomas F. Mathews, *The Early Churches of Constantinople: Architecture and Liturgy* (University Park: The Pennsylvania State University Press, 1971); Yoram Tsafrir, "The Development of Ecclesiastical Architecture in Palestine," in *Ancient Churches Revealed*, ed. Yoram Tsafrir (Jerusalem: Israel Exploration Society, 1993), 1–16; Ousterhout, *Eastern Medieval Architecture*, 10–19.

37. Unlike house churches, which were often inconspicuously located in residential areas of a city, monumental basilicas were frequently built in centralized and prominent locations such as forums, marketplaces, and close to the seats of government authority. In late Roman and Byzantine Palestine (especially Jerusalem), such churches were also built at locations associated with the life of Jesus or other saints as destinations for pilgrims to visit and connect with events of the biblical past. See John Wilkinson, "Constantinian Churches in Palestine," in *Ancient Churches Revealed*, ed. Yoram Tsafrir (Jerusalem: Israel Exploration Society, 1993), 23–27.

38. To demonstrate the triumph of Christianity over traditional Greco-Roman polytheism, imperial patrons of the fourth and fifth centuries would occasionally construct monumental churches over the sites of earlier pagan

temples (which they destroyed in the process) or convert pagan temples into churches by making architectural renovations and rededicating the space to an analogous Christian saint. See Garth Fowden, "Bishops and Temples in the Eastern Roman Empire A.D. 320–435," *Journal of Theological Studies* 29 (1978): 53–78.

39. Some of the earliest Christian basilicas—such as the Church of the Holy Sepulchre in Jerusalem—were oriented eastward (with their entryways facing east and their apses on the west end of the building) in imitation of the Jerusalem temple. However, the orientation of most monumental churches quickly changed to a westward orientation (with their entryways facing west and apses on the east end of the building) so that during Eucharistic services worshippers could face east (the direction of the rising sun and Jesus's anticipated Second Coming). See Wilkinson, "Constantinian Churches," 26–27.

40. On the developing use of hanging veils in churches of this period, see box 5.5 and Mathews, *Early Churches of Constantinople*, 162–71; Urs Peshlow, "Dividing Interior Space in Early Byzantine Churches: The Barriers between the Nave and Aisles," in *Thresholds of the Sacred: Architectural, Art Historical, Liturgical, and Theological Perspectives on Religious Screens, East and West*, ed. Sharon E. J. Gerstel, Dumbarton Oaks Byzantine Studies (Washington, DC: Dumbarton Oaks Research Library and Collection, 2006), 53–71; Elizabeth S. Bolman, "Veiling Sanctity in Christian Egypt: Visual and Spatial Solutions," in *Thresholds of the Sacred: Architectural, Art Historical, Liturgical, and Theological Perspectives on Religious Screens, East and West*, ed. Sharon E. J. Gerstel, Dumbarton Oaks Byzantine Studies (Washington, DC: Dumbarton Oaks Research Library and Collection, 2006), 73–104. Mosaic depictions of hanging curtains within sixth-century churches throughout Jordan can be seen in Michele Piccirillo, *The Mosaics of Jordan* (Amman: American Center of Oriental Research, 1997), 160–61, 165, 209, 234–35, 242–43, 246, 270, 276, 288–89, 292. For fourth- to sixth-century references to the use of various veils, curtains, and cloth coverings within Christian churches, see Eusebius, *Ecclesiastical History* 10.4.44; Egeria, *Itinerarium Egeriae* 25.8; John Chrysostom, *Homilies on First Corinthians* 36.5.1–5; *Homilies on Ephesians* 3.5.6–10; see also John Chrysostom, *On the Incomprehensible Nature of God* 4.4; Theodoret of Cyrrhus, *Ecclesiastical History* 5.21; Epiphanius, *Epistula* 51.9; Evagrius, *Ecclesiastical History* 6.21.

41. See, for example, Emma Loosely, *The Architecture and Liturgy of the Bema in Fourth- to Sixth-Century Syrian Churches* (Leiden: Brill, 2012).

42. For more on the development of domed roofs on churches—including

structures that fused basilica features with centrally planned domes, such as at the sixth-century Hagia Sophia in Constantinople—see Mathews, *Early Churches of Constantinople*, 43–111; Robert Ousterhout, "New Temples and New Solomons: The Rhetoric of Byzantine Architecture," in *The Old Testament in Byzantium*, ed. Paul Magdalino and Robert Nelson (Washington, DC: Dumbarton Oaks Research Library and Collection, 2010), 223–53 (esp. 239–51).

43. For aspects of church iconography, architecture, and liturgy that were designed to foreshadow Jesus's return and eschatological kingdom, see John Herrmann and Annewies van den Hoek, "Apocalyptic Themes in the Monumental and Minor Art of Early Christianity," in *Pottery, Pavements, and Paradise: Iconographic and Textual Studies on Late Antiquity*, ed. Annewies van den Hoek and John Herrmann Jr. (Leiden: Brill, 2013), 327–82.

44. For discussions on church architecture being symbolic of the cosmos (combining heaven and earth), the significance of architectural domes as representing the celestial canopy in which God dwells (which transforms the church liturgy into a heavenly drama), and the role of *Christ Pantocrator* (who is often depicted in the dome) as the mediator of heavenly and earthly realms, see Robert Ousterhout, "The Holy Space: Architecture and the Liturgy," in *Heaven on Earth: Art and the Church in Byzantium*, ed. Linda Safran (University Park, PA: The Pennsylvania State University Press, 1998), 88–91, 97–99; Ousterhout, "New Temples," 239–51. Examples of contemporary sources that describe this symbolism can be found in a Syriac hymn for the Church at Edessa (circa AD 550) and Maximus the Confessor, *Mystagogia* 1–24 (circa AD 650).

45. For detailed descriptions of the liturgical activities that occurred within churches of the fourth century onward, see Mathews, *Early Churches of Constantinople*, 111–15, 138–76; Ousterhout, "Holy Space," 81–120; Ousterhout, *Eastern Medieval Architecture*, 37–79.

46. It is not always clear from the literary and archaeological evidence how, exactly, the congregation occupied the various parts of the church interior. It is possible, for example, that some congregations gathered together in the nave, aisles, or both and that others may have been segregated by gender (either through use of the aisles or an upper balcony); see Mathews, *Early Churches of Constantinople*, 117–34.

47. For lectures from the mid-fourth century designed to prepare those who would soon be baptized (catechumens) on subsequently receiving the mysteries (the "Second Entrance") they would experience in the Eucharistic services, see Cyril of Jerusalem, *Procatechesis* 1–17 and *Mystagogical Catechesis* 1–5.

48. For sources on the veiling of the sanctuary during the consecration of the Eucharist, see note 40.

49. See Cyril of Jerusalem, *Mystagogical Catechesis* 5.6; *Apostolic Constitutions* 7.35.1–10; 8.12.6–27; Judith H. Newman, "Holy, Holy, Holy: The Use of Isaiah 6.3 in *Apostolic Constitutions* 7.35.1–10 and 8.12.6–27," in *Of Scribes and Sages: Early Jewish Interpretation and Transmission of Scripture*, vol. 2, *Later Versions and Traditions*, ed. Craig A. Evans (London: T&T Clark, 2004), 123–34.

50. For more on the veiled chancel screen being viewed as representing the gate of heaven (connecting earthly and heavenly realms), see Bolman, "Veiling Sanctity," 73–104; Irina Shalina, "The Entrance to the Holy of Holies and the Byzantine Sanctuary Barrier," in *The Iconostasis: Origins–Evolution–Symbolism*, ed. Alexei Lidov (Moscow: Progress-Tradition, 2000), 52–84 (in Russian, with English summary on pp. 719–20).

51. John Wilkinson, "Christian Worship in the Byzantine Period," in *Ancient Churches Revealed*, ed. Yoram Tsafrir (Jerusalem: Israel Exploration Society, 1993), 21–22. For descriptions of these actions at the veiled chancel screen, see John Chrysostom, *Homilies on First Corinthians* 36.5.1–5; *Homilies on Ephesians* 3.5.6–10; see also John Chrysostom, *On the Incomprehensible Nature of God* 4.4. In an additional description of these ritual activities, Cyril of Jerusalem instructs celebrants to receive the Eucharistic elements from the bishop with their right hand while holding out their hallowed left hand underneath it in the shape of a throne (so as to symbolically receive the royal body of Christ through the Eucharist); see Cyril of Jerusalem, *Mystagogical Catechesis* 5.21.

52. See Kilde, *Sacred Power, Sacred Space*, 49–52.

53. For more detailed explorations of this theme, see John Wilkinson, *From Synagogue to Church: The Traditional Design* (London: Routledge, 2002), 23–36, 114–61, 189–212; Ousterhout, "New Temples," 223–53; Jonathan Bardill, "A New Temple for Byzantium: Anicia Juliana, King Solomon, and the Gilded Ceiling of the Church of St. Polyeuktos in Constantinople," *Late Antique Archaeology* 3, no. 1 (2006): 339–70; Martin Harrison, "From Jerusalem and Back Again: The Fate of the Treasures of Solomon," in *'Churches Built in Ancient Times': Recent Studies in Early Christian Archaeology*, ed. Kenneth Painter (London: Society of Antiquaries of London and the Accordia Research Center, 1994), 239–48.

54. Ancient Jewish sources describing the layout and significance of Herod's temple in Jerusalem include Josephus, *War* 5.184–247; *Antiquities* 15.380–425; Mishnah *Middot* 1–5. For comparisons of these and other ancient accounts, see Lee I. Levine, "Josephus's Description of the Jerusalem

Temple: *War, Antiquities*, and Other Sources," in *Josephus and the History of the Greco-Roman Period: Essays in Honor of Morton Smith*, ed. F. Parente and J. Sievers (Leiden: Brill, 1994), 233–46.

55. First-century Jewish commentary on the cosmic significance of key features of the Jerusalem temple (including the temple courts, menorah, table of showbread, and veil, as well as the priestly garments) can be found in Josephus, *War* 5.212–18, 231–36; *Antiquities* 3.180–87; see also Philo, *De Vita Mosis* 2.101–05, 109–35; *De Specialibus Legibus* 1.66–67, 84–96; *Quaestiones in Exodum* 2.73–81. For further consideration of these and related passages, see C. T. R. Hayward, *The Jewish Temple: A Non-Biblical Sourcebook* (London: Routledge, 1996).

56. For descriptions of the temple's sacrificial rituals and priestly personnel, see Menahem Haran, *Temples and Temple-Service in Ancient Israel: An Inquiry into Biblical Cult Phenomena and the Historical Setting of the Priestly School* (Winona Lake, IN: Eisenbrauns, 1985), 205–45, 289–348.

57. See Wilkinson, *From Synagogue to Church*, 114–28; Ousterhout, "New Temples," 233–39.

58. See John Wilkinson, "Paulinus' Temple at Tyre," *Jahrbuch der Österreichischen Byzantinistik* 32, no. 4 (1982): 553–61; Ousterhout, "New Temples," 226–27. For further discussion on the role of the chancel screen in demarcating sacred space within the church in a way that is analogous to the veil of the Jerusalem temple, see Bolman, "Veiling Sanctity," 73–104; Ousterhout, "New Temples," 231; Shalina, "Entrance to the Holy of Holies," 52–84, 719–20.

59. See note 44.

60. See Ousterhout, "New Temples," 230. For sixth-century mosaic depictions and inscriptions from churches in Jordan that associate the Eucharistic service with the daily sacrifice of the Jerusalem temple, see Piccirillo, *Mosaics of Jordan*, 151, 160–61, 165.

61. For example, Eusebius claimed that Bishop Paulinus—the builder of the church at Tyre—was a "new Solomon and Zerubbabel" (Eusebius, *Ecclesiastical History* 10.4) and, in competitive rhetoric, the political rivals Anikia Juliana and Justinian in sixth-century Constantinople both compared the respective churches they built to the efforts of Solomon. See Bardill, "New Temple for Byzantium," 339–70; Ousterhout, "New Temples," 239–51.

62. See also note 33.

63. See Wilkinson, *From Synagogue to Church*, 51–69, 114–28, 161.

64. For fourth-century literary references to this symbolism—including the apse being seen as the heavenly throne room, the altar being seen as the heavenly throne, the veil being drawn aside during the Eucharist to reveal

the type of angelic liturgy occurring in God's presence, and the Eucharistic services allowing the congregation to join in that liturgy—see John Chrysostom, *Homilies on First Corinthians* 36.5.1–5; *Homilies on Ephesians* 3.5.6–10; see also, John Chrysostom, *On the Incomprehensible Nature of God* 4.4. Wilkinson notes that this imagery was sometimes supported by the presence of deacons who stood on both sides of the Eucharistic altar holding fans decorated as cherubim to represent the angels surrounding God's throne in the visions of Isaiah, Ezekiel, and John the Revelator; see Wilkinson, "Christian Worship," 21.

65. For the legacy of Byzantine church architecture and liturgy in subsequent centuries—and how many of these developments came to influence the varieties of Christian worship into the modern day—see Kilde, *Sacred Space*, 61–129, Ousterhout, *Eastern Medieval Architecture*, 245–713.

* 6 *

CONNECTING WITH CHRIST

Rituals and Worship

Mark D. Ellison

All the believers devoted themselves to the apostles'
teaching, and to fellowship, and to sharing in meals
(including the Lord's Supper), and to prayer. . . . They
worshiped together . . . and shared their meals with
great joy and generosity.

—Acts 2:42, 46
New Living Translation

A small group of people, about fifteen to twenty in number, gathers in a house somewhere in the first-century Mediterranean world.[1] They crowd together in a dining room, or maybe they sit among columns encircling an open-air atrium. If it is early morning or night, torches and small oil lamps provide faint, flickering light. We see women and men, old and young: the host who owns the house, the household slaves, children, a crying baby or two, a few of the host's relatives and longtime friends, and some new acquaintances. They have gathered to worship. They pray. They chant psalms and hymns. They listen to the stories and teachings of a visiting apostle. A reverent fire moves members of the group to prophesy, speak words of edification, give messages of comfort. They share a meal together, taking special care to pray over a round loaf of flat bread and a cup of wine, which everyone shares. There is a joyful, familial feeling to the group. They are "Christians" (Acts 11:26; see also Acts 26:28; 1 Peter 4:16), "Nazarenes" (Acts 24:5), "the Way" (Acts 9:2 NLT; see also Acts 19:9, 23; 22:4; 24:14, 22)—followers of Jesus of Nazareth—and in gatherings like this across the ancient world, they enacted the earliest forms of the rituals of Christian worship.[2]

Jesus's first followers were a movement within Judaism, but by the end of the first century, their numbers included many Gentile converts throughout the Mediterranean world, and they were gradually growing distinct from their Jewish roots. They no longer prayed and offered sacrifices at the Jerusalem temple, which a Roman army had destroyed in AD 70. Their predecessors had worshiped in synagogues as well as in houses. Now they increasingly met in believers'

BOX 6.1 ## Why It Matters

We often think of religion in terms of belief. When we learn about other religious traditions, we tend to ask, "What do they believe?" But beliefs are only part of religion. Practices matter too. Jesus emphasized heartfelt, righteous actions more than doctrine (though of course both are important). The Latin saying *lex orandi lex credendi* (the law of what is to be prayed [is] the law of what is to be believed) means that it is worship—including the symbolism, imagery, and forms of worship rituals—that expresses Christian beliefs. Our actions, including our acts of worship, reveal the essence of our faith. Learning how ancient Christians worshiped helps us more fully appreciate their faith and gives us an opportunity to examine and deepen our own worship experiences. We might ask ourselves:

- How well do my own worship practices express my faith in Christ?
- How can the worship practices of our spiritual ancestors of the ancient church enrich my own worship experiences?

homes, rented halls, and other spaces. Later, in the third century, some Christian communities remodeled houses to serve as church buildings, and from the fourth century forward they worshiped in specially-constructed basilicas, baptisteries, prayer chapels, and other structures that could be large and awe-inspiring or smaller and intimate (see chapter 5). In all these spaces, the rituals of Christian worship developed in form and meaning, and Christian theologians, clergy, and laypersons thought deeply about the importance and effects of their worship activities.

As we Latter-day Saints learn about these developments, we should keep in mind that mere changes in forms of worship or rituals are not necessarily signs of error or apostasy—our own worship

Sources Historians Use to Study Ancient Christian Worship

- The New Testament
- Treatises, sermons, and letters written by Christians after the New Testament
- Church orders (texts with doctrinal teachings and procedural instructions on how to conduct worship services, baptize, ordain, and so forth; "church handbooks" that were expanded and updated over the years). Examples: the *Didache* (late first/early second century), the *Didascalia Apostolorum* (*Teachings of the Apostles,* third century), the *Apostolic Tradition* (third century), the *Apostolic Constitutions* (late fourth century)
- Catechetical and mystagogical lectures (teachings bishops gave people in the weeks before and after their baptism discussing the meanings and details of worship practices, especially baptism and the Eucharist)
- Pilgrimage diaries that describe rituals and worship in places pilgrims visited. Example: the diary of Egeria, a Spanish nun who traveled to the Holy Land (late fourth century)
- Liturgies (written outlines for congregational worship) and commentaries on liturgy
- Archaeology, the architecture of worship spaces, visual art decorating those spaces, and artistic depictions of early Christian rituals

procedures have evolved over our short history. Some changes in ancient Christianity that we may not agree with, in light of the revelations of the Restoration, might have been motivated by people trying their best in their circumstances, with the amount of understanding they had at the time, rather than by that outright, deliberate sense of rebellion denoted in the term *apostasia* (we should be judicious and cautious in using that term).[3] For historians, it is often difficult to trace the precise origins of worship practices and their subsequent changes,[4] but what is more evident and worthy of our attention is what our spiritual ancestors of ancient Christianity were seeking to do through these forms of worship. Through prayer (private and communal), hymn singing, baptism, the Eucharist (the sacrament), and other worship practices, ancient Christians sought to connect with Jesus Christ and their fellow believers and to emulate Christ in their transformed lives.

Prayer

We do not know her name, but her painted portrait is one of the most beautiful, well-known, and intriguing works of early Christian art. She died sometime in the third century and was laid to rest in a tomb within a small family burial chamber in Rome's Priscilla catacomb (an underground cemetery). Her relatives, wanting to remember her as a woman of piety, commissioned a painting of her—standing, veiled, and clothed in a long, purple tunic, with her arms raised and her hands open as her eyes look upward toward heaven (see fig. 6.1). This painting depicts the common posture of prayer (standing and "lifting up holy hands" [1 Timothy 2:8; see also 1 Kings 8:22; Mark 11:25]), and this *orant* pose was one of the most popular forms of portraiture in early Christian art.[5] Prayer—approaching God with empty, outstretched hands in reflection of a yearning heart and mind—expressed the believer's faith and devotion.

In the environment in which Christianity emerged, prayer was an element in ancient religions generally. Observant Jews recited the *shema* (see Deuteronomy 6:4–9) morning and evening and prayed three times a day (see Daniel 6:10).[6] Prayer was a central practice in Jesus's religious observance, and his teachings guided the practice of prayer among his followers. What distinguished the prayers of early Christians from those of their neighbors was the way they sought connection with God through Jesus Christ as mediator.

The Lord's Prayer (see Matthew 6:9–13; Luke 11:2–4) served as both a pattern and a formula for early Christians.[7] By the late first

century, some Christians were urging its recitation in thrice-daily prayers.[8] It became a key part of the teachings that missionaries and bishops gave people before and after their baptism.[9] Early Christians recognized that each line of the prayer evokes moments from Jesus's own life, teachings, and ministry. Tertullian (active circa AD 200), for instance, wrote that the Lord's Prayer embraces "almost every discourse of the Lord, every record of his discipline; so that, in fact, in the prayer is comprised an epitome of the whole gospel."[10] Therefore, when ancient Christians recited this prayer thoughtfully, it led them to reflect on Jesus and to be drawn into emulating him.

Early Christians recognized that even in private prayer, saying, "*Our* Father," with the plural pronoun, urged the believer from the very start of prayer to approach God mindful of others—to see oneself in prayer as one of countless other individuals, each needing heaven's help, and to see oneself as one member of God's larger family.[11] Plural pronouns later in the prayer—"Give *us* this day *our* daily bread," "forgive *us* our debts, as *we* forgive *our* debtors," "lead *us* not into temptation, but deliver *us* from evil"—likewise helped believers think of community and consider their own needs alongside the needs of others. From start to finish, the prayer brought individuals into proper orientation with both God and neighbor—yet another way it drew believers into following Jesus, who taught that love of God and neighbor forms the heart of true religious life (see Matthew 22:34–40; Luke 10:25–28; italics added).

Ancient Christians practiced both private and communal prayer. Privately in their homes, they prayed multiple times a day. While the *Didache* (late first/early second century) encouraged thrice-daily prayers, Tertullian (active circa AD 200) encouraged prayer at more frequent intervals.[12] Inspired by scriptures that referred to regular hours for prayer (see Daniel 6:10; Acts 2:1, 15; 3:1; 10:9) and

BOX 6.3	Connecting with Christ through the Lord's Prayer
Lines of the Lord's Prayer	**Jesus's life and teachings and early Christian reflections**
"Our Father which art in heaven" (Matthew 6:9)	Jesus addressed God in prayer as "Father" (see, for example, Mark 14:36; Matthew 11:25–26; John 12:27; 17:1–26). By adopting this practice, Jesus's followers were invited into his own experience of close, intimate relationship with God as a personal, caring parent.[13] They could call God "Father" because of their connection to Christ (see Romans 8:14–17; Galatians 4:6). Early Christians saw that their lives should be guided by that identity: "Remember," wrote the bishop Cyprian (circa AD 252), "that when we call God Father, we ought to act as God's children."[14]
"Hallowed be thy name" (Matthew 6:9)	Jesus's life and ministry made God's "name" (identity, character) known to people (see John 1:18; 5:43; 12:28; 17:6). Early Christians understood this petition as an expression of love, adoration, and respect for God, as well as a plea that this love might spread throughout the world: "When we say, 'Hallowed be thy name,'" wrote Tertullian (circa AD 198), "we pray this; that it may be hallowed *in us* who are in Him, as well as in all others for whom the grace of God is still waiting."[15]
"Thy kingdom come" (Matthew 6:10)	The essence of Jesus's teaching was proclamation of "the kingdom of God" or "the reign of God" (Mark 1:14–15; see also Isaiah 52:7). Praying "may thy kingdom come" represented signing onto Jesus's message, in effect asking God to reign in one's own heart and actions and in the lives of all people: "God is invited to make the soul His home," wrote Augustine (circa AD 393–95); to pray "thy kingdom come" is to pray that God's reign may "be made manifest to men."[16] For Gregory of Nyssa (circa AD 335–395), when God's kingdom (reign) comes into a person's life, one is "no more tyrannized by evil" or "captive through sin," but "the pangs and sighs of sorrow vanish, and life, peace, and rejoicing enter instead."[17]

Lines of the Lord's Prayer	Jesus's life and teachings and early Christian reflections
"Thy will be done on earth as it is in heaven" (Matthew 6:10)	In Gethsemane Jesus prayed, "Not my will, but thine, be done" (Luke 22:42; see also Mark 14:36; Matthew 26:39, 42). Praying "thy will be done" was a way for ancient Christians to remember how Jesus submitted his will to his Father's and to seek their own submission to God's will. Cyril of Jerusalem (circa AD 313–86) wrote: "In effect you mean this by the prayer, ... 'be it done on earth in me, O Lord.'"[18]
"Give us this day our daily bread" (Matthew 6:11)	Jesus was "the bread of life" (John 6:35, 48), fed multitudes in the wilderness (see Mark 6:34–44; 8:1–9), and reassured his followers that they could trust in God's daily providence and not fret about how they would obtain food, drink, clothing, or strength for the future (see Matthew 6:25–34). The earliest commentary on the Lord's Prayer, written by Tertullian circa AD 198, teaches Christians that praying "give us this day our daily bread" should prompt them to remember these truths.[19]
"And forgive us our debts, as we forgive our debtors" (Matthew 6:12)	Jesus used "debt" as a metaphor for sin (see Matthew 6:14–15; Luke 11:4), told the parable of the unforgiving servant (see Matthew 18:21–35), and taught that receiving God's mercy requires us to be merciful to others (see Matthew 5:7; 7:1–2; Luke 6:36–38). Early Christians connected these teachings to this line of the Lord's Prayer.[20] Gregory of Nyssa saw the practice of forgiveness as one way humans become more like God: "The forgiving of debts is the special prerogative of God, since it is said, *No man can forgive sins, but God alone* [Mark 2:7]. If therefore a man imitates in his own life the characteristics of the Divine Nature, he becomes somehow that which he visibly imitates."[21]
"And lead us not into temptation, but deliver us from evil" (Matthew 6:13)	Jesus withstood temptations (see Matthew 4:1–11; Luke 22:28; Hebrews 4:15–16) and told his disciples in Gethsemane to be watchful and pray to avoid entering into temptation (see Matthew 26:41). The earliest commentary on the Lord's Prayer connects these details to this line of the Lord's Prayer, pointing to the disciples' sleeping

Lines of the Lord's Prayer	Jesus's life and teachings and early Christian reflections
(CONTINUED...)	(CONTINUED...) in Gethsemane as a cautionary story for followers of Christ, who should stay spiritually awake. It also connects this petition to the previous one—together they ask for forgiveness of past sins and help in avoiding future sins. It clarifies the phrasing of the petition: "*Lead us not into temptation*: that is, suffer us not to be led into it, by him (of course) who tempts; but far be the thought that the Lord should seem to tempt."[22]

people who devoted their lives to prayer (see Luke 2:37; Acts 6:4; 1 Timothy 5:5), Christians in monastic settings developed the Liturgy of the Hours, or Divine Office, a sequence of public services held at regular times of day for communal praying, hymn singing, and scripture reading. The *Rule* that Benedict of Nursia wrote in AD 516 to organize the practices of monastic communities prescribed eight hours for prayer: Lauds (daybreak), Prime (about 6:00 a.m.), Terce (about 9:00 a.m.), Sext (noon), None (about 3:00 p.m.), Vespers (sunset), Compline (completion of the work day), and Midnight.[23] These services were obligatory for clergy and monastic men and women but optional for lay believers.[24] Observing this routine of prayer and worship throughout each day, year after year, was one way the church collectively sought to live the ideal "pray without ceasing" (1 Thessalonians 5:17). At the same time, Christian writers encouraged individual believers to "pray without ceasing" by practicing silent prayer along with their formal prayers as they went through each day.[25] "Thus will you pray without ceasing," wrote Basil of Caesarea (AD 330–379), "if you pray not only in words, but unite yourself to God through all the course of life and so your life is made one ceaseless and uninterrupted prayer."[26]

A Prayer of the Christian Community: Rome, AD 96

"We ask you, Master, to be our helper and protector. Save those among us who are in distress; have mercy on the humble; raise up the fallen; show yourself to those in need; heal the sick; turn back those of your people who wander; feed the hungry; ransom our prisoners; raise up the weak; comfort the discouraged. . . . Forgive us our sins and our injustices, our transgressions and our shortcomings. . . . You, who alone are able to do these and even greater good things for us, we praise through the high priest and benefactor of our souls, Jesus Christ, through whom be the glory and the majesty to you both now and for all generations."[27]

Lamp Lighting in Private and Communal Prayers

One practice associated with prayer in households was a ritual of lighting lamps at the close of day. In our modern world, where houses, streets, vehicles, and cities are lit by millions of electric lights, it is difficult to appreciate the impact that night brought to the ancient world. Darkness was profound, halted normal activity, and brought a host of anxieties. "The eye in darkness hungers for light," wrote the fourth-century Christian teacher and hymnwriter Ephrem the Syrian; therefore, "after the sun sets, then there is the lamp."[28] Small, hand-size oil lamps made of clay were inexpensive and ubiquitous; even their dim, flickering light enabled some limited vision and movement after sunset, so they were among the most important household goods (see Matthew 5:15; Luke 15:8). Lighting lamps in the home at evening was a ritual across religious traditions: "Christian homes would have sparkled with the ritual lamps of evening alongside their pagan and Jewish neighbors," writes one historian.[29] Some sources indicate that lamp lighting was the special duty of women.[30] It was a

▲ **FIGURE 6.2** Oil lamp decorated with the christogram (☧), fourth or fifth century, Cyprus. Photo: Metropolitan Museum of Art, New York, metmuseum.org, (public domain)

moment that invited prayer: "At the sunsetting and at the decline of day, of necessity we must pray again," wrote Cyprian (circa AD 200–258). "When we pray and ask that light may return to us again, we pray for the coming of Christ, who will give us the grace of everlasting light."[31] From the third century forward, ceramics workshops began producing lamps decorated with distinctively Christian symbols and imagery. From the fourth century onward, these symbols could include the superimposed Greek letters *chi* (X) and *rho* (P), which are the first two letters in *christos* (ΧΡΙΣΤΟΣ, χριστός, "Christ"; see fig. 6.2). The popularity of such lamps suggests that ancient Christians remembered Jesus Christ as "the light of the world," who promised: "Whoever follows me will never walk in darkness but will have the light of life" (John 8:12 New Revised Standard Version).[32]

▲ **FIGURE 6.3** Modern-day worshipers at the Church of the Holy Sepulcher, Jerusalem. Photo: Custodia Terrae Sanctae © Marie-Armelle Beaulieu/CTS

Lamp lighting and its symbolism were also important elements in some communal prayers.[33] In Jerusalem, believers gathered nightly for evening prayer services at the Church of the Holy Sepulcher, built in the fourth century over the place believed to be the site of Jesus Christ's Resurrection. Egeria, a woman from a monastic community in Spain, visited the Holy Land in the late fourth century and wrote in her pilgrimage diary that "a lamp is always burning day and night" in the tomb, and at evening prayers, "all the people congregate." A flame is brought from the lamp in the tomb, and using it, "the lamps and candles are all lit, which makes it very bright" in the church.[34] A monk named Bernard writing a few centuries later described a similar service held during the Easter vigil: a flame brought out from the tomb kindled the lamps and candles of all the assembled worshipers, "and thus each one has light where he is standing."[35] (This tradition continues to this day in the Ceremony of the Holy Fire; see fig. 6.3.) The flame, passed from the place of Christ's Resurrection to person after person throughout the congregation, gradually illuminating the whole church, created a beautifully symbolic moment. With imagery of the flame of fire that rested upon each of the disciples on the day of Pentecost (see Acts 2:3), the ritual mirrored the spreading of faith and testimony throughout the world, one transformed life at a time, and vividly illustrated the power of the combined prayers of all who believe in Christ.

Hymn Singing

The sacred music, psalms, and hymns that had long been elements in Israel's worship were naturally part of Jesus's own life. You could even say that Jesus's life began and ended with hymns, as did the Gospels.[36] Luke recorded Mary's words of praise in a poetic form that became a Christian canticle, "My spirit rejoices in God my Savior" (Luke 1:47 NRSV), and angels sang "Glory to God in the highest" at Jesus's birth (Luke 2:14).[37] At the Last Supper, Jesus and his disciples sang a hymn (see Mark 14:26; perhaps they sang the Hallel passages of Psalms 113–118), and as Jesus suffered on the cross, he cried out the heartbreaking words of Psalm 22, "My God, my God, why hast thou forsaken me?" (Mark 15:34).

Jesus's followers worshiped with hymns from the start (see 1 Corinthians 14:26; Ephesians 5:19; Colossians 3:16), and several early Christian hymns seem to be quoted in books of the New Testament. Some of these hymns (see John 1:1–18; Philippians 2:5–11; Colossians 1:15–20; 2 Timothy 2:11–13; 1 Peter 2:21–25) share recurring themes, giving us insight into what early Christians held to be most important: the hymns praise Jesus Christ, quote scripture, refer to Jesus's premortal divinity, celebrate Jesus's role in showing

Augustine (AD 354–430): "Do you know what a hymn is? It is a song in praise of God. If you praise God and do not sing, you do not utter a hymn; if you sing and do not praise God, you do not utter a hymn."[38]

the world what God is like, describe how Jesus humbled himself and suffered a salvific death on the cross, and testify that Jesus brings life, reconciliation, healing, and freedom from sins.[39]

Around the year AD 112, the Roman governor Pliny the Younger mentioned in a letter that when Christians meet to worship they "sing responsively a hymn to Christ as God" (*Letters* 10.96–97). This seems to describe antiphonal singing, with lines sung alternately by a soloist or small group and the entire congregation. Pliny's reference to "a hymn to Christ as God" calls to mind New Testament hymns that emphasize Christ's divinity:

- "In the beginning was the Word, and the Word was with God, and the Word was God" (John 1:1; the New English Bible's translation of the final clause conveys the sense of the Greek: "and what God was, the Word was").
- "In him all the fullness of God was pleased to dwell" (Colossians 1:19 NRSV).
- "Christ Jesus . . . was in the form of God" (Philippians 2:5–6).[40]

(For more on understandings of Jesus's divinity, see chapter 8). Some hymns were written by church leaders, but many may have been written by ordinary believers unknown to us, giving us a glimpse at the faith of laypersons who made their own contributions to church life.

One of the earliest Christian hymns outside the New Testament is *Phos hilaron*, Greek for "Joyous Light" (*Lumen hilare* in the Latin

BOX 6.6 An Ancient Evening Hymn: *Phos hilaron* (Joyous Light)

"Joyous light of the holy glory
of the immortal Father, heavenly,
holy, Jesus Christ;
Having come to the sun's setting
(and) beholding the evening light,
we praise God, Father, Son
and Holy Spirit.
It is fitting at all times that you
should be praised with auspicious
voices, Son of God, Giver of
Life: Wherefore the world
glorifies You."[41]

West), which believers sung at the evening lighting of lamps in homes or in church settings. When it first appears in a fourth-century text, it is already regarded as very ancient; it may date originally to the second or third century. Still sung today in the evening services of Eastern Orthodox churches and other liturgical traditions, it demonstrates (like the hours of prayer) how ancient Christians sought to organize their daily lives around remembrance of Jesus Christ.

A scrap of papyrus discovered at Oxyrhynchus, Egypt in 1918 contains the earliest text of a Christian hymn with musical notation (an ancient system quite different from modern staff music; see fig. 6.4). Dating to the late third century, the lyrics of this hymn call for the reverent silence of all beings, stars, winds, and rivers during the singing to the Father, Son, and Holy Spirit, in a hymn praising God as the "giver of all good things."[42] Musicologists have reconstructed the melody, and recordings of this "Oxyrhynchus hymn" can be

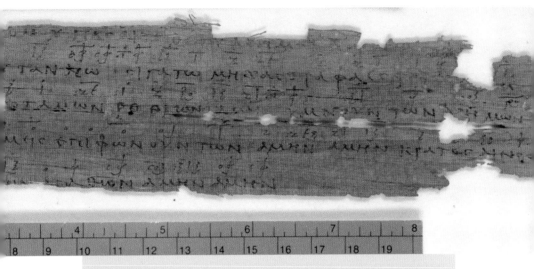

▲ **FIGURE 6.4** Cropped photo of the Oxyrhynchus Papyrus 1786, late third century. Photo: Courtesy of Wikimedia Commons (PD-US-unpublished)

found online, giving us modern Christians another way to imagine the world of our ancient predecessors by hearing what their singing might have sounded like.[43]

One of the greatest hymnwriters and poets of the early Christian centuries was Ephrem the Syrian (circa AD 306–373). Over four hundred of his hymns survive, many of them works that he wrote for women's choirs after seeing that women were not experiencing opportunities equal to men to participate in worship. Ephrem shared the same theological interests as his contemporaries, but his writing expressed his faith mostly through poetic works rather than in the form of treatises or creeds favored by many. His hymns, rich with symbolic imagery and scriptural connections, invited singers and worshipers into the experience of awe, joy, and wondrous consideration of a world filled with signs of God's work—quite different from the experience of reading philosophical definitions of God. Through hymns, Ephrem was "able to transcend frozen formulas."[44] In this contrast between hard-nosed rationality and a more mystical

BOX 6.7　An Ancient Morning Hymn: *Aeterne rerum conditor* (Eternal Founder of the World)

"The herald of the day now sounds out . . .
Roused by his call, the sun dissolves the sky from darkness . . .
It was at cockcrow that the very rock of the church washed white
　his sin . . .
When the cock crows hope returns, health is restored to the sick . . .
and faith returns to the fallen.
Look on us, Jesus, in our wavering, and seeing us correct us;
for if you look on us our sins leave us and our guilt is washed away
　in tears.
Be you a light, shine into our minds, and dispel sleep from our souls.
May the first act of our voices be to sing of you,
and so may we keep our promises to you."[45]

contemplation, we see in Ephrem one example of how human beings throughout history have been moved to express their experience of the divine in artistic forms—music, singing, poetry, visual art, architecture—as well as in prose (see a hymn by Ephrem in chapter 12).[46]

In the West, Ambrose, bishop of Milan in the fourth century, helped spur the development of hymn singing in Latin Christianity. One of Ambrose's hymns, *Aeterne rerum conditor* ("Eternal Founder of the World"), was written to be sung at dawn prayer services. Using the image of the rooster crowing to signal the dawn of a new day, Ambrose drew a connection to the Gospel accounts of Peter's denials of Jesus, the rooster's crow after the third denial, Peter's tears of remorse, and the Lord's forgiveness and renewal of Peter's call (see John 18:15–27; 21:15–19). Like the first-century Christians who knew that the chief apostle loved Jesus but was not perfect, and preserved the story of Peter's denials in all four Gospels, Ambrose and the fourth-century believers with him drew inspiration from the story of Peter, who as a model disciple gave them hope that they could repent of their own failures and be renewed each day in their efforts to follow Christ. Singing this hymn at the start of a new day (perhaps when roosters could be heard crowing in their city), early Christians gave voice to the hope that faith in Jesus Christ brought them.[47]

Baptism

Jewish practice at the time of Jesus did not include rituals exactly like Christian baptism, though many Jews did observe the practice of ritual bathing—individuals would immerse themselves in water for the purpose of becoming ritually clean (not hygienically or morally clean but purified after contact with things regarded as "unclean" in the Law of Moses). The baptisms performed by John the Baptist differed from Jewish ritual bathing in being baptisms "of repentance for the remission of sins" (Mark 1:4) performed by the physical guidance of another person. In the New Testament church, baptism was a submersion in water performed with little ceremony by an authorized person immediately upon a new convert's acceptance of the gospel.[48] The act held rich doctrinal importance for New Testament authors: baptism signified repentance, profession of faith in Jesus Christ, forgiveness and purification from sin, spiritual rebirth, dying to sin and rising to new life in Christ, preparation to receive the gift of the Holy Spirit, reception of salvation, and formally joining the church.[49] As the rite of initiation and entrance into the church, it was the most foundational and important early Christian ritual.

By the third century, the process and ritual of baptism had developed (and continued to develop in the fourth century) in ways that built upon the New Testament's doctrinal foundation and sought to enhance the convert's experience. Some Christian communities began building baptisteries where the sacred rite could be held in private. The earliest baptistery yet discovered was built around AD 240 at Dura Europos, a Roman outpost on the banks of the Euphrates River in Syria (see chapter 5).[50] Even with a large body of water nearby where baptisms could have been performed, the Christian community at Dura felt the baptismal rite called for privacy.

For Christians from the third century forward, there usually needed to be a time of formal teaching before baptism, months or years in duration. The night before Easter had become the favored occasion for baptism, a sacred time that heightened the symbolism of burial and rising with Christ (see Romans 6:3–4; Ephesians 2:5–6; Colossians 2:12–13). Generally, the ritual went as follows: After a prayer inviting the Holy Spirit to rest upon the baptismal waters, the candidate disrobed; vocally renounced Satan; received an anointing with oil; entered the font; and while standing or kneeling in the water, confessed faith in God the Father, Jesus Christ, and the Holy Spirit (see Matthew 28:19) and was immersed after each confession by bending forward into the water, guided by the person administering baptism (usually the bishop). Following this, the newly baptized received the laying on of hands with another anointing of oil, was clothed in a white robe, and then joined the waiting congregation to receive the Eucharist for the first time just as the sun was rising on Easter morning—a moment signifying the new life in Christ.[51]

There were regional variations in the rite. In Syria, Christians emphasized the prebaptismal anointing. Female deacons assisted in the anointing and baptism of women.[52] In some places the neophytes carried lit oil lamps or candles as they processed to join the congregation (see Luke 11:36; Hebrews 10:32), and as part of that service they might drink milk and honey, symbolizing entry into the promised land (see Exodus 3:8). The newly baptized often attended postbaptismal lectures by their bishop. The late fourth-century pilgrim Egeria describes the joyful, noisy response of neophytes in Jerusalem as their bishop explained to them, step by step, the spiritual meanings of the ritual they had just experienced: "The bishop relates what has been done, and interprets it. As he does so, the applause is so loud that it can be heard outside the church. Indeed, the way he expounds the mysteries and interprets them cannot fail to move his hearers."[53] The white robe worn by the newly baptized alluded to Paul's teaching, "All of you who were baptized into Christ

▲ **FIGURE 6.5** Reconstruction of the Dura-Europos baptistery, ca. 240. Photo: Used with permission, Yale Art Gallery

have clothed yourselves with Christ" (Galatians 3:27 New American Standard Bible; see also Revelation 7:9–17; the Greek verb for "to clothe or to put on" is *enduō*, from which we get the English *endow* and *endowment*). The symbol of the robe developed particular richness in the Syriac tradition of a "Robe of Glory" that Adam and Eve had originally worn in Eden but had lost: "At his or her baptism, the individual Christian, in 'putting on Christ,' puts on the Robe of Glory, thus reentering the terrestrial anticipation of the eschatological Paradise, in other words, the Church; finally, at the Resurrection

▲ FIGURE 6.6   Line drawing of the Good Shepherd painting above the font of the Dura-Europos baptistery, ca. 240. Image: Used with permission, Yale Art Gallery

of the Dead, the just will in all reality reenter the celestial paradise, clothed in their Robes of Glory."[54]

The art and design of early Christian baptisteries reveal many facets of what baptism meant to those who built and used those spaces and what their baptismal experience might have been like. At Dura Europos, the font lay directly beneath a painting of a shepherd carrying a sheep on his shoulders toward a flock grazing and drinking at a river (see figs. 6.5, 6.6): to be baptized was to be rescued by the

Good Shepherd (see Luke 15:4–6; John 10:11) and brought into the church fold, where one found "living water" and nourishment to body and soul (see Psalm 23; John 4:10–14; 7:37–39; 21:15–17). Visually, the rescued sheep is aligned vertically with the shepherd and moves horizontally toward the flock, suggesting the vertical and horizontal relationships formed in baptism—the creation of a covenant bond with Christ and with the family of Christ's followers (compare 2 Nephi 31:10–20; Mosiah 18:8–10). Other paintings in the baptistery, such as Adam and Eve (beneath the Good Shepherd), the healing of the paralytic, Jesus and Peter walking on the water, and David slaying Goliath, also had baptismal connections: baptism was a reversal of the Fall and a return to Paradise; baptism was a healing and passage from death to life (see John 5:1–9, 24); baptism was a rescue in water (Matthew 14:28–33); baptismal anointing brought power to conquer spiritual foes like David conquered Goliath after being anointed and receiving the spirit of the Lord (see 1 Samuel 16:13; 17:31–51).[55] People baptized in this space were immersed in vivid imagery tied to their own ritual actions. It would have been an impressive, multisensory experience.

From the fourth century forward, eight-sided baptismal fonts and baptisteries became popular in Christian architecture. The octagon called to mind the eighth day, or first day of the new week (when Christ rose from the dead), thus symbolizing rebirth and new creation.[56] In the fifth-century orthodox baptistery at Ravenna (see fig. 6.7), a stunning mosaic decorates the domed ceiling directly above the octagonal font (see fig. 6.8). Within a circle portraying the Twelve Apostles is a scene of Jesus being baptized by John the Baptist, as a dove (the Holy Spirit) descends upon Jesus (see Matthew 3:16–17; Mark 1:9–11; Luke 3:21–22). Christians in late antiquity who were baptized here would have seen directly over their heads a reminder that they were following the Savior, being "baptized into Christ Jesus . . . buried with him by baptism into death, so that, just as Christ was raised from the dead by the glory of the Father," they too "might walk in newness of life" (Romans 6:3 NRSV; see also Galatians 3:27–28).

Restoration work on the mosaic in the nineteenth century

▲ **FIGURE 6.7**　Octagonal Orthodox Baptistery, Ravenna, Italy, ca. 450–70. Photo: Mark D. Ellison

rendered John the Baptist pouring water on Jesus's head, but the original mosaic probably portrayed John's hand on Jesus's head, as seen elsewhere in early Christian art.[57] Nevertheless, pouring as a method of baptism had emerged as early as the late first century: the *Didache* encouraged immersion in a body of running water, but if none was available, "then pour water on the head three times in the name of Father and Son and Holy Spirit."[58] Historians debate whether the practice in the early centuries was usually immersion (plunging, perhaps not always a full submersion), sometimes affusion (pouring) or aspersion (sprinkling), or a combination of these (such as kneeling "immersed" in water while receiving pouring).[59] Affusion may have particularly served those at the point of death, including infants whose parents urgently wished to have them baptized

▲ **FIGURE 6.8**   Mosaic, the baptism of Jesus Christ, Orthodox Baptistery, Ravenna, Italy, ca. 450–70. Photo: Mark D. Ellison

before they died. Cyprian (mid-third century) defended accommodations such as pouring or sprinkling with water, calling them "divine abridgements" (*compendia*) that were acceptable "when necessity compels," such as when a person was too ill to be immersed and when there was "full and entire faith both of the giver and receiver." In such cases, "God bestows his mercy." As support, Cyprian cited Ezekiel 36:25–26: "Then will I sprinkle clean water upon you, and ye shall be clean. . . . A new heart also will I give you, and a new spirit will I put within you."[60]

Throughout the history of Christianity, believers have debated about the proper procedures for baptism, and we Latter-day Saints can easily recognize differences between our norms and ancient practices. We should also recognize that God has never stopped loving

BOX 6.8 Infant Baptism

It is difficult to identify exactly when the practice of baptizing infants began or what motivated it. Christian sources of the first two centuries make no explicit mention of infant baptism. Several second-century Christian writers express the view that little children are innocent.[61] The earliest unmistakable reference to baptizing infants comes from Tertullian, writing around AD 206. Tertullian is aware of the practice and opposes it, yet he implies that one scripture motivating Christians to baptize their infant children is Jesus's statement: "Suffer the little children to come unto me, and forbid them not" (Mark 10:14).[62]

Some Christians found support for infant baptism in the biblical precedent of circumcising male children eight days after birth (see Genesis 17:12).[63] Still other scriptural passages may have led sincere, believing parents to the conviction that they should have their newborns baptized. John 3:5, "Except a man be born of water and of the Spirit, he cannot enter into the kingdom of God," signaled the necessity of baptism for salvation.[64] Psalm 51:5 may have raised doubts about human innocence: "I was born guilty, a sinner when my mother conceived me" (NRSV).[65] In that time when infant mortality was high, life expectancy was always tenuous, and baptism was understood to be a requirement for entering the kingdom of God, parents of an infant, especially one in poor health, might understandably have felt an urgent need for their child to be baptized. Further, they may have believed that this practice was a way of demonstrating that the Atonement of Christ can cover all people, including infants. As Irenaeus wrote (AD 180): "For he came to save all by means of himself—all, I say, who by him are born again to God—infants, children, adolescents, young people, and old people."[66]

However, historical records suggest that the practice of infant baptism preceded any formal development of theological rationales for the practice. When Augustine articulated his doctrine of original sin (early fifth century), it was well after the practice of infant baptism had become widespread, and Augustine appealed to the existing practice to support his doctrine—not the other way around.[67]

Infant baptism was probably less common than adult baptism in the early Christian period, since baptismal liturgies assume that baptismal candidates can act for themselves. Parents would have spoken as proxies on behalf of their infants.[68]

Though we Latter-day Saints have a different position on this issue (because of Restoration scripture that early Christians did not have, such as Moroni 8 and Doctrine and Covenants 68:27), the idea of accommodations in the performance of ordinances is not foreign to Latter-day Saint thought or practice.[69] Doctrine and Covenants 137:9–10 assures us that children who die before the age of accountability will inherit the celestial kingdom—and also that the Lord "will judge all men according to their works, according to the desire of their hearts." Surely this includes the heartfelt concerns of parents for the eternal well-being of their little children. The argument against infant baptism in Moroni 8 is important, but it is not directed against ancient Christians in the Old World, nor modern Christians, but against Nephites who Mormon thought should have known better.

and blessing people who desired to turn to him; whenever people have believed in Christ and followed him to the extent available to them, the Lord has recognized their efforts and blessed them.[70]

Eucharist

One of the earliest-attested practices of Christian worship is the blessing and partaking of bread and wine in remembrance of Jesus Christ's death and Resurrection. The earliest Christian communities participated in this practice in the context of a common meal shared by the house-church congregation (see Acts 2:42, 46; 1 Corinthians 11:17–34; Jude 1:12). Later this ceremony was separated from the meal and became the high point of a more formal worship service

BOX 6.9　Baptism and a Changed Life

A letter that Cyprian wrote to his friend Donatus shortly after Cyprian's baptism (around AD 246) gives us a glimpse at the great blessings baptism brought into his life:

> "While I was still lying in darkness and gloomy night, wavering here and there, . . . I used to regard it a difficult matter, especially regarding my character at that time, that a man should be capable of being born again. . . . *How,* said I, *is such a conversion possible?* . . . I was held in bonds by the innumerable errors of my previous life, from which I did not believe that I could possibly be delivered. . . . But by the help of the water of new birth, the stain of former years was washed away, and a light from above, serene and pure, was infused into my reconciled heart. . . . Then, in a wondrous manner, doubtful things at once began to assure themselves to me, hidden things to be revealed, dark things to be enlightened, what before had seemed difficult began to suggest a means of accomplishment, what had been thought impossible, to be capable of being achieved. . . . I was animated by the Spirit of holiness."[71]

that, like baptism, evolved over the early Christian centuries. In the New Testament the ritual is variously called the Lord's Supper (see 1 Corinthians 11:20), communion (see 1 Corinthians 10:16), or the breaking of bread (see Acts 2:42, 46); later, it was called the Eucharist (from the Greek *eucharistéō,* "giving thanks"; see Matthew 26:27), a *mystērion* (Greek, meaning "mystery" or "rite"), or the Latin equivalent *sacramentum,*[72] from which we get the English word *sacrament.*

The early practice of having the sacrament as part of a communal meal preserved its original setting at the Last Supper, where Jesus instituted the sacrament and instructed, "Do this in remembrance of me" (1 Corinthians 11:23–26; Luke 22:19–20). This practice also recalled the Last Supper's setting at Passover, another symbolic meal that ritually remembered God freeing his people from bondage (see Exodus 12–14). Early house-church sacrament meetings were further enriched by cultural connotations of dining together. In the biblical world, sharing a meal meant much more than merely satisfying hunger and thirst; it implied sharing a bond of friendship and trust, "a sharing of one's life."[73] During his ministry, Jesus had often used meals as ways to proclaim the good news of the kingdom and invite all, even the marginalized and despised, to join the heavenly feast.[74] Jesus's inclusive table fellowship, along with his feeding miracles (see Mark 6:30–44; 8:1–10; John 6) and institution of the sacrament, was a symbolic anticipation of the joyful, abundant messianic feast in the age to come (see Isaiah 25:6–10; Matthew 26:29). Early Christians were mindful of these rich connections to their own celebration of the Eucharist.

For an example of this, let us visit the Church of the Multiplication on the shore of the Sea of Galilee. This small church commemorates the traditional site of the feeding of the five thousand. It stands on the site of a fourth-century church whose altar (for blessing the bread and wine) stood over a rock where Jesus was believed to have blessed the loaves and fishes. A fifth-century mosaic floor preserved this memory with a depiction of two fish and a basket of small, round loaves of bread, and this part of the ancient mosaic is still visible in the present-day church, directly in front of the altar (see figs. 6.9, 6.10). Curiously, the basket of bread in the mosaic depicts only four loaves, while the Gospel accounts relate that there were five. Careful observers have suggested that this might be intentional—perhaps the fifth loaf is the real one that would have been placed upon the altar above the mosaic. The living church with its living worshipers completed

◀ **FIGURE 6.9** Loaves and fishes mosaic, Church of the Multiplication, Tabgha, Israel, fifth century. Photo: Mark D. Ellison

◀ **FIGURE 6.10** Loaves and fishes mosaic with altar, Church of the Multiplication, Tabgha, Israel. Mosaic: fifth century; altar and church: twentieth century, built upon the floor plan of the fifth-century church, above the location of the earlier fourth-century church. Photo: Mark D. Ellison

the scene.[75] Scripture, sacred space, art, and ritual converged here, urging believers to see themselves in worship as if they were participants in the miraculous feeding of the five thousand and all its meaningful connections to the sacrament—celebrating Jesus's joyful proclamation of the kingdom, his bestowal of overflowing grace, his provision of "daily bread," his promise of the heavenly abundance to come, his identity as "the bread of life" (John 6:35).[76] Whether the miracle had actually taken place at this spot is not as important as the ties that early Christians who worshiped there sought to maintain between themselves and Jesus Christ. Ritual can link the past and present: it can connect the living worship community to people and events of the past. It can bridge the distance between earth and heaven.

Over the first Christian centuries, a Sunday liturgy gradually developed as a worship service built around the ritual of the Eucharist. In the mid-second century, Justin Martyr described a relatively simple service that included scripture readings, sermons, and prayers before the blessing and sharing of bread and wine (see box 6.10).

When Christians began constructing majestic basilical churches in the fourth century, it solidified developments in the liturgy that were already evident in the third century. In these settings that evoked reverential awe, there was no longer a communal meal shared by a small group; rather, larger congregations followed a formal sequence

Sunday Worship in the Second Century

Justin Martyr (circa AD 151–155) described a typical Sunday worship service:

> "On the day called Sunday, all who live in cities or in the country gather together to one place, and the memoirs of the apostles [the Gospels] or the writings of the [Old Testament] prophets are read, as long as time permits. Then, when the reader has ceased, the president verbally instructs, and exhorts to the imitation of these good things. Then we all rise together and pray. . . . When our prayer is ended, bread and wine and water are brought, and the president in like manner offers prayers and thanksgivings, according to his ability, and the people assent, saying Amen. There is a distribution to each, and a participation of that over which thanks have been given, and to those who are absent a portion is sent by the deacons."[77]

of prayers, hymns, readings from scripture, and a sermon leading to the climactic high point near the end of the service—the blessing and partaking of bread and a cup of wine (a token meal) before a concluding blessing. The unbaptized were dismissed before the Eucharist, which was kept private, only for the baptized. The main weekly gathering occurred on Sunday morning, but in some places smaller gatherings celebrated the Eucharist daily. Generally there were no pews, benches, or chairs for the congregation, who stood throughout the service. There were regional variations in the liturgy over time, but it is possible to list some general commonalities (see box 6.11; this basic form is still followed today in liturgical churches—Catholic, Orthodox, Anglican/Episcopalian, Lutheran, and so forth).[78]

BOX 6.11 Sunday Worship in the Fourth-Fifth Centuries: A Basic Outline of the Liturgy

Entrance
- Congregation files into the church, stands in aisles and sides of nave
- Clergy process down the center of the nave, bishop sits at center of apse, priests sit beside him in the apse (see fig. 6.10)

Liturgy of the Word
- Initial greetings, prayers, and songs
- Readings from Old and New Testaments, interspersed by responsorial chanting of psalms
- Sermon (by bishop or an appointed priest)
- Dismissal of all the nonbaptized

Liturgy of the Eucharist
- Intercessory prayers of the congregation (led by a deacon), then prayer of the bishop
- Preparation of the bread and wine
- Prayers, including recitation of the Lord's Prayer
- Kiss of peace (congregation members wish each other peace with a traditional kiss of greeting; see Romans 16:16; 1 Corinthians 16:20; 2 Corinthians 13:12; 1 Thessalonians 5:26; 1 Peter 5:14)
- Blessing and distribution of the bread and wine (congregation members come forward to receive the bread and wine at the chancel rail between the altar and the nave)
- Benediction (blessing upon the congregation)

Exit
- Bishop and clergy process out of the church down the center of the nave, followed by the laity

BOX 6.12 **Connections between Ancient Christian Rituals and Latter-day Saint Temple Worship?**

If you are familiar with Latter-day Saint temple worship, you have probably noticed as you have read this chapter that there are intriguing resemblances between Latter-day Saint practices and elements of ancient Christian rituals—especially in the ancient baptismal liturgy (its washing and anointing ceremonies and symbolic white robes) and the Eucharistic liturgy (with its formalized sequence, solemn processions, communal prayers, and climactic end—only for the baptized—representing communion with deity). Some Latter-day Saint scholars have drawn attention to such similarities and have hinted or speculated that early Christian rituals may have been remnants of rites comparable to those practiced in Latter-day Saint temples—that is, ancient rites restored in our time.[79]

However, there are reasons Latter-day Saints should be cautious on this question. First, passages in the Doctrine and Covenants state that some of our doctrines and practices were never revealed before but were reserved for our time. These passages strongly imply that Latter-day Saint temple ordinances are among the revelations that were not previously known and were reserved for "the dispensation of the fullness of times" (Doctrine and Covenants 124:39–42; see also Doctrine and Covenants 121:26–27; 128:16–18).

Further, many seeming parallels between ancient rituals and Latter-day Saint practices do not appear so convincing when examined closely in context.[80] Some Latter-day Saint scholars who have speculated about temple connections have been critiqued for committing methodological errors such as selectively citing seeming parallels while ignoring counter evidence and ancient contexts.[81] It is better historical practice to start with the evidence and proceed to interpretation rather than to start with a theory and seek evidence to prove it. If we take seriously the Latter-day Saint aspiration to turn our hearts to our ancestors, we will try to understand them for who they were rather than try to imagine them exactly as we are in order to serve our own purposes (see Doctrine and Covenants 128:15, 17). Approaching history in this more cautious, charitable way enables us to appreciate differences and learn from them (we cannot learn from people if we assume they are exactly like us). This approach also helps us see more clearly the Lord's "line upon line" incremental revelation over time (see 2 Nephi 28:30) and more fully appreciate all that is distinctive and wonderful in the Restoration. Meanwhile, we can still recognize similarities between ancient and modern forms of worship, ponder them, and allow them to inform and enrich our own worship experiences.

Conclusion: The Legacy of Ancient Christian Worship

There are other early Christian forms of worship and ritual that space here will not permit us to explore. Ancient Christians developed a liturgical calendar organized around Easter, Christmas, and other feasts and fasts.[82] They went on pilgrimages to holy sites and the graves of martyrs and saints.[83] They anointed the sick, following New Testament precedents (see Mark 6:13; James 5:14–15).[84] They practiced traditional and new funerary rites (see chapter 11).[85] From the fourth century forward, they asked their bishops to pronounce blessings on the bride and groom at weddings (traditionally private celebrations in the home), which led to the development of marriage liturgy and brought weddings within the sphere of church ritual.[86] Christians developed rites for the ordination of clergy and consecration of virgins (see chapter 4).[87] These early Christians also began developing a system of penance with formal procedures by which those guilty of grave sins could be restored to good standing in the church—like most forms of worship, this would be further developed in medieval and early modern Christianity.[88] But the forms of worship discussed here—prayer, hymns, baptism, the Eucharist— were the basic, foundational practices that defined the religious lives of the vast majority of ancient Christians.

BOX 6.13   A Personal Reflection on Ancient Christian Ritual and Latter-day Saint Worship

I saw the Lord sitting on a throne, high and lofty; and the hem of his robe filled the temple. Seraphs were in attendance above him; each had six wings. . . . And one called to another and said: "Holy, holy, holy is the Lord of hosts; the whole earth is full of his glory." . . . And I said: "Woe is me! I am lost, for I am a man of unclean lips, and I live among a people of unclean lips; yet my eyes have seen the King, the Lord of hosts!" Then one of the seraphs flew to me, holding a live coal that had been taken from the altar with a pair of tongs. The seraph touched my mouth with it and said: "Now that this has touched your lips, your guilt has departed and your sin is blotted out." Then I heard the voice of the Lord saying, "Whom shall I send, and who will go for us?" And I said, "Here am I; send me!"

—Isaiah 6:1–3, 5–7 NRSV

The following is one way that ancient rituals have enriched my own worship experiences. There is a fascinating tradition in Eastern Christianity (Byzantine and Syriac) in which details and imagery from Isaiah's vision of God in the heavenly temple were gradually brought into Eucharistic liturgy. The hymn of the angelic seraphim, "Holy, holy, holy, is the Lord of hosts" (Isaiah 6:3), was an element of Jewish and Christian worship from very early on (see Revelation 4:6–8) and suggested that when the worship community on earth sang these words in church, they joined their voices with the heavenly hosts (see Doctrine and Covenants 109:79).[89] In the fourth century, some Christians were comparing the Eucharistic bread to the coal that the seraph touched to Isaiah's "unclean lips" with the words, "This has touched your lips; your iniquity is taken away, and your sin purged" (Isaiah 6:7).[90] By the sixth century, liturgies made frequent reference to details in Isaiah 6, and liturgical vessels and spaces were decorated with images of the seraphim and cherubim that surrounded God's throne.[91] These ritual elements encouraged worshipers to imagine themselves in the role of Isaiah, approaching the throne of God as they approached the church altar, receiving forgiveness and purification anew through the Eucharist, and being transformed into people who could, like Isaiah, go forth with newfound confidence to bear testimony of God's word to the world (see Isaiah 6:8–9; see fig. 6.11).

This beautiful connection that ancient Christians saw between Isaiah's transformative vision and their own experience of Eucharistic worship continues to move me, centuries later. Sometimes I feel lost and hopeless, a bit like Isaiah when he sensed his own uncleanness before God and cried out: "Woe is me! for I am undone" (Isaiah 6:5). Yet, as I sit in my relatively simple Latter-day Saint sacrament meeting and take the small piece of bread, I feel led to recall the angelic words: "This has touched your lips; your iniquity is taken away, and your sin purged" (Isaiah 6:7 New King James Version). I think of the many ways the Lord has changed my life, and as I consider the good that God wants me to do in the world, I feel myself renewed to say in my heart: "Here am I, Lord; send me."

Ancient Christian rituals were multisensory experiences that engaged the whole person: body, mind, and spirit. Physical actions and postures, words spoken or chanted or sung, the hearing of these words and melodies, the experience of feeling water or oil on the skin, tasting bread and wine, breathing in the fragrance of incense, seeing light and images and architecture, sensing sacred space, listening to instruction on the meanings of rituals—all these immersed worshipers in learning, remembering, feeling, and expressing religious devotion. Later Christians would theorize more deeply about how these rituals worked, developing theologies of sacraments; debating whether unworthy officiators invalidated rituals; asking whether ritual elements were mere symbols, memorials, or actual vehicles of divine grace; and so forth.[92] These conversations have their beginnings in early Christianity but extend well beyond it into the medieval and early modern periods.

▲ **FIGURE 6.11**   Jesus Christ enthroned between six-winged seraphim as an angel gives the coal (as if sacramental bread) to Isaiah. Nineteenth-century drawing of a sixth-century painting, *Vatican Codex of Cosmas Indicopleustes*. Image: Raffaele Garrucci, *Storia della arte cristiana nei primi otto secoli della chiesa*, vol. 3 (Prato: Guasti, 1876), Tav. 148.2. Vat.gr.699, 72 verso, (public domain)

Nevertheless, even our brief look at the worship and ritual of the early Christians enables us to discern a consistent theme: a central focus on Jesus Christ, scripture, and the formation of lives of faith as individuals and communities. If worship and ritual reveal the heart of a people's shared conviction, this recurring theme comprises a testimony left by ancient Christians, spoken not only in word but also in the actions of worship. Augustine's reflections on the annual celebration of the Easter vigil might apply as well to the prayers that recalled Jesus's life and teachings, the hymns that sang of his works and salvation, the baptism that symbolized dying and rising with him, and the Eucharist that memorialized his atonement and anticipated his feast to come: "Christ died once for us. . . . And yet this solemnity repeats it as the years go round. . . . By celebrating it regularly, the solemnity renews it for loving hearts."[93]

Notes

1. The following abbreviations are used in these endnotes: *ACW*=Ancient Christian Writers; *ANF*=Ante-Nicene Fathers; *NPNF 1*=*Nicene and Post-Nicene Fathers*, series 1; *NPNF 2*=*Nicene and Post-Nicene Fathers*, series 2; PG=Patrologia Graeca, ed. Jacques-Paul Migne, 161 vols. (Paris, 1857–86).

2. For New Testament passages referring to the worship activities described in this paragraph, see Acts 1:14–15; 2:1–18, 42, 46; 21:8–9; 1 Corinthians 11:4–5; 14:3, 26; Ephesians 5:18–20; Colossians 3:16. For a study of New Testament house churches by two New Testament scholars, see Carolyn Osiek and David L. Balch, *Families in the New Testament World: Households and House Churches* (Louisville, KY: Westminster John Knox Press, 1997). The Church of Jesus Christ of Latter-day Saints uses the word *ordinances* to refer to rituals or ceremonies such as baptism, confirmation, the sacrament of the Lord's Supper, ordination, blessing the sick, and temple rites: "In the Church, an ordinance is a sacred, formal act or ceremony performed by the authority of the priesthood." Gospel Topics, s.v. "Ordinances," accessed February 12, 2022, https://www.churchofjesuschrist.org/study/manual/gospel-topics/ordinances. However, the Hebrew and Greek words that were translated as *ordinance* or *ordinances* in the King James Version of the Bible refer not to ceremonies but to decrees, laws, judgments, regulations, statutes, rules, traditions, and so forth. The Oxford English Dictionary defines *ordinance* as (1) "something decreed, ordained [set in place], or prescribed," (2) "an authoritative direction, decree, or command," (3) "that which is ordained or decreed by God," (4) "a practice or usage authoritatively enjoined or prescribed, esp. a religious or

ceremonial observance," including, "(chiefly in the Baptist church) either of the sacraments of baptism or communion." This fourth usage appears to have entered the English language in the fourteenth century. *Oxford English Dictionary*, s.v. "ordinance," accessed February 26, 2021 https://www.oed.com/view/Entry/132352.

3.   See Walter Bauer, William F. Arndt, F. Wilbur Gingrich, and F. W. Danker, *A Greek-English Lexicon of the New Testament and Other Early Christian Literature*, 3rd ed. (BDAG), (Chicago: University of Chicago Press, 2000), s.v. "ἀποστασία (*apostasia*)": "defiance of established system or authority, *rebellion, abandonment, breach of faith*." From ἀπό (*apo-*, "apart") and ἵστημι (*hístēmi*, "stand"), literally "stand apart," figuratively "rebel," the word is used twice in the New Testament: once in Acts 21:21, where Jewish-Christians in Jerusalem have heard that Paul teaches people "to forsake [*apostasia*] Moses"; and once in 2 Thessalonians 2:3, where Paul says that the day of the Lord "shall not come, except there come a falling away [*apostasia*] first." Though many Latter-day Saints have used 2 Thessalonians 2:3 as a proof text for a general apostasy of the entire church, the verse in context may refer to a more particular, proximate event; see Grant Hardy, "The King James Bible and the Future of Missionary Work," *Dialogue* 45, no. 2 (2012): 30–31. The word *apostasy* does not appear in the Book of Mormon; rather, a standing-related metaphor the Book of Mormon uses to describe the standing of post-New Testament Christians is "stumble" (1 Nephi 13:29, 34; 2 Nephi 26:20), which invites us to consider people who were trying to make forward progress in rough terrain. We can choose to be charitable readers, remembering that if we judge ancient Christians harshly, in the worst possible light, that is how we, too, will be judged (see Matthew 7:1–2). For a thorough, responsible study of the concept of apostasy in Christianity as it has been discussed by Latter-day Saints, see Miranda Wilcox and John D. Young, eds., *Standing Apart: Mormon Historical Consciousness and the Concept of Apostasy* (New York: Oxford University Press, 2014). For informed reconsiderations of what Christian "apostasy" might have entailed, see James E. Faulconer, "The Concept of Apostasy in the New Testament," in *Early Christians in Disarray: Contemporary LDS Perspectives on the Christian Apostasy*, ed. Noel B. Reynolds (Provo, UT: Brigham Young University Press, 2005), 133–162; Nicholas J. Frederick and Joseph M. Spencer, "Remnant or Replacement? Outlining a Possible Apostasy Narrative," *BYU Studies Quarterly* 60, no.1 (2021): 105–27. For faithful, broad ways of understanding Christian history and the Restoration, see Philip Barlow, "To Mend a Fractured Reality: Joseph Smith's Project," *Journal of Mormon History* 38, no. 3 (2012): 28–50; Patrick Q.

Mason, *Restoration: God's Call to the 21st-Century World* (Meridian, ID: Faith Matters Publishing, 2020); see also chapter 1 in this volume.

4. See Paul F. Bradshaw, *The Search for the Origins of Christian Worship: Sources and Methods for the Study of Early Liturgy*, 2nd ed. (Oxford: Oxford University Press, 2002); Bradshaw, *Reconstructing Early Christian Worship* (Collegeville, MN: Liturgical Press, 2009).

5. See A. M. Giuntella, "Orans," in *The Encyclopedia of the Early Church*, ed. Angelo Di Berardino, trans. Adrian Walford (Cambridge: Oxford University Press, 1992), 2:615; Robin M. Jensen, *Understanding Early Christian Art* (London: Routledge, 2000), 35–37. Other postures of prayer mentioned in the Bible include kneeling (see Luke 22:41; Acts 9:40; 20:36) and, most humbly, full prostration, with one's face to the ground (see Matthew 26:39; see also Luke 5:12; 17:16). Early Christians prayed facing east, the biblical location of Paradise or Eden (see Genesis 2:8), the direction of the rising sun, and the direction from which it was believed Christ (the Light of the World) would return (see Matthew 24:27; Ezekiel 43:1–2; Zechariah 14:4–5; Origen, *On Prayer* 32; Gregory of Nyssa, *Sermon 5 on the Lord's Prayer* [ACW 18, 76–77]; Augustine, *The Lord's Sermon on the Mount* 2.5.18). The modern posture of folded hands originated in the late tenth century; see Kevin Madigan, *Medieval Christianity: A New History* (New Haven: Yale University Press, 2015), 109. On postures of prayer, see N. T. Wright, *The Lord and His Prayer* (Grand Rapids, MI: Eerdmans, 1996), 21. For discussions of the *Donna Velata* (veiled lady) in the Priscilla Catacombs, see Nicola Denzey, *The Bone Gatherers: The Lost Worlds of Early Christian Women* (Boston: Beacon Press, 2007), 75–88; Christine Schenk, *Crispina and Her Sisters: Women and Authority in Early Christianity* (Minneapolis, MN: Fortress, 2017), 133–39; Mark D. Ellison, "Visualizing Christian Marriage in the Roman World" (PhD diss., Vanderbilt University, 2017), 91–102.

6. See also *Berakoth* 1.1–2; 4.1.

7. Origen mentioned "a pattern of how we ought to pray"; Origen, *On Prayer* 18.2, in Henry Chadwick and J. E. L. Oulton, eds., *Alexandrian Christianity*, The Library of Christian Classics (Philadelphia: Westminster, 1954), 275; see also Origen, *On Prayer* 22.5. Cyprian referred to "a form of praying"; Cyprian, *On the Lord's Prayer* 2 (ANF 5:448).

8. See *Didache* 8.

9. See, for example, Cyril of Jerusalem, *Catechetical Lectures* 23.11–18.

10. Tertullian, *On Prayer* 1 (ANF 3:681). "In summaries of so few words, how many utterances of the prophets, the Gospels, the apostles—how many discourses, examples, parables of the Lord, are touched on!" Tertullian, *On*

Prayer 9 (*ANF* 3:684). "This prayer . . . serves as a lens through which to see Jesus himself, and to discover something of what he was about. When Jesus gave his disciples this prayer, he was giving them part of his own breath, his own life, his own prayer. The prayer is actually a distillation of his own sense of vocation, his own understanding of his Father's purposes." Wright, *The Lord and His Prayer*, x.

11. Cyprian wrote, "The Teacher of peace and the Master of unity would not have prayer to be made singly and individually, as for one who prays to pray for himself alone. For we say not 'My Father, which art in heaven,' nor 'Give me this day my daily bread;' nor does each one ask that only his own debt should be forgiven him; nor does he request for himself alone that he may not be led into temptation, and delivered from evil. Our prayer is public and common; and when we pray, we pray not for one, but for the whole people, because we the whole people are one. The God of peace and the Teacher of concord, who taught unity, willed that one should thus pray for all." Cyprian, *On the Lord's Prayer* 8 (*ANF* 5:449). Augustine stated that people cannot pray Our Father with true piety unless they recognize that other people are their brothers and sisters; see Augustine, *The Lord's Sermon on the Mount* 4.16 (*ACW* 5:106).

12. See *Didache* 8. Tertullian encouraged prayer at sunrise, the third hour (9:00 a.m.), the sixth hour (noon), the ninth hour (3:00 p.m.), sunset, before meals, and before bathing; see Tertullian, *On Prayer* 24–25; see also *Apostolic Tradition* 35, 41. But there was then (like now) diversity in people's actual practice—bishop Gregory of Nyssa preached a series of sermons prompted by concern that most Christians were neglecting their prayers; see Gregory of Nyssa, *The Lord's Prayer, Sermon 1* (*ACW* 18, 21–34).

13. God is called father in the Old Testament. See, for example, Hosea 11:1; Malachi 2:10. However, *father* is not used as a term of address in prayer in the Old Testament. Typical Old Testament terms of address include "O Lord God of Abraham, Isaac, and of Israel, our fathers" (1 Chronicles 29:18), "O Lord God of Israel" (2 Chronicles 6:13–14), "O Lord God of hosts" (Psalm 84:8), and "O God of our salvation" (Psalms 65:5; 79:9; 85:4; 1 Chronicles 16:35). Some early Christians claimed that Jesus was the first to address God in prayer as "Father"; see Origen, *On Prayer* 22–23; Augustine, *The Lord's Sermon on the Mount* 2.4.15. For a caution against exaggerating the difference between Jesus's practice and Judaism, see Amy-Jill Levine, *The Sermon on the Mount: A Beginner's Guide to the Kingdom of Heaven* (Nashville: Abingdon, 2020), 70–72.

14. Cyprian, *On the Lord's Prayer* 11 (*ANF* 5:450); see also Tertullian, *On Prayer* 2; Origen, *On Prayer* 22–23; Augustine, *The Lord's Sermon on the*

Mount 2.4.16.

15. Tertullian, *On Prayer* 3 (*ANF* 3:682); see also Cyril of Jerusalem, *Catechetical Lectures* 23.12. When the Lord's name is introduced in the Old Testament, it is in the context of his statement to Moses: "I have surely seen the affliction of my people which are in Egypt, and have heard their cry by reason of their taskmasters; for I know their sorrows; and I am come down to deliver them" (Exodus 3:7–8). Jesus, too, saw people, heard them, knew their sorrows, and came down to deliver them. To hallow God's name is to love and revere God as one who sees, hears, understands, and delivers.

16. Augustine, *The Lord's Sermon on the Mount* 2.5.18, 2.6.20 (*ACW* 5:108–9). Compare Russell M. Nelson, "Let God Prevail," *Ensign*, November 2020, 92–95.

17. Gregory of Nyssa, *Sermon 3 on the Lord's Prayer* (*ACW* 18:51–52).

18. Cyril, *Catechetical Lectures* 23.14 (*NPNF* 2/7:155); see also Tertullian, *On Prayer* 5. Gregory of Nyssa taught, "We . . . say to God: Thy Will be done also in me"; Gregory of Nyssa, *Sermons on the Lord's Prayer* 4 (*ACW* 18, 59).

19. Tertullian, *On Prayer* 6 (*ANF* 3:683). The teachings to "take no thought" (Matthew 6:25–34) would be better translated as "do not worry." For Latter-day Saint commentary on this petition, see D. Todd Christofferson, "Give Us This Day Our Daily Bread," January 9, 2011, Brigham Young University, https://speeches.byu.edu/talks/d-todd-christofferson/give-us-this-day-our-daily-bread/.

20. See, for example, Tertullian, *On Prayer* 7; Augustine, *The Lord's Sermon on the Mount* 8.28–29.

21. Gregory of Nyssa, *Sermon 5 on the Lord's Prayer* (*ACW* 18:71). For more early Christian thought on becoming like God, see chapter 10 in this volume.

22. Tertullian, *On Prayer* 8; see also Augustine, *The Lord's Sermon on the Mount* 9.30; James 1:13. The Joseph Smith Translation also changes this line to: "And suffer us not to be led into temptation." The final doxology, "For thine is the kingdom, and the power, and the glory, for ever. Amen" (Matthew 6:13), is not in the oldest manuscripts of Matthew and seems to have been added later. Nevertheless, it does reflect the way Jesus gave glory to the Father (see Mark 10:17–18; John 17:1–4) and urged his followers to do so, too (see Matthew 5:16). For the follower of Jesus in prayer, it logically follows, after praying for forgiveness, today's needed sustenance, and deliverance from evil, to acknowledge reliance upon God's strength for all these forms of help.

23. See *Rule of Benedict* 16. L. Edward Phillips, tracing the origins of the set hours of prayer, observes that the times may have originated as "merely

conveniences," such as "waking in the middle of the night anyway, or wanting protection before going to sleep, and so forth. Christians prayed at sunrise because the sun was up, and that could be reason enough. Yet preachers and theologians who had time to ponder such actions would soon find biblical and thematic reasons for the connection: the rising sun is a type of Christ's resurrection (Cyprian, *Dom. or.* 35). The explanations might be historically arbitrary but, nonetheless, evocative of divine purpose. Educated leaders, and probably not a few uneducated believers, made the connections because the practice was already there waiting to be interpreted. By proposing typological or scriptural precedents and interpretations, patristic commentators were attempting to give affective, imaginative depth to habitual practice that was forever in danger of drifting into the banal through sheer repetition." Phillips, "Early Christian Prayer," in *The Oxford Handbook of Early Christian Ritual*, ed. Risto Uro, Juliette J. Day, Richard E. DeMaris, and Rikard Roitto (Oxford: Oxford University Press, 2019), 580.

24. Maybe this is not much different from the situation in Latter-day Saint temples: called temple workers go to the temple at prescribed times to participate in worship and ordinances, while ordinary Church members may choose on their own when to attend the temple.

25. Clement of Alexandria, *Stromata* 7.7.40, 49; Origen, *On Prayer* 12; John Chrysostom, *Homilies on Prayer* 1–2.

26. Basil, Homily 5, *In Martyrem Julittam* (PG 31:244; *NPNF* 2/8:69; modernized).

27. *1 Clement* 59.4; 60.1, 3, in *The Apostolic Fathers: Greek Texts and English Translations*, 3rd ed., trans. Michael W. Holmes (Grand Rapids, MI: Baker, 2007), 125–29.

28. Ephrem, *Hymns on Virginity* 5.5, in Kathleen E. McVey, trans., *Ephrem the Syrian: Hymns*, (New York: Paulist, 1989), 283.

29. Kim Bowes, *Private Worship, Public Values, and Religious Change in Late Antiquity* (Cambridge: Cambridge University Press, 2008), 54.

30. Tosefta, *Ketubot* 5.8; Jerusalem Talmud, *Shabbat* 2.4, 6; *Avot de-Rabbi Nathan*, version B, 9; cited in Amit Assis, "The Lamp—Its Use and Significance in Jewish Tradition," in *Let There Be Light: Oil-Lamps from the Holy Land*, ed. Joan Goodnick Westenholz (Jerusalem: Bible Lands Museum, 2004), 8, 21.

31. Cyprian, *On the Lord's Prayer* 35 (*ANF* 5:457; altered). "At the time when the sun sets they are to pray. . . . Again when one lights the lamps in the evening they are to pray." *Canons of Hippolytus* 25. See also Paul F. Bradshaw, Maxwell E. Johnson, and L. Edward Phillips, *The Apostolic Tradition:*

A Commentary, ed. Harold W. Attridge (Minneapolis, MN: Fortress Press, 2002), 199; Basil, Homily 5, *In Martyrem Julittam* (PG 31:244; *NPNF* 2/8:69); Kristina Sessa, *Daily Life in Late Antiquity* (Cambridge, UK: Cambridge University Press, 2018), 200–205.

32. "In the darkness, then, of this life in which we are journeying away [that is, apart] from the Lord while we walk by faith and not by vision, the Christian soul ought to regard itself as desolate so that it does not cease to pray, and it should learn to turn the eye of faith to the words of the divine and holy scriptures, as if to a lamp set in a dark place, until the day dawns and the morning star rises in our hearts [see 2 Peter 1:19]. For the ineffable source, so to speak, of this lamp is that light which shines in the darkness so that the darkness does not grasp it [see John 1:5], and in order to see it hearts must be cleansed by faith." Augustine, *Epistle* 130.5, in *Letters 100–155*, trans. Ronald Teske, part 2, vol. 2 in The Works of St. Augustine: A Translation for the 21st Century series (Hyde Park, NY: New City Press, 2003), 186.

33. See *Apostolic Tradition* 25.

34. Egeria, *Itinerarium Egeriae* 24.4, in Lester Ruth, Carrie Steenwyk, and John D. Witvliet, eds., *Walking Where Jesus Walked: Worship in Fourth-Century Jerusalem*, The Church at Worship: Case Studies from Christian History series (Grand Rapids, MI: Eerdmans, 2010), 48. See Anne McGowan and Paul F. Bradshaw, *The Pilgrimage of Egeria: A New Translation of the Itinerarium Egeriae with Introduction and Commentary* (Collegeville, MN: Liturgical Press, 2018), 99.

35. John Wilkinson, *Jerusalem Pilgrims before the Crusades* (Warminster: Aris and Philips, 1977), 266.

36. See John Anthony McGuckin, *At the Lighting of the Lamps: Hymns of the Ancient Church* (Harrisburg, PA: Morehouse, 1995), ix.

37. Luke's account of the annunciation and birth of Christ is structured around four psalm-like texts that may have been early Christian hymns. They have come to be known in Western Christian tradition by their first words in Latin: the *Magnificat* (Mary's hymn of praise; see Luke 1:46–55), the *Benedictus* (Zecharias's hymn of blessing; see Luke 1:68–79), *Gloria in excelsis* (the angels' hymn; see Luke 2:14), and *Nunc dimittis* (Simeon's prayer, "Now let thy servant depart in peace"; see Luke 2:29–32). For a Latter-day Saint discussion of these hymns in the context of Luke's narrative, see Eric D. Huntsman, "Glad Tidings of Great Joy," *Ensign*, December 2010, 52–57.

38. Augustine, *Exposition on the Psalms* 148.11 (trans. J. E. Tweed, *NPNF* 1/8: 677; modernized).

39. See Thomas A. Wayment, "'Each Person Has a Hymn': The Creator-Savior

Hymns," in *Thou Art the Christ, the Son of the Living God: The Person and Work of Jesus in the New Testament*, ed. Eric D. Huntsman, Lincoln H. Blumell, and Tyler J. Griffin (Provo, UT: Religious Studies Center, Brigham Young University; Salt Lake City: Deseret Book, 2018), 192–215; Joshua W. Jipp, "Hymns in the New Testament," Bible Odyssey, accessed February 14, 2022, https://www.bibleodyssey.org/en/passages/related-articles/hymns-in-the-new-testament.

40. "Psalms and hymns written by faithful Christians from the beginning celebrate Christ the Word of God, speaking of him as Divine." Eusebius (circa AD 324), *Ecclesiastical History* 5.28.5–6 (*NPNF* 2/1:247; altered).

41. Antonia Tripolitis, trans., "*Phos Hilaron*: Ancient Hymn and Modern Enigma," *Vigiliae Christianae* 24, no. 3 (1970): 189.

42. "Oxyrhynchus hymn," Papyrus 1786; Charles H. Cosgrove, *An Ancient Christian Hymn with Musical Notation* (Tübingen: Mohr Siebeck, 2011), 37.

43. For example, see Gregorio Paniagua, "Hymne Chrétienne d'Oxyrhynchus," *Musique de la Grèce antique*, YouTube video, 5:05, https://www.youtube.com/watch?v=ENj_OWfinPU; for a stirring modern rearrangement, see Sean Kiner and Dean Kiner, "Oxyrhynchus Hymn," *Early Christian Schisms*, YouTube video, 1:12, https://www.youtube.com/watch?v=SeZ6VJ-bQ80.

44. John Meyendorff, "Preface," in McVey, *Ephrem the Syrian*, 2.

45. "Early Monastic Chant," UC Davis, accessed July 1, 2021, http://medieval.ucdavis.edu/20a/music.html. For Latin text and an English translation of *Aeternae rerum conditor*, see Peter G. Walsh with Christopher Husch, ed. and trans., *One Hundred Latin Hymns: Ambrose to Aquinas* (Cambridge, MA: Harvard University Press, 2012), 2–5.

46. Latter-day Saint readers may also be interested in another Syriac hymn from early Christianity, the "Hymn of the Pearl," which was quoted in the third-century *Acts of Thomas* and relates an allegorical life journey that resonates with Latter-day Saint ways of thinking about the plan of salvation. For a discussion and English translation of this hymn, see John W. Welch and James V. Garrison, "The 'Hymn of the Pearl': An Ancient Counterpart to 'O My Father,'" *BYU Studies* 36, no. 1 (1996–97): 127–38, https://byustudies.byu.edu/article/the-hymn-of-the-pearl-an-ancient-counterpart-to-o-my-father/.

47. For an insightful Latter-day Saint discussion of Peter's denials, see Eric D. Huntsman, "The Accounts of Peter's Denial: Understanding the Texts and Motifs," in *The Ministry of Peter, the Chief Apostle*, ed. Frank F. Judd Jr., Eric D. Huntsman, and Shon D. Hopkin (Provo UT: Religious Studies Center, Brigham Young University; Salt Lake City: Deseret Book, 2014), 127–149, https://rsc.byu.edu/ministry-peter-chief-apostle/accounts-peters-

denial-understanding-texts-motifs.

48. See Acts 2:37–42; 8:35–39; 16:14–15, 30–33.

49. See Acts 2:38; 18:8; Hebrews 10:22; John 3:5; Romans 6:1–11; Titus 3:5; 1 Peter 3:21; 1 Corinthians 12:13.

50. L. Michael White identifies the probable date of the house's initial construction as AD 232/233 and its renovation into a *domus ecclesiae* (domestic space converted into a church) as 240/241; see White, *The Social Origins of Christian Architecture*, vol. 2, *Texts and Monuments for the Christian Domus Ecclesiae in Its Environment* (Valley Forge, PA: Trinity Press, 1997), 124.

51. The summary in this paragraph draws upon those in Robin M. Jensen, *Baptismal Imagery in Early Christianity: Ritual, Visual, and Theological Dimensions* (Grand Rapids, MI: Baker, 2012), 2–3; Everett Ferguson, *Church History*, vol. 1, *From Christ to Pre-Reformation* (Grand Rapids, MI: Zondervan, 2005), 148–52; Everett Ferguson, *Baptism in the Early Church: History, Theology, and Liturgy in the First Five Centuries* (Grand Rapids, MI: Eerdmans, 2009), 855–56. See also Andrew B. McGowan, *Ancient Christian Worship: Early Church Practices in Social, Historical, and Theological Perspective* (Grand Rapids, MI: Baker, 2014), 135–82. Sources indicate efforts to avoid scandal and maintain sexual propriety by segregating male and female baptismal candidates during the parts of the ritual when they were disrobed and naked; see Jensen, *Baptismal Imagery*, 168–69.

52. The assistance of women deacons in baptismal rites is described in *Didascalia Apostolorum* (*Teachings of the Apostles*) 16 (third century) and *Apostolic Constitutions* 3.16.1–2, 4; 8.28.6 (fourth century); see Kevin Madigan and Carolyn Osiek, eds. and trans., *Ordained Women in the Early Church: A Documentary History* (Baltimore: Johns Hopkins University Press, 2005), 111–12, 115–16; *ANF* 7:431, 494. Other ministerial duties and qualities of female deacons are mentioned in many places in these documents; see Madigan and Osiek, *Ordained Women*, 106–16. For ancient inscriptions mentioning female deacons, see Ute E. Eisen, *Women Officeholders in Early Christianity: Epigraphic and Literary Studies* (Collegeville, MN: Liturgical Press, 2000), 158–198. The earliest written prayer for the ordination of women deacons, recorded in *Apostolic Constitutions* 8.19–20, evokes the biblical precedents of Miriam, Deborah, Anna, Huldah, Mary, and women who were gatekeepers of the ancient tabernacle and temple (*ANF* 7:492, https://www.newadvent.org/fathers/07158.htm). In the New Testament, Phoebe, evidently the person who delivered Paul's epistle to the Romans and likely read it to the members of the church in Rome, is called a deacon (Greek διάκονος, *diakonos*, translated "servant" in the KJV; see Romans 16:1). Pliny's Letter to Trajan (*Letters* 10.96), written circa AD 112,

mentions that Pliny tortured two female Christian slaves who were called deacons (Latin *ministrae*). For a thorough discussion of evidence of women deacons in early Christianity, see Madigan and Osiek, *Ordained Women*, 25–162. For more discussion in this volume about women and leadership in the ancient church, see chapter 4.

53. Egeria, *Itinerarium Egeriae* 47.2, in Ruth, Steenwyk, and Witvliet, *Walking Where Jesus Walked*, 61; see also McGowan and Bradshaw, *Pilgrimage of Egeria*, 114.

54. Sebastian Brock, *St Ephrem the Syrian: Hymns on Paradise* (Crestwood, NY: St Vladimir's Seminary Press, 1990), 67.

55. For a thorough, insightful examination of the art of the Dura baptistery, see Michael Peppard, *The World's Oldest Church: Bible, Art, and Ritual at Dura-Europos, Syria* (New Haven: Yale University Press, 2016).

56. See *Epistle of Barnabas* 15.8–9 (early second century); Justin, *Dialogue with Trypho* 138.1 (mid-second century); Augustine, *Epistle* 55.9.17, 13.23, 15.28; Augustine *Sermon* 260C.2–3; Jensen, *Baptismal Imagery*, 204–9. For other shapes of early Christian baptismal fonts, such as cruciform or womb-shaped fonts (and their symbolism), see Jensen, *Baptismal Imagery*, 160–65.

57. For example, see Jensen, *Baptismal Imagery*, 14–16, fig. 1.1; 70, fig. 2.1; 132–33, figs. 3.7–8.

58. *Didache* 7.3, in *The Apostolic Fathers: Greek Texts and English Translations*, 3rd ed., trans. Michael W. Holmes (Grand Rapids, MI: Baker, 2007), 355.

59. See, for example, Robin M. Jensen, "Material and Documentary Evidence for the Practice of Early Christian Baptism," *Journal of Early Christian Studies* 20, no. 3 (2012): 371–405; Jensen critiques Ferguson, *Baptism in the Early Church*, who had argued that immersion (submersion) was nearly always the practice.

60. Cyprian, *Epistle* 69.12 [75.12] (*ANF* 5:400–401); Ferguson, *Baptism in the Early Church*, 355.

61. *Shepherd of Hermas, Similitudes* 9.29-1-3=106.1–3; *Epistle of Barnabas* 6.11; Athenagoras, *On the Resurrection* 14. "When a child has been born to one of them [Christians], they give thanks to God; and if it should die as an infant, they give thanks the more, because it has departed life sinless." Aristides, *Apology* 15.11, *Early Christians Speak: Faith and Life in the First Three Centuries*, 3rd ed., trans. Everett Ferguson (Abilene, TX: Abilene Christian University Press, 1999), 53–54.

62. See Tertullian, *On Baptism* 18; see also *Apostolic Constitutions* 6.15, where this same rationale appears in a late fourth-century source. A few decades after Tertullian, both Origen (*Commentary on Romans* 5.9; *Homily on*

Leviticus 8.3) and Cyprian (*Epistle* 64 [58]) approved of infant baptism.

63. See also Galatians 3:27–29; 6:15; Cyprian, *Epistle* 64.2, 4 [58.2, 4].

64. See Origen, *Homily on Luke* 14.5.

65. See Origen, *Homily on Leviticus* 8.3.

66. Irenaeus, *Against Heresies* 2.22.4, in Ferguson, *Early Christians Speak*, 54.

67. See Augustine, *On the Merits and Forgiveness of Sins, and on the Baptism of Infants*, 1.23, 28, 39; 3.2, 7. See also the discussion in Ferguson, *Early Christians Speak* (1999), 57–60.

68. "They shall baptize the little children first. And if they can answer for themselves, let them answer." Tertullian, *On Baptism* 18, in Ferguson, *Early Christians Speak*, 55. See also *Apostolic Tradition* 21.3–5. In AD 418 the Council of Carthage forbade teachings that opposed infant baptism, and in the early sixth century the emperor Justinian made infant baptism mandatory.

69. For example, deaf Latter-day Saint priesthood holders using American Sign Language as they perform ordinances involving the laying on of hands may begin by laying on hands, then remove the hands to pronounce the words of confirmation and blessing in ASL, and then reimpose hands at the close of the prayer (with thanks to Doug Stringham for his assistance on this point). In April 2020, when the Church adjusted to the social distancing guidelines during the COVID-19 pandemic, it permitted a number of accommodations to ordinances, including, for example, allowing a priesthood leader who is responsible to oversee ordinances to observe them online when necessary; see "First Presidency Provides Guidance on How to Administer the Church in Challenging Times," Newsroom, The Church of Jesus Christ of Latter-day Saints, April 17, 2020, https://newsroom.churchofjesuschrist.org/article/guidance-administer-the-church-in-challenging-times.

70. Joseph Smith stated, "God judges men according to the use they make of the light which He gives them." Andrew Jensen, ed., *The Historical Record: A Monthly Periodical*, vol. 7 (Salt Lake City, 1888). See also Doctrine and Covenants 137:9. Paul said that prophecy would end, but charity, Christ's pure love, never would (see 1 Corinthians 13:8; compare Moroni 7:46–47). We Latter-day Saints may wonder whether baptisms of ancient Christians "counted." We are not their judges. Perhaps the Lord looked upon ancient Christians with a generosity similar to that expressed to Methodist minister James Covel in 1831: "I have looked upon thy works and I know thee. . . . Thine heart is now right before me at this time; and, behold, I have bestowed great blessings upon thy head" (Doctrine and Covenants 39:7–8). Compare with the words of Latter-day Saint scholar Stephen Robinson: "When Sidney Rigdon came to Joseph Smith in 1830, a month

after converting to Mormonism from being a Campbellite minister, he was told that his ministry *as a Protestant* had been like that of John the Baptist, who prepared the way for the fullness of the gospel (Doctrine and Covenants 35:4–5)." Craig L. Blomberg and Stephen E. Robinson, *How Wide the Divide? A Mormon and an Evangelical in Conversation* (Downers Grove, IL: InterVarsity Press, 1997), 165.

71. Cyprian, *Treatise 1* (trans. Ernest Wallis, ANF 5:275–76; altered).
72. See Cyprian, *Epistle 62*.
73. James D. G. Dunn, *Unity and Diversity in the New Testament: An Inquiry into the Character of Earliest Christianity*, 2nd ed. (London: SCM Press, 1990), 162; see also Paul J. Achtemeier, ed., *HarperCollins Bible Dictionary* (New York: HarperCollins, 1985), 616.
74. See, for example, Matthew 9:10–13; 11:19; Luke 7:36–50; 15:1–2; 19:1–10.
75. See Michael Peppard, "Early Christian Art and Ritual," in *The Routledge Handbook of Early Christian Art*, ed. Robin M. Jensen and Mark D. Ellison (London: Routledge, 2018), 275–76; see also Livia Bevilacqua, "Symbolic Aspects of the Mosaics in the Church of the Multiplication of the Loaves and Fishes at Tabgha," *Envisioning Worlds in Late Antique Art: New Perspectives on Abstraction and Symbolism in Late-Roman and Early-Byzantine Visual Culture (c. 300-600)*, ed. Anna Cecilia Olovsdotter (Berlin: DeGruyter, 2019), 208–28.
76. Additional connections between the feeding miracles and the sacrament of the Lord's Supper include the identical sequence of verbs in both stories. In Mark 6:41 (the feeding of the five thousand), Jesus *took* the bread, *blessed* it, *broke* it, and *gave* it to his disciples; Mark 14:22 states that at the Last Supper "Jesus took bread, and blessed, and brake it, and gave to them, and said, Take, eat: this is my body." Similarly, when Jesus dines with the two disciples he had met on the road to Emmaus, Luke 24:30 presents the same sequence of verbs: "And it came to pass, as he sat at meat with them, he took bread, and blessed it, and brake, and gave to them." Early Christians consciously connected Eucharistic worship with episodes from Jesus's ministry in which he shared food and drink with people; "he was known of them in breaking of bread" (Luke 24:35). For Christians in the centuries following the New Testament, Christ continued to be known in the breaking of bread—the sacrament/Eucharist.
77. Justin, *1 Apology 67* (circa AD 151–55; ANF 1:186; altered).
78. The outline in the box 6.11 draws upon Robin M. Jensen and J. Patout Burns, "The Eucharistic Liturgy in Hippo's Basilica Major at the Time of Augustine," in *Augustine through the Ages*, ed. Allan D. Fitzgerald (Grand Rapids, MI: Eerdmans, 1995), 335–38; Andrew B. McGowan, *Ancient*

Christian Worship: Early Church Practices in Social, Historical, and Theological Perspective (Grand Rapids, MI: Baker, 2014), 60–62; Ferguson, *Church History*, 248.

79. For example, see Hugh Nibley, *Mormonism and Early Christianity* (Salt Lake City: Deseret Book, 1987), 45–99, 355–434; Marcus von Wellnitz, "The Catholic Liturgy and the Mormon Temple," *BYU Studies* 21, no. 1 (1981): 3–35; Stephen E. Robinson, *Are Mormons Christians?* (Salt Lake City: Bookcraft, 1991), 96–103; Barry Robert Bickmore, *Restoring the Ancient Church: Joseph Smith and Early Christianity* (Ben Lomond, CA: Foundation for Apologetic Information and Research, 1999), 283–351; C. Wilfred Griggs, "Rediscovering Ancient Christianity," *BYU Studies* 38, no. 4 (1999): 73–90; see also the works cited in Gaye Strathearn, "The Valentinian Bridal Chamber in the Gospel of Philip," *Studies in the Bible and Antiquity* 1 (2009): 84n1.

80. See, for example, Strathearn, "The Valentinian Bridal Chamber," 83–103; Gaye Strathearn, "The Gnostic Context of the Gospel of Judas," *BYU Studies* 45, no. 2 (2006): 26–34.

81. See, for example, Kent P. Jackson, "Hugh Nibley, Old Testament and Related Studies [review]," *BYU Studies* 28, no. 4 (1988): 114–19; Douglas F. Salmon, "Parallelomania and the Study of Latter-day Scripture: Confirmation, Coincidence, or the Collective Unconscious?," *Dialogue: A Journal of Mormon Thought* 33, no. 2 (2000): 129–56; Taylor G. Petrey, "Siding with Heretics: Evaluating Hugh Nibley Today," *Studies in the Bible and Antiquity* 7 (2015): 66–70. However, some of these critiques may more fairly apply to scholars who have followed in Hugh Nibley's wake rather than to Nibley himself; for a careful analysis of Nibley's own methodology and thought, see Joseph Spencer, *Hugh Nibley*, Introductions to Mormon Thought series (Urbana, IL: University of Illinois Press, forthcoming).

82. Thomas J. Talley, *The Origins of the Liturgical Year* (New York: Pueblo, 1986); McGowan, *Ancient Christian Worship*, 217–260. For a book on the traditional Christian celebrations of Holy Week for Latter-day Saint readers, see Eric D. Huntsman and Trevan G. Hatch, *Greater Love Hath No Man: A Latter-day Saint Guide to Celebrating Holy Week* (Provo, UT: Religious Studies Center, Brigham Young University, forthcoming).

83. See, for example, Melito of Sardis, in Eusebius, *Ecclesiastical History* 4.26.14; Jerome, *Epistle* 46; Egeria, *Itinerarium Egeriae*; McGowan and Bradshaw, *The Pilgrimage of Egeria*; Edward David Hunt, *Holy Land Pilgrimage in the Later Roman Empire: AD 312–460* (Oxford: Clarendon, 1982); Wilkinson, *Jerusalem Pilgrims before the Crusades*; Dennis Trout, "Saints, Identity, and the City," in *Late Ancient Christianity*, ed. Virginia

Burrus, vol. 2 in A People's History of Christianity series (Minneapolis, MN: Fortress, 2005), 165–87.

84. See *Apostolic Tradition* 24.

85. See Robin M. Jensen, "Dining with the Dead: From the Mensa to the Altar in Christian Late Antiquity," in *Commemorating the Dead: Texts and Artifacts in Context. Studies of Roman, Jewish, and Christian Burials*, ed. Laurie Brink and Deborah Green (Berlin: De Gruyter, 2008), 107–143.

86. See Thomas Fisch and David G. Hunter, "Echoes of the Early Roman Nuptial Blessing: Ambrosiaster, *De peccato Adae et Evae*," *Ecclesia Orans* 11 (1994): 225–44; Mark Searle and Kenneth W. Stevenson, *Documents of the Marriage Liturgy* (Collegeville, MN: The Liturgical Press, 1992); David G. Hunter, "Wedding Rituals and Episcopal Power," in *The Oxford Handbook of Early Christian Ritual*, ed. Risto Uro, Juliette J. Day, Richard E. DeMaris, and Rikard Roitto (Oxford: Oxford University Press, 2020), 627–43; Philip L. Reynolds, *How Marriage Became One of the Sacraments* (Cambridge, UK: Cambridge University Press, 2016).

87. See *Apostolic Tradition* 2–3, 7–8, 12; Gregory of Nyssa, *On the Baptism of Christ*; Augustine, *On Baptism, Against the Donatists* 1.1.2; Ambrose, *On Virgins* 3.1.1; Ambrose, *On Virginity* 5.26; 7.39.

88. On early developments in the penitential system, see J. N. D. Kelly, *Early Christian Doctrines*, rev. ed. (New York: Harper and Row, 1978), 198–99, 436–40. Penance did not become a sacrament until the twelfth century.

89. Forms of this Trisagion (thrice-holy) hymn appear in the earliest liturgies; see, for example, *Anaphora of Addai and Mari* (third century) 21–22, in A. Gelston, *The Eucharistic Prayer of Addai and Mari* (Oxford: Clarendon Press, 1992), 119; *Liturgy of St James* 28 (*ANF* 7:543–44). On the joining of human and angelic prayers, see Origen, *Against Celsus* 8.34; R. M. M. Tuschling, *Angels and Orthodoxy: A Study in Their Development in Syria and Palestine from the Qumran Texts to Ephrem the Syrian* (Tübingen: Mohr Siebeck, 2007), 177–205 (chapter 3, "Angels and Human Prayers").

90. See Ephrem, *Hymns on Faith* 10.8, 10, 17; see Sebastian P. Brock and George A. Kiraz, ed. and trans., *Ephrem the Syrian: Select Poems* (Provo, UT: Brigham Young University Press, 2006), 200–13 (esp. 207); Sebastian Brock, ed. and trans., *Treasure-House of Mysteries: Explorations of the Sacred Text through Poetry in the Syriac Tradition* (Yonkers, NY: St Vladimir's Seminary Press, 2012), 275–79; *Liturgy of St James* 3, 42 (*ANF* 7:537, 548); *Liturgy of the Blessed Apostles* 11, 18 (*ANF* 7:564, 567). Some fifth-century continuations are included in the following: Sebastian Brock, *Fire from Heaven: Studies in Syriac Theology and Liturgy* (Burlington, VT: Ashgate, 2006), 236; Narsai, Homily 21, *On the Mysteries of the Church and on*

Baptism; Narsai, Homily 32, *On the Church and on the Priesthood.*

91. For example, see the *Liturgy of Saint John Chrysostom*, such as in Sacred Archdiocese of Thyateira and Great Britain, trans., *The Divine Liturgy of our Father among the Saints John Chrysostom* (Oxford: Oxford University Press, 1995), 44. For art, see Gabriele Mietke, "44A, B. Pair of Liturgical Fans (Rhipidia)," in *Byzantium and Islam: Age of Transition, 7th–9th Century*, ed. Helen C. Evans and Brandie Ratliff (New York: Metropolitan Museum of Art, 2012), 73; Marlia Mundell Mango, *Silver from Early Byzantium: The Kaper Koraon and Related Treasures* (Baltimore: Walters Art Gallery, 1986), 147–49, no. 31; Susan A. Boyd, "Art in the Service of the Liturgy: Byzantine Silver Plate," in *Heaven on Earth: Art and the Church in Byzantium*, ed. Linda Safran (University Park, PA: Pennsylvania State University Press, 1998), 160–62, 177–78; *Paten with the Communion of the Apostles*, AD 565–578, silver, 35 x 35 x 3.2 cm, 908 g, Cleveland Museum of Art, loan from the Dumbarton Oaks Collection, BZ. 1924.5 22.2019.

92. J. N. D. Kelly surveys the general theory of sacraments in the fourth through fifth centuries and its application to baptism, confirmation/chrism, penance, the eucharistic presence, and the eucharistic sacrifice: "In the fourth and fifth centuries little or no attempt was made, in East or West, to work out a systematic sacramental theology. The universal, if somewhat vague, assumption was that the sacraments were outward and visible signs marking the presence of an invisible, but none the less genuine, grace." Kelly, *Early Christian Doctrines*, 422; see also 422–55.

93. Augustine, *Sermon* 220, in *Sermons (184-229Z)*, ed. John E. Rotelle, trans. Edmund Hill, part 3, vol. 6 of The Works of Saint Augustine: A Translation for the 21st Century series (New York: New City Press, 1993), 200–201; syntax altered.

✳ 7 ✳

HUMAN
NATURE

Creation and the Fall

Gaye Strathearn

For as many as are led by the Spirit of God, they are
the sons [and daughters] of God. For ye have not
received the spirit of bondage again to fear; but ye
have received the Spirit of adoption whereby we cry,
Abba, Father. The Spirit itself beareth witness with
our spirit, that we are the children of God: And if
children, then heirs; heirs of God, and joint-heirs with
Christ; if so be that we suffer with him, that we may
be also glorified together.

—Romans 8:14–17[1]

As the psalmist contemplates the magnificence and wonder of God and his heavenly creations, he wonders why God takes an interest in humanity. "What are human beings that you are mindful of them, mortals that you care for them?" (Psalm 8:4 New Revised Standard Version). The psalmist's response to his own question reflected a very positive understanding of human nature: God made humans "a little lower than" himself, "crowned them with glory and honor," and gave them dominion over all his other creations (Psalm 8:5–8 NRSV).[2] The early Christians were fascinated with the nature of God's creations, especially of humans, and with the question of *why* God placed humans in a privileged position over his other creations. What is humanity's connection with God? What made them different from the rest of God's creations? These were important questions because the answers have significant implications for understanding not only the nature of human beings but also the broader topics of the natures of God and Christ, the role of free will in humans, the existence of evil, and the opportunity for our salvation (see box 7.1).[3]

In their efforts to better understand these issues, early Christian writers used the best tools that were available to them: scripture and the teachings of the Apostles. The scripture they used was the Septuagint—that is, the Greek translation of the Old Testament. The teachings of the Apostles were found in the burgeoning library of Christian texts, including many texts that would eventually become part of the New Testament.[4] The difficulty, however, was that while these texts gave important insights and clues for the questions, they were not systematic treatises that provided a definitive account of human nature;

Why It Matters

The early Christian writers had lots of questions about the nature of humanity and why they need Christ's work of salvation. There were a variety of ways that ancient Christians understood the implications of what it means that (1) humanity is created in the image of God and after God's likeness and that (2) humanity needs a Redeemer who can overcome the effects of sin. As Latter-day Saints, when we take time to study our questions and the answers we formulate, we can find nuggets of truth that can deepen our own understanding of our divine heritage and our potential as sons and daughters of God.

rather, they gave fragmentary hints, leaving it to later generations to put together into a coherent whole. The texts needed to be interpreted. Thus, some of their important interpretive tools included using scripture to interpret scripture, looking for "types" in the Old Testament, and using allegory to interpret scriptural stories and teachings. In addition, they drew on the best practices in human inquiry that were available from Greco-Roman philosophy (see box 7.2).

In discussing the nature of humanity, the foundational scriptural events that the early Christian writers turned to are the Genesis accounts of the creation of Adam and Eve and their experiences in the Garden of Eden. In particular, they concentrated on Genesis 1:26–27: "God said, 'Let us make humankind in our image, according to our likeness; and let them have dominion over the fish of the sea, and over the birds of the air, and over the cattle, and over all the wild animals of the earth, and over every creeping thing that creeps upon the earth.' So God created humankind in his image, in the image of God he created them; male and female he created them" (NRSV).[5] These verses place humans in an intermediary role between God and creation. On the one hand, like the declaration of the psalmist, early

> ### BOX 7.2 Philosophy and Early Christianity
>
> At the beginning of the second century, Justin Martyr calls Chris-
> tianity the one true philosophy and argues that this "philosophy is
> indeed one's greatest possession, and is most precious in the sight of
> God, to whom it alone leads us and to whom it unites us, and they in
> truth are truly holy men who have applied themselves to [this] phi-
> losophy."[6] Origen, writing in the third century, describes philosophy
> as a "handmaid" to Christianity (*Philocalia of Origen* 13.1).[7] At the
> beginning of the third century, Tertullian distanced the Church from
> philosophy when he famously asked: "What indeed has Athens to
> do with Jerusalem?" (*Prescription against Heretics* 7). In our day the
> First Presidency has taught that "philosophers including Socrates,
> Plato, and others, received a portion of God's light."[8] And we are
> taught: "Seek ye diligently and teach one another words of wisdom;
> yea, seek ye out of the best books words of wisdom; seek learning,
> even by study and also by faith" (Doctrine and Covenants 88:118).

Christian writers emphasize a theomorphic (see box 7.3) view of humanity that connects them with God. At the same time, humans are
also linked with the rest of God's creations, over whom they were giv-
en stewardship. Whereas God created each animal species "after their
kind" (Genesis 1:21, 24–25), humans were created distinct from the
rest of God's creations—they alone were created in his image, according to his likeness.

As foundational as this Genesis passage is for the early Christian
understanding of human nature, it also raised important questions
for early Christian theologians. What is the "image of God," and how
should it be understood? Should it be identified with the human
mind or soul, the body, the whole person, or moral virtue? Does the
image refer to humans or to Christ, and if the latter, does it refer to the
incarnate Christ or the transcendent Word of God?[9] What is God's

BOX 7.3   Theomorphism vs. Anthropomorphism

The term *theomorphism* refers to humans who have been created in the image of God. It stands in contrast to *anthropomorphism*, which refers to the idea that humans have created gods according to their own form and leads to "a certain humanization of God."[10] This approach, anthropomorphism, is evident in the description of the gods in the early writings of Homer and in a famous statement by Xenophanes: "If oxen <and horses> or lions had hands or could draw with hands and complete the works which men do, horses would draw pictures of gods like horses, and oxen like oxen, and they would make the bodies (of their gods) the sort which they themselves have in form."[11]

likeness? Is it synonymous with the image, or does the image and likeness each refer to unique characteristics? The reality is that Christians had different ways of understanding this passage. In the discussion that follows, we will look at some examples of early Christians' writings and see how they interpreted both the image and the likeness of God and what it meant for their understanding of humanity.

The second major aspect of understanding human nature deals with the Fall. As with the creation, the biblical account does not provide systematic answers and frequently leads to even more questions. When did the Fall take place? Who is responsible for the introduction of sin and death into the world created by God? Does responsibility for sin ultimately fall on God since he created humans with a nature that had a propensity to sin? Or on Adam and Eve, because of their choices in the Garden of Eden? Does each human bring sin and death to themselves because of their choices? Or is it a combination of all three? In asking these types of questions, early Christian writers were honestly trying to understand the nature of humans and their relationship with deity.

In contrast to the biblical text, the Book of Mormon authors frequently refer to the Fall of Adam and Eve even before the coming of Christ. The Brother of Jared taught that "we are unworthy before [the Lord]; because of the fall our natures have become evil continually" (Ether 3:2). Lehi taught that "the way is prepared from the fall of man" and that "the Messiah cometh in the fulness of time, that he may redeem the children of men from the fall" (2 Nephi 2:4, 26). Jacob taught that "the resurrection must needs come unto man by reason of the fall; and the fall came by reason of transgression; and because man became fallen they were cut off from the presence of the Lord" (2 Nephi 9:6). Alma taught Corianton that "the fall had brought upon all mankind a spiritual death as well as a temporal, that is, they were cut off from the presence of the Lord" (Alma 42:9).

It may be surprising to some that the term *Fall* is not found in the biblical text of Genesis 3, nor anywhere else in the Bible, to describe Adam and Eve's actions in the garden (see box 7.4). Rather, our earliest Jewish commentaries on the biblical story portray Adam as a patriarch, a hero, and a man of great wisdom (see Sirach 17:1–12; Wisdom of Solomon 10:1–2).[12] Prior to the fifth century AD, there was no notion that *all* human nature had been corrupted as a result of Adam and Eve's disobedience. Rather, the earliest Christians placed their emphasis on the redemption that comes through Christ. They are generally aware of the events in Genesis, but they do not make an effort to systematically interpret them. Adam is simply understood as a type for all humans. Just as his choices had implications for him, so likewise the choices for each human has implications for each of Adam and Eve's progeny. Rather than blaming God for creating humans with a sinful nature or condemning Adam for introducing sin into the world, early Christians turned to the serpent as the cause of sin and Cain's killing of Abel as the cause of death in mortality. After all, God cursed Cain for his actions (see Genesis 4:1–11; see also Moses 5:16–25), but there is no evidence in the biblical text that he cursed Adam and Eve for their actions.[13] Methodius, bishop of Olympus (AD 260–311), a town in southwest Turkey, may have been the first to use the term *Fall* to describe Adam and Eve's transgression: "But when it came to pass that, by transgressing the commandment (of God), *[Adam] suffered a terrible and destructive fall, being thus reduced to a state of death*, for this reason the Lord says that He came from heaven into (a human) life, leaving the ranks of the armies of angels."[14]

In what follows, I have chosen three early Christian theologians who give us some sense of the variety of interpretations: Irenaeus, a second-century Christian of Lyon (circa AD 130–202), Origen of Alexandria (circa AD 185–254), and Augustine, a fourth- and fifth-century theologian and philosopher as well as bishop of Hippo in Roman North Africa (AD 354–430). Both Irenaeus and Origen view Christ as the archetypal image of God and see a distinction between the image and the likeness. They also acknowledge that in some way either the image or the likeness was marred by humanity's use of their free will, which can only be fully rectified in Christ. But it was ultimately Augustine's view of "original sin" that became the most influential understanding of human nature, particularly in the Western Church.

Irenaeus

Irenaeus is one of the most influential Christian theologians during the second century.[15] His important five-volume work, commonly known as *Against Heresies*, was written toward the end of the second century (circa AD 185), with the aim of identifying and systematically overthrowing the teachings of other Christian groups whose theology Irenaeus strongly disputed. These groups taught, for instance, that the body was evil and that humans became spiritual only when "their flesh has been stripped off and taken away."[16] They also taught that God made some humans with a good nature and others with one that was inherently bad and that those with a bad nature are outside the scope of any type of salvation.[17] In order to refute these views, Irenaeus had to explain his own understanding of human nature—as created in the image and likeness of God.

Before discussing Irenaeus's view of humans as created in the image and likeness of God, it is important to recognize that, like many of the early Christian thinkers, he believed Christ was the image of the invisible God (see 2 Corinthians 4:4; Colossians 1:15). In addition, he believed that by nature Jesus was the *only* being who was eternally like God. "Who else is superior to, and more eminent than that man who was formed after the likeness of God, except the Son of God?"[18] So, when Irenaeus discusses God's creation of humans, his starting point is Christ, "who is the perfect image and likeness of God the Father." Therefore, when Irenaeus talks of humans as created in the image and likeness of God, he means that they are "created in the image and likeness of the Son" (compare Moses 2:27).[19]

His major emphasis is that human nature is "made up of soul and body," both of which are holy and can be saved.[20] Even though he makes a distinction between the image and likeness of God, he stresses that neither of them can achieve salvation without the other. It is the combination of the two of them that renders humans spiritual and perfect:

> Now God shall be glorified in His handiwork, fitting it so as to be conformable to, and modelled after, His own Son. For by the hands of the Father, that is by the Son and the Holy Spirit, man, and not [merely] a *part* of man, was made in the **likeness of God**. Now the soul and the spirit are certainly a part of *the* man, but certainly not the man; for the **perfect man** consists in the commingling and the union of the soul receiving the spirit of the Father, and the admixture of that fleshly nature which was molded after the image of God.[21]

Irenaeus identifies the human body as being formed after the "image of God," which he emphasizes again when he teaches that God "gave

Plato's *Cratylus* purportedly records a conversation between Socrates and Hermogenes: "For some say that the body is the grave . . . of the soul which may be thought to be buried in our present life. . . . Probably the Orphic poets were the inventors of the name, and they were under the impression that the soul is suffering the punishment of sin, and that the body is an enclosure or prison in which the soul is incarcerated, kept safe, as the name *sōma* [Greek for 'body'] implies, until the penalty is paid."[22] The Jewish historian Josephus describes the teachings of the Essenes using this idea: "For the view has become tenaciously held among them that whereas our bodies are perishable and their matter impermanent, our souls endure forever, deathless: they get entangled, having emanated from the most refined ether, as if drawn down by a certain charm into the prisons that are bodies. . . . sharing the view of the sons of Greece."[23]

[Adam's] frame the outline of His own form that the visible appearance too should be godlike—for it was as an image of God that man was fashioned and set on earth."[24] Thus, Irenaeus directly argues against those who taught that humans become spiritual only when "their flesh has been stripped off and taken away."[25] In his mind, the body is the vehicle that enables humans to perform righteous acts, so any view of a state of eternal righteousness must include the body.[26] For Irenaeus, therefore, people become spiritual, not because their nature is divested of their body but because they "partake of the spirit."[27] Thus, Irenaeus views the body as something to be embraced and as an important part of human nature. This interpretation of the divine image counters the platonic philosophical view that the image of God is located in the immaterial soul or intellect and that "the body is a tomb" that will eventually be discarded (see box 7.5).[28]

As important as the divine image in humans is to Irenaeus, he

▲ **FIGURE 7.1**   Relief carving of the creation of Eve, detail from the Vatican "Dogmatic" Sarcophagus, ca. 325, Museo Pio Cristiano. Christ rests his hand upon the head of the newly-created Eve in a gesture of blessing, as God the Father (seated) makes a speaking gesture that might also have been seen as a blessing. The image suggests a relatively positive view of human nature. Eve's diminutive size also suggests her child-like status, similar to how Irenaeus described Adam and Eve as created with "an innocent and childlike mind." Photo: Mark D. Ellison

also recognizes the importance of the "likeness of God," which he understands to include a spiritual aspect that encompasses both the soul and the image. Irenaeus taught that this spiritual element was given to humans when God breathed into them the breath of life that enabled them to become living souls (see Genesis 2:7).[29] Further, he taught that without this spiritual element a human was imperfect since by itself the soul may include the image of God but not the likeness.[30] Irenaeus sometimes understands this "likeness" or spiritual element to refer to humanity's rationality and freedom of choice, while at other times he sees it more specifically as the potential for what humans can ultimately become—the perfect human.[31] The combined elements of the flesh and the breath in the creation were intended so that humanity "became like God in inspiration as well as in frame."[32]

One of the central elements in Irenaeus's understanding of Adam and Eve's creation is that God endowed them with free will to obey "God voluntarily, and not by compulsion. For there is no coercion with God, but a good will [toward us] is present with Him continually."[33] This concept of humanity's free will is Irenaeus's refutation against those Christians who taught that God made some humans with a good nature and others with one that was inherently bad.[34] It does not make sense to Irenaeus that some humans were created with a good nature because they will not be able to comprehend good if their nature does not allow them the opportunity to choose

---

BOX 7.6   Opposition and Agency

Irenaeus's teachings have parallels with Lehi's teachings in the Book of Mormon. "For it must needs be, that there is an opposition in all things. If not so, my first-born in the wilderness, righteousness could not be brought to pass, neither wickedness, neither holiness, nor misery, neither good nor bad" (2 Nephi 2:11).

something different.[35] Likewise, if humans have been created good, then there is no merit in doing good—it is just the result of their nature. Similarly, if some humans are created with a bad nature, then neither can their actions be reprehensible.[36]

Irenaeus was aware of how Adam and Eve's choices were depicted while they were in the Garden of Eden (see Genesis 3). He acknowledges that their decision to eat of the fruit of the tree of knowledge of good and evil was in direct disobedience to God's command: "But of the tree of the knowledge of good and evil, thou shalt not eat of it" (Genesis 2:17).[37] But Irenaeus argues that although God had created Adam and Eve in his "image, after [his] likeness" and had endowed them with free will, he had not created them as fully developed beings. Rather, he argues, God created humans with a neutral nature, whereby they could either choose God's goodness or reject it.[38] To be sure, in their creation they were given tremendous responsibility to be stewards over all of God's creations—both the earth and the animals—but they still had to learn how to understand God and his commandments before they could reach their full potential. Irenaeus viewed Adam and Eve in the garden as children whose thoughts "were innocent and childlike" and "had need to grow so as to come to [their] full perfection."[39] Thus, Irenaeus understood their decisions in the Garden of Eden not as an act of rebellion but as an act of ignorance. Therefore, Adam and Eve could not be culpable for their choice to partake of the fruit of the tree of knowledge of good and evil because they were unable to conceive of, let alone understand, the nature of wickedness. As a result of their innocence, they were "easily led astray by [Satan]," whom Irenaeus describes as being jealous of "the man and looking on him with envy because of God's many favors which He had bestowed on the man."[40] Since Irenaeus claims that Adam repented of his disobedience, he argues that it is Satan, rather than Adam and Eve, who is the "the head and fount of sin."[41]

God's prohibition against partaking of the fruit was not to prevent Adam and Eve from having knowledge of good and evil. To a certain extent, the serpent was correct when he told Adam and Eve that if they partook of the fruit they would "be as the gods, knowing

▲ **FIGURE 7.2** Detail from the Vatican "Dogmatic" Sarcophagus, Museo Pio Cristiano, ca. 325. Relief carving of Christ giving Adam and Eve the symbols of their labors—a sheaf of wheat for Adam (symbolizing farming), and a sheep to Eve (symbolizing wool work); both symbols also foreshadow Christ as the "bread of life" and "lamb of God" who would redeem Adam and Eve and all humanity. Adam and Eve look towards Christ and do not appear ashamed or afraid but seem to be listening; off to the right, the serpent is coiled around a tree, set off by himself. Irenaeus held that it was the serpent, not Adam and Eve, who was "the author and originator of sin." Photo: Mark D. Ellison

good and evil" (Genesis 3:4). The problem was in the timing. Adam and Eve were still "unaccustomed to, and unexercised in, perfect discipline."[42] Drawing upon Paul's metaphor in 1 Corinthians 3:2 that he had to feed the Corinthian Saints milk before he could feed them meat, Irenaeus argues that Adam and Eve also needed time to grow before they would be ready to receive the knowledge of good and evil. The condemnation of their choice that later comes in Augustine's doctrine of original sin is not found in Irenaeus's writings. Instead, he emphasizes that God's response to their choice was to curse the earth and Satan, not Adam and Eve.[43]

However, Irenaeus did acknowledge that there were consequences for Adam and Eve's actions. They were cast out of the garden, removing them from the presence of God. In their new world they had to toil in the field to cultivate food and labor to bring forth children (see Genesis 3:14–19). In addition, Irenaeus understands their expulsion from the garden in a spiritual sense of them losing their God-likeness.[44] In part, the loss of the likeness meant that Adam and Eve's focus was no longer exclusively on God but was now diluted to some extent by the need to survive in a mortal environment: they now had to focus on the earthly choices before them.[45] As a result, even though they were made in the image of God, they were now removed from his presence and were, therefore, in need of a spiritual regeneration. For Irenaeus, while Adam and Eve are not the cause of sin in humanity, they did become types for the rest of humanity. "But this is Adam, if the truth should be told, the first formed man, of whom the Scripture says that the Lord spake, 'Let Us make man after Our own image and likeness,' and we are all from him: and as we are from him, therefore have we all inherited his title."[46]

Irenaeus argues that there are two interrelated ways that the likeness of God can be regained and perfected. On the one hand, this return to a state of likeness with God comes as people use their free will to receive and act upon the word of God.[47] But, on the other hand, he also emphasizes the important role that Christ played in helping humans recover what was lost by Adam and Eve. "When He [Christ] became incarnate, and was made man, he . . . furnished us, in a brief, comprehensive manner, with salvation; so that what we had lost in Adam—namely, to be according to the image and likeness of God—that we might recover in Christ Jesus."[48]

In summary, when Irenaeus thinks about the nature of humanity, he does not view it as being corrupted at the time of Adam and Eve's disobedience. Instead, he sees that event as a moment of learning for them. As a result, he does not limit his focus to a single moment; instead, he views human nature over the process of time—from their potential at creation to their growth and progress, until humans can eventually become regenerated beings.

> By this arrangement, therefore, and these harmonies, and a sequence of this nature, man, a created and organized being, is rendered after the image and likeness of the uncreated God—the Father planning everything well and giving His commands, the Son carrying these into execution and performing the work of creating, and the Spirit nourishing and increasing [what is made], but man making progress day by day, and ascending towards the perfect, that is, approximating to the uncreated One. For the Uncreated is perfect, that is, God. Now it was necessary that man should in the first instance be created; and having been created, should receive growth; and having received growth, should be strengthened; and having been strengthened, should abound; and having abounded, should recover [from the disease of sin]; and having recovered, should be glorified; and being glorified, should see his Lord. For God is He who is yet to be seen, and the beholding of God is productive of immortality, but immortality renders one nigh unto God.[49]

As Thomas G. Weinandy explains, Irenaeus gives us a very positive view of nature. Being human "clothes us with a dignity that is inconceivable, a dignity that pertains not to some spiritual aspect of our being, but to our very created humanness. It is the very humanness of human beings that, for Irenaeus, reflects who and what God is, for in making us human he made us in his likeness."[50]

Origen

The second example of a Christian author thinking about the nature of humanity is an Egyptian scholar and theologian named Origen Adamantus, more commonly known as Origen of Alexandria (circa AD 185–254). He was a brilliant thinker and a prolific writer.[51] Origen comes to the idea of human nature from a very different place than Irenaeus. While Irenaeus's view is grounded in the Genesis account of the creation of Adam and Eve and their actions in the Garden of Eden, Origen focuses his interpretations on the creation and a fall of souls outside of time as we know it. He was one of the first Christians to argue for, and develop, a systematic theology of the preexistence of souls in his work entitled *On First Principles.*

Origen's conclusions about the human soul's preexistence came from a combination of his nuanced reading of the scriptural texts and the philosophy of Plato, his work to understand and explain the origin of evil in the world, and especially his effort to understand how God could judge people as either good or evil before they came into being. If God is just and fair, he argued, then how can we explain the unequal states into which rational creatures are born? Origen specifically wanted to understand scriptural passages that say that God chose Jacob over Esau (see Genesis 25:22–26), even "loved Jacob and hated Esau" (Romans 9:11–14), and that God filled John the Baptist with the Holy Ghost (see Luke 1:41), while all of them were still in the womb—before they had time to act one way or another to merit those judgments. "How could they have been 'known by God'" if they had not yet been born? Without some type of existence before birth, he writes, "it would seem that God fills some with the Holy Spirit neither by judgement nor according to merits, and sanctifies [them] undeservedly."[52]

The difficulty that Origen found is that there is little in the Bible to suggest a premortal existence. One of the places that he turned to was Jeremiah 1:5: "Before I formed thee in the belly I knew thee; and before thou camest out of the womb I sanctified thee, and I ordained thee a prophet unto the nations."[53] But there does not appear to be a common interpretation of this verse among the Church

▲ **FIGURE 7.3** Mosaic of Jeremiah, San Vitale, Ravenna, sixth century. The Old Testament prophet Jeremiah unfurls a scroll representing his prophecies. He is represented along with Abraham and Moses as witnesses to God's covenant. Photo: Alamy

Fathers—Origen is the only one I have found who interprets it as referring to a premortal existence for Jeremiah instead of as referring to God's foreknowledge. Perhaps this is one reason why he introduced *On First Principles* by saying there are some things about which the scriptures do not contain very much information, and "while on other points [the Apostles] stated that things were so, [while] keeping silence about how or whence they are."[54] Origen recognizes the difficulty of going beyond what the scriptures and Apostles had taught and acknowledges that although he wrote "with great fear and caution," he felt comfortable "as best as we can, in matters of a kind needing discussion rather than definition."[55] This topic needed discussion because, for Origen, the righteousness of God was at stake.

Origen found the beginnings of a solution to this scriptural conundrum in Plato's teachings about the preexistence of souls (see box 7.7).[56] Plato believed that the essence of humans was found in the soul, which he identifies as an immaterial, intellectual essence. The human body, for Plato, was a "tomb" that entrapped the soul during its mortal phase of existence.[57] In addition, because he considered souls to be eternal, Plato accepted that there must be some type of premortal existence. With this concept of souls, Origen found tools to help him explain human nature in a way that would both explain the origin of evil while still vindicating the perfection and goodness of God and, at the same time, explain how God could legitimately judge people before they were born into mortality.[58]

Origen accepted Plato's general concept of souls: they are rational beings who possess "free will and volition" and "according to their proper nature, [are] bodiless," although he argues that they never exist without some form of a body.[59] Origen argues that although souls are immortal, in the premortal realm they were created by God.[60] This characteristic was important for Origen since some early Christians were uncomfortable with the notion of preexistent souls because they felt such a teaching blurred the lines between souls and God. Origen's insistence that they were created beings was intended to make a clear statement that he did not consider them to be eternal beings of the same nature as God. "Uncreated" and "eternal" were terms reserved

> **BOX 7.7**   **What Is a Soul?**
>
> When ancient Christians used the term *soul*, they did so in a differ-
> ent way than members of The Church of Jesus Christ of Latter-day
> Saints often understand it today. For example, Doctrine and Cove-
> nant 88:15 teaches that "the spirit and the body are the soul of man."
> But ancient Christians made a distinction between human body and
> the soul. The Bible uses "soul" (Hebrew *nephesh*; Greek *psyche*) in a
> variety of ways, including the life force that animates God's creations
> (see Genesis 2:7; 9:10, 16) and departs at the time of death (see Luke
> 12:20), human feelings or emotions (see Matthew 26:38; John 12:27;
> Romans 2:9), the part of humanity that is subject to temptation (see
> 1 Peter 2:11), and the part of humans that receives salvation from
> death (see 1 Peter 1:9). In these aspects, the use of the term *soul*
> is closer to some of its uses in the Book of Mormon (see 2 Nephi
> 4:15–17, 26–28, 30–31; Alma 36:12, 15–16).

for the Godhead: the Father, Christ, and the Holy Spirit. In contrast
to Irenaeus's view of explaining human nature through his interpretation of the creation of humanity in Genesis 1–2, Origen sees the locus
of human nature situated in these preexistent souls.

Origen's understanding of a "fall" is also situated outside of the
Genesis description of the events in Eden. Like Irenaeus, Origen also
disavows the argument of some Christians that God is responsible
for the existence of evil in the world because he created some souls
that were evil by nature.[61] For Origen this position is untenable: God
is by nature wholly good and, therefore, is unable to create evil.[62]
Instead, Origen argues that souls possess free will whereby they are
capable of making choices, which they are accountable for and which
either draw them closer to the goodness of God or move them away
from it.[63] Although Origen claims that Christ also has a rational soul,
he argues that Christ "chose to love righteousness" and "adhered

to it unchangeably and inseparably, so that the firmness or purpose and immensity of affection and inextinguishable warmth of love destroyed all thought of alteration or change," which means that Christ's soul did not have "any thought or possibility of sin."[64] In this, Christ is unique. All other souls, to one extent or another, make choices that move them away from the good that exists in God, resulting in a type of fall. Origen describes this fall as a "cooling" that comes as the soul's choices move it away from the divine fire, resulting in a hierarchy of souls.[65] For example, Origen describes the devil as "one of the wicked spirits" and then goes on to ask, "What can be found colder than these?"[66] Just as hot air rises and cold air falls, so too, for Origen, all souls, with the exception of Jesus Christ, turn from the warmth of God's light, and they fall. But Origen is clear that even if a

---

BOX 7.8 **We Are All Adam and Eve**

Origen viewed Adam as a symbol for all humanity. Discussing Paul's teachings in Corinthians 15:21–22, he teaches: "For 'in Adam' (as the Scripture says) 'all die', and were condemned in the likeness of Adam's transgression, the word of God asserting this not so much of one particular individual as of the whole human race. For in the connected series of statements which appears to apply as to one particular individual, the curse pronounced upon Adam is regarded as common to all (the members of the race), and what was spoken with reference to the woman is spoken of every woman without exception. And the expulsion of the man and woman from paradise, and their being clothed with tunics of skins (which God, because of the transgression of men, made for those who had sinned), contain a certain secret and mystical doctrine (far transcending that of Plato) of the soul's losing its wings, and being borne downwards to earth, until it can lay hold of some stable resting-place" (*Against Celsus* 4.40; emphasis original).

▲ **FIGURE 7.4** Wall fresco of Psyche and Cupid, Catacomb of Domitilla, Rome, third century. In Roman art, Psyche (depicting the soul) was personified as a winged female; many Romans, including Roman Christians, asked that the image of Psyche be depicted on their tombs, perhaps to represent the departed soul (psyche) of the deceased. Photo: Josef Wilpert, *Die Malereien der Katakomben Roms* (Freiburg: Herder, 1903), Taf. 53 (public domain)

soul has cooled down, it "has not lost the power of restoring itself to that condition of fervor in which it was at the beginning."[67]

This concept of the soul's creation and fall outside of time influences the way that Origen understands the creation account in Genesis. He argues that Genesis describes two separate and distinct creations, reflecting his dualist understanding of humanity consisting of a soul and a body. He interprets Genesis 1:26–27 as a description of the first creation—a creation of souls, "our inner person, invisible, incorporeal, incorruptible, and immortal which is made 'according to the image of God.'"[68] The second creation takes place in Genesis 2:7, where the physical body is formed out of "the dust of the ground" and animated when the breath of life is breathed in its nostrils.[69]

Origen does not agree with Irenaeus's view that Genesis 2:7 is a positive continuation of the creation of humans. Although Origen argues that both the soul and the material body are created, he views them as being different. The soul is the seat of human nature, but the body is a source of corruption: "Wherever bodies are, corruption follows immediately."[70] He views the body as something that "weighs down the soul" and adversely affects its ability to understand the things of righteousness. Furthermore, the mortal body will ultimately be discarded, ceasing to exist after death.[71] Only the soul is resurrected (based on his reading of 1 Corinthians 15:44–50).[72] Origen therefore insists, "We do *not* understand . . . this man indeed whom Scripture says was made 'according to the image of God' to be corporeal. For the form of the body *does not* contain the image of God."[73] This differs from Irenaeus.

Like Irenaeus, however, Origen also makes a distinction between the image and the likeness of God. He uses Genesis 1:26–27 as his proof text for this distinction. Although God planned to make "humans in our image, after our likeness," he only made them "in his image" according to Genesis 1:27. Origen then notes that God "was silent about the *likeness*."[74] He construes this silence to mean that the likeness will only be fully attained by the believers at the end of the world: while humans "received the honor of God's image in his first creation . . . the perfection of God's likeness was reserved for [them] at the consummation" of the world.[75]

Like Plato before him, Origen understood that the highest good "towards which every rational being hastens . . . is to become as far as possible like God"—although Origen insists that Genesis 1:26 taught this principle long before the philosophers such as Plato.[76] Origen's perspective on rational beings, as we would expect, includes a Christian modification. Since the Word is the true image of God and eternal Son of God, he is like God in a way that humans are not: he is eternal, "born of [God] but is yet without any beginning," and is the "Son by nature" rather than "through adoption in the Spirit," which is how humans become "the children of God" (see Romans 8:15).[77]

In contrast, humans are not like God in the same sense that Jesus

BOX 7.9 **Origen and the Premortal Fall**

Origen discusses a "fall" in the context of preexistence, so he only deals briefly with the biblical account in Genesis 3. He acknowledges Eve's part in the events in Eden—"Sin began from the woman and then spread to the man" (compare Sirach 25:24; 1 Timothy 2:14)—but then he goes on to connect Eve with Elizabeth and Mary, the mother of Jesus Christ. "In the same way, salvation had its first beginnings from women. Thus the rest of women can . . . imitate as closely as possible the lives and conduct of these holy women [Elizabeth and Mary] whom the Gospel now describes."[78]

is. By Origen's definition, humans are souls who "through negligence . . . [fall] away from the pure and complete reception of God." But he acknowledges that even in that fallen state, the human soul "always contains within itself some seeds," which have the potential for goodness. Mortality is, thus, a time for the fallen souls to cultivate those seeds and bring them to a full spiritual fruition with "diligence and the imitation of God." As they do so, the soul "is renewed according to the image and likeness of God who created him." These spiritual rebirths enable souls to eventually return to their initial unity with God.[79] Thus, Origen emphasizes that through Christ, the true image and likeness of God, the human potential to be transformed and return to God's presence, can be unlocked.

Another time, he compared the man who descended from Jerusalem to Jericho in the story of the good Samaritan (see Luke 10:25–37) to "Adam who was driven from paradise into the exile of this world."[80] If understood in terms of his teachings on the fall of the soul, this comparison may imply that Origen understood paradise to be in heaven.[81]

Origen does not see human nature as something that is either

▲ **FIGURE 7.5** Embroidered Roundel with the Annunciation and Visitation, Victoria and Albert Museum, London, seventh or eighth century. This silk embroidered linen roundel was likely once part of a tunic worn in either an ecclesiastical setting or by a lay person. Mary is identifiable by her striped maphorion (garment covering her head and shoulders) dotted with stars. She holds her spindle and has a textile basket next to her as she is greeted by Gabriel on the left; this is the moment she becomes Theotokos or Mother of God. On the right, Mary embraces Elizabeth who recognizes Mary's blessed nature as she bears the child Jesus, also recognized by John leaping in her womb. Photo: Scala/Art Resource NY

Latter-day Saints vs. Origen on the Preexistence

While it is true that Latter-day Saint readers will resonate with some aspects of Origen's teachings on preexistent souls, they will likely not agree with all his interpretations. We Latter-day Saints derive our understanding of the premortal life from our unique Restoration scripture that was unavailable to Origen (see Moses 3:5; 4:1–4; 6:51; Abraham 3:22–26; Doctrine and Covenants 93:29; 138:53–56). Origen, however, developed his ideas about premortality from a careful reading of the Bible but also from Platonism, which argued that our existence on earth is just a shadow of a higher spiritual plane where immortal, invisible, and infinite souls preexist its entry into a body.[82]

static or eternally predetermined. Rather, he sees the potential for fallen souls in mortality to grow, with the free will to make choices that will enable them to draw into closer contact with the goodness of God, with the goal of becoming like him. This likeness is more than an intellectual likeness, although it is certainly that, but it is also an ethical and moral likeness, where humans seek to attain many of the virtues that are contained in God's transcendent goodness.

Later Christians ultimately rejected Origen's explanation on the origin of the soul in premortality because, they argued, it was based on Platonism and not scripture. It was eventually condemned as heresy by the Second Council of Constantinople in AD 553. As John Anthony McGuckin noted, "While Origen himself felt he was always working within the tradition of ecclesiastical wisdom, as it had been established by the Scriptures and apostles on the basis of the teachings of Jesus . . . his successors were not so sure he had always followed his own advice."[83] Origen's fall from favor, long after his death, seems to have been impacted by the developing political and religious emphasis on doctrinal unity, greater emphasis on a literal interpretation of scripture, and the rise in importance of Plato's student, Aristotle, who argued that the true self consisted of both the body and the soul and that some parts of the soul cannot be separated from the body.[84]

Early Christians proposed a number of alternate interpretations to that of Origen's creation of souls, but two seem to have gained the most long-lasting traction in Christian thought.[85] First, Tertullian and Gregory of Nyssa argued that souls are transmitted from parents to children in the act of conception.[86] This doctrine, known as *traducianism*, was, according to Jerome, the major interpretation in the Western Church in his day.[87] Second, Jerome himself advocated for the doctrine of *creationism*, which argues that God is continually making souls for each individual at the time of their "conception, birth, or sometime in between."[88]

Both Irenaeus and Origen are examples of Church Fathers who viewed evil as something that is outside of God's creation of humanity. It was something that came into existence because of moral weakness on the part of humans—or in Origen's case, their souls—because of their independent use of their free will. In the fourth and fifth centuries, the tide began to change, and although not the first to talk about original sin, the most influential proponent of it was a North African theologian and philosopher by the name of Augustine.

Augustine

Augustine was a convert to Christianity. He grew up in a family with a Christian mother and a pagan father.[89] He was baptized in AD 387 by Ambrose, Bishop of Milan (AD 374–397).

In his early writings, Augustine seems to have had a positive view of human nature as it is found in the human soul: "Of all things the soul is nearest to God."[90] As we have seen with both Irenaeus and Origen, Augustine also understands the soul in terms of its reasoning capacity. Augustine views the importance of this reasoning capacity in two ways: (1) it is the essential characteristic that makes humans superior to God's other creations, and (2) it is the vehicle by which humans can become immortal.[91] "Souls will return to bodies in which no unhappiness can be left. Such bodies can only be those which God has in mind when He promises to make souls in union with their immortal bodies, blest forever."[92] Like others before him, it is the soul or "the interior man, where reason and intellect reside" that is the image of God.[93]

The formulation of Augustine's teachings on original sin developed over time and seems to have been influenced by his own sense of sinfulness and need for the grace of Christ.[94] Like many of the Greek Fathers, including Irenaeus and Origen, Augustine also believes that Adam and Eve were born into a state where they had free will and, thus, had the ability to cleave unto God and not to sin. In addition, Augustine argues that through complacency or pride they turned from the light of divine wisdom and so were deceived. Thus, pride was the result of Adam and Eve's misuse of their free will to cleave to God. Romans 5:12 became an important scriptural text for him: "By one man sin entereth into the world." Unlike Irenaeus, Augustine views Adam as fully culpable because he "sinned knowingly and deliberately."[95] Even more significantly, Augustine rejects the idea that Adam is only a type for the rest of humanity, who also sin. Instead, he argues that Adam's guilt is passed down to all of humanity: "By the evil will of that one man all sinned in him, since all were that one man, from whom, therefore, they individually derived original sin."[96] For Augustine, it was not just that Adam's guilt was passed on to humanity; it was also that the subsequent corruption to his nature was inherited by his posterity. This corruption means that humanity is motivated by self-love more than their love of God. Augustine feels that this state of corruption cannot be changed by a simple act of free will or a choice to change. He firmly believes that this corrupted human nature could only be healed by divine grace—something that humans must trust in and actively seek to obtain (compare Mosiah 3:19).

While the concept of original sin is not found in the Bible (although certain passages are later interpreted through that lens), there

▲ **FIGURE 7.6**   Adam and Eve vignette from the Junius Bassus sarcophagus, 359 (Vatican Treasury Collection, Saint Peter's Basilica), depicting Adam and Eve turning away from each other and looking downward, details that emphasize the ideas of shame, sin, fallenness, and the need for redemption. Photo: Scala/Art Resource NY

is evidence that in the Western Church some foundational ideas for Augustine were introduced by his predecessors.[97] Two examples of people whose teachings laid the foundation for Augustine's doctrine of original sin are Tertullian and Ambrosiaster (or Pseudo-Ambrose).

Unlike Origen, Tertullian believes that souls consist of bodies that mirror the physical body and that they are created from the souls of their parents at the moment of conception.[98] This is a theory of seminal identity, which imagines that every soul derives from Adam, and is then disseminated among his posterity; every soul, therefore, "by reason of its birth, has its nature in [fallen] Adam until it is born again in Christ."[99] Seminal identity laid one of the foundations for Augustine's idea of original guilt.

Another important precursor is Ambrosiaster, a late fourth-century commentator on Romans. We know little about this author's life, but it is his mistranslation of Romans 5:12 that provides "the scriptural proof-text for Augustine's theology."[100] The Greek text of Romans 5:12 reads, "Therefore, just as sin came into the world through one man, and death came through sin, and so death spread to all *because* [Greek *eph hō*] all have sinned" (NRSV; emphasis added). The emphasis here is that like Adam, all have sinned. That sense is dramatically changed in the Latin translation and Ambrosiaster's subsequent interpretation. The Greek text's *eph hō* (because) is translated in the Latin version as *in quo* (in whom). Ambrosiaster's commentary on this translation reads as follows:

> "*In whom*—that is, in Adam—*all sinned*" [Romans 5:12]. Although he is speaking of the woman, he said *in whom* because he was referring to the race, not to a specific type. It is clear, consequently, that *all sinned in Adam as a lump* (*quasi in massa*). Once he was corrupted by sin, those he begat were all born under sin. All sinners, therefore, derive from him, because we are all from him.[101]

Ambrosiaster's interpretation becomes one of the bedrocks upon which Augustine develops his doctrine of original sin. Seven or eight years after his baptism, we see something of the influence of Ambrosiaster's commentary on Augustine as he begins to think about the impact of sin on human nature. In writing to counter the teaching of some "heretics," Augustine teaches:

> Given that our nature sinned in paradise, we are [now] formed through a mortal begetting by the same Divine Providence, not according to heaven, but according to earth . . . not according to the spirit, but according to the flesh, and *we have all become one mass of clay . . . a mass of sin.* Since therefore we have forfeited our reward through sinning, and since, in the absence of God's mercy, we as sinners deserve nothing other than eternal damnation, who then does the man from this mass think he is that he can answer God and say: "Why have you made me this way?"[102]

Notice the similarity of thought between Ambrosiaster's "all sinned in Adam *as a lump*" and Augustine's "because our nature sinned in paradise," all humans have "all become one mass of clay, a mass of sin." His understanding of the effect of Adam and Eve's choices in the Garden of Eden was very different from the Greek Fathers, such as Irenaeus, who believed that humanity shared in the effects of our first parents' choice but not the collective guilt that Augustine espoused.[103] As we have already seen, Origen argued that souls were punished for their individual sins.

Perhaps one of the aspects of Augustine's teachings on original sin that may seem harsh to modern readers is his certainty "that every soul, *even the soul of an infant*, requires to be delivered from the binding guilt of sin." Yet, as Augustine continues this explanation, we see the reason for his emphasis on human guilt: "There is no deliverance except through Jesus Christ and Him crucified."[104] Further, "By the water . . . which holds forth the sacrament of grace in its outward form, and by the Spirit who bestows the benefit of grace in its inward power, cancelling the bond of guilt, and restoring natural goodness, the man deriving his first birth originally from Adam alone, is regenerated in Christ alone."[105] Infant baptism was practiced long before Augustine, but he was the one who provided the theological underpinnings for its practice (see box 6.8).[106] Augustine concluded that if death is the punishment for sin, and some infants die, then they

BOX 7.11 Pelagianism

Not everyone agreed with Augustine's teachings. Opposition primarily came from a group of Christians known as the Pelagians. Their
leader, Pelagius, was a British monk who went to study law in Rome
in AD 380. His rigorous practice of asceticism and his oratory skills
helped him to become well known and praised as a man of great
moral standing. His reputation was known to Augustine (see Augustine, *Proceedings of Pelagius* 46). In AD 410 Pelagius fled from Rome
to escape the invading Visigoths and moved to Africa and then on to
Palestine, where he died. His theological teachings were carried on
by his followers. Pelagius taught that human nature is fundamentally
good and that sin only comes about through personal actions (see
Pelagius, *A Letter of Pelagius to Demetrius* 2–3; Augustine, *On Nature
and Grace* 19.21).[107] Ultimately, Pelagianism was condemned at the
First Council of Ephesus in AD 431.

must need the Atonement of Jesus Christ to be redeemed from death.

Augustine's teachings on original sin were confirmed by many
Councils, especially the Second Council of Orange (AD 529), and his
teachings became doctrine in the Western Church. But if that was all
modern readers knew about Augustine's teachings, they would miss
the mark. His teachings on original sin were a means to an end rather
than the end itself. The "end" for him was to help people understand
the vital need for divine grace. He is most famous for his focus on the
remission of Adam's sin, but he also recognized that humans sin individually, for which they are also indebted to God's grace. For Augustine, even if theoretically humans never sinned, they would still need
access to Christ; human choice will never be sufficient to change human nature. That change can only come from God, through his Son,
and his grace is sufficient to overcome both the sin of Adam and Eve
and our personal sins.

Conclusion

In this chapter we have touched on just three examples to represent some of the various ways the Church Fathers struggled to understand more deeply the implications of biblical passages about the nature of humanity. The variety of interpretations developed because the biblical record lacks any systematic doctrine of human nature. While the Genesis accounts of the creation and the events in the Garden of Eden provide some clues, they also raise questions about the scriptural meaning and the implications for understanding the age-old questions about the relationship between God and humans, the purpose of creation, the role of evil, and the eventual destiny for humanity.

Irenaeus, Origen, and Augustine each devoted their lives to the study of the scriptures and the apostolic interpretations of them. Rather than focusing on the *differences* between the way they understood the question of human nature, there is value in honoring their dedication and consecration in their search to better understand the nature of humanity. Although modern Latter-day Saint readers may disagree with some of their conclusions, we can find areas in which we resonate with their teachings—for example, Origen's view that before mortality God created intelligences who had agency, and the use of that agency had implications for their mortal experience; Irenaeus's view that the human body was the "image of God" and that Adam and Eve were in a state of innocence in the garden of Eden; and Augustine's emphasis on humanity's critical dependence on the atoning sacrifice of Jesus Christ. We can also resonate with all of their teachings on the goodness of God and the expectation that whatever our nature, because of Christ, we can have hope that eventually we can also become good, as God and Christ are.

Notes

1. I would like to thank the peer reviewers who made very helpful suggestions. I would also like to especially thank Jason Combs for all of the help that he gave me with this chapter.

2. This NRSV translation reflects the reading found in the Septuagint (LXX). The King James version, however, uses the Masoretic text and therefore reads, "For thou hast made him a little lower than the angels."

3. On the natures of God and Christ, see chapter 8.

4. For more detailed discussions on the authoritative texts used by the early Christians, see Daniel Becerra, "The Canonization of the New Testament," in *New Testament History, Culture, and Society: A Background to the Texts of the New Testament*, ed. Lincoln H. Blumell (Provo, UT: Religious Studies Center, Brigham Young University; Salt Lake City, UT: Deseret Book, 2019), 772–85. See also chapter 3 in this volume.

5. The King James version of the Bible uses an androcentric translation. At times, as here in their translation of Genesis 1:26–27, both the language and the context indicate a more inclusive meaning. In Hebrew the word *'adam* has numerous meanings. It can refer to a specific man called Adam, but it can also refer to the broader concept of humanity in general, which seems to be the case here when Genesis 1:27 specifically says that both male and female were created in the image of God. Therefore, I have chosen to use gender-inclusive language in this chapter. Some early Christian writers were somewhat ambiguous on whether women were also created in the image of God. John Chrysostom, for example, noted that "when God formed her [Eve], he also used the same words in both the fashioning of man [male] and the making of the woman. For just as He said in man's regard, 'Let us make man [humankind] in our image and likeness' and not 'Let there be man [humankind]' so also He did not say in her regard, 'Let there be a woman,' but rather, 'Let us make a helper for him'—not simply a helper but, 'one like unto him,' showing again [her] equality of honor." Chrysostom, *Patrologia Graeca* 54:594, in Frederick G. McLeod, *The Image of God in the Antiochene Tradition* (Washington, DC: Catholic University of America Press, 1999), 198–99. Others interpreted Genesis 1:26–27 through the lens of 1 Corinthians 11:7–9; see Maryanne Cline Horowitz, "The Image of God in Man: Is Woman Included?," *Harvard Theological Review* 72, no. 3/4 (1979): 175–206.

6. *Dialogue with Trypho* 2 in *Saint Justin Martyr: The First Apology, The Second Apology, Dialogue with Trypho, Exhortation to the Greeks, Discourse to the Greeks, The Monarchy or The Rule of God*, trans. Thomas B. Falls, vol. 6 in The Fathers of the Church: A New Translation series (Washington, DC:

Catholic University Press, 1948), 149.

7. *The Philocalia of Origen*, comp. St. Basil of Caesarea and Gregory Nazianzen, trans. Rev. George Lewis (Edinburgh: T. & T. Clark, 1911), 57.

8. "Statement of the First Presidency regarding God's Love for All Mankind," February 15, 1978, quoted in James E. Faust, "Communion with the Holy Spirit," *Ensign*, May 1980, 12.

9. Frances Young, "From Image to Likeness: Incarnation and Theosis," in *God's Presence: A Contemporary Recapitulation of Early Christianity* (New York: Cambridge University Press, 2013), 149.

10. Christoph Markschies, *God's Body: Jewish, Christian, and Pagan Images of God*, trans. Alexander Johannes Edmonds (Waco, TX: Baylor University Press, 2019), 21.

11. Fragment 15 in Hermann Diels, *Die Fragmente der Vorsokratiker: Griechisch und Deutsch,* 7th ed., ed. Walther Kranz (Berlin: Weidmannsche Verlagsbuchhandlung, 1954). For a more detailed discussion, see Markschies, *God's Body*, 20–25.

12. See the discussion in John E. Toews, *The Story of Original Sin* (Eugene, OR: Pickwick Publication, 2013), 15–40; Igal German, *The Fall Reconsidered: A Literary Synthesis of the Primeval Sin Narratives against the Backdrop of the History of Exegesis* (Eugene, OR: Pickwick Publications 2016), 34–51.

13. In Genesis 3, the serpent is cursed (3:14) and the ground is cursed (3:17), but Adam and Eve are not cursed. See Irenaeus, *Against Heresies* 3.23.3; see also Henri Rondet, *Original Sin: The Patristic and Theological Background*, trans. Cajetan Finegan (Staten Island, NY: Alba House, 1972), 39–40.

14. Methodius of Olympus, *The Banquet of the Ten Virgins*, Discourse 3–*Thaleia* 6; emphasis added; William R. Clark, trans., *Ante-Nicene Fathers* 6:318. I am grateful for Jason Combs in helping me with this reference.

15. See Toews, *The Story of Original Sin*, 51.

16. Irenaeus, *Against Heresies* 5.6.1. English translation *Ante-Nicene Fathers*, vol. 1. In this chapter, all quotations from Irenaeus, *Against Heresies* are from this source.

17. Irenaeus, *Against Heresies* 4.37.2. Origen also argued against these teachings of divergent natures; see Origen, *First Principles* 2.9.6. For a discussion of the three groups of humans in Irenaeus, see Denis Minns, *Irenaeus* (Washington, DC: Georgetown University Press, 1994), 13–15. See also Irenaeus, *Against Heresies* 1.5.1; 1.7.5; Clement of Alexandria, *Excerpts from Theodotus* 54.1–2; 56.1–4.

18. Irenaeus, *Against Heresies* 4.33.4.

19. Thomas G. Weinandy, "St. Irenaeus and the *Imago Dei*," *Logos: A Journal of Catholic Thought and Culture* 6, no. 4 (2003): 19.

20. Irenaeus, *Demonstration of Apostolic Preaching* 2. In this chapter, all quotations from this source are from *St. Irenaeus: Proof of the Apostolic Preaching*, trans. Joseph P. Smith, vol. 16 in The Ancient Christian Writers (New York: Newman Press, 1952).

21. Irenaeus, *Against Heresies* 5.6.1; emphasis original. See also Irenaeus, *Against Heresies* 4.preface.4. Methodius also saw human nature as consisting of both the soul and the body. At the creation, humans were different from other living creatures because they were "given the form and image of God, with every part accurately finished, after the very original likeness of the Father and the only-begotten Son." Methodius, *Discourse on the Resurrection* 3.4–5.

22. Plato, *Cratylus* 400C; Benjamin Jowett, trans., in *Plato: The Collected Dialogues, including the Letters*, ed. Edith Hamilton and Huntington Cairns, Bollingen Series 71 (Princeton: Princeton University Press, 1994).

23. Josephus, *Jewish War* 2.154–55 (2.8.11); Steve Mason, trans., *Flavius Josephus: Translation and Commentary, vol. 1B; Judean War 2* (Leiden: Brill, 2008), 123–24.

24. Irenaeus, *Demonstration of the Apostolic Preaching* 11.

25. Irenaeus, *Against Heresies* 5.6.1.

26. Irenaeus, *Against Heresies* 2.29.2.

27. Irenaeus, *Against Heresies* 5.6.1.

28. Peter C. Bouteneff, *Beginnings: Ancient Christian Readings of the Biblical Creation Narrative* (Grand Rapids, MI: Baker Academic, 2008), 82. An exception to the general patristic view may be found in a fourth-century group of Christians known as the sect of the Audians. These Christians were anthropomorphists and believed that God had a bodily form which the human body replicates; see Epiphanius, *Refutation Against All Heresies* 70.9; see also Theodoret, *Ecclesiastical History* 4.9.

29. See Irenaeus, *Demonstration of the Apostolic Preaching* 11.

30. Irenaeus, *Against Heresies* 5.6.1.

31. For "likeness" as humanity's rationality and freedom of choice, see Irenaeus, *Demonstration of Apostolic Preaching* 11; Smith, *St. Irenaeus, Proof of the Apostolic Preaching*, 33; *Against Heresies* 4.4.3; 37.4; 38.4. For "likeness" as the potential for what humans can ultimately become, see Irenaeus, *Against Heresies* 5.6.1.

32. Irenaeus, *Demonstration of the Apostolic Preaching* 11.

33. Irenaeus, *Against Heresies* 4.37.1.

34. See Irenaeus, *Against Heresies* 4.37.2.

35. See Irenaeus, *Against Heresies* 4.37.1.

36. See Irenaeus, *Against Heresies* 4.37.2.

37. See Irenaeus, *Demonstration of the Apostolic Preaching* 16.

38. See Irenaeus, *Against Heresies* 4.37.1; see also Matthew 23:37.

39. Irenaeus, *Demonstration of the Apostolic Preaching* 12, 14.

40. Irenaeus, *Demonstration of the Apostolic Preaching* 16; see also Theophilus of Antioch, *To Autolycus* 2.26; Clement of Alexandria, *Stromata* 4.23; 6.12; *Exhortation to the Greeks* 11.1–2.

41. Irenaeus, *Demonstration of the Apostolic Preaching* 16. On Adam repenting, see Irenaeus, *Against Heresies* 3.23.5.

42. Irenaeus, *Against Heresies* 4.38.1. See Toews, *The Story of Original Sin*, 52; Bouteneff, *Beginnings*, 77–85.

43. See Irenaeus, *Against Heresies* 3.23.1–5; *Demonstration of the Apostolic Preaching* 16.

44. See Irenaeus, *Against Heresies* 5.16.2. Most of the other early Christian writers (with the exception perhaps of Origen) do not make a distinction between the image and the likeness, so they emphasize instead that it is the image that was marred in the garden.

45. See Irenaeus, *Against Heresies* 4.4.3.

46. Irenaeus, *Against Heresies* 3.23.2.

47. See Irenaeus, *Against Heresies* 5.10.1.

48. Irenaeus, *Against Heresies* 3.18.1.

49. Irenaeus, *Against Heresies* 4.38.3.

50. Weinandy, "St. Irenaeus," 17.

51. Origen was "one of the most prolific writers of the early Church Fathers." Thomas W. Toews, "Biblical Sources in the Development of the Concept of the Soul in the Writings of the Fathers of the Early Christian Church, 100–325 C.C." (PhD diss., Andrews University, 2011), 228.

52. Origen, *First Principles* 1.7.4. In this chapter all quotations from this source are from John Behr, ed. and trans., *Origen, On First Principles*, Oxford Early Christian Texts (Oxford: Oxford University Press, 2017), 2:247. See also Origen, *Commentary on John* 2.25.

53. Origen, *First Principles* 1.7.4. The idea of divine election before birth in Jeremiah 1:5 has parallels in other ancient Near Eastern texts; see Dana M. Pike, "Before Jeremiah Was: Divine Election in the Ancient Near East," in *A Witness for the Restoration: Essays in Honor of Robert J. Matthews*, ed. Kent P. Jackson and Andrew C. Skinner (Provo, UT: Religious Studies Center, Brigham Young University, 2007), 33–59.

54. Origen, *First Principles* 1.preface.3.

55. Origen, *First Principles* 1.6.1.

56. According to Porphyry, as quoted by Eusebius, Origen studied under Ammonius Saccas, who was reportedly the founder of Neoplatonism; see

Eusebius, *Ecclesiastical History*, 6.19. Although Origen's argument for the premortality of souls answered some theological questions mentioned here, it also creates additional ones. For a discussion of some of these additional questions, see James L. Sieback, "Philo, Augustine, and Classical Varieties," review of *When Souls Had Wings: Pre-mortal Existence in Western Thought*, by Terryl L. Givens, *BYU Studies* 50, no. 4 (2011): 137.

57. Plato, *Cratylus* 400C. See also *The Oxford Dictionary of the Christian Church*, ed. F. L. Cross, 3rd rev. ed., ed. E. A. Livingstone (Oxford: Oxford University Press, 1997), s.v. "soul."

58. Origen's teachings are complex. It should be noted that he does not specifically mention the term preexistence and often speaks in cyclical terms with the end referring to a return to the beginning. In such cyclical terms, the concept of a preexistence seems out of place. John Behr, for one, prefers to speak of Origen's "antecedent causes" rather than a preexistence; see Behr, *Origen*. But, on other occasions, Origen talks of souls existing outside of time as we know it. Even so he also insists that they were *created* by God, meaning that there was a "time" in which they did not exist. Once they came into existence, they exercised their free will in ways that divided them into different types of souls; see Origen, *First Principles* 2.6.5. In his *Commentary on John*, Origen argues: "He who is careful to do nothing unjustly, or by chance or caprice, must admit that John's soul, being older than his body and subsisting prior to it, was sent to the ministry of testimony concerning light." He continues to speak of "the general theory concerning the soul . . . that is, that it has not been sown with the body but exists before it." Origen, *Commentary on John* 2.181–82, trans. Ronald E Heine in vol. 80 of The Fathers of the Church: A New Translation series (Washington, DC: Catholic University Press, 1948), 143–144. Certainly, Church Fathers such as Jerome and Augustine understood that Origen was teaching that souls existed in an earlier life, even though they rejected it; Augustine, *Letters* 166: *On the Origin of the Soul* 27; Jerome, *Letters* 165: *To Marcellinus and Anapsychia* 1.

59. Origen, *First Principles* 1.preface.5; 1.7.1; see also *First Principles* 1.6.4; 2.2.2; 4.3.15; 4.4.8. Behr, *Origen*, 1:121n3.

60. See Origen, *First Principles* 1.7.1; 2.9.2.

61. See Origen, *First Principles* 2.9.5.

62. See Origen, *First Principles* 1.2.13; 1.5.3.

63. See Origen, *First Principles* 1.8.3; 2.6.5; 1.5.2–3.

64. Origen, *First Principles* 2.6.5.

65. See Origen, *First Principles* 2.8.3.

66. Origen, *First Principles* 2.8.3.

67. Origen, *First Principles* 2.8.3.

68. Origen, *Homily on Genesis* 1.13, in Origen, *Homilies on Genesis and Exodus*, trans. Ronald E. Heine, vol. 71 in The Fathers of the Church: A New Translation series (Washington, DC: The Catholic University of America Press, 1982), 63. In this chapter all English quotations from *Homilies on Genesis* are from this edition. For Genesis 1:26–27 as a description of the creation of souls, see Origen, *Against Celsus* 6.63.

69. See Origen, *Homily on Genesis* 1.13.

70. Origen, *First Principles* 3.6.1.

71. See Origen, *Epistle of Romans* 3.3.14. Origen quotes the Jewish apocryphal text the Wisdom of Solomon to explain the negative effects of a physical body on the ability of a person to understand the things of righteousness: "For the reasoning of mortals is worthless, and our designs are likely to fail; for a perishable body weighs down the soul, and their earthly tent burdens the thoughtful mind" (Wisdom 9:14–15 NRSV).

72. See Origen, *First Principles* 2.3.3; *Against Celsus* 2.60.8. For a discussion about the body of Jesus after the Resurrection, see Markschies, *God's Body*, 283–319; see also chapter 8 in this volume.

73. Origen, *Homily on Genesis* 1:13 (emphasis added). Philo makes a similar distinction in *On the Creation* 134.

74. Origen, *First Principles* 3.6.1; emphasis original.

75. Origen, *First Principles* 3.6.1.

76. See Origen, *First Principles* 3.6.1. See also Plato, *Theaetetus* 176B.

77. On the Word as the true image of God, see Origen, *First Principles* 4.4.10; *Commentary on John* 1.105. On the Word as eternal, "born of [God] but is yet without any beginning," see *First Principles* 1.2.2; and for the Word being the "Son by nature" rather than "through adoption in the Spirit," see *First Principles* 1.2.4.

78. Origen, *Homilies on Luke* 8.1, English translation from in Origen, *Homilies on Luke, Fragments on Luke*, trans. Joseph T. Lienhard, vol. 94 of Fathers of the Church: A New Translation series (Washington, DC: The Catholic University of America Press, 1996), 33.

79. Origen, *First Principles* 4.4.9. Origen used the word *apokatastasis* to describe this final condition. Some have interpreted Origen's teachings to allow the possibility that even the devil could ultimately choose goodness and be saved. For a discussion on Origen's teachings about the devil being saved, see Lisa R. Holliday, "Will Satan Be Saved? Reconsidering Origen's Theory of Volition in *Peri Archon*," *Vigiliae Christianae* 63 (2009): 1–23.

80. Origen, *Homily on Joshua* 6, trans. Barbara J. Bruce, vol. 105 of Fathers of the Church: A New Translation series (Washington, DC: The Catholic

University of America Press, 2002), 72.

81. See Rondet, *Original Sin*, 76.

82. See Plato, *Republic* 7; *Phaedo* 76–77.

83. John Anthony McGuckin, ed., *The Westminster Handbook to Origen*, The Westminster Handbooks to Christian Theology (Louisville, KY: Westminster John Knox Press, 2004), 25.

84. See Aristotle, *On the Soul* 2.1, 412b6–9, 413a3–5.

85. See Augustine, *Letters* 166: *On the Origin of the Soul* 27; Jerome, *Letters* 165: *To Marcellinus and Anapsychia* 1.

86. See Tertullian, *On the Soul* 27; Gregory of Nyssa, *The Making of Man* 28–29.

87. Jerome, *Letters* 165: *To Marcellinus and Anapsychia* 1.

88. Jerome, *Against John of Jerusalem* 22; see also Augustine, *Letters* 166: *On the Origin of the Soul* 8; Jerome, *Letters* 165: *To Marcellinus and Anapsychia* 126.1.

89. See Augustine, *Confessions* 11.17.

90. Augustine, *On a Happy Life* 1.4, in Augustine, *The Happy Life; Answer to Skeptics; Divine Providence and the Problem of Evil; Soliloquies*, trans. Ludwig Schopp, Denis J. Kavanagh, Robert P. Russell, and Thomas F. Gilligan, vol. 5 in The Fathers of the Church: A New Translation series (New York: Cima Publishing Co., Inc., 2008), 48. Augustine's early writings are the so-called Cassiciacum dialogues. The Cassiciacum dialogues received their name from a country estate north of Milan where Augustine, in preparation for his upcoming baptism, conducted informal philosophical dialogues that were compiled by a secretary and eventually became the basis for *Contra Academicos* (*Against the Academics*), *De beata vita* (*On a Happy Life*), *De ordine* (*On Order*), *Soliloquies*, and *On the Immortality of the Soul*. For a general introduction to the Cassiciacum dialogues, see Michael P. Foley, trans., *On the Happy Life: Saint Augustine's Cassiciacum Dialogues* (New Haven: Yale University Press, 2019), 2:xxiii–xxviii.

91. On reason making humans superior, see Augustine, *On Order* 2.19.49. See also the discussion in Michael P. Foley, *On Order, St. Augustine's Cassiciacum Dialogues*, vol. 3 (New Haven: Yale University Press, 2020), 204–08. Tertullian also taught that it is the soul that separates humans from God's other creations; see Tertullian, *On the Soul* 19.

92. Augustine, *The City of God and Christian Doctrine* 22.27; trans. Gerald G. Walsh and Daniel J. Honan, in *Saint Augustine The City of God, Books XVII–XXII*, vol. 24 in The Fathers of the Church: A New Translation series (Washington, DC: The Catholic University of America Press, 1954), 494.

93. Augustine, *On Genesis against the Manichaeans* 1.17.28, in Augustine, *On Genesis: Two Books on Genesis Against the Manichees and on the Literal*

Interpretation of Genesis: An Unfinished Book, trans. Roland J. Teske, vol. 84 in The Fathers of the Church: A New Translation series (Washington, DC: The Catholic University of America Press, 1991), 76.

94. See Augustine, *Confessions* 5.8–9; 10.16. See Toews, *The Story of Original Sin*, 76; Paul Rigby, *Original Sin in Augustine's Confessions* (Ottawa, ON: University of Ottawa Press, 1987), 2.

95. Augustine, *City of God* 14.11, trans. Gerald G. Walsh and Grace Monahan in *Saint Augustine, The City of God Books VIII–XVI*, vol. 14 in The Fathers of the Church: A New Translation series (Washington, DC: The Catholic University of America Press, 1952), 378.

96. Augustine, *On Marriage and Concupiscence* 2.5.15. English translation from *Nicene and Post-Nicene Fathers* series 1, vol. 5.

97. See Toews, *The Story of Original Sin*, 62–72.

98. See Tertullian, *On the Soul* 9.

99. Tertullian, *On the Soul* 19, 40. English translation from *Ante-Nicene Fathers*, vol. 3.

100. Towes, *The Story of Original Sin*, 69.

101. Ambrosiaster, *Commentary on Romans* 5.12(2a–3), in *Ambrosiaster's Commentary on the Pauline Epistles: Romans*, trans. with notes Theodore S. de Bruyn, introduction by Theodore S. de Bruyn, Stephen Andrew Cooper, David G. Hunter, vol. 41 in the Writings from the Greco-Roman World series (Atlanta: SBL Press, 2017), 96–97; emphasis added.

102. Augustine, *Eighty-Three Different Questions* 68.3, in Augustine, *Eighty-Three Different Questions*, trans. David L. Mosher, vol. 70 in The Fathers of the Church: A New Translation series (Washington, DC: The Catholic University of America Press, 1982), 158–62; emphasis added.

103. Paul M. Blowers, "Original Sin," in *Encyclopedia of Early Christianity*, 2nd ed., ed. Everett Ferguson (New York: Routledge, 1999), 839. For Irenaeus's view that humanity shared in the effects of our first parents' choice, see Irenaeus, *Against Heresies* 3.18.7.

104. Augustine, *Letters* 166.3.7; emphasis added. English translation from *Nicene and Post-Nicene Fathers* series 1, vol. 1.

105. Augustine, *Letters* 98.2. English translation from *Nicene and Post-Nicene Fathers* series 1, vol. 1

106. See Everett Ferguson, "Baptism," in *Encyclopedia of Early Christianity*, 2nd ed., ed. Everett Ferguson (New York: Routledge, 1999), 162.

107. Blowers, "Original Sin," 840. For an English translation of *A Letter of Pelagius to Demetrius*, see "A Letter from Pelagius," Epistolae, https://epistolae.ctl.columbia.edu/letter/1296.html. For a more detailed discussion of teachings of Pelagius and his followers, see Pier Franco Beatrice, *The*

Transmission of Sin: Augustine and the Pre-Augustine Sources, trans. Adam Kamesar (New York: Oxford University Press, 2013), 15–37; Joanne McWilliam, "Pelagius and Pelagianism," *Encyclopedia of Early Christianity*, 2nd ed., ed. Everett Ferguson (New York: Routledge, 1997), 887–89; John Ferguson, *Pelagius: A Historical and Theological Study* (New York: AMS Press, 1978).

DIVINE NATURE

Father, Son, and Holy Spirit

Jason R. Combs

In the beginning was the Word, and the Word was with God, and the Word was God. . . . And the Word was made flesh, and dwelt among us.

—John 1:1, 14

"Whom say ye that I am?" Simon Peter responded, "Thou art the Christ, the Son of the living God" (Matthew 16:16; see also Mark 8:29; Luke 9:20). Even as Peter spoke these words he did not yet fully comprehend their meaning.[1] A fuller understanding of the nature of Christ, and therefore also the nature of God (see Colossians 1:15), would come to Jesus's disciples slowly—line upon line.[2] By the time Paul wrote his letter to the Philippians (circa AD 54–64), Christians sang praises that Jesus Christ was "in the form of God" and "equal with God" (Philippians 2:6). Yet, as this poetic passage continues, "[Jesus] made himself of no reputation, and took upon him the form of a servant, and was made in the likeness of men" (Philippians 2:7). Jesus was understood as somehow both human and divine. Paul also proclaimed, "To us there is but one God, the Father ... and one Lord Jesus Christ" (1 Corinthians 8:6). Yet the earliest Christians also joined with their fellow Jews in proclaiming that there is one God and that he alone should be worshiped (see Deuteronomy 6:4; Mark 12:29).[3] God was understood somehow both as three—Father, Son, and Holy Spirit—and as one.

As ancient Christians pondered the words of Paul and the Gospels, as well as the words of the Old Testament, they often were left with questions.[4] And the more carefully they read, the more questions emerged. Was Jesus fully divine because he was "equal with God," or was he only like God being "in the form of God" (Philippians 2:6)? Was Jesus fully human, or was he only "made in the likeness of men" (Philippians 2:7)? Some Christians emphasized the humanity of Jesus while others emphasized his divinity. Still others

BOX 8.1 **Why It Matters**

"We believe in God, the Eternal Father, and in His Son, Jesus Christ, and in the Holy Ghost" (Article of Faith 1). Reading what our ancient Christian ancestors wrote about God the Father, Jesus Christ, and the Holy Ghost can help us to reflect on the beauty and profundity of our beliefs and to look upon Christians who differ from us with Christ-like love. Similarly, learning the history behind the early Christian creeds can help us to understand more precisely how we Latter-day Saints differ from other Christians as well as how certain terminology and descriptions of God came to be considered orthodox.

took these views to an extreme. Some insisted that Jesus was a mere human being (psilanthropism; from the Greek *psilōs*, "merely," and *anthrōpos*, "human") who was so righteous that God adopted him to be his son (adoptionism) at baptism or the Resurrection. Others insisted that Jesus was so divine and incorruptible that he would not or could not take upon himself a corruptible mortal human body in any real way. They thought Jesus appeared to be human when in fact he was only divine (docetism; from the Greek *dokeō*, "to seem" or "to appear"). Both adoptionism and docetism were declared heresies. Between these two opposing positions, other Christians affirmed, somewhat paradoxically, that Jesus Christ was both fully human (but without sin) and fully divine. These Christians did not describe Jesus as half-human and half-god—like the demigods of Greek and Roman mythology—but fully both human and God (see box 8.2).

This affirmation that Jesus Christ is both fully human and fully divine is paradoxical because Christians saw a great difference between humanity and divinity. One obvious difference is God's sinlessness, but divinity is also different from humanity in other ways. God is far greater than humanity in knowledge, power, glory, and so

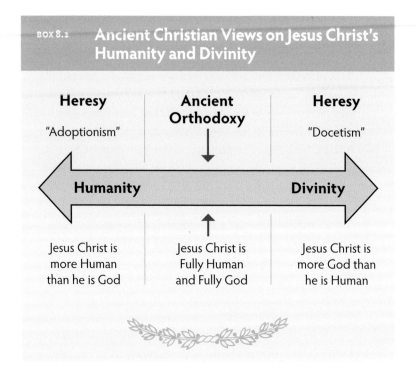

BOX 8.1   Ancient Christian Views on Jesus Christ's Humanity and Divinity

Heresy	Ancient Orthodoxy	Heresy
"Adoptionism"		"Docetism"

Humanity ⟵   ⟶ **Divinity**

| Jesus Christ is more Human than he is God | Jesus Christ is Fully Human and Fully God | Jesus Christ is more God than he is Human |

on. All of these are attributes of the Father, Son, and Holy Spirit, attributes which set the divine nature apart from human nature. Some ancient Christians came to emphasize these differences between humans and God, in part, as a way to explain the absolute necessity of Jesus Christ and his salvific work. Regardless of any similarity human beings bear to God, being created in God's image and likeness (see Genesis 1:26–27), our distance from God could not be overcome without the aid of a savior. For humanity to have a chance to be united with God, we would have to be transformed by God the Son taking on (or "assuming") humanity. "For that which [Christ] has not assumed [taken upon himself], he has not saved," explained the fourth-century theologian Gregory of Nazianzus.[5] To affirm Jesus's *full* humanity, therefore, was to affirm that the divine Word of God, Jesus Christ, redeemed humanity completely. But how are we to understand a being who is simultaneously the Lord God Almighty and a babe in a manger, the Everlasting God and the crucified Messiah? How might Christians make sense of this paradox?

▲ **FIGURE 8.1**   Icon of Christ, Saint Catherine's Monastery, Sinai, sixth century. Viewers have long observed that the right and left sides of Christ's face are depicted differently. One theory is that this represents an artist's attempt to portray Christ's human and divine natures. Photo: Alamy

The ancient church councils at Nicaea, Constantinople, Ephesus, and Chalcedon were each an attempt to summarize the message of scripture in response to such questions. This chapter is about these councils and how ancient Christians labored in faith to understand the message of scripture regarding the nature of God—to describe in human language the God whose ways are higher than our ways (see Isaiah 55:8–9).[6]

From Tertullian to the Council of Nicaea

Writing at the beginning of the third century (AD 200), Tertullian became the first important Christian theologian to write in Latin. And Tertullian wrote a lot. Residing in the city of Carthage on the northern shore of the African continent (in modern-day Tunisia), Tertullian wrote more than forty-five lengthy treatises. A number of these works provide a good summary of the theological debates of the second century. For discussions about the nature of God and Christ, one key treatise is Tertullian's *Against Praxeas*.

We know little about this Praxeas. Tertullian only says that Praxeas brought his wrong-headed ideas to Rome from Asia Minor (modern-day Turkey). We do, however, know quite a bit about Praxeas's view of God. It has been called modalism, monarchianism, and Sabellianism (see box 8.3).[7] According to Tertullian, Praxeas believed that "the Father [is] identical with the Son in the sense that both are one person."[8] This view is called modalism because Praxeas believed that there could only be one person called God who manifests himself in different "modes" (modalism) at different times: at one time, in the mode of the Father, at another, in the mode of the Son, and so on. Quoting from Psalm 2:7, Tertullian envisions God the Father speaking to his Son, Jesus Christ: "Thou *art* my Son; this day have I begotten thee." But Tertullian mocks his modalist opponent by altering that psalm: "If you want me to believe [the one God] to be both the Father and the Son, show me some other passage where it is declared, 'The Lord said unto himself, I am my own Son, today have I begotten myself.'"[9] Of course, nothing like that is found in scripture. Tertullian's point is that modalists are foolish.

BOX 8.3 Key Figures in the Modalism Debate

- **Praxeas, who lived in Rome (circa AD 200),** believed that God the Father, Jesus Christ, and the Holy Ghost are one person who is manifest at different times in different modes: in the mode of the Father or of the Son or of the Spirit (this heresy is called modalism). Other names for modalism:
  - **Monarchianism,** so-called because some modalists believed that God's "monarchy"—God as sole ruler of all—depended on the existence of only one person called God.
  - **Sabellianism,** named after Sabellius (circa AD 220) who likewise argued against any distinction between the persons of God the Father and his Son, Jesus Christ. Sabellius even called God the "Son-Father."
- **Tertullian of Carthage (circa AD 200)** believed that God the Father, Jesus Christ, and the Holy Ghost are three distinct persons who are one in essence (*substantia*), condition, and power. The Godhead is a "tri-unity" or Trinity. Jesus Christ is subordinate to God the Father (see *Against Praxeas* 9.2)—this subordinationism is later declared a heresy.

For Tertullian, scripture bears clear witness to the threeness of God: God the Father, Jesus Christ, and the Holy Spirit are three distinct persons.[10] Yet Tertullian also accepts scripture's affirmation that God is one.[11] How does Tertullian make sense of this apparent paradox—God who is both three and one? He suggests that the Father, Son, and Holy Spirit should be understood as one in terms of their shared essence (*substantia*), condition, and power, and they should also be understood as three in regard to their position, form, and appearance.[12] Tertullian summarizes this view of God as a "tri-unity," the Trinity.[13] In fact, Tertullian is the first to use the Latin *trinitas* (Trinity) for the Godhead. And he does so in order to argue against

BOX 8.4 Ancient Christian Views on the Oneness and Threeness of God

Heresy	Ancient Orthodoxy	Heresy
"Monarchianism"		"Paganism"

God is One ⟵   ⟶ **God is Three**

Modalism— One God who manifests Godself in three forms or modes	God is one nature (*ousia*) in three persons (*prosōpa*)	Polytheism— Many gods with their own natures, personalities, and purposes

the modalist view that the Father, Son, and Holy Spirit are all one person (see box 8.4). For Tertullian, "all the Scriptures attest the clear existence of the Trinity and a distinction between (the persons of) the Trinity."[14]

Much of Tertullian's writing sets the stage and established the Latin terminology for future discussions about the nature of God. One of Tertullian's personal views, however, was later declared to be heresy. In his efforts to defend the threeness of God against the modalists, Tertullian suggested that God is three in regard to "position" (Latin *gradus*, "position," "station," or "degree"). For Tertullian, Jesus does not stand in a position entirely equal with God the Father but is subordinate to him: "As [Jesus] himself professes, *Because my Father is greater than I*" (quoting John 14:28).[15] This subordinationist thinking was later declared heresy. In fact, one could say that subordinationism is precisely the question at stake in the Council of Nicaea.

Arius, Alexander, and the Council of Nicaea

By the time of the Nicene Council (AD 325), the status of Christians in the Roman Empire had changed dramatically.[16] Twelve years earlier, official persecution of Christians had come to an end, and Christianity became one of the legal religions of the Roman Empire (Edict of Milan, AD 313). Only one year before the Council of Nicaea, Constantine defeated his coruler, became the sole emperor of the entire Roman Empire, and made Byzantium—soon to be dedicated as "Constantinople"—his new capital city (AD 324). Constantine's coruler had controlled the eastern half of the empire. With Constantine now assuming full control, he had to deal with new challenges arising in the east. Among them was a rapidly spreading controversy about the nature of God and Christ.

The debate had originated in Alexandria, Egypt, between Alexander, bishop of Alexandria, and Arius, a local presbyter and popular teacher (see box 8.5). Both accepted that Jesus Christ is divine, but they disagreed on how best to describe his relation to God the Father.[17] Is Christ just as much God as God the Father or is he in some

---

BOX 8.5 **Key Figures from the Council of Nicaea**

The Council of Nicaea (AD 325) was called by Roman Emperor Constantine.

- **Arius, presbyter in Alexandria, Egypt**, believed that Jesus, as the "Son" of God, is of a lesser divine status because he was "created" by the Father. Jesus is not as much God as is God the Father.
- **Alexander, bishop of Alexandria, and the Nicene Creed** affirmed that Jesus Christ is consubstantial with the Father and that he is *not* of a lesser divine status, because he was "begotten" by the Father. Jesus is just as much God as is God the Father.

way inferior to the Father? For Arius, the answer was clear: Jesus, as the "Son" of God, is inferior to the Father because he was "created" by the Father: "The Son . . . created before ages and established, was not before he was begotten . . . he alone was constituted by the Father. He is not eternal or coeternal . . . with the Father, nor does he have his being together with the Father."[18]

For Alexander, Arius's theology was dangerous. Arius demeaned Christ's divinity when he suggested that the Only Begotten was "created" or "constituted" by God or that "there was a time when Christ was not."[19] Moreover, if Christ was not fully divine, how could he have the power to rescue humanity from sin and death? Alexander's answer was that scripture affirmed not that Christ was "created" by the Father, but that Christ was "begotten" by him. Christ was, therefore, just as much God as God the Father—of the same nature or essence. And yet Christ was distinct from the Father, whom Alexander called the Unbegotten. As the Only Begotten and Creator of the world, Christ had a unique connection with both the Father and the world. As the Only Begotten, Christ could fully represent the Father and mediate between the Father and humanity (see Colossians 1:15–17; 1 Timothy 2:5).[20]

Arius and Alexander each accused one another of heresy. Arius accused Alexander of overemphasizing Christ's divinity and his oneness with the Father to the point of docetism and modalism. Alexander accused Arius of overemphasizing Christ's humanity and his distinction from the Father to the point of subordinationism, or even adoptionism and polytheism.[21] Had this debate stayed between these two church leaders in Alexandria, it is unlikely that it would have drawn the attention of the emperor Constantine. But the conflict spread. According to Constantine's ancient biographer, "In every city bishops were engaged in obstinate conflict with bishops, and people rising against people."[22] In order to settle this dispute about the nature of God and Christ, as well as another dispute about the proper time to celebrate Easter, Constantine called for a council of bishops to gather at the city of Nicaea (in the northwestern part of modern-day Turkey, not far from ancient Byzantium/Constantinople).[23] Between 200 and 300

BOX 8.6 **What Is a Creed?**

Creed comes from the Latin credo (I believe) and is a statement of faith. Some creeds, such as the Niceno-Constantinopolitan Creed, eventually became part of worship and were recited by members as part of a church service—beginning in the fifth century in the East and eleventh century in the West. Such creeds functioned as a public affirmation of beliefs, similar to the Articles of Faith for Latter-day Saints, and as a means to maintain allegiance to orthodox belief, similar to temple recommend interviews for Latter-day Saints.

bishops gathered from throughout the empire and beyond, from as far west as Spain and as far east as Persia.[24] The Council began on May 20, AD 325. This was the first great ecumenical council—a council of different churches. It was the first time that representatives of various churches throughout the empire could gather in one place to discuss the affairs of the Church. This was not possible in the period of persecution, nor was it possible without the financial and political support of the emperor. One of the results of this first great ecumenical council was the Nicene Creed (see box 8.6).

The Nicene Creed was intended to serve at least two purposes. First, it functioned to exclude the views of Arius that were perceived to be a dangerous heresy. The creed originally concluded with a series of statements that Christians should reject. "But those who say [that is, Arius and his followers], 'there was a time when [the Son] was not,' and 'before he was begotten he was not,' and that 'he came to be out of what was not,' or who say that he is from another subsistence [*hypostasis*] or essence [*ousia*], or that the Son of God is a 'creation' or 'changeable' or 'alterable,' these the holy, universal, and apostolic church condemns."[25]

A second purpose of the Nicene Creed was to ensure that the Christian message was preached the same in every corner of the

▲ **FIGURE 8.2** Fourth-century mosaic from the Catacomb of Domitilla, Rome, depicting Christ seated between Peter and Paul. An inscription bordering the mosaic reads, "You who are called the Son are found to be also the Father," which appears to represent modalistic ideas (the Son is a "mode" or earthly representation of God the Father) that evidently were still in circulation even after the Council of Nicaea. Photo: Alamy

world; in other words, this council served a similar purpose as the Correlation Department in The Church of Jesus Christ of Latter-day Saints does today.[26] Prior to the Council of Nicaea, local churches each developed their own criteria for what a new member of the Church needed to know and affirm before baptism. With this First Council of Nicaea, the churches now had an opportunity to be more united, to truly become one universal Church.

To develop a unified summary of the Christian message, the authors relied heavily on the words of scripture. The Nicene Creed begins, "We believe in one God [see Deuteronomy 6:4], Father Almighty, creator of all things both visible and invisible [see Colossians

BOX 8.7   Ancient Creeds[27]

Nicene Creed	Niceno-Constantinopolitan Creed
"We believe in one God, Father Almighty, creator of all things both visible and invisible.	"We believe in one God, Father Almighty, creator of heaven and earth, and of all things both visible and invisible.
"And in one Lord Jesus Christ, the Son of God, begotten from the Father, only-begotten, that is, out of the essence [ousia] of the Father, God from God, light from light, true God from true God, consubstantial ["same essence" (ousia)] with the Father, through whom all things came into being, both things in heaven and things on earth. Who, for us human-beings and for our salvation, descended, and became incarnate, and became human, and he suffered and rose on the third day according to the Scriptures, and ascended to heaven, and he is coming to judge the living and the dead;	"And in one Lord Jesus Christ, the Son of God, only-begotten, begotten from the Father before all time, light from light, true God from true God, begotten not created, consubstantial ["same essence" (ousia)] with the Father, through whom all things came into being. Who, for us human-beings and for our salvation, descended out of heaven and became incarnate from the Holy Spirit and the virgin Mary, and became human, and was crucified for us under Pontius Pilate, and suffered and was buried, and rose on the third day according to the Scriptures, and ascended to heaven, and is seated on the right of the Father, and he is coming again in glory to judge the living and the dead, whose rule will have no end.
"And in the Holy Spirit.	"And in the Holy Spirit, the Lord and the life-giver, who, going out from the Father, being worshipped and glorified with the Father and the Son, spoke through the prophets.

Nicene Creed	Niceno-Constantinopolitan Creed
"But those who say, 'there was a time when he was not,' and 'before he was begotten he was not,' and that 'he came to be out of what was not,' or who say that he is from another subsistence [*hypostasis*] or essence [*ousia*], or that the Son of God is a 'creation' or 'changeable' or 'alterable,' these the holy, universal, and apostolic church condemns."	"In one, holy, universal and apostolic church; we profess one baptism for the forgiveness of sins; we look forward to the resurrection of the dead and to life in the world to come. Amen."

1:16]. And in one Lord Jesus Christ [see 1 Corinthians 8:6], the Son of God, begotten from the Father, only-begotten [see John 1:14]."[28] So the Creed continues, weaving scriptural language together as a testimony of God the Father and Jesus Christ. Yet in its purpose to summarize the biblical witness regarding God, the Nicene Creed fell short. Since the Council of Nicaea was assembled primarily in response to Arius's view of God the Father and Jesus Christ, the Creed included little about the Holy Spirit. This was remedied by the First Council of Constantinople (AD 381), which created the Niceno-Constantinopolitan Creed (see box 8.7).[29] In its purpose to stay true to the language of scripture, however, the Creed largely succeeded.

The Nicene Creed rarely veers away from scriptural language. Nonscriptural language appears primarily when scripture required clarification because of a disagreement over its interpretation. Arius had interpreted scripture describing Christ as "begotten" to mean that Christ is not like the Father, that he is not "eternal or coeternal . . . with the Father."[30] For Arius, to speak of Christ as begotten was to speak of a time that God "made" Christ. For the authors of the Nicene Creed, however, "to beget" and "to make" are two different things. For example, a potter "makes" a pot but "begets" a son; and that son of the potter would be much more like the potter than any pot could ever be. A "begotten son" inherits the nature of his father. So, in response to Arius's (mis)interpretation of the word *begotten*, the Nicene Creed attempted to clarify how that term should be understood. It explains that "only-begotten" means "out of the essence [*ousia*] of the Father" and "consubstantial [*homoousios*] with the Father."[31] The Greek word *homoousios* (from the Greek *homo*, "same," and *ousia*, "substance" or "essence"), which is often translated as "consubstantial" (from the Latin *cum*, "with," and *substantia*, "substance" or "essence"), is not used in scripture. The term was adopted to refute Arius's interpretation of scripture.[32]

One might mistakenly assume that the word consubstantial (*homoousios*) in the Nicene Creed implies Jesus Christ and God the Father are one and the same person.[33] That was not the intent. In fact, that would be the heresy called modalism, which the Church had long rejected. The Council of Chalcedon (AD 451) clarifies that Jesus Christ is not only *homoousios* with the Father but also *homoousios* with us human beings (I will discuss the Chalcedonian Definition next). This definition makes it clear that *homoousios* should not be read to mean that Jesus and the Father are one person, any more than it means that Jesus is one person with all of us humans. But this reading was not clear at the time of the Nicene Council. It took many years and many more councils to reach the conclusion of the Council of Chalcedon.

From the Council of Ephesus to the Council of Chalcedon

By the time we arrive at the Council of Chalcedon (AD 451), the Roman Empire and the Church's position within the Empire had again changed dramatically. Christianity was no longer just one among many religious options. In AD 380, Emperor Theodosius I declared Christianity to be *the* official religion of the Roman Empire.[34] With that declaration came all of the privileges and complications that accompany being both a religion and the ruling class. And, over the next

▲ **FIGURE 8.3** Many coins feature Aelia Pulcheria as Augusta or empress. Her imperial authority is accentuated by the hand of God crowning her from heaven. On the reverse, a winged victory figure stands with a bejeweled cross, indicating the Orthodox victory at Councils like Ephesus and Chalcedon supported by the empress. Photo: Used with permission, wildwinds.com, ex Gemini I auction, Jan 2005

few decades, ruling became very complicated. Theodosius I awarded the empire to two of his sons. One was to rule the western half of the empire from Rome, and the other, the eastern half from Constantinople. By AD 410, the great city of Rome, capital of the western empire, was raided by Visigoth tribes, forcing the western imperial family to flee from Rome to Ravenna, Italy. In the east, Theodosius I's other son had died in AD 408, just two years before the sack of Rome, leaving a nine-year-old daughter, Pulcheria, and a seven-year-old son, Theodosius II, to rule in his place. So Theodosius II was crowned emperor, but his older sister Pulcheria was the power behind the throne.[35] Pulcheria was directly involved in the next major ecumenical councils at Ephesus and Chalcedon.[36]

The First Council of Ephesus (AD 431) set the stage for the
Council of Chalcedon (AD 451). Both of these councils focused on
the significance of Jesus Christ's dual nature, his divinity and humanity. During Jesus's mortal ministry, did his humanity accomplish some
things without the involvement of his divine nature? Or did his divinity fully take over his humanity? Or were both his divinity and
humanity somehow fully present in everything he did? The Council
of Ephesus, which convened at the instigation of Pulcheria and others, began to answer these questions. Its most forceful answer came
in the condemnation of Nestorius, bishop of Constantinople. For
Nestorius, Jesus's humanity and divinity operated separately. Nestorius argued, for instance, that Christ is God but not in such a way that
Mary could be called Theotokos (Mother of God). Nestorius saw
Jesus's birth as an expression of his humanity, not his divinity.[37] The
Council of Ephesus rejected the idea that Jesus's humanity accomplished some things without his divine nature.[38] But this was only the
beginning of the debate. Next came Eutyches.

Eutyches was the head of an important monastery in Constantinople. He had attended the Council of Ephesus and spoken in opposition to Nestorius. He was convinced that Nestorius had been
convicted of heresy not only for describing Christ as a dual person
but also for describing Christ as having two natures after the Incarnation—when Christ assumed a mortal body.[39] Eutyches explained
his own position as follows: "I acknowledge that our Lord came into
being from two natures before the union [the Incarnation]; but after
the union I acknowledge one nature."[40] That one nature, for Eutyches,
was Christ's divine nature.[41] He affirmed the Niceno-Constantinopolitan Creed that Christ was of the same substance (*homoousios*)
with the Father (a divine *ousia*), but he thought it blasphemous to
suggest that Christ was also of the same substance (*homoousios*) with
humanity (possessing a human *ousia*).[42] For Eutyches, Christ's condescension was taking on human flesh, but Christ remained foremost
the divine Word of God.

Word of Eutyches's teachings reached Leo, the bishop of Rome.[43]
Concerned, Leo wrote a letter to the new bishop of Constantinople

Key Figures from Ephesus to Chalcedon

First Council of Ephesus (AD 431) was called by eastern Emperor Theodosius II and his sister Pulcheria.

- **Nestorius, Bishop of Constantinople**, believed that Jesus Christ is consubstantial with God and humanity, with his divine and human natures functioning independently.
- **Council of Ephesus** declared that it is heresy to describe the human and divine natures of Jesus Christ in such a way that would depict him as two different people.

Council of Chalcedon (AD 451) was called by eastern Emperor Marcian and Empress Pulcheria (Theodosius II's sister).

- **Eutyches, head of a monastery in Constantinople**, believed that Jesus Christ is one divine nature after the Incarnation; Christ is consubstantial with God, not humanity (this belief is called monophysitism, and it was declared a heresy).
- **Leo the Great, bishop of Rome, and the Chalcedonian Definition** affirmed that Jesus Christ is consubstantial with God and humanity—acknowledged in two natures joined, but not mixed, into one person, into one subsistent being (*hypostasis*). Later, this view of Christ's nature is called the hypostatic union.

and presented the theological problems with Eutyches's position (see box 8.8). This letter is now known as Leo's *Tome*. For Leo, the teachings of Eutyches were perilous. He writes in his *Tome* how dangerous it is "to believe the Lord Jesus Christ to be merely God."[44] For Christ to save us humans, Leo explains, it was necessary for him to retain the distinctness of both human and divine natures in his person such that "lowliness is assumed by majesty, weakness by power, mortality by eternity." Leo continues, "In order to pay the debt of our condition, the unchangeable nature has been united to the changeable, so that, as the appropriate remedy for our ills, one and the same 'mediator between God and humankind, the human Christ Jesus' (1 Timothy 2:5), might from one element be capable of dying, and from the other be incapable."[45] Eutyches argued that after the Incarnation there was nothing human left in Christ. But if Christ bore nothing of our human nature to the cross, then how could we humans be saved by him?

The heresy of Eutyches was serious. Writing to the bishop of Constantinople would not be enough. So Leo also sent a letter to Pulcheria, asking her to intervene.[46] And Pulcheria soon found her opportunity. In July AD 450, Theodosius II was riding his horse on a hunting expedition when the horse stumbled, and Theodosius was badly injured. He died soon after, leaving no heir to his throne. Pulcheria moved quickly. She married Marcian, a well-respected senator who had been a personal assistant and friend to the commander of the eastern army. With Marcian as emperor, Pulcheria was now officially empress. Marcian publicly agreed that he would honor Pulcheria's vow of celibacy, so she retained her religious authority while gaining additional political power.[47] One of her first acts was to have Marcian convene a Church council at Chalcedon, a suburb of Constantinople.

The Council of Chalcedon (AD 451) was tasked with resolving the Christological issues that remained after the Council of Ephesus and with addressing the new concerns that had arisen around the teaching of Eutyches. A detailed account of the sixteen sessions of that council still exists today. The work of the council commenced on Monday, October 8th AD 451. The 300 to 520 bishops in attendance read and sustained the doctrinal affirmations of Nicaea and Constantinople. They also read and accepted as doctrinally accurate Cyril of Alexandria's *Second Letter to Nestorius* and the *Tome of Leo*. By Monday, October 22nd, they had presented, discussed, modified, and accepted a new definition of faith—the Chalcedonian Definition (see box 8.9), clarifying the Niceno-Constantinopolitan Creed.[48]

One can see in the Chalcedonian Definition language that avoids the position of Nestorius ("not parted or divided into two persons")

BOX 8.9   The Chalcedonian Definition (AD 451)

"Following, therefore, the holy fathers, we all in harmony teach confession of one and the same Son our Lord Jesus Christ, the same perfect in divinity and the same perfect in humanity, truly God and the same truly human, of a rational soul and body, consubstantial [*homoousios*] with the Father as regards his divinity, and the same consubstantial [*homoousios*] with us as regards his humanity, like us in all things apart from sin, begotten from the Father before the ages as regards his divinity, and the same in the last days for us and for our salvation from the Virgin Mary the *Theotokos* as regards his humanity, one and the same Christ, Son, Lord, Only-Begotten, acknowledged in two natures without confusion, change, division, or separation (the difference of the natures being in no way destroyed by the union, but rather the distinctive character of each nature being preserved and coming together into one person and one subsistent-being [*hypostasis*]), not parted or divided into two persons, but one and the same Son, Only-Begotten, God, Word, Lord, Jesus Christ, even as the prophets of old and Jesus Christ himself taught us about him and the creed of the fathers has handed down to us."[49]

and language that avoids the view of Eutyches ("acknowledged in two natures without confusion, change, division, or separation"). The resulting description of Christ is beautiful in its symmetry. It does not avoid but embraces the paradox of scriptural affirmations: Jesus is fully human (he thirsted, grew weary, he suffered pain, and bled for us), and Jesus is fully divine (he created the world as the Word of God, and during his mortal ministry, he forgave sins, atoned for our sins, and had the power to lay down his life and take it up again). Although it would be logical for two different natures to result in two different hypostases, or persons, the miracle of Christ's Incarnation—as declared in this Chalcedonian formula—is that both the

▲ **FIGURE 8.4** Ivory diptych. Constantinople, mid-sixth century. Ivory diptychs were often used for private devotion within elite Christian settings. Here, representations of the incarnate Jesus, son of Mary on the right, and Christ, the Divine Word made flesh on the left, are presented together, underscoring discussions like those at Chalcedon. Photo: Courtesy of Picasa, Wikimedia Commons

human nature and the divine nature come together (unmixed) into the one person and one *hypostasis,* Jesus Christ. This description of Christ's unified natures is called the *hypostatic union.* Although this term itself is unscriptural, it represents the earnest work of ancient Christians to summarize the message of scripture concerning the nature of Jesus Christ, the Son of God.

The Council of Chalcedon ended on November 1, AD 451, and Pulcheria died two years later (AD 453). The Niceno-Constantinopolitan Creed as clarified by the Council of Chalcedon has become a standard summary of the Christian message. It is professed by Christians of various denominations throughout the world even today.

After Chalcedon

The intent of these ancient councils was to unite Christians throughout the world, but they often resulted in new divisions. The Visigoths who sacked Rome were Christians who followed the teachings of Arius, who had been condemned at the First Council of Nicaea. Some eastern churches separated after the Council of Chalcedon because of too much emphasis in the Chalcedonian Definition on the distinction between Jesus's two natures after the Incarnation; their own position is called miaphysitism, a belief in Christ's one nature (*mia* and *physis*) that is uniquely both human and divine. The Second (AD 553) and Third (AD 680–81) Councils of Constantinople were convened to

---

BOX 8.10 A Latter-day Saint Christology

Latter-day Saints tend to emphasize the divinity of our Lord and Savior, Jesus Christ. We also celebrate that Jesus Christ, the Word of God, became flesh and dwelt among us and that he experienced all that it means to be human but was without sin. We believe that Jesus is one with the Father just as he desires us to be one with him. Latter-day Saints have not developed a Christological creed that defines Christ's divine and human natures in a way similar to the Councils of Ephesus and Chalcedon. We would likely differ from these definitions of faith primarily in our doctrine of the innate divine potential of human nature—that we are spirit children of Heavenly Parents (see Doctrine and Covenants 93:29–40; Abraham 3:22–23).

remedy this rift between the east and west. These councils resulted in greater theological precision; for instance, the Third Council took up the question of Jesus's will and concluded that he had two wills: one human, the other divine (see Luke 22:42).[50] But with greater theological precision came additional divisions between churches. By AD 1054, Greek Orthodox and Roman Catholic Christians formally divided, in part, over the question of whether the Holy Spirit proceeds from the Father alone or equally from both the Father and the Son (*filioque*).[51] Later Protestant councils reinforced their separation from Roman Catholicism with new creeds of their own. In fact, some of the traditional Christian beliefs that Latter-day Saints consider most troubling only appear as "creeds" in these much later Protestant councils—for instance, the statement that God is "without body, parts, or passions" (see box 8.10).

A God "without Body, Parts, or Passions"?

The statement that God is "without body, parts, or passions" does not appear in Christian creeds until the Lutheran Augsburg Confession (AD 1530)—more than a thousand years after the authors and events that were discussed in this chapter.[52] Nevertheless, discussions about God the Father's "impassability" (emotionlessness or being uncontrolled by passions) and His "incorporeality" (existing without a body) began as early as the second and third centuries AD.

The descriptions of God as impassible and incorporeal belong to a theological tradition called apophatic theology (from the Greek *apophasis*, "denial" or "negation"). Also called negative theology, apophatic theology is an attempt to describe God by describing what God is not. For example, God is defined by some Christians as "not passible" and as "not corporeal." Although these specific definitions of God do not appear explicitly in scripture, apophatic theology does appear in scripture. According to Paul's letters, God's judgments are "unsearchable" (Romans 11:33) and his great gift "unspeakable" (2 Corinthians 9:15), and God is "invisible" (Colossians 1:15), "immortal," and "unapproachable" in his glory (1 Timothy 6:18). If the

▲ **FIGURE 8.5** Depiction of the Trinity creating Eve and Adam; detail from a carved stone sarcophagus, ca. 325, Musée départemental Arles Antique. The three figures at the left represent (left to right) the Holy Spirit, the Father (seated), and the Son, whose hand rests upon the head of Eve (damaged) in a gesture of blessing. Eve and Adam are depicted in diminutive scale, reflecting their newly-made status (as if newborn). At far right the balding male whose hand rests upon Adam's shoulder has been interpreted as the Apostle Paul, who wrote that Adam's Fall brought death and sin into the world, which Christ as the new Adam overcame through his death and resurrection (Romans 5:12–21; 1 Corinthians 15:21–22). Two other male figures seen faintly in the background reflect a convention of early Christian frieze sarcophagi, which sculptors filled with figures of anonymous onlookers and witnesses to the biblical scenes in the foreground. The Christian patrons who commissioned this sarcophagus, and the sculptors who created it, were comfortable depicting the Father, Son, and Holy Spirit anthropomorphically and corporeally. Photo: Mark D. Ellison

things of this world, human things, are searchable, speakable, visible, mortal, and approachable, and if God's ways are higher than our ways (see Isaiah 55:8–9), then—so the logic goes—God cannot be any of these things. Extending this logic, one can see how a Christian might arrive at the conclusion that God is bodiless and emotionless. But that is only part of the story. The ideas of a passionless and bodiless God began with Christians defending themselves against paganism.

The idea that God is impassible arose out of Christian apologetics in the second century. As Christians wrote defenses (Greek *apologiai*) of their beliefs against pagan polytheists, they often contrasted God with the mythological gods of the pagans. Anyone familiar with Greek or Roman mythology knows that the gods of Mount Olympus were less than virtuous. In fact, the great myths of Greece and Rome often describe gods as being overcome by their passions and acting out of lust, anger, or envy. When Christians contrasted God with the impassioned gods of the pagans, the point was not to argue that God is without feeling but that God is not controlled by base human passions.[53] For these Christians, God experiences love but not lust, godly sorrow but not paralyzing grief, righteous-anger but not uncontrollable rage. For many early Christians, the claim that God was "without passions"

BOX 8.11   Divine Impassibility and the Possibility of Repentance

John Chrysostom (circa AD 370) taught: "For if the wrath of God were a passion, one might well despair as being unable to quench the flame which he had kindled by so many evil doings; but since the Divine nature is unimpassioned, even if He punishes . . . He does this not with wrath, but with tender care, and much loving-kindness; therefore, we should be of much good courage, and to trust in the power of repentance."[54]

meant that the Father was not subject to the whims of emotion (see box 8.11). Most Latter-day Saints would likely be sympathetic to this view. Other Christians, however, held more extreme views and believed that God could not experience anything comparable to human emotion because God did not have a body.

Scripture describes God as creating humans in his image (see Genesis 1:26–27); as possessing a face (see Exodus 33:11), a back (see Exodus 33:23), and wings with feathers (see Psalm 91:4); as a giant (see Isaiah 66:1), as "spirit" (John 4:24), and "a consuming fire" (Hebrews 12:29; see also Deuteronomy 4:24). Debates over which passages to interpret literally and which metaphorically were central to Christian discussions about God's body. In these debates, Christian discourse paralleled discussions among non-Christian philosophers about the nature of God. The Christian theologian Tertullian, for instance, appears closest to the views of Stoicism when he reads scripture to mean: "Everything that exists is body of some kind or another. Nothing is incorporeal except what does not exist."[55] For Tertullian, even fire and spirit are bodies or matter.[56] By contrast, Origen seems closest to contemporaneous developments in Platonism when he writes against Christians whom, he says, have a "degraded conception of God" because they believe God has a body. For Origen, this view demeans God because, he argues, all bodies are "divisible and material and corruptible," and it would be most impious to attribute corruptibility to God.[57]

Latter-day Saints have sometimes argued that philosophy corrupted the Christian notion of God.[58] We have seen here that the truth is more complicated. Some Christians read philosophy and participated in theological discussions that parallel, in some respects, the debates of philosophers.[59] But correlation does not imply causation! These two opposite examples, Tertullian and Origen, suggest that philosophy did not corrupt the Christian notion that God has a body any more than philosophy corrupted the Christian notion that God does *not* have a body. All Christian theologians relied on a careful

▲ **FIGURE 8.6** Fifth-century mosaic from a baptistery in Albegna, Italy, depicting three concentric circles, each containing a christogram with the Greek letters alpha and omega. This illustrates how ancient Christian artists experimented with abstract ways they might visually express their beliefs in the oneness and threeness of God. Photo: Wilpert, Die römischen Mosaiken und Malereien Bd3 Tafeln Mosaiken (1916), Taf. 88.1

BOX 8.12   A Latter-day Saint Theology

As Latter-day Saints, we affirm that God the Father and Jesus Christ have tangible bodies that are immortal, incorruptible, and glorious (Doctrine and Covenants 130:22). We affirm that God can be present in a distinct location, as Christ was through his Incarnation or as God the Father and Jesus Christ were in their manifestation to Joseph Smith in the Sacred Grove, and that simultaneously there is nowhere God's presence cannot reach. We affirm these things because of our interpretation of both the Bible and the revelations granted to the Prophet Joseph Smith. Understanding God's embodied nature gives us hope in his great plan for us mortal, embodied human beings—it nourishes the hope we have for our salvation through the resurrected, glorified, and embodied Savior, Jesus Christ. Even while we may disagree with other Christians about the nature of God as embodied, we can still admire their use of apophatic theology to glorify God.

reading of Christian scripture to reach their conclusions. And Christians found evidence for both these views in the Bible (for a Latter-day Saint view, see box 8.12).

Conclusion

For Latter-day Saints, some of the questions and answers of our ancient Christian ancestors may seem too speculative. It may seem as though they are looking beyond the mark or seeking to understand things that are beyond human understanding. Why did ancient Christians engage in such inquiry? For one, such questions were not mere intellectual curiosities. These questions go straight to the heart of faith in our redemption through Christ Jesus. If Jesus Christ were not completely human, could he completely ransom humanity? If Jesus Christ were not entirely divine, could he fully unite us with

BOX 8.13 **Words Matter**

Latter-day Saints and those Christians who affirm the Niceno-Constantinopolitan Creed and the Chalcedonian Definition share similar beliefs about God and Jesus Christ, but we often misunderstand each other because we, Latter-day Saints, can be less familiar with traditional Christian theological vocabulary.

Example 1: Many Christians, including Latter-day Saints, would agree that God is three distinct persons. Yet, if a Latter-day Saint were to describe this idea by saying, "God is three distinct *beings* (Greek *ousia*; Latin *essentia*)," Nicene Christians might hear that statement as implying that the Father, Son, and Holy Spirit have three different natures and/or purposes, similar to the various pagan gods of antiquity—something we Latter-day Saints do not believe.

Example 2: A Latter-day Saint might casually describe Christ as being half-human and half-God. To many Christians this would sound like we consider Jesus a demigod, like Hercules. Even more concerning, this language ("half") could denigrate the power of the Atonement of Jesus Christ. If Jesus is only half human, then he only redeemed half of what it means to be human. And if he is only half God, how could he make a statement such as "he that hath seen me, hath seen the Father" (John 14:9)? Christians, including Latter-day Saints, can jointly affirm that Jesus Christ participates fully in the Godhead (the divine nature) and experienced all that it means to be human, apart from sin. Jesus Christ is fully human and fully divine.

God? Ancient Christians asked questions about the divine nature because they wanted to understand God and to nurture their hope in redemption. For Latter-day Saints, there is value in learning how our ancient Christian ancestors talked about these questions—even when they differ from us (see box 8.13).

A second reason why our ancient Christian ancestors strove to understand the nature of God was the sincere belief that this labor of love would bring them closer to God. For many early Christians, to be created in the image of God meant, in part, that we are endowed with reason (Greek *logos*)—an aspect of the divine Logos or Word of God within us, the light of Christ. The effort to engage our God-gifted reason in order to understand our Heavenly Father nurtures that which is godlike within us. Gregory of Nazianzus, one of the great Christian theologians who helped to craft the Niceno-Constantinopolitan Creed, wrote: "In my opinion [the true essence and nature of God] will be discovered when that within us which is Godlike and divine, I mean our mind and reason, shall have mingled with its like, and the image [of God, you and I,] shall have ascended to the archetype [God himself], of which it has now the desire. And . . . 'we shall know even as we are known' [1 Corinthians 13:12]."[60]

Notes

1. When Jesus explained that being the Christ meant he would have to suffer, die, and rise again (see Matthew 16:21; see also Mark 8:31; Luke 9:22), Peter refused to accept it (see Matthew 16:22; see also Mark 8:32). See also John 12:16.

2. Jesus's followers came to understand him with greater clarity after the Resurrection (see Luke 24:21, 25–32) and with more certainty after the endowment of the Holy Spirit at Pentecost (see Acts 1:8, 2:1–36).

3. On the complexity of ancient Jewish monotheism, see Alan F. Segal, *Two Powers in Heaven: Early Rabbinic Reports about Christianity and Gnosticism* (1977; repr., Leiden: Brill, 2002); Peter Schäfer, *Two Gods in Heaven: Jewish Concepts of God in Antiquity*, trans. Allison Brown (Princeton, NJ: Princeton University Press, 2020).

4. On second-century Christology, see Jason R. Combs, "'Christ' after the

Apostles: The Humanity and Divinity of the Savior in the Second Centu-ry" in *"Thou Art the Christ, the Son of the Living God": The Person and Work of Jesus in the New Testament—Sperry Symposium 2018*, ed. Eric Huntsman, Lincoln Blumell, and Tyler Griffin (Provo, UT: Religious Studies Center, Brigham Young University, 2018), 303–34. For more detailed treatments of early Christologies, see the foundational work, Aloys Grillmeier, *Christ in the Christian Tradition: From the Apostolic Age to Chalcedon (451)*, 2nd rev. ed., trans. J. Bowden (1965; repr., Atlanta: John Knox, 1975); see also Larry W. Hurtado, *Lord Jesus Christ: Devotion to Jesus in Earliest Christianity* (Grand Rapids, MI: Eerdmans, 2003); James L. Papandrea, *The Earliest Christologies: Five Images of Christ in the Postapostolic Age* (Downers Grove, IL: IVP Academic, 2016).

5. Gregory of Nazianzus, *Epistle* 101.32; trans. adapted from Christopher A. Beeley, *Gregory of Nazianzus on the Trinity and the Knowledge of God: In Your Light We Shall See Light* (Oxford: Oxford University Press, 2008), 127.

6. For previous studies of ancient Christian conceptions of the nature of God by Latter-day Saints, see especially Lincoln H. Blumell, "Rereading the Council of Nicaea and Its Creed" in *Standing Apart: Mormon Historical Consciousness and the Concept of Apostasy*, ed. Miranda Wilcox and John D. Young (New York: Oxford University Press, 2014), 196–217; for addi-tional bibliography, see Blumell, "Rereading the Council of Nicaea and Its Creed," 209–10n1. See also Keith Norman, "Ex Nihilo: The Development of the Doctrines of God and Creation in Early Christianity," *BYU Studies* 17, no. 3 (1977): 275–90.

7. For more on Sabellius, see Epiphanius, *Against Heresies* 62.2.2 (GSC 31:390). For more on modalism, see J. N. D. Kelly, *Early Christianity Doc-trines*, rev. ed. (New York: HarperSanFransisco, 1978), 110–23; Rebecca Lyman, "Monarchianism" in *Encyclopedia of Early Christianity*, 2nd ed., ed. Everett Ferguson (New York: Routledge, 1999), 764–65; John Anthony McGuckin, *The Westminster Handbook to Patristic Theology* (Louisville, KY: Westminster John Knox, 2004), 225–27.

8. Tertullian, *Against Praxeas* 10; translation from Ernest Evans, *Tertullian's Treatise Against Praxeas* (Eugene, OR: Wipf & Stock, 1948).

9. Tertullian, *Against Praxeas* 11.3, trans. Peter Holmes (*Ante-Nicene Fathers* 3:605).

10. See Tertullian, *Against Praxeas* 11.4; 25.1.

11. See Tertullian, *Against Praxeas* 25.1.

12. See Tertullian, *Against Praxeas* 2. For more on Tertullian's theology, see Eric Osborn, *Tertullian, First Theologian of the West* (Cambridge: Cam-bridge University Press, 1997), 116–39.

13. See Tertullian, *Against Praxeas* 2.
14. Tertullian, *Against Praxeas* 11.4, trans. Peter Holmes (*Ante-Nicene Fathers* 3:606); adapted.
15. Tertullian, *Against Praxeas* 9; trans. Evans, *Tertullian's Treatise Against Praxeas*. For more on Tertullian's theology and subordinationism, see Geoffrey D. Dunn, *Tertullian* (London: Routledge, 2004), 24–26; Eric Osborn, *Tertullian, First Theologian of the West* (Cambridge: Cambridge University Press, 1997), 116–43.
16. For a more thorough treatment of the Nicene and Niceno-Constantinopolitan Creeds, see Lewis Ayres, *Nicaea and Its Legacy: An Approach to Fourth-Century Trinitarian Theology* (Oxford: Oxford University Press, 2004); R. P. C. Hanson, *The Search for the Christian Doctrine of God: The Arian Controversy, 318–381* (1988; repr., Grand Rapids, MI: Baker Academic, 2005).
17. For Arius, Jesus is rightfully called God but is inferior to the Father: "Thus the Son who was not, but existed at the paternal will, is only-begotten God, and he is distinct from everything else"; Extracts from the Thalia of Arius—Athanasius, *On the Synods of Ariminum and Seleuceia* 15; trans. J. Stevenson and W. H. C. Frend, *A New Eusebius: Documents Illustrating the History of the Church to AD 337* (Grand Rapids, MI: Baker, 2013), 374–75.
18. Arius, *Letter to Alexander of Alexandria*; trans. adapted from Edward Rochie Hardy, ed., *Christology of the Later Fathers* (Louisville, KY: Westminster John Knox Press, 1954), 333.
19. See box 8.7 for the refutations of Arian language in the Nicene Creed.
20. See Alexander of Alexandria, *Letter to Alexander of Byzantium [Constantinople]* 44.
21. For more on the "epistolary war" between Arius and Alexander, see Henryk Pietras, *Council of Nicaea (325): Religious and Political Context, Documents, Commentaries* (Rome: Gregorian & Biblical Press, 2016), 39–99.
22. Eusebius, *Life of Constantine* 3.4; trans. Ernest Cushing Richardson (*Nicene and Post-Nicene Fathers* 2/1:520).
23. On the debate about the celebration of Easter, see Eusebius, *Life of Constantine* 3.5; on the summons to council, see Eusebius, *Life of Constantine* 3.6.1. Celebration of Emperor Constantine's twentieth year of rule may have been the primary impetus for the summons to the Council of Nicaea in AD 325 rather than the ostensibly insignificant debates over Arianism and the date of Easter; see Pietras, *Council of Nicaea (325)*, 147.
24. See Eusebius, *Life of Constantine* 3.7; for more on the number of attendees, see Hubertus R. Drobner, *Fathers of the Church: A Comprehensive Introduction*, trans. Siegfried S. Schatzmann (Peabody, MA: Hendrickson, 2007),

239.

25. In this chapter, English translations of the Nicene and Niceno-Constantinopolitan Creed are my own based on the Greek found in Hubertus R. Drobner, *Fathers of the Church: A Comprehensive Introduction*, trans. Siegfried S. Schatzmann (Peabody, MA: Hendrickson, 2007), 292–94. The Niceno-Constantinopolitan Creed adds that Christ was "begotten before time," making him the eternal Son of the Eternal Father; see box 8.7.

26. For more information on the Church's Correlation Department, see Frank O. May Jr., "Correlation of the Church, Administration" in *Encyclopedia of Mormonism*, vol. 1, ed. Daniel H. Ludlow (New York, NY: Macmillan, 1992), 323–25; Daniel H. Ludlow, "Correlation" in *Encyclopedia of Latter-day Saint History*, ed. Arnold K. Garr, Donald Q. Cannon, and Richard O. Cowan (Salt Lake City, UT: Deseret Book, 2000), 250–51.

27. Translation my own; see note 25.

28. Translation my own; see note 25. For more on how much of the Nicene Creed is supported not only by the Bible but also by the Book of Mormon and other Restoration scripture, see Blumell, "Rereading the Council of Nicaea and Its Creed," 203–205.

29. For more on the Council of Nicaea and the First Council of Constantinople, see Leo Donald Davis, *The First Seven Ecumenical Councils (325–787): Their History and Theology* (Collegeville, MN: Liturgical Press, 1983), 28–100. See also Lewis Ayres, *Nicaea and Its Legacy: An Approach to Fourth-Century Trinitarian Theology* (Oxford: Oxford University Press, 2004), 187–221, 244–269.

30. Arius, *Letter to Alexander of Alexandria*; trans. adapted from Hardy, *Christology of the Later Fathers*, 333.

31. Translation my own; see note 25. The elided section borrows language directly from scripture: "God from God, light from light [see 1 John 1:5], true God from true God [see 1 John 5:20]."

32. Within the context of the Nicene Creed, however, *ousia* functions as a synonym for *hypostasis*, and that word does appear in scripture. In Hebrews 1:3, Jesus Christ is described as "the express image of [God the Father's] person [*hypostasis*]." That said, the Nicene Creed moves beyond the language of Hebrews when it describes Jesus as "one substance" (*homoousios*) with God the Father.

33. Marcellus of Ancyra, for instance, interpreted the homoousios language of Nicaea in the direction of modalism; although he would reject that description. See Ayres, *Nicaea and Its Legacy*, 62–69; Jörg Ulrich, "Nicaea and the West," *Vigiliae Christianae* 51 (1997): 10–24.

34. *Cunctos populos*, also called the Edict of Thessalonica (*Theodosian Code*

16.1.2); see J. Stevenson and W. H. C. Frend, ed., *Creeds, Councils, and Controversies: Documents Illustrating the History of the Church, AD 337–461* (Grand Rapids, MI: Baker Academic, 2012), 174–75.

35. Recent studies of this period have demonstrated that even though Theodosius II was officially made the emperor of the east, Pulcheria wielded a tremendous amount of political and religious power. See Philip Jenkins, *Jesus Wars: How Four Patriarchs, Three Queens, and Two Emperors Decided What Christians Would Believe for the Next 1,500 Years* (New York: HarperOne, 2010), 118–120; Kathryn Chew, "Virgins and Eunuchs: Pulcheria, Politics and the Death of Emperor Theodosius II," *Historia: Zeitschrift für Alte Geschichte* 55, no. 2 (2006): 207–27; Stephen J. Shoemaker, *Mary in Early Christian Faith and Devotion* (New Haven: Yale University Press, 2016).

36. For more on the political situation in the early fifth century, see Peter Brown, *The World of Late Antiquity: AD 150–750* (New York: W. W. Norton & Co., 1989), 115–35; Fergus Millar, *A Greek Roman Empire: Power and Belief under Theodosius II (408–450)* (Berkeley: University of California Press, 2006), 1–123.

37. See Nestorius, *Letter to Cyril of Alexandria* 6; trans. John I. McEnerney, *Saint Cyril of Alexandria: Letters 1–50*, Fathers of the Church 76 (Washington, DC: Catholic University of America Press, 1987), 45. For more on the significance of the Theotokos debate, see Brian E. Daley, "Christ and Christologies," in *The Oxford Handbook of Early Christian Studies*, ed. Susan Ashbrook Harvey and David G. Hunter (Oxford: Oxford University Press, 2008), 886–905, esp. 896.

38. See Cyril of Alexandria, *Third Letter to Nestorius* 19. For more on the Council of Ephesus, see Davis, *The First Seven Ecumenical Councils*, 102–27. For more on the Christology of Cyril of Alexandria and Nestorius, see John A. McGuckin, *Saint Cyril of Alexandria, The Christological Controversy: Its History, Theology, and Texts* (Leiden: Brill, 1994).

39. See Nestorius, *Bazaar of Heracleides* 2.2; translation from G.R. Driver and Leonard Hodgson, *Nestorius: The Bazaar of Heracleides* (Oxford: Oxford University Press, 1925), 339.

40. Acts of Chalcedon 1.527; translation from Michael Gaddis and Richard Price, ed., *The Acts of the Council of Chalcedon* (Liverpool: Liverpool University Press, 2005), 222.

41. For the influence of Cyril of Alexandria and an Apollinarian forgery on Eutyches's Christology, see Christopher A. Beeley, *The Unity of Christ: Continuity and Conflict in Patristic Tradition* (New Haven: Yale, 2012), 275–76.

42. See Nestorius, *Bazaar of Heracleides* 2.2; Acts of Chalcedon 1.516.

43. Leo, who had attended the Council of Ephesus as a deacon and envoy of the bishop of Rome, by AD 440 became bishop of Rome.

44. Leo, *Tome* 5; trans. Hardy, *Christology of the Later Fathers*, 366.

45. Leo, *Tome* 3; trans. adapted from Hardy, *Christology of the Later Fathers*, 363.

46. For a summary of this correspondence see Chew, "Virgins and Eunuchs," 224, 226, n. 91.

47. See Jenkins, *Jesus Wars*, 117; Chew, "Virgins and Eunuchs," 207–27.

48. Gaddis and Price, *The Acts of the Council of Chalcedon*, 1:44 (table 3).

49. Acts of Chalcedon 5.34; trans. adapted from Gaddis and Price, *The Acts of the Council of Chalcedon*, 2:204. For more on the Council of Chalcedon, see Davis, *The First Seven Ecumenical Councils*, 129–155. For more on the Christology of Leo and Eutyches, see Bernard Green, *The Soteriology of Leo the Great* (Oxford: Oxford University Press, 2008), 188–47.

50. For more on the Third Council of Constantinople and the monothelite (one-will) controversy, see Davis, *The First Seven Ecumenical Councils*, 194–216. For a fuller treatment of dyothelite (two-wills) christology, see Demetrios Bathrellos, *The Byzantine Christ: Person, Nature, and Will in the Christology of Saint Maximus the Confessor* (Oxford: Oxford University Press, 2004).

51. For a detailed history of this controversy, see A. Edward Siecienski, *The Filioque: A History of a Doctrinal Controversy* (Oxford: Oxford University Press, 2010).

52. See Terryl L. Givens, *Wrestling the Angel: The Foundations of Mormon Thought: Cosmos, God, Humanity* (Oxford: Oxford University Press, 2015), 85. For more on the Lutheran Augsburg Confession, see Charles P. Arand, James A. Nestingen, and Robert Kolb, *The Lutheran Confessions: History and Theology of the Book of Concord* (Minneapolis, MN: Fortress Press, 2012).

53. See Justin, *1 Apology* 25.1–3; compare with Gregory of Nazianzus, *Oration* 28.11. See also Tertullian describing God as possessing more refined emotions than human beings; Tertullian, *Against Marcion* 2.16.4–7; compare with Augustine, *On Patience* 1.1. For discussion of these passages and others, see Paul L. Gavrilyuk, *The Suffering of the Impassible God: The Dialectics of Patristic Thought* (Oxford: Oxford University Press, 2004), 47–63.

54. John Chrysostom, *Letter to Theodore after His Fall* 1.4, in *Nicene and Post-Nicene Fathers* 1/9:93, adapted. See also Gavrilyuk, *The Suffering of the Impassible God*, 60–63.

55. Tertullian, *On the Flesh of Christ* 11.4; trans. in Markschies, *God's Body*, 70.

56. See Tertullian, *On the Soul* 22.2; Tertullian, *Against Praxeas* 7.7; see also

the discussion of Tertullian's view on the corporeality of the soul in Markschies, *God's Body*, 69–71, 109–11.

57. Origen, *On Prayer* 23.3; trans. Alistair Stewart-Sykes, *Tertullian, Cyprian, Origen: On the Lord's Prayer* (Crestwood, NY: St. Vladimir's Seminary, 2004), 163. For more on Origen's view on the incorporeality of God, see Markschies, *God's Body*, 54–69.

58. For instance, see Richard R. Hopkins, *How Greek Philosophy Corrupted the Christian Concept of God*, 2nd ed. (1988; repr., Springville, UT: Horizon Publishers, 2009). Latter-day Saint scholar David Paulsen has written much on divine embodiment; see David L. Paulsen, "Early Christian Belief in a Corporeal Deity: Origen and Augustine as Reluctant Witnesses," *Harvard Theological Review* 83 (1990): 107–14; the responses by Kim Paffenroth, "Paulsen on Augustine: An Incorporeal or Nonanthropomorphic God?," *Harvard Theological Review* 86 (1993), 233–35; David L. Paulsen, "Reply to Kim Paffenroth's Comment," *Harvard Theological Review* 86 (1993): 235–39. See also Carl W. Griffin and David L. Paulsen, "Augustine and the Corporeality of God," *Harvard Theological Review* 95 (2002): 97–118; David L. Paulsen, "Divine Embodiment: The Earliest Christian Understanding of God," in *Early Christians in Disarray: Contemporary LDS Perspectives on the Christian Apostasy*, ed. Noel B. Reynolds (Provo: BYU Press, 2005), 239–93. Paulsen's work has been favorably received by Stephen H. Webb, *Mormon Christianity: What Other Christians Can Learn from the Latter-day Saints* (Oxford: Oxford University Press, 2013), 160–165; Markschies, *God's Body*, 320–330.

59. As Origen advised Gregory Thaumaturgus, the best thinking of the day (philosophy) should only be the "handmaiden" to Christianity; see *Philocalia of Origen* 13.1.

60. Gregory of Nazianzus, *Second Theological Oration* 17; trans. adapted from Hardy, *Christology of the Later Fathers*, 147.

＊ 9 ＊

RECEIVING CHRIST

Atonement, Grace, and Eternal Salvation

Cecilia M. Peek

For all have sinned, and come short of the glory of
God; being justified freely by his grace through the
redemption that is in Christ Jesus: whom God hath set
forth to be a propitiation through faith in his blood.
—Romans 3:23–25

At the time Jesus was born, some expected that the Messiah would be a victorious king who would triumph over the Romans. Others believed he would come as a priest to restore the proper sacrificial order. Still others thought he would arrive as the perfect teacher of the Law.[1] All of these assumptions were based on a close reading of passages from the Jewish Bible. For early Christians, Jesus Christ fulfilled each of these expectations but not in the way many had anticipated. For them, the need for a messiah encompassed far more than politics or contemporary religious practices; the fate of humanity itself was at stake. Jesus Christ came to save humanity through his teaching, his perfect life, his sacrifice, and his triumph over sin and death. He came as God's gift of grace to the world.

One of the critical themes in Christian theology, and one that has engaged thinkers and writers from the earliest Christian era, is the relationship between grace and salvation—examining what grace is and how it makes redemption possible. These were and remain complex matters, but it is vital to investigate how ancient Christians addressed and began to resolve these questions and how their efforts and answers still resonate today (see box 9.1).

Christian conceptions of grace and its role in salvation overwhelmingly depend on Paul's use of the term in his epistles. While other New Testament authors employ the word *grace* (Greek *charis*), none does so more often than Paul. Of the more than 150 instances of the expression in the New Testament, 102 of those occur in the securely attributed Pauline corpus, with 26 of them in Romans alone. The earliest preserved Pauline use of the word occurs in 1 Thessalonians, dating to AD 50 or 51.[2] In that epistle, Paul uses *charis* twice,

Why It Matters

Authors of the New Testament texts and other early Christian writers devoted significant attention to investigating the meaning of and relationship between grace and salvation. Examining what early Christians believed grace and salvation to mean and how the writers described the relationship between them can provide us with a rich vocabulary for talking about these vitally important ideas. Encountering the depth of feeling and faith of ancient Christians as they considered the goodness of God's greatest gifts to humankind can direct us to more profound insights and experience with Jesus's Atonement ourselves.

both times in a simple greeting formula: one at the beginning and one at the end of his letter (see 1 Thessalonians 1:1; 5:28). While he links grace to God the Father and Jesus Christ, Paul does not present a doctrine of grace in this early letter. However, by the time Paul composed the epistle to the Galatians and, certainly, the epistle to the Romans, he had a developed theology of grace and salvation that would inform early Christian ideas and discussions.[3]

Charis: Pre-Christian Definitions and Paul

Paul's letters use a wide variety of Greek terms to convey notions of God's favors and gifts, but the word *charis* is the one most commonly rendered "grace" in English translations. This word had a long history before Paul appropriated it to articulate divine favor.[4] *Charis*, which is a common enough term in Greek, occurs in the earliest surviving examples of Greek literature, appearing in the works of the archaic poets Homer and Hesiod. It denotes external charm, favor, or beauty, but also means kindness, goodwill, or benevolence, as well as the favors that are inspired by that benevolence.[5]

There is notable reciprocity in *charis*.[6] While it can refer to *outward* appearance, it likewise refers to *inward* character. While it encompasses the favors motivated by kindness and goodwill, it also describes the grateful response to those favors.[7] In Paul's cultural context, this reciprocity can be seen as having delineated ideas and practices of gift giving. The practice of reciprocal giving can be found in Greek culture all the way back to Homeric epics and the principles of hospitality promoted therein.[8] The Romans likewise had well-defined ideas about the bestowing of favors and reciprocity, specifically in their system of political patronage. Someone granting a benefaction was the patron. This benefaction (*beneficium*) obliged the recipient as a client, from whom (and from whose family, friends, and allies) the patron could expect favors, including political favors.[9] The Jews also gave gifts with the "expectation of a return," and although they were also supposed to give to the poor, who might well be unable to offer a gift as repayment, they could anticipate God's blessing as recompense.[10] In all of the ancient cultures influencing Paul's milieu, there was an anticipation of some return for a benefaction bestowed.[11]

Importantly, gift giving was also regulated by the worthiness of the recipient. As John Barclay rightly observed, "Most gifts and benefits in the ancient world were distributed discriminately to fitting or worthy recipients."[12] That worthiness might be measured in a variety of ways—social status, political influence, moral goodness—but one would *not* venture to confer favor on the undeserving.[13]

From the pre-Christian notions of *charis* as kindness, benevolence, and reciprocal favor, Paul derives his application of the term to God's goodwill and favor to humankind. In his application, however, he transforms *charis*, endowing it with meaning that persists into the Christian period and shapes how Christians apply and elaborate the term ever after. For Paul, grace is not "merely an attitude

▶ **FIGURE 9.1**   Mosaic portrait of Paul, Ravenna, Archbishop's Chapel, sixth century. Paul is often depicted in early Christian art. He is recognizable in this portrait by his dark hair, beard, and receding hairline. Photo: Scala/Art Resource NY

or disposition."[14] The grace of God *is* Jesus Christ. The incarnated Son is the favor given, the active and physical manifestation of God's kindness, expressed in Christ's life, death, and Resurrection.[15]

For Paul, moreover, grace always encompasses the idea that the favor humans receive is something freely given and utterly unmerited. The Apostle's perspective is revolutionary in this regard. In sharp contrast to the idea that gifts ought to be given to someone worthy and with the anticipation of something in return, Paul, whose theology has fully evolved in his epistle to the Romans, declares: "Being justified freely by his grace through the redemption that is in Christ Jesus: whom God hath set forth to be a propitiation through faith in his blood" (Romans 3:24–25). In the King James Version of the Bible, the word translated as "freely" in English is *dōrean* in Greek, which can mean "as a gift," "as a free gift," or "without payment."[16] Significantly, Paul also says that "God commendeth his love toward us, in that, *while we were yet sinners*, Christ died for us" (Romans 5:8; italics added). Elsewhere in Romans, humans are referred to as being "without strength," "ungodly," and "enemies" (Romans 5:6, 10), affirming that Christ gave the free gift when we categorically did *not* deserve it—"while we were yet sinners."

The gracious gift identified by Paul is the means by which death is overcome and by which people can receive a remission of sins and be justified before God—to be absolved of guilt and freed from the results of sin, to be "declared or made righteous."[17] God's grace is what makes justification and, by extension, salvation possible. That salvation is not earned by human righteousness but is effected through divine favor:

> Therefore, just as sin came into the world through one man, and death came through sin, and so death spread to all. . . . Death exercised dominion from Adam to Moses, even over those whose sins were not like the transgression of Adam, who is a type of the one who was to come. But the free gift is not like the trespass. For if the many died through one man's trespass, much more surely have the grace of God and the free gift in the grace of one man, Jesus

Christ, abounded for the many. (Romans 5:12, 14–
15 New Revised Standard Version)

Paul's "benefaction ideology" influences all future discussions of grace
and salvation.[18]

Postapostolic Conceptions of Grace

Christian thinkers who succeeded the first generation of Apostles
were sincere, earnest believers striving to understand and communicate the Christian message. One cannot, however, speak of a systematic investigation of grace and salvation in the earliest generation of
postapostolic writers. Ancient Christian writers had no recognized
Atonement theories, no established definitions of grace and salvation, and no fully developed vocabulary or analogies to explain what
grace and salvation were or how they worked. These earliest Christians, to whom we look for so much of the thought and language
we now depend on to make sense of the Atonement of Jesus Christ,
were just beginning to develop an understanding of the Atonement,
relying partly on Old Testament ideas and heavily on Paul's letters.
Even without a systematic theology of the Atonement, one can detect
important references to these themes among the Apostolic Fathers
and other early Church Fathers (see box 9.2).

All of these authors grounded their understanding of the Atonement of Jesus Christ and human salvation in their close reading of
New Testament teachings on these subjects. In some cases, the authors are trying to clarify and amplify Paul's thinking for fledgling
Christian communities. "The most sustained engagement" of this
subject belongs to Augustine of Hippo (AD 354–430), and will be
discussed at the end of this chapter.[19] Only select examples of these
various references can be discussed here.

The First Epistle of Clement to the Corinthians (circa AD 95–96), a
letter purportedly written by Clement of Rome,[20] establishes a critical connection between grace and repentance: "Let us fix our eyes on
the blood of Christ and understand how precious it is to his Father,
because, being poured out for our salvation, it won for the whole

world the grace of repentance. Let us review all the generations in turn, and learn that . . . the Master has given an opportunity for repentance to those who desire to turn to him."[21] Here, Clement seems to indicate that the possibility of repentance is the unique manifestation of grace leading to salvation. Elsewhere, Clement refers to the "yoke of his grace," suggesting that Christians are bound by God's gift. Further, he reminds his readers: "The ministers of the grace of God spoke about repentance through the Holy Spirit; indeed, the Master of the universe himself spoke about repentance with an oath: 'For as I live, says the Lord, I do not desire the death of the sinner so much as his repentance' (Ezekiel 33:11)."[22] This teaching likewise links grace to repentance since it was the "ministers of grace" who spoke about that repentance, and it is implied that grace-inspired repentance can outdo death. According to Clement, grace inspires humans, obligates humans (the "yoke of grace"), and requires humans to repent for it to be fully effective. There is no explicit reference in this letter to a debate about the efficacy of grace versus the efficacy of works in human salvation, but Clement's emphasis on repentance allows for the possibility that such a debate was already happening in nascent Christianity and that Clement wanted to assure his audience that the act of repentance is the necessary result of and response to grace.

Justin Martyr, writing in the middle of the second century, was a defender and martyr of the Christian faith.[23] Justin sees the grace of Jesus Christ extending back into the pages of the Old Testament. Specifically, he addresses God's promise that Abraham would be "a father of many nations," asserting that this did not refer to Abraham as the father of specific subgroups of people, such as "of the Arabs, or the Egyptians, or the Idumaeans"—after all, Ishmael and Esau also fathered mighty nations. "What greater favor, then, did Christ bestow on Abraham," Justin asks.[24] The term here translated as "[bestowing] favor" is *charizetai* (χαρίζεται), whose root is the same as *charis*, meaning grace. So Justin asks what more *grace* did Christ bestow on Abraham. And he answers: "This: that he likewise called with his voice, and commanded him to leave the land wherein he dwelt. And with that same voice he has also called all of us, and we have abandoned our former way of life in which we used to practice evils common to all the other inhabitants of the world. And we shall inherit the Holy Land together with Abraham, receiving our inheritance for all eternity, because by our similar faith we have become children of Abraham."[25] In Justin's construct, reminiscent of Paul's invocation of Abraham in his letters, Jesus Christ is the one who bestowed grace on Abraham, and that grace takes the form of Christ calling Abraham and enjoining him to leave the land in which he was living. That land becomes a figure for sin, since we are called by that same gracious voice (or Word) to leave "our former way of life in which we used to practice evils." Christians can, with Abraham, leave behind the land of sin and "inherit the Holy Land" of salvation and eternal life, winning "our inheritance for all eternity."[26] Justin locates grace in the Old Testament context, mediated by Jesus Christ, the Word of God, and functioning as a salvific force and impulse. (For more on following the Word, Jesus Christ, as central to our salvation, see the section "Christ the Illuminator" later in this chapter.)

Irenaeus of Lyons bridged the second and third centuries. He personally knew Polycarp, one of the Apostolic Fathers, from his homeland of Smyrna. According to Irenaeus, Polycarp learned directly from the Apostle John and was appointed bishop of Smyrna by original Apostles. Irenaeus eventually made his way to Rome, where he studied and taught. From there, he went to serve in a church in Lyon.[27]

BOX 9.3 The Grace of Humanity's Divine Potential

In the second century, Irenaeus suggested that humans have the potential to become like God:

"For we cast blame upon [God], because we have not been made gods from the beginning, but at first merely men, then at length gods; although God has adopted this course out of His pure benevolence, that no one may impute to Him invidiousness or grudgingness. He declares, 'I have said, Ye are gods; and ye are all sons of the Highest' (Psalm 82:6). But since we could not sustain the power of divinity, He adds, 'But ye shall die like men' (Psalm 82:7), setting forth both truths—the kindness of His free gift, and our weakness, and also that we were possessed of power over ourselves. For after His great kindness He graciously conferred good [upon us], and made men like to Himself, [that is] in their own power; while at the same time by His prescience He knew the infirmity of human beings, and the consequences which would flow from it; but through [His] love and [His] power, He shall overcome the substance of created nature. For it was necessary, at first, that nature should be exhibited; then, after that, that what was mortal should be conquered and swallowed up by immortality, and the corruptible by incorruptibility, and that man should be made after the image and likeness of God, having received the knowledge of good and evil."[28]

For Irenaeus, the first manifestation of God's grace is "the creation of human beings in the image and likeness of God."[29] Irenaeus declares: "Man, a created and organized being, is rendered after the image and likeness of the uncreated God."[30] Speaking of the gift of creation and the eventual hope of immortality, he adds: "For after his great kindness, He graciously conferred good [upon us] and made men like to Himself," adding that "it was necessary . . . that man should be made after the image and likeness of God."[31] Grace is present in human history from the creation (see box 9.3 and chapter 7).

Central to Irenaeus's understanding of grace is his insistence that Christ is the example and source of grace. He avows that God "may, in the exercise of his grace, confer immortality on the righteous, and holy, and those who have kept his commandments, and have persevered in his love, some from the beginning, and others from their repentance, and may surround them with everlasting glory."[32] While Irenaeus allows that God's grace is already in evidence in the creation, grace increased after the arrival of Christ, and by means of that fuller grace, people may, under certain conditions, receive immortality and everlasting glory.[33] This latter point seems to be Irenaeus's way of addressing what he sees as a dangerous misconception of the Valentinians, a group he calls heretics—namely, he accuses the Valentinians of believing that with the grace they have received, they are freed from any obligation to do good works.[34] Those who have not yet obtained special knowledge (*gnōsis*) may still have to work to gain salvation, but the Valentinians believe that they have sufficient grace to be spared the labor. Irenaeus complains that they, therefore, "addict themselves without fear to all those kinds of forbidden deeds of which the scriptures assure us that 'they who do such things shall not inherit the kingdom of God.'"[35] Irenaeus goes on to describe the "forbidden deeds" in which the Valentinians participate: attending pagan religious festivals, attending gladiatorial games, and other activities Irenaeus considers unfit for followers of Christ. For Irenaeus, good works and proper Christian behavior remain important.

As "one of the first major systematic writers of Christianity," Irenaeus tried to articulate this delicate balance between how humans are saved by grace but are simultaneously accountable for their actions in order to combat what was seen as a heretical misinterpretation of the doctrine of grace and how it affected the work of salvation.[36] (For more on Irenaeus's understanding of Christ's role in our salvation, see the section "Christ the Restorer" later in this chapter.)

> **BOX 9.4   Grace and Works**
>
> "For by grace you have been saved through faith, and this is not your own doing; it is the gift of God—not the result of works, so that no one may boast. For we are what he has made us, created in Christ Jesus for good works, which God prepared beforehand to be our way of life" (Ephesians 2:8–10 NRSV).

The explicit and early connection between grace and salvation is well established. In Ephesians, it says, "By grace ye are saved" (Ephesians 2:5; see box 9.4).[37] Early Christian discussions of the work of Jesus Christ—his life, his death on the cross, his Resurrection—regard that work as the proof and embodiment of God's grace and the means by which salvation was accomplished.[38] But what was meant by salvation? How was it achieved and what did it mean for the faithful? These are questions to which early Christians gave thoughtful attention.

Sōtēria: Pre-Christian Definitions and Models of Salvation

The Greek word used in early Christian texts to express salvation (*sōtēria*) was already known in classical Greek. At that time, it referred to preservation, safety, a guarantee of security, deliverance from danger, a safe return (especially a safe return home after an absence), and bodily health.[39] In the Septuagint, which many early Christian writers knew and which was their regular source for Old Testament quotations, the word *sōtēria* stands for general safety, security, and deliverance from trouble, but it is also the specific term used to express Israel's escape at the Red Sea (see Exodus 14:13) and, therefore, often suggests God's power of deliverance in contrast to the futile "help of man."[40] In the New Testament, *sōtēria* is regularly translated as "salvation," referring to the results for humankind of the life,

▲ **FIGURE 9.2** Mosaic of Christ teaching apostles, S. Lorenzo/San Aquilino, Milan, late fourth/early fifth centuries. This apse mosaic depicts a youthful Christ enthroned, with a scrinium or box of scrolls at his feet, preaching to his apostles. Notice that the halo behind Christ's head identifies him with the Christogram (chi rho) and the Greek letters alpha and omega. Photo: Mark D. Ellison

death, and Resurrection of Jesus Christ.[41] Soteriology, which is the study of salvation, has resulted in several so-called atonement models. These classifications attempt to explain salvation and can generally be grouped into four areas: Christ the Illuminator (the educational model), Christ the Restorer (the physical model), Christ the Victor (the classic model), and Christ the Victim (sacrifice language, suggesting Christ as a sacrifice).[42] As we shall see, early Christian authors often assert and bridge more than one paradigm in their attempts to articulate and explicate the processes and results of the salvific work

BOX 9.5 **Ancient Christian Models for Describing the Atonement**

Atonement model	Problem	Solution	Related scriptures
Christ the Illuminator	Humanity is lost or ignorant without a guide and pursues false religion and sin.	Christ comes to illuminate us, to show and teach us how to live as God intended for us.	Matthew 16:24; John 17:3; 1 Peter 2:21 (see also 2 Nephi 31:16; 3 Nephi 27:27)
Christ the Restorer	Humanity, created in the image and likeness of God, lost that "God-likeness" through sin.	Christ restores humanity to our "God-likeness" by becoming human, by living a perfect life, and by his Resurrection.	John 11:25–26; Romans 5:12–21; 1 Corinthians 15:22 (see also 2 Nephi 2:26; Mosiah 3:19; 16:4–10; 27:25–26)
Christ the Victor	Satan and demons form a very real force, as do sin and death, that literally attack humans and keep them from reaching God.	Christ defeats Satan and demons, as well as sin and death, through his death and Resurrection.	Matthew 8:29–32; John 16:33; Romans 2:8; 1 Corinthians 15:54–57; Colossians 2:14–15 (see also Mosiah 15:8; Alma 22:14; 27:28; Mormon 7:5; Doctrine and Covenants 138:18, 23)
Christ the Victim	Humanity's sins merit death and divine wrath; humanity's fallen trajectory is toward corruption and destruction.	Christ offers himself as a sacrifice to propitiate divine wrath; or takes upon himself the punishment humanity deserves.	Romans 3:25; Galatians 3:13; Hebrews 8–10; 1 John 2:2 (see also 2 Nephi 2:7; Mosiah 15:9; Alma 42:15; Doctrine and Covenants 19:16)

of Jesus Christ. Each of these models grew out of the careful reading of scripture (see box 9.5).

Christ the Illuminator

Notions of Christ as the illuminator or educator treat multiple concerns. First of all, these views comprehend the idea that Jesus Christ is the perfect paradigm, and his disciples are freed from ignorance, false religion, and sin by following his example and teachings. This model also maintains that Christ brought the true knowledge (*gnōsis*) or reason (*logos*) and illumination through which the true God is revealed, and this is part of how humanity is rescued from ignorance of God's purposes. The idea of Christ as an educator and exemplar can be traced back at least to the texts of the New Testament and the Apostolic Fathers.[43] For instance, in the Gospel of John salvation is gained through a knowledge of God and Christ: "And this is life eternal, that they might *know* thee the only true God, and Jesus Christ, whom thou hast sent" (John 17:3; emphasis added). Both the *Didache* and the *Epistle of Barnabas* make reference to "two ways of life," indicating that the path marked by Jesus Christ is the true way. The *Didache* affirms: "There are two ways, one of life, and one of death."[44] It goes on to communicate moral directives for the Christian life.[45]

The view of Christ as the illuminator appears in the Church Fathers as well. Irenaeus declares: "We could have learned in no other way than by seeing our Teacher and hearing His voice with our own ears, that, having become imitators of His works as well as doers of His words, we may have communion with Him."[46] Jesus Christ provided direction in his teachings and in his life. This belief is relevant, as Frances Young observed, not least because of the possibility of persecution and martyrdom in the early Christian era, which tested the ability of Christians to imitate Christ not only by living well but also by dying well, if needed.[47] Biblical texts could be cited to highlight the death of Christ (and not just his life) as a behavioral example (see 1 Peter 2:21).[48]

As early as *The First Epistle of Clement to the Corinthians*, discussed previously, Christ as the illuminator is expressed in less practical and more metaphysical terms: "Through him our foolish and darkened mind springs up into the light; through him the Master has willed that we should taste immortal knowledge."[49] Justin Martyr and another Clement, Clement of Alexandria, continue this trend, pronouncing Christ as the Logos. This notion envisions Christ as the divine reason (*logos*) that makes truth known and saves humans by revealing the will and knowledge of the true God and inspiring the recipient of this knowledge to repent and turn to God.[50]

Clement of Alexandria, who lived in the late second and early third centuries, was a theologian who looked to detect connections between Christianity and Greek culture. He seems to have become the head of an independent school, wherein Christianity was offered as "the true philosophy."[51] It is perhaps more than coincidence, therefore, that Clement sees education (pedagogy) as central to God's saving grace. Clement, according to Matyáš Havrda, "elaborates the model of 'pedagogical' cooperation between the will of God and human effort towards the fulfillment of the goal of divine activity in the history of salvation."[52] God teaches us what we must do to achieve God's goal (our salvation), and we cooperate with God by doing it. Clement compares human "cooperation" in the process of salvation to a patient's cooperation with a doctor in the process of regaining health: "And as the physician ministers health to those who co-operate with him in order to heal, so also God ministers eternal salvation to those who co-operate for the attainment of knowledge and good conduct; and since what the commandments enjoin are in our own power, along with the performance of them, the promise is accomplished."[53]

In the fifth book of the *Stromata*, Clement maintains that humans must choose perfection, but he acknowledges that perfection can still only "be achieved by grace."[54] As Clement writes: "The free-will which is in us, by reaching the knowledge of the good, leaps and bounds over the barriers, as the gymnasts say; yet it is not without eminent grace that the soul is winged, and soars."[55] God and humans must cooperate through a careful interaction of grace and free will to enable salvation.

In Clement, the grace that is manifest in the life, death, and Resurrection of Jesus Christ demands something of human beings, as it does in the theologies of other early Christian thinkers, including efforts toward repentance and ongoing obedience. But for Clement, that gracious interaction requires an even greater response:

> God himself is love, and for the sake of this love, he made himself known. And while the unutterable nature of God is as a Father, his sympathy with us is as a Mother. . . . For this [the Son] came down, for this he assumed human nature, for this he willingly endured the sufferings of humanity, that by being reduced to the measure of our weakness, he might raise us to the measure of his power. And just before he poured out his offering, when he gave himself as a ransom, he left us a new testament: 'I give you my love' (John 13:34; 14:27). What is the nature and extent of this love? For each of us he laid down his life, the life which was worth the whole universe, and he requires in return that we should do the same for each other.[56]

According to Clement's reasoning, willingness to sacrifice oneself is an additional aspect of the response to grace, which, though given freely and generously, requires something of its recipients. Not only are Christ's life and death proof of God's love for humankind, but they constitute "a demand that humanity demonstrate comparable love for God" and for one another.[57]

In this model, God's gracious act was to send the Savior as a guide to show humanity a better path—a path that leads to God and salvation. Redemption is about both how the Christian lives and what the Christian knows. Redemption is illumination, and Jesus Christ, the Illuminator.[58]

Christ the Restorer

Of course, many early Christian thinkers believed, as Paul did, that "the wages of sin is death" (Romans 6:23). Knowledge, even divinely revealed knowledge, was not sufficient in itself. While a correct understanding of the true God and the true way might direct the

> **BOX 9.6** **Enacting Salvation: Atonement Models and Worship Rituals**
>
> Ancient Christians expressed their various models of the Atonement in their rituals of worship. The following are a few examples relating to the rites of baptism and the Eucharist (also called the sacrament or communion):
>
> **Christ the Illuminator**: Ancient Christians often referred to baptism as "illumination," to baptismal candidates as "those about to be enlightened," and to baptisteries as *phōtistēria* (places of illumination).[59] Oil lamps and torches lit the spaces in which the ceremonies of baptism and the Eucharist took place and were sometimes held by participants in those rites, heightening the symbolism of being illuminated by Christ.
>
> **Christ the Restorer**: Depictions of Adam and Eve were popular in early Christian art and sometimes appeared by baptismal fonts or in company with images of baptism, the Eucharist, and Christ. These visual juxtapositions suggested that Christ's Atonement reverses the Fall and redeems humanity, a redemption that humans receive through baptismal and Eucharistic rites. Irenaeus, for example, wrote that when ordinary bread "which is produced from the earth" is blessed, it "is no longer common bread, but the Eucharist, consisting of two realities, earthly and heavenly; so also our bodies, when they receive the Eucharist, are no longer corruptible, having the hope of the resurrection to eternity" (*Against Heresies* 4.18.5 [*Ante-Nicene Fathers* 1:486]).
>
> **Christ the Victor**: In early Christian art, many depictions of Christ include a victor's crown held over his head; similar crowns are depicted in baptismal settings. For example, a mosaic on the ceiling of the fourth-century Baptistery of San Giovanni in Fonte, Naples, depicts the hand of God extending a crown of life, visually conveying the idea that those baptized in the font below participate in Christ's victory over death and sin and echoing the testimony of Paul: "Thanks be to God, who gives us the victory through our Lord Jesus Christ" (1 Corinthians 15:57 NRSV; see also Romans 6:1–5).

Christ the Victim: From at least the late first century forward, ancient Christians regarded the Eucharist as the distinctively Christian sacrifice (Greek *thysia*) corresponding to and replacing the sacrificial offerings of animals that priests had formerly performed in the Temple of Jerusalem. The church table that held the bread and wine of the Eucharist was called an altar. Those who faithfully partook of the blessed bread and wine were "held to be united and assimilated to Christ, and so to God," receiving "the gift of eternal life, the remission of sins, and the imparting of heavenly joy."[60]

For more about ancient Christian worship and ritual, see chapter 6.

believer's actions and understanding, some remedy for the mortality introduced to humanity by Adam was still needed. Salvation must involve the Christian being delivered from death. This view of salvation—the physical model—likewise has its roots in the earliest Christian writings, both in New Testament texts and in the Church Fathers.[61] In *The First Epistle of Clement to the Corinthians* we read: "How, then, can we consider it to be some great and marvelous thing if the Creator of the universe shall bring about the resurrection of those who have served him in holiness?"[62] The *Didache*, which we saw above emphasizes Christ as Illuminator, also includes the physical aspect of Christ's Atonement: "We give thanks, Holy Father . . . for the knowledge and faith *and immortality* that you have made known to us through Jesus your servant."[63] Originally, the focus on immortality seems to have been eschatological—anticipation of immortality at some future time—but increasingly, their concern became the present life in Christ, wherein humans are actively being recreated by Christ (see box 9.6).[64]

While the physical model includes the idea that salvation answers the problem of death, it, more specifically, affirms that immortality is made possible through the Incarnation—the *physical* life—of Christ.

▲ **FIGURE 9.3** Detail from a fourth-century gold-glass medallion (excised gold foil between two layers of glass) that originally formed the base of a shallow glass dish. The scene depicts Christ beside Eve and Adam, extending his wonder-working staff (like the rod of Moses) towards Eve and Adam, suggesting that his transforming, life-giving miracles extend to the first parents (and all humanity). Photo: Scala/Art Resource NY

Of the ancient figures who elaborated this physical view of salvation, Irenaeus is perhaps the most important. Regarding the Incarnation, he says: "When [Christ] became *incarnate*, and was made man, He commenced afresh the long line of human beings and furnished us ... with *salvation*; so that what we had lost in Adam—namely, to be according to the image and likeness of God—we might recover in Christ Jesus."[65] Irenaeus asserts that Christ wins back for humankind what was lost by Adam. Irenaeus's explanation for Christ's Atonement is commonly called recapitulation. The name comes from the Latin verb *recapitulo*, which means "to go over the main parts of a thing again, to recapitulate."[66] The central idea is that Christ recapitulates the whole history of Adam, but in every particular in which Adam failed, Christ succeeds and restores the salvation of man that was lost in Adam.[67] Building on the teachings of Paul in his letter to the Romans, Irenaeus writes: "For as by the disobedience of the one man . . . the many were made sinners, and forfeited life; so was it necessary that, by the obedience of one man . . . many should be justified and receive salvation (Romans 5:19). Thus, then, was the Word of God made man. . . . God recapitulated [*recapitulavit*] in Himself the ancient formation of man, that He might kill sin, deprive death of its power, and vivify man."[68] Yet something more than immortality seems to be at issue in Irenaeus's conception of salvation. Elsewhere, he observes that "the Word of God, our Lord Jesus Christ . . . did, through His transcendent love, become what we are, *that He might bring us to be even what He is himself.*"[69] More than a century later, Athanasius is more explicit when he declares that Christ "became human that we might become divine."[70] While it is not absolutely clear what Athanasius had in mind with this declaration, it does seem to suggest that he believed the incarnate Christ created the possibility not only of immortality but also of the divinization of fallen man (for more on becoming like God through Jesus Christ, see chapter 10).

Athanasius, whose life spanned much of the fourth century (died AD 373), underscores the vital importance of Christ's physicality and mortality: "The Word perceived that corruption could not be got rid of otherwise than through death; yet He himself, as the Word, being immortal and the Father's Son, was such as could not die. For this reason, therefore, He assumed a body capable of death."[71] Athanasius's discussion of our salvation in Christ, however, focuses less on Christ as a restorer and more on Christ as a victor.

Christ the Victor

Early Christian writers frequently describe Christ's work as a victory: *Christus Victor.*[72] In this view, Christ's life, death, and Resurrection are the "culminating act[s] in the cosmic struggle between the hosts of God and Satan and his angels."[73] This struggle is regularly articulated in the language of warfare, with Christ characterized as the conquering hero while sin and death as well as the devil and demons are the defeated foes.[74] For some ancient Christians, demons threatening the

▲ **FIGURE 9.4** Mosaic of Christ, haloed, clothed like a solider, treading upon a lion and a serpent. Archbishop's Chapel, Ravenna, Italy, early sixth century. The image draws upon Psalm 91:13: "You will tread on the lion and the adder, the young lion and the serpent you will trample under foot" (other similar images depicted Christ treading upon four beasts). For Christians, this psalm referred to Christ's victory over the forces of evil in general, and specifically over Satan, whom New Testament writers described as a snake, serpent, dragon, and lion (1 Peter 5:8; Revelation 12:9; 20:2). Photo: © JoséLuiz Bernardes Ribeiro, Wikimedia Commons

souls of men is central to Christian thought, and Christ's miracles of casting out evil spirits (see, for example, Mark 1:23–27, 34, 39; 3:11–12) in conjunction with his death and Resurrection can be seen as the conquest of demonic forces.[75] Justin describes Christ's ascension as a victory.[76] Origen avows that the very conception of Christ in the Virgin Mary constituted a victory over demons and declares that through the Resurrection, Christ destroyed the kingdom of death.[77] Irenaeus, quoted above, affirms that Christ's work of recapitulation was undertaken "that He might kill sin, deprive death of its power, and vivify man."[78]

Athanasius treats Christ's victory over death in detail, asserting Christ had slain death itself.[79] He describes Jesus's death on the cross "as the mark of victory and the triumph over death."[80] He affirms that death is "done away by the power of the Savior," that "death is destroyed, and that the Cross has become the victory over it," and that "death has been brought to naught and conquered by the very Christ that ascended the Cross."[81] For Athanasius, the willingness of Christians to be martyred for their faith is evidence of Christ's victory over death:

> For as when a tyrant has been defeated by a real king, and bound hand and foot, then all that pass by laugh him to scorn, buffeting and reviling him, no longer fearing his fury and barbarity, because of the king who has conquered him; so also, death having been conquered and exposed by the Savior on the Cross, and bound hand and foot, all they who are in Christ, as they pass by, trample on him, and witnessing to Christ scoff at death, jesting at him, and saying what has been written against him of old: "O death, where is thy victory? O grave, where is thy sting" (1 Corinthians 15:55).[82]

Christ's victory over death becomes a refrain in Athanasius's writing.

For some ancient Christian authors, Christ's triumph results from a deception. For these authors, Satan was responsible for Jesus's death, but Satan did not realize that his apparent victory—killing Jesus on the cross—would actually be his own ruin. Gregory of Nyssa, who was a learned theologian and the bishop of Nyssa in the late fourth century, compares the deception to a fish being lured to its capture by taking the unseen bait.[83] In the case of Christ, "deity was hidden under the veil of our [human] nature that, as is done by greedy fish, the hook of the deity might be gulped down along with the bait of the flesh and thus life be introduced into the house of death."[84] Augustine, bishop of Hippo in North Africa, writing in the late fourth and early fifth centuries, elaborated: "The devil exulted when Christ died, and by that very death of Christ the devil was overcome: he took food as it were from a trap.... The cross of the Lord became a trap for the devil; the death of the Lord was the food by which he was ensnared. And behold our Lord Jesus Christ rose again."[85]

Later, more fanciful accounts detail Christ's visit to hell (or the underworld) after His death and before His resurrection. The apocryphal *Gospel of Nicodemus*, for example, represents a conversation between Satan and Hades, in which Hades expresses fear that Christ is coming to raise the dead and that, if he is allowed into their realm, none of the dead will remain. Finally, Hades chides Satan, saying: "Turn and see that not one dead man is left in me, but all that you gained through the tree of knowledge you have lost through the tree of the cross. . . . You wished to kill the King of glory, but have killed yourself."[86] For many early Christian thinkers, the achievement of Christ is best expressed as a triumph over the powers of Satan, sin, and death that have held humankind in bondage since the disobedience of Adam.[87] Recalling Paul's teachings about Adam and Christ in Romans 5, proponents of Christ the Victor suppose that Adam, by his submission to the devil, was conquered; Christ, by his perfect obedience to the Father conquered the devil, thus divesting him of his power and assuming power over death for himself.

Christ the Victim

Finally, drawing on the imagery of the Old Testament and on New Testament texts such as Romans and Hebrews, some early Christian Fathers see Christ's death on the cross as an effective sacrifice.[88] This idea that Christ's suffering can be understood on analogy with temple

▲ **FIGURE 9.5** The Maskell Passion Ivory, Crucifixion panel, British Museum, London, ca. 420–430. The earliest surviving depiction of the crucifixion of Jesus Christ in narrative art is this small scene carved in ivory around 420–430 in Rome. Christ is shown on the cross, a halo encircling his head beneath a plaque inscribed in Latin, REX IVD, "King of the Jews." Mary and John approach sorrowfully from the left (see John 19:26–27), as a soldier to the right pierces Christ's side with a spear (now missing, though the wound in Christ's side is visible; see John 19:34). At left, Judas hangs from a tree (see Matthew 27:3–5). The image presents Christ as simultaneously victim and victor. Photo: Scala/Art Resource NY

sacrifices is also implied by the word translated as "propitiation" in Romans 3:24–25: "Christ Jesus: Whom God set forth to be a propitiation." The word translated as "propitiation" (Greek *hilastērion*) refers to "a sin offering," "that which serves as an instrument for regaining the goodwill of a deity."[89] It can also refer to the site of that propitiation, as it is the word used in the Septuagint version of Exodus to express the lid (mercy seat) on the ark of the covenant, that same

▲ **FIGURE 9.6** Lamb of God relief from a sarcophagus at Sant'Apollinare in Classe (near Ravenna, Italy), with cross and bird with crown, fifth to sixth century. The right short end of this sarcophagus features the innocent Lamb of God juxtaposed with a bejeweled cross with the sign of the Rho completing a type of staurogram. The dove of peace, a heavenly messenger, carries an honorific laurel crown in its beak. This iconography demonstrates a sophisticated understanding of Christ's victory over death, signifying God's sacrifice in the flesh. Photo: Mark D. Ellison

covering that is sprinkled with blood on the Day of Atonement.[90] Hebrews affirms that Christ performs his atoning sacrifice for humanity as both priest and offering: "But when Christ came as a high priest . . . he entered once for all into the [heavenly] Holy Place, not with the blood of goats and calves, but with his own blood, thus obtaining eternal redemption" (Hebrews 9:11–12 NRSV). Christ completes the final, perfect sacrifice to satisfy God's justice and win His favor for all humankind, however undeserving humankind may be.[91] Christ's sacrifice is the ultimate expression of God's grace.

Athanasius understands Christ's sacrifice as comparable to the Passover lamb and as a worthy sacrifice for humankind: "[Christ] became incarnate for our sakes so that He might offer himself to the Father in our place, and redeem us through His offering and sacrifice.... This is he who, in former times, was sacrificed as a Lamb, having been foreshadowed in that lamb. But afterwards He was slain for us."[92]

Athanasius works out the logic of Christ's sacrifice more fully in his work *On the Incarnation*. First, he explains the need for a sacrifice. God created humanity, gave humans commandments, and stipulated that death would be the punishment for breaking the commandments (Genesis 2:17; Deuteronomy 24:16; Romans 6:23; James 1:15). Humanity broke commandments and became subject to death and corruption. For Athanasius, God had created humanity out of nothing, and now that humans had turned from God, humanity was moving back toward nothingness—toward corruption and death. Yet God wanted humans to live—*why else would he have created us?* And God loves humanity, so he did not desire humans to devolve into nothingness. At the same time, God cannot go against his own word, so death had to remain as a punishment. Some have described this as a "divine dilemma."[93]

The solution to this divine dilemma comes in the person of Jesus Christ. According to Athanasius, Christ, as the Word of God who created this world, was the only one worthy to satisfy justice: "For being Word of the Father, and above all, he alone of natural fitness was both able to re-create everything, and worthy to suffer on behalf of all and to be ambassador for all with the Father."[94] So Christ took upon himself a mortal human body and "gave it over to death in the stead of all ... [that] the law involving the ruin of men might be undone (inasmuch as its power was fully spent in the Lord's body, and had no longer holding ground against men, his peers)."[95] Despite Athanasius's strong focus on the logic behind Jesus the Victim, he does not rely exclusively on this model. His statement about Christ giving "over to death in the stead of all [his human body]" is immediately followed by another statement that relies on the model of Christ the Restorer: "Whereas [humans] had turned toward corruption, [Christ] might turn them again toward incorruption, and quicken them from death by the appropriation of his body and by the grace of the resurrection, banishing death from them like straw from the fire."[96] Christ the Victim remained one model among many for ancient Christians and their understanding of God's grace, especially the salvific work of Jesus Christ.

BOX 9.7   Why So Many Atonement Models?

As Latter-day Saints, we affirm with other Christians that one can experience and know the power of the Atonement of Jesus Christ through repentance, prayer, and other spiritual practices and that we should seek to understand that Atonement even though full comprehension lies beyond our human capacity. The Atonement models reviewed in this chapter represent ancient Christian efforts to understand the redemptive role of Jesus Christ.

Elder Bruce R. McConkie declared: "We do not know, we cannot tell, no mortal mind can conceive the full import of what Christ did in Gethsemane. . . . We know that in some way, incomprehensible to us, his suffering satisfied the demands of justice."[97]

President James E. Faust affirmed: "Our salvation depends on believing in and accepting the Atonement. Such acceptance requires a continual effort to understand it more fully. . . . The nature of the Atonement and its effects is so infinite, so unfathomable, and so profound that it lies beyond the knowledge and comprehension of mortal man."[98]

President Dallin H. Oaks taught: "The magnificent and incomprehensible effect of the Atonement of Jesus Christ is based on God's love for each of us. . . . His plan motivated by love must be received with love."[99]

The Lasting Influence of Augustine of Hippo

The models of the Atonement of Jesus Christ reviewed so far represent a variety of attempts to explain how Jesus opened to *humanity* the possibility of salvation. In the late fourth and early fifth century, a debate between Augustine of Hippo and the monk Pelagius shifted the focus slightly and attempted to explain how the *individual* Christian gains for herself or himself the salvation that Christ's Incarnation, death, and Resurrection made possible. In other words, both Augustine and Pelagius presuppose Christ's atoning work for *humanity*, but they disagree about how the *individual* Christian obtains the prize of that atoning work. The dispute between them is known as the Pelagian controversy.[100] Their argument highlighted questions about human nature, sin, and grace, as well as the role of grace in human salvation. Pelagius's view might be called perfectionism. For him and his followers, because humans were created in God's image and likeness, they have complete freedom and are left without excuse if they sin:

> We cry out at God and say, "This is too hard! This is too difficult! We cannot do it! We are only human and are hindered by the weakness of the flesh!" What blind madness! What blatant presumption! By doing this we accuse the God of knowledge of a two-fold ignorance—ignorance of God's own creation and of God's own commands. . . . No one knows the extent of our strength better than the God who gave us that strength. . . . God has not willed to command anything impossible.[101]

This perspective suggests, as theologian Alister McGrath remarks, that "since perfection is possible it is obligatory," and failure to perform God's will, which God made us capable of doing, will result in eternal punishment. Pelagian grace consists of "natural human faculties" and "external enlightenment." The latter comes in the form of commandments and Jesus's example, which, for Pelagius, is all we need to make us capable of perfect obedience.[102] Grace is, therefore, "external and passive."[103]

While Pelagius emphasized the image of God, Augustine objected that Pelagius did not sufficiently consider the effect of the Fall. Augustine asserted that the grace described in the New Testament clearly means more than mere human faculties and external enlightenment, even if that external enlightenment comes from divine commandments and the divine example provided by Jesus Christ. Augustine sees grace as including divine help, what McGrath calls "the real, redeeming presence of God in Christ within us"; in this construct, grace is "internal and active."[104] Augustine presents a merciful God who is striving to "heal and restore wounded human nature."[105] Humankind was created innocent but fell from God. God himself graciously came to save his creation. For Augustine, the very faith by which the Christian is made righteous is a gift—even our best work is the result of God working within us: "But God, who is rich in mercy, on account of the great love with which He loved us, even when we were dead through our sins, raised us up to life with Christ, by whose grace we are saved. But this grace of Christ, without which neither infants nor grown persons can be saved, is not bestowed as a reward for merits, but is given freely, which is why it is called grace."[106] When Paul says that we are justified by faith, Augustine understands him to mean that God gives us the very faith by which we believe in the promise of forgiveness and of eternal life.

Conclusion

And with that, the discussion has come full circle. Paul's paradigm suggested that the grace of God is a free and undeserved gift, quite in contrast to the traditional reciprocity of gift giving and the typically required worthiness of a gift's recipient. As early Christian writers continued to consider and probe the implications of that, some seem to have worried that if salvation were seen as the free gift of grace, Christians might not feel required to turn from a life of sin. Church Fathers began, therefore, to emphasize the response grace should evoke in humanity: to repent, to obey, to be baptized, to remain faithful to the end. With Pelagius, the pendulum had swung too far, and we encounter a doctrine claiming that humans, with their own faculties, already have the ability to obey God perfectly, aided only by external orders and Jesus's example. Augustine counters this perspective by recalling and amplifying Paul's teachings and reminding Christians that we cannot be liberated from sin and saved by our own powers, but only by the grace of God revealed in Christ. This sentiment has continued to fascinate and move humanity—we marvel at a God willing to offer his Son and at a divine Son willing to be sacrificed for human salvation, even when that gift is wholly unmerited.

Latter-day Saint theology participates in these historical currents of religious thought. Some Latter-day Saints have emphasized works, wary of cheap grace and sensing the necessity of Christ's Atonement having real, transformative effects in our mortal lives. Others have recognized that overemphasis on works may miss the "good news" of the gospel, lead to "toxic perfectionism," and overlook the witness of our ancient Christian predecessors that grace is the unmerited gift of God—the divine love that moves us, works within us, and invites and enables us to respond.[107]

Notes

1. For a brief overview of messianic expectation in the time of Jesus, see David B. Levenson, "Messianic Movements" in *The Jewish Annotated New Testament*, 2nd ed., ed. Amy-Jill Levine and Marc Zvi Brettler (Oxford: Oxford University Press, 2017), 622–28. For a fuller treatment, see Adela Yarbro Collins and John J. Collins, *King and Messiah as Son of God: Divine, Human, and Angelic Messianic Figures in Biblical and Related Literature* (Grand Rapids, MI: Eerdmans, 2008); John J. Collins, *The Scepter and the Star: The Messiahs of the Dead Sea Scrolls and Other Ancient Literature* (New York: DoubleDay, 1995).

2. Indeed, 1 Thessalonians may be the oldest known New Testament text. For the dating of the epistle, see Raymond E. Brown, *An Introduction to the New Testament* (New York: Doubleday, 1997), 457. This chapter will assume the traditional chronology for Paul's life and letters; see Brown,

Introduction to the New Testament, 428. For general commentaries on the letters to the Thessalonians, see James E. Frame, *Thessalonians* (*International Critical Commentary*) (Edinburgh: T&T Clark, 2002); F. F. Bruce, *1 & 2 Thessalonians*, Word Biblical Commentary (Dallas: Word Books, 1982). For Paul's life, see Jerome Murphy-O'Connor, *Paul: A Critical Life* (Oxford: Oxford University Press, 1996); Daniel Boyarin, *A Radical Jew: Paul and the Politics of Identity* (Berkeley: University of California Press, 1997).

3. For the date of Galatians, see Brown, *Introduction to the New Testament*, 468. For the date of Romans, see James D. G. Dunn, *Romans 1–8*, Word Biblical Commentary (Dallas: Word Books, 1988), xliii-xliv.

4. On Paul's Greek education, see Murphy-O'Connor, *Paul*, 46–51. See also Brown, *Introduction to the New Testament*, 69–70; Dunn, *Romans*, xxxix-xli.

5. See Henry George Liddell, Robert Scott, and Henry Stuart Jones, *A Greek-English Lexicon*, 9th ed. (Oxford: Clarendon, 1996), s.v. "χάρις (*charis*)." Henceforward, this source will be referred to as LSJ. See also Homer, *Odyssey* 2.12; Hesiod, *Works and Days* 65. In legal documents of the Roman imperial period, *charis* is used to designate grants made by the Roman emperor. See LSJ, s.v. "χάρις (*charis*)," for uses in the Roman imperial period. For the use of the term as an imperial grant from the first-century AD Egypt, see Wilhelm Dittenberger, ed., *Orientis graeci inscriptiones selectae* (*OGI*) (Leipzig: Hirzel, 1903-05), 669.44.

6. On the reciprocity of grace, see Cilliers Breytenbach, *Grace, Reconciliation, Concord: The Death of Christ in Graeco-Roman Metaphors* (Leiden: Brill, 2010), 146; John M. G. Barclay, *Paul and the Power of Grace* (Grand Rapids, MI: Eerdmans, 2020), 1–9.

7. The Latin term for "grace" (*gratia*) conveys the same array of ideas encompassed by *charis*, including the same two-sidedness and is the obvious root of the English word *gratitude*.

8. See Christopher Gill, Norman Postlethwaite, and Richard Seaford, eds. *Reciprocity in Ancient Greece* (Oxford: Oxford University Press, 1998); Sitta von Reden, *Exchange in Ancient Greece* (London: Routledge, 1995).

9. See Michael Peachin, *The Oxford Handbook of Social Relations in the Roman World* (Oxford: Oxford University Press, 2014); Koenraad Verboven, *The Economy of Friends: Economic Aspects of Amicitia and Patronage in the Late Roman Republic* (Brussels: Latomus, 2002).

10. Barclay, *Paul and the Power of Grace*, 8–9.

11. For the Greeks and Romans, this reciprocity is also true of the relationship between humans and gods, where humans offer sacrifice and worship to their deities and are granted blessings in return. See Barclay, *Paul and the*

Power of Grace, 6. See also Richard Seaford, *Reciprocity and Ritual: Homer and Tragedy in the Developing City-State* (Oxford: Clarendon, 1994).

12. Barclay, *Paul and the Power of Grace*, xiv.

13. See Barclay, *Paul and the Power of Grace*, 6–7. For ancient discussions of the standards for generosity, see Aristotle, *Nicomachean Ethics* 4; Cicero, *On Moral Duties* 2.62–62.

14. Dunn, *Romans*, 17.

15. See Karen Jo Torjesen, "Grace," in *Encyclopedia of Early Christianity*, 2nd ed., ed. Everett Ferguson (New York: Routledge, 1999), 481; see also Barclay, *Paul and the Power of Grace*, xiii. For Latter-day Saints, the atoning sacrifice of Jesus Christ is "infinite and eternal" (Alma 34:10, 14), and its reach stretches back to the deliverance of ancient Israel and forward to today. The power of that sacrifice is not confined to the mortal manifestation of Jesus Christ.

16. Since—as indicated by papyri of the Roman imperial period—*charis* designated a grant from the emperor, the word could have had particular relevance to the audience of the epistle to the Romans, for whom the benefactions described by Paul could be seen as a kind of imperial patronage. See Hans Conzelmann, "Χάρις (*charis*)," in *Theological Dictionary of the New Testament*, vol. 9 (Grand Rapids, MI: Eerdmans, 1974), 387–401; Stephan Joubert, *Paul as Benefactor: Reciprocity, Strategy, and Theological Reflection in Paul's Collection* (Tübingen: Mohr, 2000), 17–70.

17. Anthony Meredith, "Justification," in *Encyclopedia of Early Christianity*, ed. Everett Ferguson, 2nd ed. (New York: Routledge, 1999), 646. See also *Merriam-Webster.com Dictionary*, s.v. "justify," https://www.merriam-webster.com/dictionary/justify.

18. See James R. Harrison, *Paul's Language of Grace in Its Graeco-Roman Context* (Tübingen: Mohr, 2003), 346.

19. Alister E. McGrath, ed., *The Christian Theology Reader*, 5th ed. (Malden, MA: Wiley-Blackwell, 2017), xxvii.

20. Tradition labels this Clement as the third bishop of Rome after Peter; see Eusebius, *History of the Church* 3.15.34. The letter has no internal identification of the author, but "ancient tradition and most manuscripts identify it as the work of Clement." Michael W. Holmes, trans., *The Apostolic Fathers: Greek Texts and English Translations*, 3rd ed. (Grand Rapids, MI: Baker Academic, 2007), 34. Unless otherwise noted, English translations of *1 Clement* and *Didache* are taken from this edition of *Apostolic Fathers* translated by Holmes.

21. *1 Clement* 7:4–5.

22. *1 Clement* 8:1–2.

23. Justin, who was martyred around AD 165, wrote, among other things, a defense of Christianity addressed to the Roman emperor Antoninus Pius, urging him to put an end to the persecution of people for being Christian. For general information about Justin, see Alister E. McGrath, *Christian Theology: An Introduction*, 2nd ed. (Cambridge: Blackwell, 1997), 10–11.

24. Justin Martyr, *Dialogue with Trypho* 119, in Justin Martyr, *Dialogue with Trypho*, ed. Michael Slusser, trans. Thomas B. Falls, vol. 3 in Selections from the Fathers of the Church series (Washington, DC: Catholic University of America, 2003), 179. In this chapter, all English translations of *Dialogue with Trypho* come from this edition translated by Falls.

25. Justin Martyr, *Dialogue with Trypho* 119.

26. Justin Martyr, *Dialogue with Trypho* 119.

27. For more on Irenaeus, see McGrath, *Christian Theology*, 11; Mary T. Clark, "Irenaeus," in *Encyclopedia of Early Christianity*, ed. Everett Ferguson, 2nd ed. (New York: Routledge, 1999), 587–88. On Polycarp, see Graydon F. Snyder's entry in *Encyclopedia of Early Christianity*, ed. Everett Ferguson, 2nd ed. (New York: Routledge, 1999), 933–34.

28. Irenaeus, *Against Heresies* 4.38.4 (*ANF* 1:522); see chapter 10 in this volume.

29. Torjesen, "Grace," 481.

30. Irenaeus, *Against Heresies* 4.38.3 (*ANF* 1:521–22). Unless otherwise indicated, all translations of Irenaeus, *Against Heresies* are from Alexander Roberts and James Donaldson, ed., *The Ante-Nicene Fathers*, 10 vols. (1885–1887; repr. Peabody, MA: Hendrickson, 2012). For Irenaeus, the grace of creation and the grace of redemption are of a piece—God's grace is present in creation as much as it is in forgiveness.

31. Irenaeus, *Against Heresies* 4.38.4 (*ANF* 1:522).

32. Irenaeus, *Against Heresies* 1.10.1 (*ANF* 1:330–1).

33. See Matthew Knell, *Sin, Grace, and Free Will: A Historical Survey of Christian Thought*, vol. 1, *The Apostolic Fathers to Augustine* (Cambridge: James Clarke & Co., 2018), 43–44.

34. Valentinian Gnostics were a Christian group who came to be viewed as opponents to orthodox Christian teachings and as heretics. They focused on obtaining personal spiritual knowledge (*gnosis*), privileging that knowledge over the traditions and authority of institutional religion. For a fuller description of Valentinians and other so-called Gnostic groups, see David Brakke, *The Gnostics: Myth, Ritual, and Diversity in Early Christianity* (Cambridge, MA: Harvard University Press, 2010).

35. Irenaeus, *Against Heresies* 1.6.3 (*ANF* 1:324).

36. Knell, *Sin, Grace, and Free Will*, 46.

37. For additional New Testament examples, see also Acts 15:11; 2 Timothy 1:9–10; Titus 3:4–7; 1 Peter 1:9–11. For Clement of Alexandria on Ephesians 2:5, see Matyáš Havrda, "Grace and Free Will According to Clement of Alexandria," *Journal of Early Christian Studies* 19, no. 1 (2011): 21–48, esp. 41.

38. See McGrath, *Christian Theology*, 387.

39. See LSJ, s.v. "σωτηρία (*sōtēria*)." The notion of salvation as "a safe return home" is in evidence, among other places, in the text of the fifth-century Athenian historian, Thucydides. The author portrays a deadly naval battle between the Athenians and Syracusans, describing the Athenian boatswains as urging their men to show their courage and "seize a safe return home (*sōtērias*) to their country." Thucydides, *History of the Peloponnesian War* 7.70.7. *Sōtēria* as physical well-being is common in surviving papyri. See, for example, *Berliner griechische Urkunden* 423.12; *Oxyrhynchus Papyrus* 939.20.

40. W. Barclay, *New Testament Words* (Louisville, KY: Westminster John Knox Press, 1964), 268–69.

41. Frederick W. Danker, Walter Bauer, William F. Arndt, and F. Wilbur Gingrich, *A Greek-English Lexicon of the New Testament and Other Early Christian Literature*, 3rd ed. (BDAG) (Chicago: University of Chicago Press, 2000), s.v. "σωτηρία (*sōtēria*)." This lexicon will further be referred to as "BDAG." The term *sōtēria* occurs forty-six times in the New Testament, not including uses of the related Greek terms *sōtēr* (savior) and *sōzō* (to save).

42. See H. E. W. Turner, *The Patristic Doctrine of Redemption: A Study of the Development of Doctrine during the First Five Centuries* (London: A.R. Mowbry and Co., 1952), 28; Frances Young, "Atonement," in *Encyclopedia of Early Christianity*, ed. Everett Ferguson, 2nd ed. (New York: Routledge, 1999), 143–46.

43. For the significance of the Apostolic Fathers in writing about Christ the Teacher, see Turner, *Patristic Doctrine of Redemption*, 43–44. The *Didache*, whose full title is either *The Teaching of the Lord to the Gentiles by the Twelve Apostles* or *The Teaching of the (Twelve) Apostles*, is a notoriously problematic, anonymous text. A number of dates have been suggested for its composition and compilation, ranging from AD 50 to the third century. As Holmes observes, it is likely that the text took "its present form as late as 150, though a date considerably closer to the end of the first century seems more probable." It is generally agreed that the materials from which the *Didache* was originally composed reveal Christian thought from an even earlier time. Holmes, *Apostolic Fathers*, 337. See also Everett Ferguson, "Didache," in *Encyclopedia of Early Christianity*, ed. Everett Ferguson, 2nd

ed. (New York: Routledge, 1999), 328. The *Epistle of Barnabas* likewise presents the ideas of an anonymous author. Although the manuscript tradition gives it the title *Epistle of Barnabas*, modern scholars mostly reject the idea that it is the work of the Barnabas of the New Testament. The document is usually dated to the AD 130s; see Holmes, *Apostolic Fathers*, 372–373; Everett Ferguson, "Barnabas, Epistle of," in *Encyclopedia of Early Christianity*, ed. Everett Ferguson, 2nd ed. (New York: Routledge, 1999), 167–68.

44. *Didache* 1.1. For the "two ways" in the *Epistle of Barnabas*, see *Epistle of Barnabas* 18.1–20.2. For certain moral guidelines, see *Epistle of Barnabas* 4.9–14.

45. See, for example, *Didache* 1.2–6.1.

46. Irenaeus, *Against Heresies* 5.1.1 (*ANF* 1:526).

47. Young, "Atonement," 144. See also Turner, *Patristic Doctrine of Redemption*, 29–34.

48. See also Ignatius, *Epistle to the Ephesians* 21:1.

49. *1 Clement* 36.2.

50. See Justin, *1 Apology* 46, 50–51; Clement of Alexandria, *Stromata* 6.14.109. See also S. R. C. Lilla, *Clement of Alexandria: A Study in Christian Platonism and Gnosticism* (Oxford: Oxford University Press, 1971); Turner, *Patristic Doctrine of Redemption*, 39–42.

51. Walter H. Wagner, "Clement of Alexandria," in *Encyclopedia of Early Christianity*, 2nd ed., ed. Everett Ferguson (New York: Routledge, 1999), 262–64. In his intellectualism, Clement held certain views that might be considered similar to the Gnostics, but he explicitly distinguishes his form of Christianity from the Gnostics.

52. Havrda, "Grace and Free Will According to Clement of Alexandria," 47.

53. Clement of Alexandria, *Stromata* 7.7.4; see Havrda, "Grace and Free Will According to Clement of Alexandria," 43.

54. Havrda, "Grace and Free Will According to Clement of Alexandria," 41. See also Clement of Alexandria, *Stromata* 5.1.7.

55. Clement of Alexandria, *Stromata* 5.13.1.

56. Clement of Alexandria, *The Rich Man's Salvation* 37; trans. McGrath, *The Christian Theology Reader*, 287.

57. McGrath, *Christian Theology*, 407.

58. See Turner, *Patristic Doctrine of Redemption*, 40.

59. Michael Peppard, "The Photisterion in Late Antiquity: Reconsidering Terminology for Sites and Rites of Initiation," *Journal of Ecclesiastical History* 71, no. 3 (2020): 463–83.

60. J. N. D. Kelly, *Early Christian Doctrines*, rev. ed. (San Francisco: Harper and

Row, 1978), 450.

61. Of many possible New Testament examples, see 1 Corinthians 6:14; 15:21; Acts 24:15; John 11:25–28.

62. *1 Clement* 26:1.

63. *Didache* 10.2; emphasis added.

64. See Young, "Atonement," 144. The Eucharist played an important role in this re-creation; see Irenaeus, *Against the Heresies* 4.18.5.

65. Irenaeus, *Against the Heresies* 3.18.1; emphasis added.

66. Charlton T. Lewis and Charles Short, *A Latin Dictionary*, Perseus, University of Chicago, s.v. "recapitulo," https://artflsrv03.uchicago.edu/philologic4/LewisShort521/navigate/17/217/. See also McGrath, *Christian Theology: An Introduction*, 286; Turner, *Patristic Doctrine of Redemption*, 47–69.

67. See Irenaeus, *Demonstration of the Apostolic Teaching* 12, 15–16.

68. Irenaeus, *Against Heresies* 3.18.7, 3.21.10 (*ANF* 1:393, 398).

69. Irenaeus, *Against Heresies* 5, preface (*ANF* 1:464; emphasis added).

70. Athanasius, *On the Incarnation* 54, in Archibald Robertson, trans., "Athanasius, On the Incarnation of the Word" in *Christology of the Later Fathers*, ed. Edward Rochie Hardy and Cyril C. Richardson (Louisville, KY: Westminster John Knox, 1954), 55–110. Unless otherwise indicated, all translations of Athanasius's *On the Incarnation* are taken from this edition translated by Robertson. The Greek verb used by Athanasius and translated as "become divine" is *theopoieō*, which means "to make divine." Here, in the passive voice, it suggests "to be made divine" or, perhaps, "to be made a god."

71. Athanasius, *On the Incarnation* 9. For more on Athanasius, see Charles Kennengiesser, "Athanasius," in *Encyclopedia of Early Christianity*, 2nd ed., ed. Everett Ferguson (New York: Routledge, 1999),137–39.

72. See Gustaf Aulen, *Christus Victor: An Historical Study of the Three Main Types of the Idea of the Atonement* (Eugene, OR: Wipf and Stock, 2003), 4. Aulen calls this perspective the "classic idea of the Atonement." See Young, "Atonement," 145.

73. Aulen, *Christus Victor*, 4.

74. John Chrysostom uses elaborate military metaphors to communicate not only the victory of Christ but also the role of the believing Christian in his exegetical homilies on Ephesians. See John Chrysostom, *Homilies on Ephesians* 23, 24.

75. See Ignatius, *Epistle to the Trallians* 5. See also, Ignatius, *Epistle to the Ephesians* 19.1.

76. See Justin, *Dialogue with Trypho* 36.

77. See Origen, *Against Celsus* 1.60; Origen, *Commentary on the Epistle to the Romans* 5.1; Turner, *Patristic Doctrine of Redemption*, 49.

78. Irenaeus, *Against Heresies* 3.18.7 (*ANF* 1:393). See Aulen, *Christ the Victor*, 19.

79. See Athanasius, *On the Incarnation* 26–30.

80. Athanasius, *On the Incarnation* 26.1.

81. Athanasius, *On the Incarnation* 26.6; 27.1; 29.2.

82. Athanasius, *On the Incarnation* 27.4.

83. See David L. Balás, "Gregory of Nyssa," in *Encyclopedia of Early Christianity*, ed. Everett Ferguson, 2nd ed. (New York: Routledge, 1999), 495–97.

84. Gregory of Nyssa, *The Great Catechisim* 17–23; quoted in Young, "Atonement," 145. See also Aulen, *Christus Victor*, 47–55.

85. Augustine, *Sermon* 263, in Augustine, *Sermons on the Liturgical Season*, trans. Mary Sarah Muldowney, vol. 38 in The Fathers of the Church: A New Translation series (Washington, DC: Catholic University of America, 1959), 392–93. For more on Augustine, see Margaret R. Miles, "Augustine," in *Encyclopedia of Early Christianity*, ed. Everett Ferguson, 2nd ed. (New York: Routledge, 1999), 148–53.

86. *Gospel of Nicodemus (The Pilate Cycle): The Descent into Hell* 7(23).1, in *The Apocryphal New Testament: A Collection of Apocryphal Christian Literature in an English Translation*, trans. J. K. Elliott (Oxford: Clarendon, 1993), 188–89.

87. There are two schools of thought about the nature of that Satanic captivity. Irenaeus represents one school, characterizing Satan as a usurper, who has no rights to human souls. In this view, God and Christ are taking back what is rightfully theirs. Compare Tertullian, *Concerning the Flight under Persecution* 2, which also suggests that the devil has rights. See also Turner, *Patristic Doctrine of Redemption*, 54–55.

88. McGrath, *Christian Theology*, 251–52. For Hebrews references, see Hebrews 4–12, esp. 9:1–28; 10:1–18.

89. BDAG, s.v. "ἱλαστήριον (*hilastērion*)."

90. See BDAG, s.v. "ἱλαστήριον (*hilastērion*)." See also Exodus 25:16–22; Leviticus 16:14.

91. See Hebrews 9:1–28; 10:1–18. For a later explication of the "satisfaction theory of the atonement," see Anselm of Canterbury, *Why God Became Man*.

92. Athanasius, *Festal Letters* 7, quoted in McGrath, *Christian Theology*, 252. Augustine likewise elucidated the notion of Christ as a sacrifice: "To take then away the separating wall, which is sin, that Mediator has come, and the priest has Himself become the sacrifice. And because He was made a sacrifice for sin, offering Himself as a whole burnt-offering on the cross of His passion." Augustine, *Tractates on the Gospel of John* 41.5; partly quoted in McGrath, *Christian Theology*, 252.

93. Young, "Atonement," 146.

94. Athanasius, *On the Incarnation* 7.

95. Athanasius, *On the Incarnation* 8.

96. Athanasius, *On the Incarnation* 8.

97. Bruce R. McConkie, "The Purifying Power of Gethsemane," *Ensign*, May 1985, https://www.churchofjesuschrist.org/study/ensign/1985/05/the-purifying-power-of-gethsemane

98. James E. Faust, "The Atonement: Our Greatest Hope," *Ensign*, November 2001, 18–20.

99. Dallin H. Oaks, "What Has Our Savior Done for Us," *Ensign*, May 2021, 75–77.

100. See Joanne McWilliam, "Pelagius, Pelagianism," in *Encyclopedia of Early Christianity*, ed. Everett Ferguson, 2nd ed. (New York: Routledge, 1999), 887–89.

101. Pelagius, *Letter to Demetrias*, cited in McGrath, *The Christian Theology Reader*, 350.

102. McGrath, *Christian Theology*, 430.

103. McGrath, *Christian Theology*, 430

104. McGrath, *Christian Theology*, 430

105. McGrath, *Christian Theology*, 429.

106. Augustine, *Of Nature and Grace* 3–4, cited in McGrath, *The Christian Theology Reader*, 349.

107. See Stephen E. Robinson, *Believing Christ: The Parable of the Bicycle and Other Good News* (Salt Lake City: Deseret Book, 1992); Robert Millet, *Life in Christ* (Salt Lake City: Bookcraft, 1990); Bruce C. Hafen, *The Broken Heart: Applying the Atonement to Life's Experiences* (Salt Lake City: Deseret Book, 1989); Dieter F. Uchtdorf, "The Gift of Grace," *Ensign*, May 2015, 107–10; Jeffrey R. Holland, "Be Ye Therefore Perfect—Eventually," *Ensign*, November 2017, 40–42.

10

BECOMING LIKE GOD

Incarnation, Moral Formation, and Eternal Progression

Daniel Becerra

His divine power has given us everything needed
for life and godliness, through the knowledge of him
who called us by his own glory and goodness. Thus
he has given us, through these things, his precious
and very great promises, so that through them you
may escape from the corruption that is in the world
because of lust, and may become participants of the
divine nature.

—2 Peter 1:3–4
New Revised Standard Version

What does it mean to become like God? For many Latter-day Saints, this question can conjure visions of eternal families, the creation of worlds, and the continuation of God's plan of happiness throughout eternity. In this sense, we tend to think about becoming like God as primarily a *future* possibility—life in heaven. For other Christians, becoming like God relates more to a *past* event—specifically to the work accomplished by Jesus Christ in taking upon himself a human body, often referred to as the Incarnation (literally, being "made flesh"; see John 1:14). By virtue of this union, some Christians believe, Christ united a human body with the divine attributes of immortality and incorruption. Becoming like God, therefore, describes less an individual person's eternal reward and more the melding of Christ's divine nature to human nature through his miraculous birth. Still others may envision becoming like God as a process that occurs principally in the *present*: the daily small and simple acts of spiritual discipline that contribute to the cultivation of Christlike character.

These three ways of thinking are not mutually exclusive, and all have their origins in the writings of Jesus's early followers. They describe, albeit in different ways, the complex and multifaceted process by which humans have been understood to become divine in the Christian tradition. Ancient Christians referred to this process by different Greek terms—the earliest Christians wrote in Greek—including *theosis*, *theopoiesis*, and *apotheosis*, all of which are frequently translated into English as "divinization" or "deification." As one might expect, discussions regarding deification become more numerous and systematic over time. In other words, as Christians reflected on

BOX 10.1 Common Scriptures in Early Christian Discussions about Deification

"And God said, Let us make man in our image, after our likeness. . . . So God created man in his own image, in the image of God created he him; male and female created he them" (Genesis 1:26–27).

"I have said, Ye are gods; And all of you are children of the most High" (Psalm 82:6).

"Jesus answered, "Is it not written in your law 'I said, you are gods'? If those to whom the word of God came were called 'gods'—and the scripture cannot be annulled— can you say that the one whom the Father has sanctified and sent into the world is blaspheming because I said, 'I am God's Son'?" (John 10:34–36 New Revised Standard Version).

"Be ye therefore perfect, even as your Father which is in heaven is perfect" (Matthew 5:48).

"For all who are led by the Spirit of God are children of God. For you did not receive a spirit of slavery to fall back into fear, but you have received a spirit of adoption. When we cry, "Abba! Father!" it is that very Spirit bearing witness with our spirit that we are children of God" (Romans 8:14–17 New Revised Standard Version).

"And all of us, with unveiled faces, seeing the glory of the Lord as though reflected in a mirror, are being transformed into the same image from one degree of glory to another; for this comes from the Lord, the Spirit." (2 Corinthians 3:18 New Revised Standard Version).

"Behold, what manner of love the Father hath bestowed upon us, that we should be called the sons of God: therefore the world knoweth us not, because it knew him not. Beloved, now are we the sons of God, and it doth not yet appear what we shall be: but we know that, when he shall appear, we shall be like him; for we shall see him as he is" (1 John 3:1–2).

"Thus he has given us, through these things, his precious and very great promises, so that through them you may escape from the corruption that is in the world because of lust, and may become participants of the divine nature" (2 Peter 1:4 New Revised Standard Version).

scriptures—such as Genesis 1:26–27; 3:5; Psalm 82:6; John 10:34–36; Matthew 5:48; Romans 8:14–17; 2 Corinthians 3:18; 1 John 3:1–2; and 2 Peter 1:4 (see box 10.1)—and applied all the intellectual tools available to them to understanding God's word, views about deification evolved and distilled.[1] This chapter traces some of this development of thought through the first centuries of the Church and in the writings of several influential theologians.

Given the brief nature of this chapter, my goal is not to be exhaustive but to identify several broad themes relating to deification and to briefly describe how different Christian theologians talked about them. My choice of themes and theologians reflects my effort to both highlight significant developments in Christian thought and to feature theological discussions which I think will be of some interest to Latter-day Saints. As will become apparent below, discussions about deification in the early Church did not exist in a theological vacuum but were linked in significant ways to other beliefs. For this reason, one cannot talk about deification without also addressing, at least to a small degree, assumptions about the nature of God and Christ, human nature, grace, agency, ethical life, and life in heaven. To this end, this essay proceeds in three parts. Part one addresses deification as a past event, meaning the deifying effect of Christ's Incarnation on human nature generally. Part two examines deification as a present process and focuses on the moral formation of individuals through living an ethical life. Part three then turns to deification as a future possibility and examines two ideas relating to heavenly life and eternal progression.

Incarnation and Deification

The New Testament does not contain fully developed teachings about deification. What it does contain, however, are broad themes that will be developed more systematically in subsequent years under the theological umbrella of deification.[2] These themes include the notion that Christ's premortal divine status, birth, death, and resurrection enable humans to be reconciled to God, that salvation involves imitating Christ, and that participation in the ordinances of the Church and living a good life unite believers to God and one another.[3] At the heart of many New Testament teachings was the assumption that Christ, being both divine and human, is distinct from the rest of humankind and that his nature enables him to bless, heal, save, and relate to humans in unique ways.

The earliest surviving Christian literature outside of the New Testament is clearly informed by this assumption. Christian authors who lived after the earliest New Testament texts were written were committed to the idea that Jesus Christ had both human and divine qualities and that his dual nature makes human flourishing and salvation possible.[4] By the turn of the second century, for example, the bishop Ignatius of Antioch (died circa AD 110) taught that Jesus is "both flesh and spirit, born and unborn, God in man . . . both from Mary and from God."[5] And for this reason, Christ is able to serve as a "physician" to humankind.[6] Several decades later, the apologist Justin Martyr (died before AD 167) similarly emphasized the importance of Christ's Incarnation and dual nature for enabling a human to "become a god," which is the first time such language appears so explicitly in early Christian literature.[7] Justin is perhaps most famous for his efforts to articulate

▲ **FIGURE 10.1**   Virgin and Child, Tokali Church, Göreme, Turkey (ca. AD 960). This fresco from Cappadocia depicts Mary and Jesus, cheek to cheek, in a tender embrace. The tactile gestures call to mind the corporeal humanity shared by the mother and child while Mary's outward gaze to us as viewers recalls the gravity of his divine mission and destiny. Photo: Alamy

and defend the Christian faith by use of scripture and philosophical reasoning.[8] Commenting on Psalm 82:6, which reads, "Ye are gods; and all of you are children of the most High," Justin taught that all humans are capable of progressing toward godhood, a state which is only fully realized in the resurrection.[9] This progression is possible because humans possess the *logos spermatikos*, a Greek philosophical term referring to the seed of divinity present in human beings.[10]

Within a decade or two after Justin lived, the bishop Irenaeus of
Lyons (writing circa AD 180) would famously teach that the Son of
God "became what we are in order to make us like himself."[11] This
teaching is sometimes referred to as the "exchange formula" and concisely represents the relationship between Christ's Incarnation and
human deification in early Christian thought. Implicit in Irenaeus's
exchange formula is the notion that God and humans are fundamentally distinct beings, which was an assumption that would pervade
Christian theology for generations to come. Irenaeus believed that
created things are inherently inferior to that which created them,
and for this reason, humans can never fully be like God, who, unlike
humans, is immortal and incorruptible by nature.[12] By taking upon
himself a human body, Christ united the divine qualities of immortality and incorruptibility to mortal and corruptible human nature.
Therefore, through this past event, humans may partake of divine
nature through uniting with Christ, who mediates these qualities to
us to the degree possible. This deifying union occurs as persons are
"adopted" by Christ (see Romans 8:22–23), something initiated at
baptism and maintained by receiving the Holy Spirit, participating in
the sacraments of the Church, and living a moral life.[13]

As may be seen in Irenaeus's writings, it was common for early
Christian authors to rely on the language of scripture, particularly the
New Testament, in their discussions of deification. Several New Testament concepts were especially influential. Paul, for example, spoke
of the faithful as being adopted as Christ's children and as becoming
alive, sanctified, and new creatures through him.[14] He also taught that
the faithful can be one with Christ and that Christ can live in them.[15]
John expressed similar sentiments in his writings[16] and 2 Peter 1:4
introduces the idea that humans can be "participants of the divine
nature" through Christ. Although somewhat abstract, the language
of unity, vitality, adoption, kinship, and participation would pervade
discussions of deification in the early years of the Church. Writing
over a century after Irenaeus, the bishop Athanasius (circa AD 296–
373) would restate Irenaeus's exchange formula, saying that the Word
of God "was incarnate [that is, made flesh] that we might be made

god."[17] Unlike his predecessors, however, Athanasius more explicitly emphasized the *full* divinity of the Son, meaning that the bishop was committed to the belief that the Son was entirely, rather than partly, divine.[18] The reason for this was that by the time of Athanasius, some Christians differed significantly in their understanding of the degree to which Jesus was human and the degree to which he was divine. Such theological differences had implications for Christians' understanding of salvation. For instance, one of Athanasius's opponents, Arius (circa AD 265–336), argued that because the Father created the Son, the Son could not be equal in divinity to the Father. Athanasius, however, reasoned that if the Son is not fully divine, then he cannot fully save humans; full divinity is necessary to enable others to become divine.

The theologian and bishop Gregory of Nazianzus (circa AD 329–390) would echo the sentiments expressed by Athanasius but also emphasize the equal importance of Jesus's *full* rather than partial humanity for deifying humans. He taught that "what has not been assumed has not been healed," meaning that to save human bodies from death and sin, Christ had to fully "assume" (that is, take upon himself) a human body and human nature through his Incarnation.[19] A formal declaration of this idea would later be made at the Council of Chalcedon in AD 451, according to which Christ was described as "perfect in divinity and humanity, truly God and truly human . . . being of one substance with the Father in relation to divinity, and being of one substance with us in relation to his humanity"[20] (see chapter 8).

For Gregory and many subsequent Christian theologians, Christ was paradoxically and necessarily both fully human and fully divine. Gregory was unique, however, in that he was the first Christian author to use the term *theosis* to refer broadly to the process of humans becoming like God.[21] The writings of Irenaeus, Athanasius, Gregory, and others demonstrate that early Christians understood human salvation to be inseparably linked to the nature and work of Christ. The reason for this is that Christ's nature was understood to be both a goal and means of human deification. Thus, while these theologians differed from one another on some of the details, they agreed that deification would not be possible without Jesus Christ intervening into human history through his Incarnation.

Comparing Ancient Christian and Latter-day Saint Teachings

You may have noticed that the teachings of Irenaeus and Athanasius appear to resemble Lorenzo Snow's statement that "as man now is, God once was; as God now is, man may be."[22] There are, however, at least two significant theological differences between these ancient and modern statements. The first difference relates to the identity of God. When these ancient authors spoke of God becoming human, they were referring to the Incarnation of Jesus Christ. Lorenzo Snow, however, appears to be referring to God the Father and alluding to a statement given by Joseph Smith in his King Follet Sermon that "God himself was once as we are now ... the Father of us all, dwelt on an earth, the same as Jesus Christ himself did."[23] While this nineteenth-century sermon is well known, it is not considered as a "doctrinal standard" in the Church, and modern Latter-day Saint leaders have not speculated further on the idea of Heavenly Father's potential "humanity."[24]

The second difference relates to human nature. Irenaeus and Athanasius understood God (as Creator) and humans (as creations) as different species, so to speak, rather than the same species albeit at different points of development.[25] Consequently, while these ancient Christian writers believed that humans could become immortal and incorruptible like God, they did not understand these divine attributes to be proper to our nature.

Moral Formation and Deification

In addition to the work accomplished by Christ's Incarnation, early Christians also believed that living a moral life was essential to becoming like God. This involved following God's commandments and cultivating attributes like faith, hope, charity, humility, patience, wisdom, and temperance. The cultivation of such attributes was frequently understood to be a journey in overcoming one's "passions," or "vices"—that is, those dispositions, desires, and emotions that lead to sin. Along this path of moral growth, many Christians saw themselves as progressing toward a more Edenic and heavenly existence. In other words, Christians spoke of moral growth as regaining God's "image" and/or "likeness" (Genesis 1:26)—creation as it existed in Eden before the Fall—and as imitating Christ and the life of heavenly angels (see Matthew 22:30).[26]

Like modern Christians, ancient followers of Jesus relied on scripture, on the inspiration of the Holy Spirit, and on guidance from ecclesiastical leaders to determine how best to live. These early Christians were also influenced by their larger cultural contexts, including their local customs and education. In an empire that spanned thousands of miles and that contained diverse peoples from different nations and tribes as well as a variety of strong-willed local and regional ecclesiastical leaders with unique pastoral concerns, differences of opinion naturally emerged regarding how best to bridge the gap between human and divine nature.

BOX 10.4 What Are God's "Image" and "Likeness"?

The early Christian theologian Origen of Alexandria (circa AD 185–254) believed that God's image and likeness in humans were two different things. The image refers to humans' potential for growth while the likeness refers to the realization of that potential. Origen explained: "Humankind received the honor of God's image in their first creation; whereas the perfection of God's likeness was reserved for them at the consummation. The purpose of this was that humans should acquire it for themselves by their own earnest efforts to imitate God, so that while the possibility of attaining perfection was given to them in the beginning through the honor of the 'image,' they should in the end through the accomplishment of these works obtain for themselves the perfect 'likeness.'"[27]

BOX 10.5   **Examples of Monastic Teachings**

"What is humility?. . . It is if you forgive a brother who has wronged you before he is sorry."[28]

"It is good to show beneficence to all, but more so to those unable to return the favor."[29]

"If trial does not come upon you, either openly or secretly, you cannot progress beyond your present measure. For all the saints, when they asked that their faith might be increased, entered into trials."[30]

"Do not pray for the fulfillment of your own wishes, for they do not necessarily accord with the will of God. But pray rather as you were taught, saying: 'Your will be done' in me (Matthew 6:10). And in every matter entreat him in this way that his will be done, for he wills what is good and beneficial for your soul, but you are not necessarily looking for this."[31]

"If, therefore the dread of some punishment continues to hold someone back from acting wrongly, it is clear that the freedom of the Spirit does not hold sway in the mind of the person who lives in such fear. For it cannot be doubted that, if he did not fear punishment, he would have acted wrongly. And so a mind which is held fast by the bondage of fear does not know the grace of freedom. For good things are to be loved for their own sakes, and not pursued because punishments are threatened."[32]

It is clear from the historical record that ancient Christians thoughtfully studied scripture with the question, What ways of living are most conducive to moral growth? Most ancient Christians would have lived as latter-day Christians do—going about their daily activities while trying their best to honor Christ's commands to love God and neighbor. Others, inspired by scriptures such as Matthew 6:25–26; 22:30; and Luke 18:22–25, gave all their possessions to the poor and separated themselves from family and society to live a life dedicated to prayer, study, and service. These men and women were called "monks," from the Greek word *monachos*, meaning "solitary."[33] Not all monks lived alone, however; some lived together in communities called monasteries, where they had "all things in common" (Acts 4:32) and were governed by a set of moral and practical guidelines called a "rule." These communities were viewed as laboratories for intellectual and spiritual formation—a kind of university of virtue and paradigm of what heavenly life might be like. Many texts that contain the moral teachings of ancient Christian monks were treasured and passed down for generations and still survive today (see box 10.5). Still other Christians dedicated themselves to service as Church officials or patrons or as teachers of scripture and theology, or they sought to imitate the itinerant lifestyle of Jesus and the Apostles by travelling and preaching. Such ways of life were understood to contribute to the moral development of those who adopted them.

As Christians reflected on what it meant to live a good life, disputes would arise periodically regarding the precise mechanics of moral development. One such dispute centered on the role of human nature, grace, and agency. At the heart of this debate was the question of whether humans were born sinful and what power they had, if any, to improve their condition. The famous theologian Augustine (AD 354–430) taught that because of the Fall of Adam and Eve, all humans (except Christ) are born sinful and lack the ability to even desire righteousness.[34] This is referred to more commonly as the doctrine of "original sin." Consequently, God must give his grace to humans to enable them to desire and do good. As Jesus says, "Apart from me you can do nothing," and "no man can come to me, except the Father which hath sent me draw him" (John 6:44; 15:5). Put simply, Augustine believed that God must heal human nature before humans could begin to develop morally and become more like God. While Augustine's views would ultimately become influential in the Western Roman Empire (see fig. 10.2), some Christian writers were concerned that his robust understanding of the role of grace might be leveraged to devalue human agency and moral responsibility.[35]

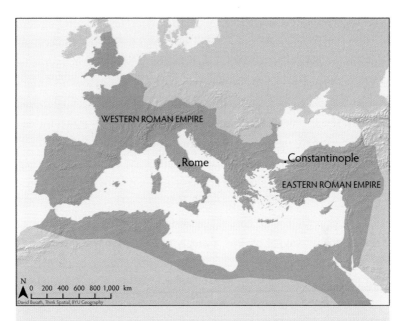

▲ **FIGURE 10.2**   Map with borders of the Roman Empire in AD 385 under Emperor Theodosius

For example, one of Augustine's contemporaries, a monk named Pelagius (circa AD 354–420), disagreed with his views. Unlike Augustine, Pelagius reasoned that humans are born sinless and inherently possess the ability to desire and do good.[36] To say otherwise would call God's goodness into question—after all, why would God create broken beings who are unable to do what he asks of them?[37] Accordingly, Pelagius taught that God's grace does not heal human nature because human nature has no need of healing. Rather, grace is expressed in God bringing to our attention what we must do *on our own* to live good lives. Such manifestations of grace include the Ten Commandments and the moral example of Jesus Christ.[38] God's grace also takes the form of forgiveness and empowerment when humans fall short. For Pelagius then, moral perfection was entirely within the grasp of human beings in mortality. All humans need is for God to tell them what to do and help them out along the way (see chapter 7).

Other ancient Christians focused their energies on better understanding what precisely the process of moral formation looks like,
asking questions such as, What virtues should Christians cultivate
and how? What vices must one overcome and how? How do different virtues and vices relate to one another? What are signs of moral
growth? The monk Evagrius of Pontus (circa AD 345–399), for example, identified eight vices that one must conquer: gluttony, lust,
avarice, sadness, anger, despondency, vainglory, and pride.[39] Other
Christians would later shorten and revise this catalog into the commonly known list of "seven deadly sins." Evagrius prescribed spiritual
exercises, or remedies, to combat each vice, including prayer, fasting,
scripture study, singing psalms, almsgiving, gift giving, and service.[40]
He reasoned that such practices could help to change one's nature
from bad to good and from good to better. Whereas some ancient
Christians, like Origen of Alexandria, believed that moral progress
entailed merely controlling one's sinful inclinations (an ideal known
as *metriopatheia*) in mortality,[41] Evagrius taught that it was possible
for humans to completely eradicate them (an ideal know as *apatheia*).
He described this ideal moral state as the "health of the soul," which
enables one to love completely, to be unperturbed by temptation and
trial, and to commune with God without distraction or interference.[42]

One of Evagrius's contemporaries, the bishop and theologian
Gregory of Nyssa (circa AD 335–395), similarly wrote about the process of moral formation. In his *Homilies on the Beatitudes*, for example, Gregory envisioned growth in godliness to correspond to Jesus's
list of "beatitudes" recorded in Matthew 5:3–10. In so doing, he further demonstrated the way in which Christians consistently sought
to understand moral progress through the lens of scripture. Gregory
taught that the beatitudes are arranged "like so many steps, so as to
facilitate the ascent from one to the other."[43] Eight attributes charac-
terize this ascent to godliness: poverty of spirit, meekness, mourning,
hunger and thirst for justice, mercy, cleanliness of heart, peacemak-
ing, and suffering persecution for righteousness' sake. Like Evagrius,

▲ **FIGURE 10.3** Ladder of Divine Ascent, Saint Catherine's Monastery, Sinai, Egypt. This icon (made in the twelfth century but representing earlier monastic ideas) vividly details the conceptual ascent toward God with some monks falling to worldly passions and demons while others are encouraged toward virtue by angels above and saints below. Photo: Courtesy of Florian Prischl via Wikimedia Commons (public domain)

Gregory saw the goal of moral life to be "communion with the God-head," meaning not only communication with but likeness to God.[44] Those who attain this state enjoy the "highest form of freedom," which is self-mastery; they become strangers to sin, possess properly ordered love, and are not enslaved by desires for worldly things.[45] For Gregory, as well as for others, however, progression toward godliness was not limited to this mortal life. It could also continue after death.

Eternal Progression

What is heavenly life like? Two prominent early Christian theologians agreed that humans continue to progress toward becoming like God after death.[46] One, however, believed that this progression eventually ends; the other believed that it does not. The first theologian, Origen of Alexandria, dedicated his life to teaching about and defending the Christian faith as he understood it. He believed that after death, the spirits of good persons will "remain in some place situated on earth, which . . . scripture calls 'paradise.'"[47] He describes this paradise as a "school for souls" in which deceased persons will learn about the nature and destiny of the earth, the stars and other heavenly bodies, and the various works of God. He speculated, for example: "He [God] will show to them, as to sons, the causes of things and the perfection of his creation, teaching them why one star is placed in its particular position in the sky and why it is separated from another by so great an interval of space."[48] Such persons will also be taught about "'the things which are not seen' (2 Corinthians 4:18)" as they progress in knowledge and will eventually ascend to see the face of God.[49]

Origen believed that the more one learns in mortality, the better equipped one will be to participate in this kind of learning in the afterlife, but he also recognized that certain kinds of learning require that a person not be hindered by the "carnal senses."[50] In other words, according to Origen, the absence of a physical body enables a person to learn differently. For this reason, after death, a human being can grow "not as it grew in this life in the flesh . . . but increasing in mind and intelligence," progressing toward "perfect knowledge" and "the

▲ **FIGURE 10.4**   Dome with Cross and Stars, Mausoleum of Galla Placidia, Ravenna, Italy, fifth century. A field of stars surround a cross and illuminate the dark blue heavenly dome. Mosaics, made up of small tesserae, were often used to decorate the interior of early Christian basilicas, mausolea, and chapels. They create a scintillating, otherworldly environment for the contemplation of the divine economy. Photo: Courtesy of Luca Sartoni via Wikimedia Commons (public domain)

contemplation and understanding of God."[51] At the end of this journey of human progression, a person becomes one with God, just "as the Father is one with the Son."[52]

When Latter-day Saints speak about oneness with God, we often speak of being united to him in purpose and power. Or perhaps we think of possessing "all that [the] Father hath" or of the similarities that will exist between God's and our own celestial bodies (Doctrine and Covenants 84:38). Origen, however, speaks of being united to God in mind—an intellectual union in which "there will no longer be any diversity" between God and those who are united to him.[53] He explains: "And he [God] will be all things in each person in such a way that everything which the rational mind . . . can feel or understand or think will be all God and that the mind will no longer be conscious of anything besides or other than God, but will think God and see God and hold God and God will be the mode and measure of its every movement; and in this way God will be all to it."[54] For Origen, then, unity means that God will be "all in all" (1 Corinthians 15:28).[55] At this pinnacle of human progression, the human mind will be completely enveloped and satiated in God. There will be a point at which humans will stop progressing and rest in God. In this sense, for Origen, progression after death is not eternal because it has an end.[56]

On this final point, Gregory of Nyssa would disagree with Origen. Like Origen, Gregory dedicated his life to teaching about the Christian faith as he understood it. He is perhaps most well-known for his teaching regarding "epectasy"—from the Greek word for "stretching" or "extension"—which relates to the soul's eternal and ever-increasing progression toward God.[57] This theological tenet rests primarily on three assumptions relating to the nature of God and human nature. First, like several of his theological forebears, Gregory believed that God is a perfect and infinite being, and that because of this, there will always exist an unbridgeable gulf between him and creation (that is, us). As created and finite beings we can certainly know some things about God, we just cannot know everything about God.[58] Consequently, we can never become like God in the fullest sense.

The good news and second assumption upon which Gregory's teaching about epectasy is based is that human nature is malleable and has an infinite capacity for growth. Gregory explains: "Human nature came into being as something capable of becoming whatever it determines upon, and to whatever goal the thrust of its choice leads, it undergoes alteration in accord with what it seeks."[59] In other words,

> **BOX 10.6 Christ Is the Light. We Are the Mirror.**
>
> Gregory of Nyssa taught that one way God reveals himself to humans is by conforming their character to his. In this way, they come to know experientially who God is—how he thinks, feels, and sees the world. He explained that as humans develop spiritually, God reveals himself "in the mirror that we are," which makes our souls to gleam "in company with the light that appears within it" and makes "the Invisible visible for us and the Incomprehensible comprehensible."[60]

if humans consistently choose to orient themselves to God and seek out his will, our nature will be changed such that we become more like him (see box 10.6). Much of this orientation will take place after death and the resurrection, when "the passions that now afflict us through the flesh do not rise up with those bodies . . . and every corporeal disposition has disappeared from our nature."[61]

Finally, because God is infinite and humans have an infinite capacity for growth, becoming like God is a never-ending process. The more we learn about God and become like him, the more we realize how much more there is to know and become. As Gregory put it, "For that which is apprehended at any given time is in all respects greater than anything that has been apprehended previously, but it does not . . . set limits to the object of the search," rather it becomes "the starting point of a search after more exalted things."[62] This process is eternal because the more we know and become like God, the more we desire to continue in our journey: "the soul that is joined to God is not satiated by her enjoyment of him," rather "the more abundantly she is filled up with his beauty, the more vehemently her longings abound."[63] Gregory's commitment to the notion that God transcends what humans can achieve was an expression of his reverence and respect for God. It also reflected his faith that even though God's greatness will ever be out of our reach, it can always be on our horizon.

▲ **FIGURE 10.5** Good Shepherd Mosaic, Mausoleum of Galla Placidia, Ravenna, Italy, fifth century. The victorious Christ occupies a paradisiacal, pastoral landscape surrounded by his sheep (followers). He is divinely and imperially garbed in gold and purple and holds the cross as a shepherd's staff. The mosaicist has chosen to include a rocky chasm in the foreground that might encourage the viewer to aspire to a similar station of disposition and repose after death and resurrection. Photo: Courtesy of Alfredo Dagli, Scala/Art Resource NY

Conclusion

Early Christian discussions of deification emerged from a deep love for God and scripture and from a desire to better understand them both. Christ was central to these discussions. Not only was his miraculous Incarnation understood to provide the means by which human nature could be divinized, but his moral life served as a model for his early followers to imitate. Like Latter-day Saints, early Christians found joy and fulfillment in searching scripture by study and by faith and in applying its teachings to their lives. They saw it as their duty to teach and defend Christian doctrine as they understood it. As we do today, they often disagreed, sometimes fiercely, on theological matters, on scripture interpretation, and on how God's word should inform disciples' lives. And just as we aspire to exercise humility when witnessing of the grandeur of God, so they recognized that knowledge of God is attained line upon line and precept upon precept, some in this life and some in the next. As modern Christians, we might more carefully consider the value of the theological literature produced by the early saints. Although certainly we can disagree with them on some accounts, their dedication to the question of how to bridge the gap between human and divine nature has and can continue to provide valuable theological tools and insights for generations of Christians, as we seek to know and become like God.

Notes

1. See Aristotle Papanikolaou, "Theosis," in *The Oxford Handbook of Mystical Theology*, ed. Edward Howells and Mark A. McIntosh (Oxford: Oxford University Press, 2020), 570.

2. See Stephan Finlan and Vladimir Kharlamov, *Theosis: Deification in Christian Theology* (Eugene, OR; Pickwick Publications), 65.

3. See Finlan and Kharlamov, *Theosis,* 51–65.

4. See Finlan and Kharlamov, *Theosis,* 65.

5. Ignatius, *Letter to the Ephesians* 7, in *The Apostolic Fathers: Greek Texts and English Translations,* trans. Michael Holmes (Grand Rapids, MI: Baker Books, 1999), 141. English translations of *Letter to the Ephesians* are taken from this edition of *The Apostolic Fathers* translated by Holmes.

6. Ignatius, *Letter to the Ephesians* 7.

7. See Justin Martyr, *Dialogue with Trypho* 124.2. For other statements relating to deification in Justin's writings, see also *1 Apology* 19.4; 21.6; *2 Apology* 8.3; 13.3.

8. Not unlike Ammon teaching Lamoni about the "Great Spirit" (see Alma 18:1–43), Justin sought to present Christianity in a way that would be most intelligible and attractive to his Greco-Roman audience.

9. See Justin Martyr, *1 Apology* 19.4.

10. See Justin Martyr, *2 Apology* 8.3; 13.3.

11. Irenaeus, *Against Heresies* 5, preface. The Latin reads: *factus est quod sumus nos, uti nos perficeret esse quod et ipse.*

12. See Irenaeus, *Against Heresies* 3.20.1; 4.11.1–2. For Irenaeus, to become like God is to regain one's state of being at the time of creation—that is, to recover the "likeness" of God, which humanity lost after the Fall. On the differences between human and divine nature, see Irenaeus, *Against Heresies* 2.24.2; 2.34.2; 3.8.3; 4.38.3.

13. Some Christians understood participation in such rituals to provide occasions for "contact with the divine" through the Holy Spirit; see Papanikolaou, "Theosis," 571.

14. Romans 8:14–15; Galatians 4:5; Ephesians 1:5, 10; 1 Corinthians 1:2; 15:22; 2 Corinthians 5:17; Norman Russell, *The Doctrine of Deification in the Greek Patristic Tradition* (Oxford: Oxford University Press, 2004), 79–85.

15. See Ephesians 1:5, 10; 1 Corinthians 1:2; 10:17; 15:22, 53; 2 Corinthians 5:17; Galatians 3:27; 4:19; Romans 13:14.

16. See John 1:12; 3:16; 5:26; 17:22–3; Russell, *Doctrine of Deification in the Greek Patristic Tradition,* 87–89.

17. Athanasius, *On the Incarnation* 54, in *On the Incarnation: Saint Athanasius,* trans. John Behr, vol. 44 in the Popular Patristics series (Yonkers, NY: St. Vladimir's Seminary Press, 2011), 107.

18. Athanasius believed that the Son is of the same nature as the Father and has always existed with the Father (that is, he is uncreated). This does not mean that the Son was not also human, only that he was not inferior to God the Father in any way.

19. Gregory of Nazianzus, *Letter* 101.32, in *Nicene and Post-Nicene Fathers*, series 2, trans. Charles Browne and James Swallow (Peabody, MA: Hendrickson, 1994), 7:440.

20. Translation quoted from Alister McGrath, ed., *The Christian Theology Reader*, 5th ed. (Malden, MA: Wiley-Blackwell, 2017), 241.

21. Gregory of Nazianzus, *Oration* 4.71. Two centuries later, Dionysius the Areopagite would concisely define *theosis* as "the attaining of likeness of God and union with him so far as is possible." Dionysius, *Ecclesiastical Hierarchy* 1.3; trans. qtd. from Papanikolaou, "Theosis," 574.

22. See Eliza R. Snow, *Biography and Family Record of Lorenzo Snow* (Salt Lake City: Deseret News Co.1884), 46.

23. For the various accounts of the sermon, see "Accounts of the 'King Follett Sermon,'" *The Joseph Smith Papers*, https://www.josephsmithpapers.org/site/accounts-of-the-king-follett-sermon?p=1.

24. See "Becoming Like God," Gospel Topics Essay, The Church of Jesus Christ of Latter-day Saints, footnote 35, https://www.churchofjesuschrist.org/study/manual/gospel-topics-essays/becoming-like-god.

25. Parley P. Pratt wrote: "God, angels and men, are all of one species, one race, one great family widely diffused among the planetary systems, as colonies, kingdoms, nations." Pratt, *Key to the Science of Theology* (Liverpool: F. D. Richards, 1855), 33.

26. The terms *image* and *likeness* were sometimes understood as distinct (see chapter 7). See, for example, Origen, *On First Principles* 3.6.1, in *On First Principles*, trans. G. W. Butterworth (Notre Dame: Ave Maria Press, 2013), 321. English translations of *On First Principles* are taken from this edition translated by G. W. Butterworth.

27. Origen of Alexandria, *On First Principles* 3.6.1.

28. *The Desert Fathers: Sayings of the Early Christian Monks*, trans. Benedicta Ward (London: Penguin Books, 2003), 163

29. See Evagrius, *Maxims* 2.16, in *Evagrius of Pontus: The Greek Ascetic Corpus*, trans. Robert Sinkewicz (Oxford: Oxford University Press, 2003), 231.

30. See Ammonas, *Letter* 9, in *The Letters of Ammonas, Successor of St. Antony*, trans. Derwas J. Chitty and Sebastian Brock (Oxford: SLG, 1979), 11.

31. See Evagrius, *On Prayer* 31, in *Evagrius of Pontus*, 196.

32. See Gregory the Great, *Regula Pastoralis* 13, in *Gregory the Great*, trans. John Moorhead (London: Routledge, 2005), 118–19.

33. On the history of Christian monasticism, see Bernice Kaczynski, ed., *The Oxford Handbook of Christian Monasticism* (Oxford: Oxford University Press, 2020).

34. See Augustine, *On the Predestination of the Saints* 7. For a concise summary

of Augustine's views, see Alister McGrath, *Historical Theology: An Intro-duction to the History of Christian Thought* (Malden, MA: Wiley-Blackwell, 2013), 67–73.

35. See McGrath, *Historical Theology*, 71.

36. See Pelagius, *In Support of Free Will*, as reported by Augustine, *On the Grace of Christ* 4.5. For a concise summary of Pelagius' views, see Alister Mc-Grath, *Historical Theology*, 69–73.

37. Pelagius writes: "God has not willed to command anything impossible, for God is righteous; and will not condemn anyone for what they could not help, for God is holy." Pelagius, *Letter to Demetrius* 16, in *The Christian Theology Reader*, ed. Allister McGrath, 5th ed. (Malden, MA: Wiley-Blackwell, 2017), 350.

38. See McGrath, *Historical Theology*, 71.

39. Evagrius, *Praktikos* 6–14.

40. Evagrius, *Praktikos* 16–39.

41. Origen of Alexandria taught that it is a "virtually impossible achievement" for humans to become morally perfect while in mortality. *On First Principles* 2.2.1. For a concise treatment of the stages of spiritual maturation in Origen's thought, see Mark Scott, *Journey Back to God: Origen on the Problem of Evil* (New York: Oxford University Press, 2012), 103–28.

42. Evagrius, *Praktikos* 56, 81, 84.

43. Gregory of Nyssa, *The Lord's Prayer, The Beatitudes*, trans. Hida C. Graef, vol. 18 in the Ancient Christian Writers: The Works of Fathers in Transla-tion series (New York: Paulist Press, 1954), 97.

44. Gregory of Nyssa, *The Beatitudes*, 85, 130.

45. Gregory of Nyssa, *The Beatitudes*, 173.

46. I am not claiming that only two believed this. Rather, I am providing only two examples here.

47. Origen, *On First Principles* 2.11.6.

48. Origen, *On First Principles* 2.11.7.

49. Origen, *On First Principles* 2.11.7.

50. Origen, *On First Principles* 2.11.4, 7.

51. Origen, *On First Principles* 2.11.7.

52. See Origen, *On First Principles* 3.6.4.

53. Origen, *On First Principles* 3.6.3, 4.

54. Origen, *On First Principles* 3.6.3, 4.

55. Origen, *On First Principles* 3.6.3, 4.

56. Origen, *On First Principles* 3.6.3, 4.

57. The participial form of this word appears in Philippians 3:13.

58. On the differences between human and divine nature, see Gregory of Nyssa, *On the Making of Man* 6.12.

59. Gregory of Nyssa, *Homilies on the Song of Songs* 4, trans. Richard Norris (Atlanta, GA: Society of Biblical Literature, 2013), 113. In this chapter, English translations of Gregory of Nyssa's homilies are taken from this edition translated by Norris.

60. Gregory of Nyssa, *Homilies on the Song of Songs* 3, 4 (Norris, 101, 115).

61. Gregory of Nyssa, *Homilies on the Song of Songs* 1 (Norris, 33).

62. Gregory of Nyssa, *Homilies on the Song of Songs* 8 (Norris, 261).

63. Gregory of Nyssa, *Homilies on the Song of Songs* 1 (Norris, 33).

11

INCLINING CHRISTIAN HEARTS

Work for the Dead

Catherine Gines Taylor

Blessed be the God and Father of our Lord Jesus Christ! By his great mercy he has given us a new birth into a living hope through the resurrection of Jesus Christ from the dead, and into an inheritance that is imperishable, undefiled, and unfading, kept in heaven for you, who are being protected by the power of God through faith for a salvation ready to be revealed in the last time.

—1 Peter 1:3–5
New Revised Standard Version

The realm of the dead has always been a foreign country. In this chapter, I want to take you along into the world of ordinary late ancient Christians and the material culture that defined the nature of their sociality. For early Christians, death impacted religious, social, and even economic norms established and perpetuated through kinship groups and long-standing material traditions.[1] Monuments, paintings deep in catacomb graves, ancient sarcophagi, and epitaphs still stand today as evidence that there were moments in which the body and soul of the departed commanded the full attention of a community. Death was an immediate and visceral reality for early Christians; they planned for it, considered carefully the fate of their souls, and even influenced the ways they would be remembered while they were yet living. There are many ways in which early Christians were taught and conditioned to anticipate their death.[2] Perhaps the same concerns and questions that confronted our kindred Saints have also crossed your mind: Might we catch a glimpse of life after death through our living rituals and intercessions? What can be done to aid the progression of souls after death? Will cherished relationships continue or be renewed in the afterlife?

As you read and consider the material evidence, I ask you to suspend ideas about who you think the early Christians were and let them represent themselves. I will ask you to value source material in the form of art and texts that may be unfamiliar to you. Engaging in this exercise should be an exciting prospect—an opportunity to reimagine this pivotal time period and interact with language and images that help us understand our own histories, for truly we are kin to these believers. You should be prepared to allow for the variety of salvific

---

BOX 11.1 Why It Matters

When Latter-day Saints hear the phrase "work for the dead," we immediately think of baptism for the dead or other vicarious work performed in our temples. Yet our work for the dead also includes genealogy, family history, the dedication of graves, preparing the bodies of our deceased for burial or cremation, and more. For ancient Christians, work for the dead is attested in the material record as well as textual sources and includes evidence for baptism as well as intercessory prayer, vicarious good works, visionary redemption, and vigil keeping. The visual record is more than a casual cultural exploration of the past; it is, in some cases, the only source we have to understand the faith of early Christians. As Latter-day Saints, we can learn from our ancient Christian ancestors how to better incline our hearts toward our faithful kindred dead, for truly "neither can we without our dead be made perfect" (Doctrine and Covenants 128:15).

---

acts that were performed by the living on behalf of the dead. So often we rely on texts alone to tell us about past ages, but the written record preserves a particular and privileged perspective that cannot speak for all Christian experience. My focus will be on merging the art historical record with the devotional realities that were at times in concert with, but at times in tension with, certain texts. I am asking you to likewise enable our faithful, kindred dead to speak to you from the grave as their memorial artistic record illuminates the past before our eyes.

Although we call the collective communities of believers early Christians, we should remember that individual believers lived and died within diverse communities. These people helped shape the systems of belief in this world and influenced the parameters of our understanding for the next. While ancient Christians thoughtfully engaged with theologies, religious practices, and the path of transformative love exemplified in the life and teachings of Jesus, they also went about their daily activities. The lives of believing women and men were impacted by very ordinary, very mortal events of life, including a mortality rate much higher than we know today. It is imperative that we consider the relationship between the living and the dead in late ancient Christianity on its own terms and that we give sufficient honor and memorial to the lives of faith that sustained it.

One of the best ways to understand how early Christians envisioned death and elicited aid for their deceased is to look at the material culture that they produced. By the year AD 200, Christians were experimenting with images and iconography to create a new visual language of devotion.[3] Most of the art that survives from this period is funerary in nature. Two material examples that best reflect the culture of death and memorial are the Roman catacombs and carved stone sarcophagi. Early Christians in the Mediterranean region were deeply influenced by Graeco-Roman culture. Sometimes they used images and personifications similar to their non-Christian friends and neighbors, but they also developed symbols of their own. One symbol called the Christogram combined the Greek letters chi and rho (see fig. 11.1) and was immediately associated with Christ as they overlapped and formed the first letters of *Christos*. Other symbols like the dove of peace, the anchor, the good shepherd, the fish, and the vine were used in both conspicuous and inconspicuous ways to identify the tombs of Christians.

The subject matter most often found in catacombs and on sarcophagi comes from the narratives of the Old and New Testaments. Salvific deliverance was symbolically represented in images of Abraham and his son Isaac, Noah and the ark, Jonah and the whale, Daniel in the lions' den, and the story of Susanna. These stories each demonstrate acts of intercession for the faithful and the power of prayer. The intercession of God on behalf of those who call upon him is clearly marked in these visual images. There was even an early Christian prayer for the dead called the Commendation of the Soul in which biblical figures are invoked when asking God to likewise deliver the soul of the deceased: "Deliver, Lord, [insert decedent's name], just as you delivered . . . [fill in the blank with Daniel, Susannah, or Noah]."[4]

▲ **FIGURE 11.1** Marble funerary stele with a female orante, the Christogram, and a dove of peace; Museo Nazionale, Rome, Italy, third to fifth century. Photo: Alamy

These images and prayers invoked remembrance of departed souls and evoked hope for similar rescue among the living.

Death, for early Christian believers, was always qualified by the Resurrection of Jesus. In the New Testament, death is the necessary companion to finding eternal life in Christ. For early Christians, because Christ was the first fruits of the grave (see Isaiah 53:5), not even death could separate them from Christ (see Romans 8:38–39); and the faithful found themselves "at home with the Lord" (2 Corinthians 5:8). Even the sharp sting of death was dulled in the image of the faithful, like Lazarus, simply having "fallen asleep" (John 11:11), waiting to awaken through the new birth of resurrection. Because death is common to humankind, the imperative given in 1 Corinthians 15:22, "For as all die in Adam, so all will be made alive in Christ," shifted the paradigm from an afterlife where the disembodied soul resided forever in bucolic revery to one in which the body was to be regained in order to participate in the eschaton and dwell with God in the heavenly city.

Care for and over the body had always been a necessary focus. To say that honoring the bodies of the deceased carried significant social weight within the Roman milieu would be an understatement. In the wake of the barbarous devastations suffered in Rome, Augustine (AD 354–430) gave new emphasis not only to the body but to the soul. For example, he particularly defines the expectation that the body will rise, in its transformed and perfected state, but as a secondary resurrection to that of the soul, which could occur in the present moment. For Augustine, the first resurrection of the soul is dependent on casting off ungodliness and being in a state of obedience, belief, and perseverance in order to be attuned to the voice of the Son of God—"and they that hear shall live."[5] In short, for early Christians the flesh mattered inasmuch as it could resurrect through its alignment with the power of Christ. Augustine continued in his *City of God* to imagine the call to all the souls of humankind: "Awake thou that sleepest, and arise from the dead, and Christ shall give thee light," for "as Christ has risen from the dead by the glory of the Father, so we also may walk in newness of life."[6]

Care for the Dead as Work for the Dead: *Vixit in Pace* (Lived in Peace), a Common Epitaph

Death in the late ancient world was a family affair. The paradigm of what heavenly life might be like was developed among devotees in varied Christian households and communities. While there are exceptional instances where the faithful are brought to the church in the wake of their death, most Christians were mourned and commemorated in their own homes and then at the place of interment.[7] The practices of the cult of the dead were intertwined with the faithful of multiple religions. So-called pagans and Christians alike buried their dead in the same cemeteries into the fourth century and mourned adjacent to each other as a normative part of ordinary life.[8]

The cult of the dead has material and textual evidence dating back centuries in the ancient Near East and in Israel. The influence of long-standing veneration at the tomb of Adam, the tombs of the patriarchs and their wives, along with the development of holy relics is evidence.[9] Even Jesus's own empty tomb was visited from early days, especially after the visit of the Empress Helena, Constantine's mother, to the Holy Land in AD 326.[10] Helena is famously known by the mid-fourth century for founding churches on sites already venerated in early Christianity, such as the sites of the Nativity and Christ's Ascension.[11] Christians of the early church were not just following after Hellenistic tradition but were continuing commemorative practices from time immemorial.

For a moment, let us turn our sights westward in the Mediterranean to fourth-century Spain. In the early decades of that century, nineteen bishops gathered at the Council of Elvira. This council is compelling because it produced eighty-one canons, or prescriptive rules,[12] that were meant to answer disciplinary questions about how early Christians were worshiping, even before the so-called Triumph of the Church under Constantine.[13] Several of these canons deal with actions associated with veneration of the dead, including rules about cemeteries, vigils, fasting, the use of images, and relationships between Christians and so-called pagans. Canon 34 states that "candles are not to be burned in a cemetery during the day. This practice is related to paganism and is harmful to Christians. Those who do this are to be denied the communion of the church."[14] Prohibiting the excessive use of candles was a canon that impacted women, though not exclusively, who were primary mourners at tombs and in cemeteries. Apart from the association with pagan practice, the light was thought to keep the souls of the dead awake and not allow them to rest.[15] While there is a plethora of ecclesiastical canons that condemn even the minute movements of pious laity, there is also a glaring lack of official ecclesiastical intercession on behalf of the ordinary dead. Many of the practices undertaken by early Christian families seem to reflect, perhaps, a dissatisfaction with the lack of official intercession by the church.[16]

It is clear that caring for the dead was considered an act of faith for ancient Christians, and in the end, it was the duty of families to organize not only funerals and burials but to also participate in the saving acts of vigil, fasting, salvific prayer, and regular commemoration.

▲ **FIGURE 11.2** Les Alyscamps Cemetery, Arles, France. This ancient cemetery in Arles takes its name from the pagan paradise of the Elysian fields. This area has been a necropolis or city of the dead since Roman times and became popular for early Christians when believers wished to be buried here near the tomb of St. Genesius. Some of the most beautiful early Christian sarcophagi were once housed here. Photo: Catherine Gines Taylor

Following the period in which the body was laid in the home (*collo-catio*), it would take its final journey outside the city walls and to its final resting place (fig. 11.2). Funerary feasts occurred at intervals of 3, 7 or 9, 13, and 365 days after death. Women began mourning immediately at death (*conclamatio mortis*) and at the burial by gathering kinswomen together. Women were primary actors in and the creators of ritual oral lament, especially as improvised within the aural/oral tradition.[17] They washed and anointed the dead and iterated the story and circumstances of death and life for the deceased.

▼ **FIGURE 11.3**   Death certificate for Lois Bradshaw Wright indicating the Relief Society as undertaker. Used with permission, Ardis Parshall

> Where was disease contracted,
> If not at place of death?
> Former or usual residence ... *Hurricane, Utah*
> 19 PLACE OF BURIAL OR REMOVAL *Hurricane*   DATE OF BURIAL *Feb 23*, 1920
> 20 UNDERTAKER *Relief Society*   ADDRESS *Hurricane*

BOX 11.2   Latter-day Saint Women and the Gates of Death

It was common for Relief Societies in the early days of The Church of Jesus Christ of Latter-day Saints to attend at births, in sickness, and at deaths as part of their spiritual duties and callings. Even with the advent of professionalized medicine and morticians, women maintained this practice because they felt at home in the ushering of souls in and out of this world. Groups of women attended the dying, washed and clothed the body, and sat for the wake until burial. Women even had dreams of Relief Society sisters easing a woman's death and then welcoming her into heaven.[18]

As long as families remembered and showed appropriate piety through celebration of the birthday (*die natalis*) of the deceased and the annual ancestor's day (*Parentalia*), it was as if the deceased lived on as part of the community.[19] The *Parentalia*, celebrated with sacrifice, was held on February 21 and invoked protective, watchful care over the deceased. A separate banquet, not connected to the sacrifice, was then enjoyed by the family near the tomb and again the next day at home. These periodic rituals, including offerings of food and drink, were intended for the well-being of the dead and helped to perpetuate relationships between the deceased, their relatives, and friends. By the fourth century, architectural dining spaces[20] were common in cemeteries, with stone tables, chairs, and even ovens permanently furnished because of the regular preparation of funerary meals.[21] These feasts were made to be beneficent to all parties and may remind modern readers of Memorial Day graveside picnics. Sarcophagi were regularly fitted with holes and graves with terracotta pipes to allow for libations to make their way to the dead, who "are nourished by our libations and whatever we bring to their tombs."[22] Even Monica, Augustine's own Christian mother, would visit the tombs of her parents to "share" some wine and make offerings on their behalf.[23]

Before Augustine, the Council at Laodicea forbade so-called *agape* feasts within the church proper, "nor to eat and to spread couches in the house of God,"[24] but these festivities continued. Augustine himself, like Paul (1 Corinthians 8:9–10), encouraged moderation at funerary banquets and even saw this kind of feasting as an opportunity for almsgiving to the poor as a vicarious act in aid to the dead. Even with censure of raucous behavior, Augustine does not forbid Christians from partaking in meals at the tombs of ordinary people.[25] In fact, he describes this kind of relationship between the living and the dead as "a solace for the dead."[26] Certainly, this kind of discourse speaks to the consensus that Christians were invested in the memory of their dead, even beyond threat of censure.

▲ **FIGURE 11.4**   Ivory panel showing St. Paul and Thecla, from a casket. Possibly from Rome, from the British Museum's collection, fourth century. Photo: Scala/Art Resource NY

Intercession and the Material Rest of the Grave

Early accounts from the second century describe how intercessory prayers of the righteous could be offered up as work for the dead, even for those who had no knowledge of Christianity in this life. The *Acts of Paul and Thecla* (circa AD 160–180) gives the account of a believing woman named Thecla who became a follower of Paul after hearing him preach in Iconium (modern-day Turkey). A Roman-style ivory plaque (see fig. 11.4) depicts the narrative scene of Thecla's conversion as she listens to Paul from inside the cloistered walls of her home.

Thecla is dressed in modest dress and makes a gesture of listening as Paul, her future preaching companion, reads from scripture. After Thecla joins forces with Paul and endures a number of ordeals, she is sentenced to die by lions (see fig. 4.5) for rejecting the unwanted advances of a nobleman. Her mother arranges for her to be watched over by a rich woman, Queen Tryphaena, in order to assure her virginal state at death. The night before she faces the lions, Thecla is paraded through the town and brought to the queen:

> After the exhibition Tryphaena received her again. For her dead daughter Falconilla had said to her in a dream, "Mother, receive this stranger, the forsaken Thecla, in my place, that she may pray for me and I may come to the place of the just."
>
> And when, after the exhibition, Tryphaena had received her she was grieved because Thecla had to fight on the following day with the wild beasts, but on the other hand she loved her dearly like her daughter Falconilla and said "Thecla, my second child, come, pray for my child that she may live in eternity, for this I saw in my sleep." And without hesitation she [Thecla] lifted up her voice and said, "My God, Son of the Most High, who are in heaven, grant her wish [desire] that her daughter Falconilla may live in eternity."[27]

After Thecla's miraculous release from the arena where lions, seals, and bulls do not harm her, the women of Iconium shouted aloud, "One is the God, who saved Thecla," and Tryphaena proclaims, "Now I believe that the dead are raised!"[28] Falconilla is then received into heaven by miraculous mercy because Thecla called upon her God, and Tryphaena likewise takes Thecla into her home to receive rest and joy. The account of Thecla was very popular among early Christians and offered a model of intercessory prayer answered on behalf of a pagan woman. Thecla lives out a long life and openly prays often for unlikely outcomes—and she is immediately answered. Although the account is fantastic and not held as historically precise,[29] it lived and breathed in the lives of early Christians, especially among women, and functioned as an exemplary text of faithful action for them.

While theologians like Augustine will be particular about who can benefit from prayers, particularly the prayers of the church, John Chrysostom (died AD 407) in Antioch is more generous in his sermons about the kind of work that Christians could do for their kin, believers or not. Chrysostom seems to envision the liminal world of the dead as one that is not ruled over by the church but is the jurisdiction of Jesus himself. Chrysostom associated funerary piety with night vigils and specifically cites women as those watchful souls who "go into the country" and "watch through the whole night."[30] The countryside journey is likely associated with vigils specifically kept in cemeteries like those censured at the Council of Elvira. Chrysostom also calls upon the imagination of his hearers to associate sleep with death and the house with the tomb.[31] The necropolis and the home were considered appropriate domiciles for the physical remains of the deceased. Some tombs and ossuary boxes were shaped to look like houses, and even the monumental structure of sarcophagi (from *sarco* and *phago*, or "flesh eater" of the ancient world) underscored the semipermanent abode for the body. It is easy to see how tight intersections between communal memorial and Christian identity were born of gathering at the tomb and within the home.

Cemeteries were crossroads where the sights, sounds, and performances common to burial were on display. In fact, "visiting tombs and participating in lament was not only to commemorate the dead. The practice of pious lament had a long tradition of invoking aid from beyond the grave for the purposes of the living."[32] Intercession, healing, invoking good fortune, accentuating fertility, and providing apotropaic or protective aid were all compelling reasons for Christians to seek communion with their beloved departed. Visions of death and the overlay of Christian narratives were not far from the eyes and imagination of early Christians. Images on sarcophagi and in catacombs call attention to the geography of the afterlife. Christians decorated environments for their dead with biblical scenes that evoked their faith in Christ's life, his miracles, his Passion, and his triumph over death.[33] Imagine the evocative experience of going underground into a catacomb lit only by oil lamps and seeing Christ depicted as a wonderworker, extending his power through a type of wand, to raise

◄ **FIGURE 11.5** Raising of Lazarus fresco, Catacomb of the Giordani, Rome, fourth century. In miracle scenes like the raising of Lazarus, Christ often appears beardless, wearing traditional Roman clothing, and wielding a wand or rod. Here he calls forth the bound Lazarus from his sepulcher. Photo: Scala/Art Resource NY

◄ **FIGURE 11.6** Marble sarcophagus with the *Traditio Legis*, last quarter of the fourth century, Rome, Musée départmental Arles Antique. Christ is presented standing on the apocalyptic mount with four rivers rushing forth as his sheep gather at his feet. The columns that frame him are entwined with living vines and the palms behind him and his apostles indicate his victory over death as the first fruit from the grave. Photo: Catherine Gines Taylor

Lazarus from the dead (see fig. 11.5). The proximity of this scene to bodies lying in repose, wrapped in linens like Lazarus, must have turned one's heart to hope.

The place of interment mattered a great deal in commemorating the dead. Official cemeteries were not the only place people were buried. Monuments and sarcophagi lined the streets leading into ancient cities like Rome and were a very conspicuous sight in the ancient world. Sarcophagi, with their iconic decoration, were accessible to viewers of all social classes. Tombs and family shrines marked the households of faith. Sarcophagi in particular occupied and helped define the liminal space where early Christian devotees envisioned their faith among the living dead. Sarcophagi were the permanent site for commemoration of and communication with the dead. The visual narratives found on their carved friezes demonstrate the rich reception of Jesus in the earliest Christian centuries. Early Christians "knew how to read, exhort, and expound upon the symbolic narrative images that they saw at regular intervals on funerary monuments."[34] Jesus was central to those narratives and was depicted in many ways on sarcophagi. For example, his Nativity was sometimes highlighted, while at other times he was imaged as a hero, a philosopher, a wonder-worker or healer, a king, and a law giver (see fig. 11.6).

In addition to material funerary paraphernalia, rites for the dead were serious business. The church was concerned generally over the commemoration of the anonymous dead, but individual families were responsible for more specific salvific acts on behalf of their individual loved ones.[35] There is one exception to this rule, and that is where the economy of death met the gathering of coin into the coffers of heaven. Offerings and almsgiving certainly caught the attention of clergy and could elicit prayers on behalf of the dead. The act of almsgiving connected the words of Jesus to the rich young man (and to early Christian devotees) asked to sell all and give to the poor. Peter Brown, the venerable scholar of the late ancient Christian world, discusses how wealthy believers were encouraged to give and could thereby hope to ascend into the starry heavens, almost by apotheosis.[36] Furthermore, one's experience in the afterlife was intimately mingled with the material ability to be remembered by token, word, and material memorial. It is not by chance that even the most vulnerable were asked to donate on behalf of their dead; Tertullian particularly mentions the need for widows to make offerings on behalf of their husbands.[37] For certain, the joining of heaven and earth by means of money affected the view of the soul. For better, but almost certainly for worse, arguments about material wealth and salvation would remain intertwined within the interior discourses of the Christian church for centuries.

There seems to be a real and authoritative line drawn between those who were privy to the mysteries of the initiated (baptized members) and those who were not. Baptized Christians alone benefited from the prayers of the institutional church,[38] which must have caused some worry for families concerned about the pastoral care and well-being of their deceased loved ones. This dividing line within the church, including numerous and arbitrary rules about who could be baptized and who could not, caused exclusionary othering within the church with no codified method of intercession. No wonder early Christians were keeping vigil in cemeteries at night. With their clusters of candles and lamps, they made offerings and prayed intercessory prayers because they believed they were efficacious, but also, perhaps, they did it out of desperation. The piously Christian could no more lay aside the memorial rituals for their dead than they could abandon hope in salvation for their loved ones or for themselves. It is difficult to know whether early Christians believed that the church as an institution could offer recourse on behalf of their dead or if they alone, in their own faithful acts and in alignment with the grace of Jesus, were responsible for the salvation of kindred souls. The fact that they were acting, even under threat of censure, is evidence that the fate of the soul must have caused some amount of anxiety.

Into Other's Hands: Saints and Martyrs

Along with Christian persecution came admiration toward those Saints who had suffered triumphantly, even unto death. Familial remembrance was adapted into the veneration of martyrs[39] who were likewise powerful agents of intercession within this new family of God. For example, there was a woman called Vibia Perpetua (see fig. 11.7) who lived in the Roman city of Carthage in Northern Africa. A young mother, she was martyred in the arena in AD 203 with her fellow Christians in honor of Geta, the son of Emperor Septimius Severus. *The Passion of Perpetua and Felicity* records her experiences in a type of diary that details her imprisonment leading up to her martyrdom. This record is not a theological treatise but instead documents Perpetua's devotion to Christianity and her unflinching belief that martyrdom would grant her a place in paradise. Perpetua's narrative includes the influence of scripture and classical texts, indicating that she was an educated person.[40]

One of the unique elements of *The Passion of Perpetua and Felicity* is a series of visions that illuminate the spiritual devotion of converts like Perpetua. Her newfound faith in Christ gives her the confidence to even intercede on behalf of her dead brother, Dinocrates. In the course of her imprisonment, she has a vision of Dinocrates. Perpetua states, "And I knew at once that I was worthy and that I ought to intercede on his behalf. And I began to pray for a long time for him and to cry out to God."[41] Perpetua sees her younger brother at seven years old, the year he died of a painful skin eruption on his face. She sees

▲ FIGURE 11.7   ▶ FIGURE 11.8   Mosaic roundels with Saints Perpetua and Felicity, first quarter of the sixth century; Sant'Apollinare Nuovo, Ravenna, Italy. Felicity was an enslaved woman imprisoned with Perpetua and a likewise faithful martyr. Photo: Wilpert, Die römischen Mosaiken und Malereien Bd3 Tafeln Mosaiken, 1916, Taf. 94 and 95 (public domain)

FELICI   TAS

him coming out from a dark place where others were also suffering. He appears hot and thirsty, and the wound in his face that had afflicted him in life still festered. Her heart is turned with compassion by this vision, and she starts to pray for her brother. She sees that there is a pool of water, even waters of life, from which he could drink if the height of the vessel was not so high. She states, "And I woke up, and I realized that my brother was in trouble. But I had faith that I was going to help him. And I was praying on behalf of him all the days until we were transferred into the military prison."[42]

▲ **FIGURE 11.9**   Fresco of Old Saint Peter's Basilica Interior, Rome, Italy (construction was completed in AD 360). This rendering presents a grand cutaway view of the nave and side aisles leading up to the sanctuary where the relics of Peter were held and venerated. Photo: Wikimedia Commons

Perpetua prays day and night for her brother; she groans and cries as she implores God to save him. Her vision of her brother continues as she spends time during her imprisonment in stocks: "I saw that place I had seen before, and Dinocrates was clean, well dressed, and looked refreshed. Where he had been wounded, I saw a scar."[43] To her relief, her brother is then able to drink from the vessel with water in it and then begins to play and rejoice as children do. Perpetua realizes that her brother was freed from pain and had received a kind of salvific deliverance because of her prayers and petitions to God. While Perpetua will continue to have additional visions, even visions of paradisical gardens where martyrs and saints greet her, the vision of her brother underscores her ability to efficaciously work for his good. This vision gives Perpetua an abiding resolve to be faithful and to act on behalf of another, even unto martyrdom.

▲ **FIGURE 11.10** Ivory Pola casket depicting the Constantinian tomb (or the ciborium) of Old Saint Peter's Basilica, ca. AD 440, Archaeological Museum, Venice, Italy. Photo: Scala/Art Resource NY

Early Christian martyrs were the venerated "celebrities" of the Christian world. Saints and martyrs likewise were associated with specific places that became iconic sites of the faith. Hundreds of martyrium churches were built over or near places of martyrdom throughout the Roman Empire. Peter was, of course, the most famous martyr of Rome. Constantine commissioned the building of Old Saint Peter's Basilica (see fig. 11.9) outside the city walls, the traditional and legal place of burial, to commemorate the site of Peter's martyrdom. Peter's relics were housed at the site and drew pilgrim visitors who came to see, touch, or be near them. Many of these pilgrims took away special "blessed" objects called eulogia that helped them remember or connect with the saint and to Christ by association.

The fifth-century ivory Pola casket depicts the acts of such devotees, perhaps even pilgrims, who descended beneath the columned ciborium in Old Saint Peter's Basilica to be near and to touch Peter's tomb (see fig. 11.10). This practice may sound strange to our ears,

▲ **FIGURE 11.11**   Marble sarcophagus of Junius Bassus, AD 359, Rome, Vatican Museum, Vatican City. Photo: Scala/Art Resource NY

but we must remember that Roman society, even Christian society, was based on patron-client relationships, and Christ was the true *Pater Patriae*, able to bestow his particular gifts and benevolence to his followers.

Almost instantly, Christians desired to be buried alongside these martyrs who, according to the language of Revelation, rest under the altar and cry with a loud voice for the Sovereign Lord to accomplish their redemption (see Revelation 6:9–11). Although in early Christian art martyrs are crowned with laurels and given palm fronds of victory, they must still abide in peace, cognizant of their waiting for *all* of God's children to find their way to safe refuge. As N. T. Wright affirmed, this "is why the Orthodox pray *for* the saints as well as *with* them, that they—with us when we join them—may come to the fulfillment of God's complete purposes."[44]

There are instances, usually reserved for clergy and important laypeople, when early Christians could be buried *ad sanctos* or in sanctity close to saints or martyrs. Receiving burial in proximity to holy people and sanctified objects or relics was thought to aid in the salvation of the deceased and was attested from the fourth century onward.[45] For example, a sarcophagus was found in Old Saint Peter's Basilica, the so-called sarcophagus of Junius Bassus, near the very tomb of Peter (see fig. 11.11).

Junius Bassus was a magistrate in Rome whose elaborate stone coffin demonstrates how Old and New Testament narratives were used together in service of both the dead and the living. Viewers could correlate the imperial representations of Christ as a new type of emperor. He is enthroned between Peter and Paul with his feet on the head of the sky god, Caelus, now acting as Christ's footstool in the center of the top register. Jesus also enters Jerusalem in the guise of the emperor *in adventus* in the lower register. Likewise, scenes of deliverance—such as the sacrifice of Isaac, Job rescued from the dung heap, and Daniel in the lion's den—all oriented the viewer toward the typology of Christian salvation.[46] Perhaps Latter-day Saint readers can relate, in some small way, to early Christian veneration of saints and holy sites by thinking of the natural impulse we might have to visit places sacred to our history, such as the Sacred Grove, Carthage Jail, Winter Quarters, Kirtland, Nauvoo, among many others. We, like our Christian forebears, turn our hearts and intuitively seek to connect, physically and spiritually, to places related to past persons who are meaningful to us and to the events that shape our identity.

Vicarious Baptism: If the Dead Rise Not at All

Some early Christians taught that postmortem evangelizing included vicarious baptism. Paul's convictions concerning Christ's Resurrection and the effectual rhetoric that the dead would rise again in a manner like unto Christ are pervasive in his ministry and letters. The bodily salvation of humankind by resurrection is at the very core of Paul's own sufferings and testimony (see 1 Corinthians 15:32; 2 Corinthians 1:8–10). One of the most perplexing arguments of eschatological doctrine attended to within the early church concerned the following question: Just exactly what were the Corinthians doing by baptizing the dead (see 1 Corinthians 15:29)? Surely Paul does not object to their practice, and the passage points to an actual rite for the benefit of a dead person.[47] A close look at early Christian scholarship suggests that the practice was rather limited and may have been particularly reserved for those who had been preparing for baptism but who had died before those rites were completed.

Baptism was not merely a cleansing ritual to heal or return the initiate to a former state of purity (see chapter 6). Baptism was an act and initiation that marked a new life and new social status.[48] To be baptized meant that you were birthed into the household of Christ. In fact, this initiation was so fundamental that the question of baptism for infants who had died came into question. Today in Brignoles, a small town in the Var region of southern France, a fifth-century stone stele bears a Latin inscription revealing religious concerns over infant salvation (see fig. 11.12). The parents of a little boy named Theodosius ask that their child, who had died before baptism, nevertheless be received by God. This stele demonstrates the tensions that were prevalent in the church at this time. Pelagius, a theologian of the fourth century, had defended the idea that children who were unbaptized were innocent of sin because of their fair and young age at death and must not go to hell. This perspective is in contrast to Augustine, who argued that even children carry within them the remnants of original sin and require baptism.[49] This poignant funerary inscription on the stele at Brignoles marks the tenderness and concern that parents applied in supplication for salvific intercession on behalf of their innocent child.

As part of the Christian community, the baptized were privy to the benefaction of God in the same way that children and other clients could call upon the name, property, and benevolence of their patron/

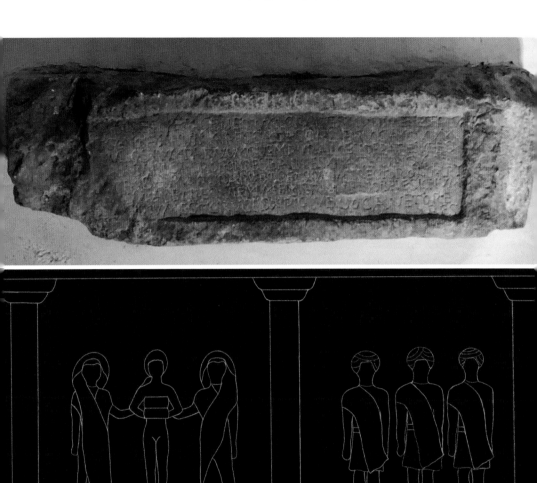

▲ **FIGURE 11.12** Stone stele of Theodosius, La Gayolle, Var Region, France, fifth century, Museum of the Counts of Provence, Brignoles, France. Photo: Catherine Gines Taylor

▲ **FIGURE 11.13** Artist rendering of the Walesby lead tank panel detail describing liturgical baptism with a woman disrobing and flanked by two veiled officiating women. Three men in short tunics are divided from the scene by columns. The Collection Museum, Lincoln, England. Artist's rendering: Holly Graff

father.[50] Paul uses the language of dying and burial when he describes baptism: "Do you not know that all of us who have been baptized into Christ Jesus were baptized into his death? Therefore we have been buried with him by baptism into death, so that, just as Christ was raised from the dead by the glory of the Father, so we too might walk in newness of life" (Romans 6:3–4 NRSV). This funerary symbolism was carried forward into the lives of early Christians. It is described in stark detail on a large lead tank from Roman Britain that features a large Christogram on the side and a scene where a female initiate lays aside her robes to enter into baptism while attended by two veiled women on either side of her (fig. 11.13). The initiate returns to her natal state, stripped bare, to be immersed and laid down into the tomb in order to rise again through water, born into new life.

While vicarious baptism was not considered a universal rite within early Christian practice, we do have patristic evidence that emphasizes it within certain regions and at certain times. For example, Tertullian hints at the practice of vicarious baptism being a ritual carried out for family members by some who also honor their dead during the traditional Roman festivals, such as *Parentalia*.[51] One group that reportedly practiced baptism for the dead was the Marcionites. Because of their dualistic beliefs and practices, these followers of Marcion, such as John Chrysostom, a theologian of the fourth century, were deemed heretical by Tertullian and others some two centuries later. Chrysostom describes the Marcionite practice being performed for uninitiated believers or catechumens who died before receiving baptism. A living Marcionite could act as proxy by laying underneath the deceased, answering the baptismal questions, and then receiving the rite by water.[52] This act was completed for those who *already* had faith and were simply not yet baptized. The contingency here was that the benefits of baptism were still reserved for those who had accepted the gospel of Jesus while they were alive.

Clearly, the earliest Christians were wrestling with Paul's writings that placed baptism at the center of salvific initiation, that acknowledged that many of God's children were absent these required rites. These Christians desired to find a universally merciful God who offered salvation to the people they loved.[53] The locus of authoritative gatekeeping via baptism was at the heart of the early church, and Christian authors and theologians continued to articulate their positions on who could and could not be allowed into God's presence through cleansing and initiation by baptism. Volumes of scholarship[54] take up the topic of vicarious baptism in greater detail than this brief discussion. As further insight, I offer a brief sampling of regional discussions in the early church (see fig. 11.14).

Far and away, the most prolific writings on vicarious baptism come from Egypt or Greek- or Egyptian-influenced theologians. Is it surprising that a culture steeped in imagery, architecture, and texts that profoundly consider the afterlife would produce thinkers for whom that same concern was at the fore? One has to wonder whether Paul's own comments on baptism were influenced by the teachings of Apollos, who "knew only the baptism of John" and was likely influenced by John the Baptist (Acts 18:25 NRSV). Apollos was from Alexandria, Egypt, and spent time teaching in Corinth. Paul's words to the Corinthians indicate that, at least in this location, Christians baptized vicariously in order to aid the deceased in the world of the dead (see 1 Corinthians 15:29). Yet, for all of this, Paul takes a relatively light hand in discussing baptism and its efficacy for the deceased. To some communities, he accepts the practice, while it is never mentioned to others.[55] Although these initiate communities may be intentionally few, perhaps, like the numbered family of Noah saved in the ark, they were still concerned about a world that God could swallow up in water.

Conclusion

Just outside of Bordeaux, France, a fourth-century epitaph was set to honor a girl called Galla who lived ten years and thirty days.[56] The title of martyr was placed at her grave along with the imperative *via in pace* (go in peace). Two doves and a Christogram with miniscule alpha and omega identify the young Galla as Christian. The impulse to eulogize and commemorate the death of a loved one was expressed in text and image as a consolation and comfort for ancient Saints as well as for

Rome, Italy

The early second-century text, Shepherd of Hermas, *Similitudes* 9:16, 5–7, reads: "These are the apostles and teachers who proclaimed the name of the Son of God, who, having fallen asleep in power and faith of the Son of God, even proclaimed to those who had previously fallen asleep and gave them the seal of the proclamation. They descended with them into the water and came up again, except that these descended alive and came up alive. Because of them, these others were enlivened and came to know the name of the Son of God. . . . They [those being baptized] fell asleep in justice and great purity, except they did not have this seal."

Interpretation of this section of Shepherd by Carolyn Osiek: "These verses, without saying so, present a good argument in favor of baptism in the name of the dead, apparently already an act of piety in first century Corinth . . . here with the pre-Christian dead, the problem is . . . they practiced virtue in their lives, but had not received baptism. Through the apostles and teachers, this problem is solved."[57]

ITALY

Rome, Italy

Ambrosiaster (late fourth century) speculates about the early practice of baptism for the dead: "Some people were at that time [when Paul wrote 1 Corinthians] being baptized for the dead because they were afraid that someone who was not baptized would either not rise at all or else rise merely in order to be condemned."[58]

ROME

AFRICA

MEDITERRAN

Carthage, North Africa

Tertullian (early-third century) wrote: "Now it is certain that they adopted this (practice) with such a presumption as made them suppose that the vicarious baptism (in question) would be beneficial to the flesh of another in anticipation of the resurrection."[59]

Later, in *Against Marcion*, Tertullian recants his previous statement when speaking in direct opposition to Marcion, who supported and practiced vicarious baptism. Marcion and his followers had communities all throughout the ancient Mediterranean, thus baptizing for the dead may have spread as evidenced in later Christian authors such as Epiphanius of Salamis and John Chrysostom in Constantinople who eventually calls the practice heretical.[60]

◄ **FIGURE 11.14**   Map of the Mediterranean region where early texts describing vicarious baptism for the dead originated or were found. Map graphic created by Ashley Pun Eveson

Alexandria, Egypt

From Didymus the Blind (mid-fourth century): "The Marcionites baptized the living on behalf of dead unbelievers, not knowing that baptism saves only the person who receives it."[61]

In his discussion of "proxy baptism by angels," Clement of Alexandria (second century) quotes Theodotus, saying: "And, they say, those who are baptized for the dead, these are the Angels who are baptized for us, so that, as we also possess the NAME, we are not bound by the Limit and the Cross, and prevented from entering Pleroma."[62]

WEST GOTHS

BLACK SEA

CIA

THRACE

ARMENIA

• CONSTANTINOPLE

PONTUS

EDONIA

ASIA

Akhmim, Egypt

In the apocryphal *Apocalypse of Peter*, God says: "I will g<ive> to my called and my elect whomever they request of me from out of punishment. And I will give them a beautiful baptism in salvation from the Acherousian Lake which is said to be in the Elysian Field, a share in righteousness with my saints."[63]

CYPRUS

CRETE

SEA

• JERUSALEM

EGYPT

Nag Hammadi, Egypt

RED
SEA

An apocryphal text called the *Apocryphon of John* has Jesus say: "I [Christ] raised and sealed the person [one of the repentant dead in hell] in luminous water with Five Seals that death might not prevail over the person from that moment on."[64]

Latter-day Saints. For example, even with its poetic simplicity, Eliza R. Snow sought to memorialize a fellow Relief Society sister in poetry:

> She has paid the last debt due to nature;
> She to earth has the casket resigned,
> That the morn of the first resurrection
> May restore it from dross all refined.[65]

The reality of the grave was readily acknowledged in late ancient Christianity right alongside faithful certainty in the coming fruits of the Resurrection. Concern for the dead receiving rest and a place of sanctity occupied the minds of our earliest Christian kin. The good news for early Christians was that the dead *could* receive a portion of efficacious work on their behalf. An early Christian source called the *Apocalypse of Peter* indicates that Saints in heaven could pray for those experiencing separation from Christ. In this work, Christ himself says that he will "give heed to the called and chosen on behalf of those in torment. And will give them a fair baptism to Salvation even a portion of righteousness with my holy ones."[66] It is necessary, generous, and sympathetic to read texts like this alongside our canonical scripture in order to view late ancient Christianity in a more complete context.

For ancient Christians, to be absent from the presence and image of Jesus was to be in darkness, to be subject to the abyss. Jesus's teachings in the New Testament focus on the Day of Judgment as an imminent state of desolation for the punishment of the wicked.[67] The righteous, on the other hand, could expect a new and eternal life in the kingdom of God. This was life in Jesus and with Jesus.[68] If the destination of one's soul was outside of paradise, it was considered bereft, in a realm of figurative darkness equated with foolishness, with ignorance. Life with God, on the other hand, was found along a narrow path, a difficult path where seeking knowledge and revelatory understanding bore fruit and led to an enlightened state, a state of wisdom. In fact, it was apocalyptically realized as fellowship with God in a place of peace, healing, comfort, and bounty (see Revelation 2:7; 22:1–5).

The vulnerable moment of death provided early Christians with grand vistas and metaphorical landscapes for the imagination. These landscapes helped them explore the realms of death, this most foreign of countries, and to reconcile hope in an afterlife they longed to understand. By inclining their hearts in work for the dead, these early Saints acted in their love for God, love for their ancestors, and love for those who would follow their example of faith. And, like the love of God, their good works through the grace of Jesus Christ could not be vanquished or overcome by time, suffering, darkness, or ignorance. For a few communities, the practice of vicarious baptism was in place, while for many others, the acts of prayer, almsgiving, good works, and supplicating the grace of Jesus were enough to offer reassurances to the living.

If we incline *our* hearts and turn *our* mind's eye toward the evidence of material culture and artistic images produced by our ancient Christian mothers and fathers, we find that across the generations, these believers celebrated and found salvific communion with their loved ones. Against all odds and censure, ancient Christians trusted that their mourning and lament, their hopeful joy, their vigilant care, and their artistic memorials could fulfill needs of physical shelter for the dead as well as providing spiritual refuge; these Christians used all available resources to call upon divine succor for themselves, their families, and their neighbors. Ultimately, early Christians depended on God made flesh, Jesus, who plumbed the depths of death and hell in order to ascend to the highest realms of glory and who did so in a resurrected body. Early Christian work for the dead depended on one alone, Jesus, who "emptied himself, taking the form of a slave, being born in human likeness. And being found in human form, he humbled himself and became obedient to the point of death—even death on a cross" (Philippians 2:7–8 NRSV). After all, it required that kind of wonderworker, that kind of realm wanderer, that kind of divine loving-kindness, to take up the mortal frame, made perfect, and save us all.

Notes

1. See Ellen Muehlberger, *Moment of Reckoning: Imagined Death and Its Consequences in Late Ancient Christianity* (Oxford: Oxford University Press, 2019), 3, esp. chapter 4: "What Remains? Situating the Postmortal." See also Peter Brown, *The Ransom of the Soul: Afterlife and Wealth in Western Christianity* (Cambridge, MA: Harvard University Press, 2015).

2. See Muehlberger, *Moment of Reckoning*, 5, esp. chapter 3: "Training for Death: Rhetorical Formation and the Cast of the Early Christian Imagination."

3. See Felicity Harley McGowan, "Death Is Swallowed Up in Victory: Scenes of Death in Early Christian Art and the Emergence of Crucifixion Iconography," in *Cultural Studies Review* 17, no. 1 (March 2011): 106.

4. Harley McGowan, "Death is Swallowed," 106n18, cites this text as found in Fernand Cabrol and Henri Leclercq, *Dictionnaire d'archéologie chrétienne et de liturgie*, vol. 14, no. 1 (Paris: Letouzey et Ané, 1907–53), columns 435–36.

5. Augustine, *The City of God* 20.6; trans. Marcus Dods (*Nicene and Post-Nicene Fathers* 1/2:425). See also John 5:25.

6. Augustine, *The City of God* 20.10; trans. Marcus Dods (*Nicene and Post-Nicene Fathers* 1/2:431). Augustine references both Romans 6:4 and Ephesians 5:14 in his rebuttal to those who think the Resurrection only pertains to bodies and not to souls.

7. See Éric Rebillard, "The Church, the Living, and the Dead," in *A Companion to Late Antiquity*, ed. Philip Rousseau (Oxford: Wiley-Blackwell, 2009), 223.

8. See Ramsay MacMullen, *Christianity and Paganism in the Fourth to Eighth Centuries* (New Haven: Yale University Press, 1997), 111.

9. Peter Brown, *The Cult of the Saints* (Chicago: University of Chicago Press, 1981), 1–22. See also Lionel Rothkrug, "The 'Odour of Sanctity,' and the Hebrew Origins of Christian Relic Veneration," in *Historical Reflections/ Réflexions Historiques* 8, no. 2 (Summer 1981): 95–142.

10. See Timothy E. Gregory, "Helena," in *The Oxford Dictionary of Byzantium* (Oxford: Oxford University Press, 1991), 909.

11. See Gregory, "Helena," 909.

12. See "The Council of Elvira, ca. 306," Catholic University of America, https://web.archive.org/web/20120716202800/http://faculty.cua.edu/pennington/Canon%20Law/ElviraCanons.htm.

13. See "The Council of Elvira, ca. 306."

14. "The Council of Elvira, ca. 306," canons 34, 35.

15. See Samuel Laeuchli, *Power and Sexuality: The Emergence of Canon Law at the Synod of Elvira* (Philadelphia: Temple University Press, 1972), 25, 40.

16. Rites for the dead are rarely recorded in association with churches, and there is a canon from the Council of Hippo in AD 393 that forbids celebrating the Eucharist in the presence of a corpse.

17. See Kathleen Corley, *Maranatha: Women's Funerary Rituals and Christian Origins* (Minneapolis, MN: Fortress Press, 2010), 43, 32–38, 57, 124–28.

18. See Susannah Morrill, "Relief Society Birth and Death Rituals: Women at the Gates of Mortality," in *Journal of Mormon History* vol. 36, no. 2 (Spring, 2010): 157.

19. See Rebillard, "The Church," 226.

20. See Ramsay MacMullen, *The Second Church* (Atlanta: Society of Biblical Literature, 2009), 25.

21. See Katharina Meineke, "Funerary Cult at Sarcophagi, Rome and Vicinity," in *Iconographie Funéraire Romaine et Société*, ed. Martin Galinier and François Baratte (Perpignan: Presses Universitaires de Perpignan, 2013), 37.

22. Lucian, *Mourning* 9, as cited in MacMullen, *Second Church*, 24n69.

23. See Rebillard, "The Church," 227.

24. See "Synod of Laodicea (4th Century)," canon 28, New Advent, https://www.newadvent.org/fathers/3806.htm

25. Local leaders do not seem to discourage veneration of the dead, including customary eating and drinking on certain feast days, because they do not want to discourage any potential catechumens. The persistence of Christian veneration looks very much like pagan veneration and is testament to the fact that both lay people and clerics deemed watchful care over the dead to be an essential act, so critical in fact that local clergy do not often comment on it except to discourage things like drunkenness near tombs. For several examples of such veneration, see Rebillard, "The Church," 226.

26. Augustine, *Epistle* 22.1.6, as cited in Rebillard, "The Church," 227.

27. *Acts of Paul and Thecla* 28–29, in *The Apocryphal New Testament: A Collection of Apocryphal Christian Literature in an English Translation*, trans. J. K. Elliott (Oxford: Oxford University Press, 1993), 369–70. In this chapter,

English translations of *Acts of Paul and Thecla* are taken from this edition translated by Elliot.

28. *Acts of Paul and Thecla* 38–39.

29. See Stephen J. Davis, *The Cult of Saint Thecla: A Tradition of Women's Piety in Late Antiquity* (Oxford. Oxford University Press, 2001), 11–18.

30. John Chrysostom, *Homilies on the Acts of the Apostles* 26.4, in *Patrologiae cursus completus*, Series graeca, ed. Jacques-Paul Migne (Paris, 1857–86), 60:202. In this chapter, the series will be abbreviated to PG and cited by volume and column number.

31. John Chrysostom, *Homilies on the Acts of the Apostles* 26.3 (PG 60:203).

32. Catherine C. Taylor, "Sarcophagi," in *The Reception of Jesus in the First Three Centuries*, vol. 3, *From Celsus to the Catacombs: Visual, Liturgical, and Non-Christian Receptions of Jesus in the Second and Third Centuries CE*, ed. Chris Keith (London: T&T Clark, 2019), 329.

33. See Taylor, "Sarcophagi," 335.

34. Taylor, "Sarcophagi," 335.

35. While intercessory prayer was communally given for the dead, it was not focused on individuals. Augustine will address this anonymous care of the dead under the guise of "the one faithful mother," who is the Church; see Augustine, *The Care to Be Taken for the Dead* 4.6, as cited in Rebillard, "The Church," 228. I suggest that in claiming this communally correlated role, the Church is subverting the role of women as active and visible agents in the landscape of death. Women enacted the public rituals necessary for the soul to pass not only into the spirit world but also to help the soul to ascend. This act was a genuine usurpation meant to assimilate lay devotion under the auspices of general and ecclesiastical authority.

36. See Brown, *Ransom of the Soul*, 45.

37. See Tertullian, *On Exhortation to Chastity* 22.2; Tertullian, *On Monogamy* 10.4; as cited in Rebillard, "The Church," 229.

38. See Rebillard, "The Church," 228–30.

39. See MacMullen, *Second Church*, 105.

40. See Barbara K. Gold, *Perpetua: Athlete of God* (Oxford: Oxford University Press, 2018), 115–19.

41. *Passio Perpetuae et Felicitatis* (*The Passion of Saints Perpetua and Felicity*) 7.2, in *Perpetua's Journey: Faith, Gender and Power in the Roman Empire*, trans. Jennifer A. Rea (Oxford: Oxford University Press, 2018), 175. In this chapter, English translations of *The Passion of Saints Perpetua and Felicity* are taken from this edition translated by Rea.

42. *The Passion of Saints Perpetua and Felicity* 7.9.

43. *The Passion of Saints Perpetua and Felicity* 8.1.

44. N. T. Wright, *For All the Saints? Remembering the Christian Departed* (London: SPCK; Harrisburg, PA: Morehouse, 2003), 24.

45. Jean Lassus, *Sanctuaires Chrétiens de Syrie* (Paris : P. Geuthner, 1947), 230f.

46. For an in-depth look at this sarcophagus, see Elizabeth Mabon, *The Iconography of the Sarcophagus of Junius Bassus* (Princeton, NJ: Princeton University Press, 1990), 3–38.

47. See Jeffrey A. Trumbower, *Rescue for the Dead: The Posthumous Salvation of Non-Christians in Early Christianity* (Oxford: Oxford University Press, 2001), 35.

48. Throughout the New Testament baptism and salvific acts are basic tenets of scripture, and baptism is a decisive act for Christian initiates. Rebirth means a new mortal existence, one that involves and is sustained in God. There are a few examples of famous individuals who waited until late in life or their deathbeds to be baptized. The delay of baptism by emperors like Constantine or theologians like Augustine was not the standard practice for ordinary Christians. However, some Christians timed their baptisms and waited until Lent to be baptized. See Rebillard, "The Church," 222. It is striking to correlate days of fasting in preparation for Holy Week, the death of Jesus, and the harrowing of hell with the act of laying down the body in baptism in the similitude of dying and then emerging from those waters being resurrected.

49. See Augustine, *The Grace of Christ, and On Original Sin* 2.19; trans. Peter Holmes (*Nicene and Post-Nicene Fathers* 1/5:243). Augustine objects to Pelagius's rejection of infant baptism: "For they neither deny the sacrament of baptism to infants, nor do they promise the kingdom of heaven to any irrespective of the redemption of Christ. . . . The real objection against them is, that they refuse to confess that unbaptized infants are liable to the condemnation of the first man, and that original sin has been transmitted to them and requires to be purged by regeneration (baptism)."

50. See Richard E. DeMaris, "Water Ritual," in *The Oxford Handbook of Early Christian Ritual*, ed. Risto Uro, Juliette J. Day, Richard E. DeMaris, and Rikard Roitto (Oxford: Oxford University Press, 2019), 399.

51. See Trumbower, *Rescue for the Dead*, 38.

52. See Trumbower, *Rescue for the Dead*, 36. See also John Chrysostom, *Homilies on First Corinthians* 40:1.

53. See Trumbower, *Rescue for the Dead*, 94.

54. For example, see Trumbower, *Rescue for the Dead*; David L. Paulsen and Brock M. Mason, "Baptism for the Dead in Early Christianity," in *Journal of Book of Mormon Studies* 19, no. 2 (2010): 22–49; Hugh W. Nibley, *Mormonism and Early Christianity* (Salt Lake City, UT: Deseret Book; Provo, UT:

FARMS, 1987), esp. chapter 4: "Baptism for the Dead in Ancient Times."

55. See 1 Corinthians 1:12–17 NRSV: "What I mean is that each of you says, 'I belong to Paul,' or 'I belong to Apollos,' or 'I belong to Cephas,' or 'I belong to Christ.' Has Christ been divided? Was Paul crucified for you? Or were you baptized in the name of Paul? I thank God that I baptized none of you except Crispus and Gaius, so that no one can say that you were baptized in my name. (I did baptize also the household of Stephanas; beyond that, I do not know whether I baptized anyone else.) For Christ did not send me to baptize but to proclaim the gospel, and not with eloquent wisdom, so that the cross of Christ might not be emptied of its power."

56. Edmond Le Blant, *Manuel d'Épigraphie Chrétienne d'après les Marbres de la Gaule* (Paris: Didier et Co., 1869), 55.

57. Text and interpretation from Carolyn Osiek, *Shepherd of Hermas: A Commentary* (Minneapolis, MN: Fortress, 1999), 232–33.

58. Ambrosiaster, *Commentary on Paul's Epistles,* in *Corpus Scriptorum Ecclesiasticorum Latinorum* 81:175; translation as found in Gerald L. Bray, ed., *1–2 Corinthians,* 2nd ed., vol. 7 in the Ancient Christian Commentary on Scripture: New Testament series (Downers Grove, IL: InterVarsity Press, 2006), 166.

59. Tertullian, *On the Resurrection of the Flesh* 48, in *Ante-Nicene Fathers* 3:581.

60. See David L. Paulsen and Brock M. Mason, "Baptism for the Dead in Early Christianity," in *Journal of Book of Mormon Studies* 19, no. 2 (2010): 32, 40.

61. Didymus the Blind, *Pauline Commentary from the Greek Church*; translation from Bray, *1–2 Corinthians,* 166.

62. Clement of Alexandria, *Excerpta ex Theodoto* 22.4 in François Sagnard, ed., *Clément D'Alexandrie: Extraits de Théodote* (Paris: Les Editions du Cerf, 1970), 103; as cited in Paulsen and Mason, "Baptism for the Dead in Early Christianity," 41.

63. Apocalypse of Peter 14; translation from the Greek Rainer Fragment in *Your Eyes Will Be Opened: A Study of the Greek (Eithiopic) Apocalypse of Peter,* trans. Dennis D. Buchholz (Atlanta: Scholars, 1988), 344–45.

64. Apocryphon of John 31.25, in the *Nag Hammadi Scriptures,* ed. Marvin Meyer (New York: Harper Collins, 2007), 131.

65. E. R. S. [Eliza R. Snow], "Sacred to the Memory of Our Beloved Sister, Mrs. Matilda Casper," *Women's Exponent* 1 (June 15, 1872): 3; as cited in Kylie Nielson Turley, "Rhetoric and Ritual: A Decade of 'Women's Exponent' Death Poetry," *Journal of Mormon History* 32, no. 3 (Fall 2006): 58.

66. *Apocalypse of Peter* 14.1.
67. See Bart Ehrman, *Heaven and Hell: A History of the Afterlife* (New York: Simon & Schuster, 2020), 154.
68. Paul's teaching on the coming Judgment is connected in some ways with the deeds of individuals. In Romans 2:6–10 glory, honor, and peace are promised to those who do good. But doing good is not enough for Paul as he articulates the frailties of the mortal condition; no one is able to be good enough. The good news for Paul is that, even though the Judgment will come, Jesus offers the gift of grace. Christ is put forth as the atoning sacrifice in flesh and blood so that believers could look forward to the coming day of judgment (see Romans 3:21–26).

✳ 12 ✳

LIVING IN THE AFTERLIFE
Heaven, Hell, and Places Between

D. Jill Kirby

And I heard a voice from heaven saying unto me,
Write, Blessed are the dead which die in the Lord
from henceforth…

— Revelation 14:13

All early Christian sources indicate expectation of a postmortem existence. Christians who came out of a Jewish matrix expected that those who were faithful could anticipate a reward, while those who chose a different path were thought to face punishment. However, the life, death, and Resurrection of Christ meant that much had to be reconsidered. Moreover, many important questions could not be resolved by a direct appeal to scripture. Who were those to whom Christ preached in the realm of the dead, wherever that was, and what did he accomplish (see 1 Peter 3:18–20)? If there were sins that could *not* be forgiven in the next life (see Matthew 12:32), what sort of expiation could be made once one had died, and how was this to be done? What was the nature of eternal punishment (see Matthew 8:12), and how could this be reconciled with the awesome power of the love of God (see Romans 8:38–39)? The martyrs certainly went straight to heaven (see Revelation 6:9), but what about the righteous who were not killed for their testimony (see Luke 16:22)?

The surviving documentary evidence of the earliest Christians makes it clear that they did *not* invent their responses to these and similar questions. They studied scripture, they pondered vigorously in private and in community, and they prayed. Their answers are based on thoughtful principles of biblical interpretation (hermeneutics) and grounded in some of the best logic ever committed to writing. As you read what follows, I encourage you to think of yourself as looking not *at* them but *with* them at the great principles of Christian hope in the gospel message. To be aware of the doctrinal differences is to be a close reader; to feel the common testimony is to be a citizen of the city of God, for death has indeed been "swallowed up in victory" (1 Corinthians 15:54; see box 12.1).

BOX 12.1   Why It Matters

Learning how various early Christian authors and communities understood what happened after death has at least three important outcomes:

1. We see thoughtful faith in their struggle to understand the implications of the life, death, and Resurrection of Jesus for their own salvation.
2. We learn that many questions for which we might like definitive answers have never been resolved and are thus reminded that we "wait upon the Lord" in all things (Isaiah 40:31).
3. We appreciate the ways in which they expressed themselves about these matters in order to create communities, build faith, and teach the gospel.

Who Were the Early Christians Whose Textual Artifacts Provide Evidence for Our Topic?

Before approaching our sources, it is necessary to specify something of the historical and cultural context of these early Christians. First, the intellectual and theological diversity of the material in our sources will make it very clear that early Christians were most definitely not a large undifferentiated group. Second, much of the material that we have is the work of, in one form or another, educated urban elites, a very small subset of the Christian population. What we know of those who were not similarly privileged usually depends on deconstructing what is said about them in the course of corrective teaching or condemnation.[1] Third, only rarely do we have evidence that speaks to the beliefs of large groups of Christians, much less anything like the entire Christian community. In this regard, Augustine's reach is unusual; it developed from the contacts he made during his time in Milan, Italy (where the imperial court was then located), as well as his prowess as a philosopher, which made him a logical interlocutor for the Roman elite. Although Augustine's prominence in the West often rendered his theological insights normative for his contemporaries and foundational for medieval European Christianity, and thus more familiar to American readers, we will see that the Greek- and Syriac-speaking Christian communities were not similarly deferential. Fourth, religion was only one of many identities available to those who lived in late antiquity, and often it was not the most important. Thus, it is not clear that baptized individuals thought of themselves as Christians except in circumstances that called for that identity.[2] Since birth, name giving, marriage, death, funeral, and burial customs were neither linked to Christian rites nor required the participation of the clergy in some areas during the first through fourth centuries, beliefs about life after death may have intersected with Christian identity very unevenly.[3] We avoid reading our insights onto all early Christian communities by noting the date and place in which they were composed or widely circulated.

That said, I have not chosen the sources for this chapter in a systematic fashion, nor do they create a comprehensive picture. Instead, I have selected sources that are foundational in some fashion, that might be of interest to Latter-day Saints, or that will expose Latter-day Saints to ideas with which they may not be familiar. Augustine is a bright thread that runs through most of the chapter because of his extraordinary influence, while the *Gospel of Nicodemus* was chosen both because of its significance for medieval Christianity and its dramatic presentation. Hell is described using two apocalypses, since that genre has a singular power to arouse feeling among both ancient and modern readers, while heaven is presented through the mystical poetry of Syriac Christianity, because the beauty thereby evoked creates a sense of longing.

The Descent of Christ to the Underworld: "Every Place Has Need of Christ"

When thinking about how the life, death, and Resurrection of Christ changed thinking about the afterlife, one might start with reflection on 1 Peter 3:18–20, in which Christ, after his death, is said to have

▲ **FIGURE 12.1**   Via Latina Catacomb fresco with Herakles bringing Alcestis back to life with dog Cerberus, fourth century. Herakles returns Alcestis, the compassionate wife of Admetus, who gave her life early in order to extend the life of her husband. Moved by this pious action, Herakles provides a type of resurrection from the underworld in a literary scene inspired by Euripedes. Photo: Scala/Art Resource NY

"preached unto the spirits in prison which sometime were disobedient, when once the longsuffering of God waited in the days of Noah," as well as 1 Peter 4:6, which asserts that "the gospel [was] preached also to them that are dead, that they might be judged according to men in the flesh, but live according to God in the spirit."[4] Such journeys into the underworld to interact with those found there are not limited to the world of early Christianity. For example, in Greek

mythology, Hermes visited Hades to plead for the return of Perse-
phone; Orpheus sought his wife, Eurydice, among the dead; and
Hercules returned from the nether world with a three-headed dog
named Cerberus. However, the descent narrative in Christian texts is
a bit different. For example, Christ's descent to the realm of the dead
was the last step in his *kenosis*—that is, the "self-emptying" spoken
of in Philippians 2:6–7 (New Revised Standard Version): "[Christ],
though he was in the form of God, did not regard equality with God
as something to be exploited, but emptied himself, taking the form of
a slave, being born in human likeness." From this, readers could affirm
Christ's humanity because the immediate circumstances of his death
were like that of any human.[5]

Beyond this, the descent narratives conveyed two basic messages, also distinct from those of the Greco-Roman descents: (1) Christ
descended to preach salvation to the dead, and (2) Christ descended
to defeat death and hell as the culmination of his redemptive activities (see 1 Corinthians 15:24–26). Presentations of the descent of
Christ are ubiquitous from the composition of 1 Peter to the end of
the fourth century, being attested in many different early Christian
communities and found in literary, liturgical, and visual formats.[6] In
illustrating this aspect of life in the afterlife, I focus only on the matter
of audiences—that is, the identification of those who heard Christ—
as a way of illustrating how the Church Fathers used both scripture
and logic (faith and reason) in their theological and pastoral endeavors (see box 12.2). In general, earlier writers were less specific about
these matters than those who came after them and had occasion to
reflect more deeply on the topics of human agency while mortal, the
freedom of the soul, and God's mercy and justice.[7]

Around the time that the last book of the New Testament was
completed, Ignatius of Antioch (died circa AD 110) used 1 Peter 4:6
as a proof text against Judaizers. Writing to the Magnesians to argue
against a Jewish Sabbath and in favor of the Lord's Day, Ignatius noted
that "by the workings of the Spirit even the Prophets were disciples
[of Christ] . . . and so he, for whom they rightly waited, came and
raised them from the dead."[8] Although terse, this statement suggests

> ### BOX 12.2 Selected Fathers on the Descent of Christ to the Realm of the Dead
>
> **Ignatius of Antioch** (died circa AD 110): Bishop of Syrian Antioch; wrote the *Letter to the Magnesians* while in confinement on his way to Rome to die in the arena.
>
> **Clement of Alexandria** (died AD 215): leader of the Christian catechetical school in Alexandria, Egypt. His work, *Stromateis* ("Miscellanies"), is a large and deliberately unorganized compendium of Christian knowledge.
>
> **Augustine of Hippo** (AD 354–430): Bishop of Hippo in North Africa and greatest of the Latin Fathers. He wrote *Eighty-three Different Questions* in AD 388, *Epistle 164* in AD 414, and *City of God* from AD 413–426, while *De Haeresibus* (*On Heresies*) was unfinished when he died.

that Ignatius believed that the idea that Christ visited and raised the prophets of ancient Israel was common knowledge among his readers.

About one hundred years later, Clement of Alexandria (died AD 215) produced a more consciously reasoned and systematic treatment of the topic. Clement's first principle was that it is Christ's work to save, and that it was his will to draw to himself *all who were willing* "by the preaching [of the gospel], to believe on Him, *wherever they were*."[9] For Clement, this included preaching to the dead, although he is unsure whether Christ personally preached to both Gentiles and ancient Israelites or only the latter. Reasoning on the matter, Clement indicated that if Christ preached only to those of Israel, then someone else must have preached to the Gentiles, and "it is plain that, since God is no respecter of persons, the apostles also, as here, so there, preached the Gospel to those of the heathen who were ready for conversion."[10] To support this arrangement, Clement cites an earlier Christian work,

▲ **FIGURE 12.2** Anastasis from the Chora Church, CP. This Byzantine-era fresco depicts Christ harrowing hell, standing on the newly ruptured gates of death amidst broken locks and atop the bound figure of Satan. The focus of the fresco is on the exultant raising of Adam and Eve from their graves. Christ appears in his resurrected state, wearing white and gold and being surrounded by a mandorla or almond-shaped body halo while John the Baptist, David, Solomon, and other righteous kings await their own resurrections. Photo: Courtesy of Till Niermann via Wikimedia Commons (public domain)

the *Shepherd of Hermas* (see box 12.3).[11] In his visions, Hermas sees a tower taking shape, which represents the Church, built with stones that portray the members. As he watches the tower's construction, he sees two groups of stones come up together through water and be fitted into the tower. When he asks about these stones, his supernatural

The *Shepherd of Hermas*

The *Shepherd of Hermas* is an early second-century Christian apocalypse, the author of which is unknown, but is sometimes identified with the Hermas of Romans 16:14. The "shepherd" in the title is the angelic guide who speaks to Hermas.

The book consists of five visions granted to Hermas, along with twelve commandments and ten similitudes.

The Ninth Similitude, quoted in this chapter, elaborates on the Third Vision, which involves the building up of the Church. It was very popular and considered authoritative by many until the 4th century.

guide tells him that the first set of stones were those who died without baptism, and so they must rise through water "to be made alive. In no other way could they enter the reign of God."[12] The second set of stones, which numbered forty, also came up from the depths and were identified as "the apostles and teachers who proclaimed the name of the Son of God, who having fallen asleep in power and faith of the Son of God, even proclaimed to those who had previously fallen asleep and gave them the seal of the proclamation [baptism]."[13]

Finally, Clement eventually follows Hermas in limiting the audience to whom the gospel message was preached to those who "fell asleep in justice and great purity."[14] According to Clement, the gospel was preached to those of ancient Israel who had kept the law, to the prophets, and to those Gentiles who had lived by philosophy, which Clement believed had prepared them for faith.[15] The idea that *all* the dead heard the gospel is, according to Clement, foolish, since "who in his senses can suppose the souls of the righteous and those of sinners in the same condemnation, charging Providence with injustice?"[16]

A little more than one hundred years later, by the middle of the fourth century, a clear shift in focus, away from Christ as preacher,

BOX 12.4   The *Gospel of Nicodemus*

The *Gospel of Nicodemus* is a pseudepigraphal work—that is, it is credited to a famous Christian figure rather than its author. It is probably dated to the late fourth or early fifth century. It consists of two main works, the *Acts of Pilate* and the *Descent of Christ*. The latter is the basis for most medieval versions of the harrowing of hell.

The *Descent of Christ* is a dramatization of Christ's visit to the realm of the dead, and it is narrated by Charinus and Lenthius, two sons of Simeon (see Luke 2:25). The appearance of Christ in the underworld is announced by Simeon, then by John the Baptist. After Christ breaks down the gates and walls of Hades, he leads out the dead, starting with Adam, and remands them to the archangel Michael, who takes them to paradise.

was in progress. In the first catechetical creed to mention the descent (AD 359), there is no mention of a gospel proclamation. Instead, Christ was "crucified and died, and descended to hell and regulated things there, Whom the gatekeepers of hell saw and shuddered."[17] This subjugation of death and hell had significant implications, which led to a new question: would anyone remain in hell once God's plans were fully implemented?[18]

Around this same time or perhaps slightly later, the pseudepigraphal *Gospel of Nicodemus* responded to this question with a resounding "no" (see box 12.4). In a dramatic oral confrontation between Satan and Hades, the Greek god of the underworld complains that Satan's scheming to cause the death of Jesus is unwise:

> Not long ago I devoured a certain dead man named Lazarus, and soon afterwards someone from the living forcefully dragged him from my intestines through

▲ **FIGURE 12.3** Raising of Lazarus (Vatican Gold Glass, ca. fourth century). Gold glass medallions (gold leaf design sandwiched between glass) were often placed within funerary contexts like catacombs as markers for Christians whose hope in salvific resurrection was often reflected in the narrative image. Here Lazarus has come forth from the sepulcher still tightly wrapped in burial clothes as Christ extends a rod toward the top of his head. Photo: Wikimedia Commons

a word alone. I suppose this was the one about whom you are speaking. If then we receive that one here, I am afraid that we might somehow be in danger with all the others. . . . It does not seem to me to be a good sign that Lazarus was previously snatched from me. For he flew out from me not like a corpse but like an eagle, so quickly did the earth cast him forth. For this reason, I adjure you, for both your benefit and mine, do not bring him here. For I think he is coming here to raise all the dead. And this I tell you, by the darkness we enjoy, if you lead him here, none of the dead will be left to me.[19]

At the appearance of Christ, the iron bars were smashed, the bronze gate crushed, and Satan was bound and handed over to Hades for torture.[20] With the ramparts of hell in disarray, at least some of the dead could no longer be detained and were thus delivered.

For the Latin West, Augustine (died AD 430) had something of the last word in these matters, and he set strict limits on who could be freed from hell. His basic dictum with respect to postmortem faith was that it was not a conversion. Those who had achieved wisdom before the coming of Christ "had been illuminated by the same truth in accord with the opportunity of their own respective periods of life."[21] Thus, those who heard Christ after death had no need of salvation after death because they had established a proper orientation toward God before their death.[22]

So, then, to whom did Christ preach? Augustine is quite tentative. In writing to fellow bishop Evodius (*Epistle 164*), Augustine admits that the descent in 1 Peter 3:18–20 disturbs him because it relates to those who lived both before and after Christ. For example, Augustine does not understand why, since many died between Adam and Christ, only those associated with the Flood are mentioned. In the end, Augustine is willing to affirm a very limited agenda: Christ was indeed "in hell, of which he loosed the sorrows whereby it was impossible that He should be held; from these it is rightly understood that He loosed and released the souls whom he chose [and finally] that He received back the body which He had left on the cross, and which had been laid in the tomb."[23] Finally, in *On Heresies*, which is Augustine's catalog of heresies and which was incomplete when he died in AD 430, he makes his most definitive statement: "Another heresy believes that upon Christ's descent into Hell the unbelievers believed and all were liberated from Hell."[24] Augustine condemns two related points: (1) that unbelievers came to faith after death and

▶ FIGURE 12.4   Portrait of Augustine, late-fifth to early-sixth centuries, St. John Lateran, Rome. Photo: Wilpert, Die römischen Mosaiken und Malereien Bd4 Tafeln Malereien (1916), Taf. 140 (public domain)

DIVER SIDIVERSA PATRES

(2) that hell was emptied. Augustine's conclusion—that the decisions of this life are spiritually definitive whether one lived before or
after Christ—set death as the "boundary of salvation" in the West
(compare Alma 34:33).[25]

Purgatory: "And the Fire Shall Try Every Man's Work of What Sort It Is" (1 Corinthians 3:13)

Although one's orientation toward Christ while living is what determined one's final state, it was also clear that only the martyrs and
other exceptionally holy people were prepared to face the consuming
fire of God at the moment of their death. Augustine believed, as have
most Christians, that the status of certain sinners could be improved
after their death, provided that their lives had been correctly oriented
toward God. One might think about it in this way: although a person
might be justified, the process of sanctification takes time, during
which death may intervene. For many of Augustine's interlocutors,
postmortem improvement was often subsumed under a broad complex of ideas about purgation—that is, a tradition of purification or
cleansing. However, these ideas were very different from those associated with purgatory in the Middle Ages, which was conceived of as a
place with some very definite ideas about accounting for the punishment due to sin (see box 12.5). As usual, these ideas about purgation
reflect close reading of scripture and considerable reflection.

Fire and water, the most common elements of purgatory, have been
perceived as retributive, probative, or purifying in traditions that are
far older than Christianity.[26] Both Testaments identify fire with God's
retributive purposes (see Leviticus 10:1–2; Deuteronomy 32:22; Luke
3:9, 17). Two passages, however, are of significant value for thinking
about a purgative experience. First, Paul refers to fire as both probative
(see 1 Corinthians 3:13–14) and purifying (see 1 Corinthians 3:15):

> For other foundation can no man lay than that is
> laid, which is Jesus Christ. Now if any man build
> upon this foundation gold, silver, precious stones,
> wood, hay, stubble; every man's work shall be made

BOX 12.5 Between Death and Resurrection

Most ancient Christians believed that humans, with the exception of the martyrs, passed to some sort of "intermediate" experience between their death and their resurrection. However, given that scripture regarding this state of existence was extremely limited, early Christians used *reason* to extend the biblical insights of *faith*. It is no surprise, then, that some details of their insights are quite different from those entrusted to us by modern revelation. We can appreciate our common testimony of the gospel if we focus on the implications of this Christian imagery.

First, we find that Christ is attested everywhere as the central figure in God's work and that his Atonement is the key to spiritual progression (see Doctrine and Covenants 138:35).

Second, we find agreement that, in death as in life, God's justice is worked out through his mercy as we continue our spiritual labors and progression after our demise, until we are finally prepared to meet God (see Doctrine and Covenants 138:25–34; 50–52).

Third, this boon has conditions; we find that the state of souls after death follows from their orientation while they lived—that is, "this life is the time for [us] to prepare to meet God" (Alma 34:32; see also Doctrine and Covenants 138:20–22)—even if that preparation is not completed before death.

Finally, we might recall what all the Church Fathers understood: our lack of revelation regarding the afterlife reflects the wisdom that wills us to be "anxiously engaged" in this life rather than experts in the next (Doctrine and Covenants 58:27–28).

manifest: for the day shall declare it, because it shall be revealed by fire; and the fire shall try every man's work of what sort it is. If any man's work abide which he hath built thereupon, he shall receive a reward. If any man's work shall be burned, he shall suffer

loss: but he himself shall be saved; yet so as by fire.
(1 Corinthians 3:11–15)

Many points separate the description in this passage from medieval purgatory. However, the earliest Christian ideas about purgatory
were built on this passage, often envisioning it as a purgative event
rather than a protracted experience in a place of torment.[27] The point
on which early Christians insisted was that, in order to benefit from
a purgatorial experience, a person's life must be founded in Christ,
which, in practical terms, meant that one must have been committed
to being a disciple of Christ while living.

A second significant passage in the development of purgatory
was Matthew 12:32: "And whosoever speaketh a word against the
Son of man, it shall be forgiven him: but whosoever speaketh against
the Holy Ghost, it shall not be forgiven him, neither in this world,
neither in the world to come" (emphasis added). Just who might benefit
from remission of sins in the afterlife was of understandable interest
to many. Once again, Augustine set the West's boundary at one's orientation toward God while living:

> There is a certain manner of living, neither good
> enough to dispense with the need for [intercession
> by family and friends], nor bad enough to preclude
> their being of advantage after death; and there is a
> certain manner of living which is so established in
> goodness as to dispense with the need for them, as
> again there is one so established in evil as to be inca-
> pable of benefiting from these when it has passed on
> from this life. *Therefore, it is here and now that a man
> acquires any merit or demerit* through which after this
> life, he becomes capable of relief or depression.[28]

By way of a concrete example of those who might anticipate the
purgatorial experience, Augustine cites the man who loves his wife,
not as Christ would have loved her but "in the world's fashion." Since,
for Augustine, the pleasure enjoyed was sin, it must be expiated, but
because it was experienced "in lawful wedlock," it is not "damnable"

as would sexual congress outside of marriage have been.[29] The means by which the living might intercede with God on behalf of the dead were established as prayers, alms, and the Eucharistic sacrifice, all three of which were traditional forms of importuning God for his mercy and, therefore, appropriate whether exercised in behalf of the living or the dead (see chapter 11).[30]

Hell and Eternal Punishment: "At Any Rate It Is Better to Escape It Than to Learn Its Nature"[31]

The interest of humans in the nature of eternal punishment far exceeds the available revelatory insight, but that imbalance has never slowed, let alone stopped, the flood of lurid speculation.[32] The earliest Christian writer, Paul of Tarsus, envisioned a judgment at which the righteous would be raised (see 1 Corinthians 15:51–52). The synoptic Gospels are the first to mention a place of punishment, typically translated as "Gehenna" or "hell" (see, for example, Matthew 5:29, 30), but they provide little description. Lastly, the book of Revelation refers to the status of the wicked in terms such as the "second death" or a place in the "lake burning with fire and brimstone" (Revelation 20:14–15) and indicates that the ascension of the smoke from the torment of those so consigned lasts forever (see Revelation 14:9–11).

While Christian scripture has relatively little to say about the realm of the damned, the katabatic (from *katabasis*, or "descent") literature of the wider Greco-Roman world was verbose. By the first century AD, Homer and Virgil were standard educational fare for students, and the works of both authors featured tours of the underworld.[33] Without a doubt, these texts were studied and memorized for their pedagogical value—that is, they motivated certain behaviors and attitudes as part of an ethical and cultural education called *paideia*. The texts persuaded readers by evoking emotion through descriptions (*ekphrasis*) delivered with vivid details (*energeia*) of sight, sound, and smell that made readers feel as if they were personally present in the netherworld. The form these narratives took was called periegetic—that is, they were journeys or tours in which a guide or

What Is an Apocalypse?

An apocalypse is a first-person narrative often featuring a supernatural guide who discloses various aspects of transcendent reality to a human companion. Biblical examples of apocalypses include Revelation and Daniel 6–12, but most apocalyptic material is not canonical.

Apocalypses come in three forms: (1) an otherworld journey, typically involving a tour of heaven, hell, or both; (2) a historical review in which events leading up to the present age are recounted; or (3) a mixed form that includes both.

The purpose of an apocalypse is to influence readers to moderate their behavior in the present in order to prosper in the future.

narrator pointed out significant features from which the audience might benefit. Since the punishments matched the sin(s) in some fashion, the audience learned to adopt certain values and behaviors associated with the social and cultural norms of the place and date of composition.[34]

Early Christian apocalypses (see box 12.6), including Revelation, functioned within the Christian community much as did the katabatic literature of authors such as Homer and Virgil. Two examples of this genre with implications in early Christian ideas about hell are the *Apocalypse of Peter* and the *Apocalypse of Paul*.[35] Both are pseudepigraphal works—that is, they are not the literary efforts of either Apostle—and both employ *ekphrasis* and *energeia* in a periegetic form to further their community *paideia*. However, because they were composed at different times, modern readers can see both what was thought of hell and how those ideas changed over time.[36]

The *Apocalypse of Peter* is framed as a prophecy, said to have been delivered by Christ to his Apostles on the Mount of Olives (see Mark 13), but Peter is the focus of the dialogue (see box 12.7).[37] By way of

The *Apocalypse of Peter*

The *Apocalypse of Peter* is a pseudepigraphal work containing descriptions of both heaven and hell. It is dated to the early second century by an allusion to Simon bar Kokhba, a Jewish revolutionary associated with the revolt of AD 132–36, and from its use by Clement of Alexandria (died circa AD 215). It was probably composed in Egypt and originally written in Greek, but only the Ethiopic version is complete.

an example, consider how the *Apocalypse of Peter* imagines punishment for abortion and infanticide:

> And near this flame there is a great and very deep pit and into it there flow all kinds of things from everywhere: judgment (?), horrifying things and excretions. And the women (are) swallowed up (by this) up to their necks and are punished with great pain. These are they who have procured abortions. . . . Opposite them is another place where the children [whom they aborted] sit, but both alive and they cry to God. And lightnings go forth from those children . . . [that pierces] the eyes of those who, by fornication, have brought about their destruction. Other men and women stand above them naked. And their children stand opposite to them in a place of delight. And they sigh and cry to God because of their parents. . . . And the milk of the mothers flows from their breasts and congeals and smells foul, and from it come forth beasts that devour flesh.[38]

The punishment for abortion and exposure of children is aligned with those acts, most strikingly by the presence of the children. The torment of the women is vividly described (*ekphrasis*) by means of the *sight* of them immersed up to their necks in excrement, the *sound* of the accusations of their children ascending to God, and the *foul smell* of putrefaction from the lake and the congealed breast milk with which they are covered (*energeia*). The reader's attention is guided around the infernal landscape to appreciate the topography ("very deep pit") by use of phrases such as "near this flame" and "opposite them" (*periēgēsis*).[39] This is certainly a memorable description—no one could doubt that abortion violated the ethical norms of those who created this work!

The catalog of sins addressed in the *Apocalypse of Peter* indicates that those whose lies betrayed the martyrs have had their lips cut off and their mouths set aflame, while those who neglected widows and orphans are dressed in rags and impaled on a pillar of fire.[40] Of note are the "hanging" punishments, among which are women hung by their hair, which they apparently used to attract their lovers, and their lovers are suspended from their thighs, while blasphemers are hung from their tongues.[41] What is most striking about this, however, is what is *not* listed. By and large, many of the sins for which punishment is detailed are typical of the wider Greco-Roman society in which Christians lived. In the *Apocalypse of Paul*, composed some two hundred years later, the types of sins listed will change.

The last of the ancient apocalyptic tours of hell, and the one that inspired the medieval imagination, is the *Apocalypse of Paul*.[42] Like the *Apocalypse of Peter*, the punishment in the *Apocalypse of Paul* is measure-for-measure, and suspending sinners from, or submerging them in fire up to, the offending body part is common.[43] In this light, consider the following excerpt:

> And there I saw a river boiling with fire. . . . And I asked and said: "Who are these, sir, who are immersed up to the knees in fire? And he answered and said to me: These are those who when they have come out of church occupy themselves in discussing strange discourses. Those, however, who are

The *Apocalypse of Paul*

The *Apocalypse of Paul* is a pseudepigraphal work containing descriptions of both heaven and hell. Since it is first attested by Augustine (died AD 430) and makes significant references to the sins of Church leaders and monastics, it is probably best dated to the fourth century. Originally composed in Greek, the most complete copies are in Latin.

immersed up to the navel are those who when they have received the body of Christ go away, fornicate and do not cease from their sins until they die. And those who are immersed up to the lips are those who when they meet in the church of God slander one another. Those who are immersed up to the eyebrows are those who give the nod to one another and (in that way) secretly prepare evil against their neighbor.[44]

Once again, the graphic description of the sin is matched by the punishment to reinforce the community's pedagogical goals. Strikingly, however, the community is now that of a Christian congregation that does not respect their communal worship, and the sins involved are those that would, if left unchecked, weaken bonds of their congregations. This difference between the two texts suggests that this community's *paideia* (cultural education) was focused more on their own social cohesion and identity and less concerned with the norms of the rest of society.[45]

This interest in Christian failings is consistent throughout the *Apocalypse of Paul* (see box 12.8). Whereas the *Apocalypse of Peter* had no sins that were unique to Christianity, punishment for such transgressions makes up about half the sins noted in the Pauline tour.[46] In addition, the attention directed toward values such as virginity and

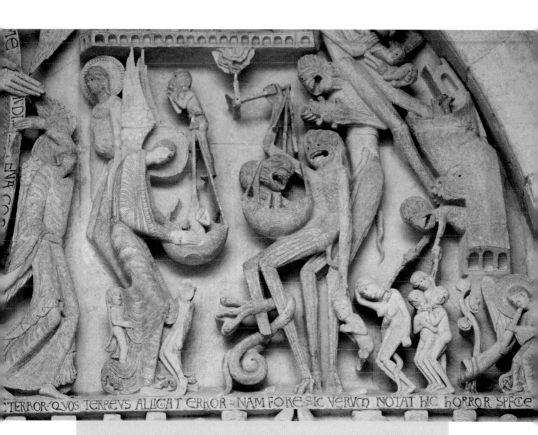

▲ **FIGURE 12.5** Tympanum of St. Lazare at Autun, France, 1130–45. The artist Ghislebertus has chosen to depict this Last Judgment scene in the tympanum space above the church portal. Later medieval art graphically depicts the judgment of souls as a contest between the Archangel Michael and the nightmarish demons that want to claim them. Here we see the naked souls of the deceased weighed on a scale to measure their righteousness. Photo: Alamy

asceticism and sins such as pride and hypocrisy are consistent with monastic values.[47] Finally, this apocalypse features the punishment of presbyters (elders), bishops, deacons, and lectors (readers), suggesting the author held some church leaders in contempt.[48] Finally, Paul is overwhelmed by the horrors of eternal punishment and weeps while the damned beg for mercy and are joined in this plea by Michael and the archangels. In response, Jesus appears and suspends punishment during Sundays for the rest of eternity as a mark of divine mercy, but no other moderation is envisioned.[49] Readers of this text were probably quite happy that their experience of hell was only a tour (*periēgēsis*) rather than a staycation.

One of the ways in which the *Apocalypse of Paul* is dated is that Augustine seems to have referred to it, by way of indicating it was spurious.[50] Against the lurid descriptions of apocalyptic imagery, Augustine is very cautious. Early on, he indicates that the punishment of the damned consists of them being deprived of their ability to reason and, therefore, being unable to confess to God. His thinking along these lines follows from the idea that eternal punishment and reward are not just God's responses to humans but "the failure and success of the rational creature's long quest . . . for the blessedness of finding his own true identity in God," just as the prodigal son discovered his identity when he returned to his father (see Luke 15:24).[51] Augustine is most concerned, however, to establish that eternal damnation is, in fact, eternal.[52] In this regard, he notes that if the "eternal" of eternal torment is a matter of being just "a very long time," then the "eternal" of one's eternal reward is also of limited duration and therefore not much of a reward (contrast with Doctrine and Covenants 19:6–12).[53]

Heaven and Eternal Reward: "Behold, the Tabernacle of God Is with Men" (Revelation 21:3)

The most striking images of heaven in Christian scripture are those of the celestial city (see Hebrews 12:22; Revelation 21:2; see also box 12.9). From a sociological standpoint, the ideas of freedom from want and distress, and of intimacy with God are at the forefront (see Revelation 22:1–9). Finally, the New Testament is split on whether there is a single celestial realm (see Revelation 4:1–4) or multiple levels of heaven (see 2 Corinthians 12:2; Hebrews 4:14; see also box 12.10). The most common metaphor for heaven is a garden, the imagery for which is found in Genesis 2. The Greeks and Romans had similar ideas of a sacred enclosed garden called a *locus amoenus*

BOX 12.9   A Celestial City on a Mountain

"For ye are not come unto the mount that might be touched, and that burned with fire. . . .

But ye are come unto mount Sion, and unto the city of the living God, the heavenly Jerusalem, and to an innumerable company of angels, To the general assembly and church of the firstborn, which are written in heaven, and to God the Judge of all, and to the spirits of just men made perfect, And to Jesus the mediator of the new covenant, and to the blood of sprinkling, that speaketh better things than that of Abel."

(Hebrews 12:18, 22–24)

(pleasant place or place of comfort and safety); the most famous example of this idea in Christianity is the description of the river and trees of the New Jerusalem in Revelation: "And he shewed me a pure river of water of life, clear as crystal, proceeding out of the throne of God and of the Lamb. In the midst of the street of it, and on either side of the river, *was there* the tree of life, which bare twelve *manner of* fruits, *and* yielded her fruit every month: and the leaves of the tree *were* for the healing of the nations" (Revelation 22:1–2).[54]

In this final section, we turn to the poetry and prose of early Christian communities in the east—that is, to Syriac Christianity (see box 12.11). Having developed in its own language and area, Syriac Christianity had some distinctive features, one of which was a certain disinterest in apocalyptic literature.[55] Thus, many Syriac texts opt to use themes and imagery from nature and to employ the values of wisdom literature (wisdom/knowledge versus folly), as may be seen in the following verses from the anonymous second-century *Odes of Solomon* which describe a righteous person:

BOX 12.10 Three Degrees of Glory in the Bible?

Some ancient Christians, such as the Apostle Paul, believed in multiple levels of heaven and degrees of glory (see, for instance, 2 Corinthians 3:18; 12:2), but there is no evidence that they understood heavenly degrees of glory in the same way it was revealed to Joseph Smith. In Doctrine and Covenants 76 and 88, Joseph came to understand heaven as divided into three distinct kingdoms: celestial, terrestrial, and telestial. Later, when working on his inspired version of the Bible, also called the Joseph Smith Translation (JST), Joseph altered the text of 1 Corinthians 15:40 to read: "Also celestial bodies, and bodies terrestrial, and bodies telestial; but the glory of the celestial, one; and the terrestrial, another; and the telestial, another." Originally, Paul had contrasted "heavenly bodies" (Latin *corpora caelestia*) such as the sun, moon, and stars, with "earthly bodies" (Latin *corpora terrestria*)—rendered in the King James Version as "celestial bodies, and bodies terrestrial" based on the Latin—in order to convince the Corinthians of the reality of bodily resurrection. The JST adapted Paul's original argument for a bodily resurrection to reinforce the modern revelation about heavenly degrees of glory. Elder Bruce R. McConkie once recommended that one should approach differences between the original biblical text and the JST with the understanding that "both of them are true" from a doctrinal or theological perspective.[56]

> And I drank from the living water that dies not, and
>   became drunk
> And my drunkenness was not without knowledge
>   But I abandoned vanities
> And returned toward the Most High, my God
>   And became rich by his gracious gift.
> And I left folly behind, dropped on the earth
>   And I stripped it off and cast it from me

> And the Lord renewed me by his garment
> And gained me by his light
> And from above he gave me imperishable rest.
> And I was like the earth that flourishes and
> laughs in its fruits.[57]

The beauty of these poetic lines is quite a change from the explicit language of sin and punishment in the apocalyptic tours of hell. In its own way, however, the totality of the phrase "and I was like the earth that flourishes and laughs in its fruits" is equally powerful in describing righteousness and in creating anticipation of a supremely pleasant existence in harmony and love shared with all of God's creations.

Two early Syriac Christian leaders are of particular interest because of their thoughts on the righteous and their eternal reward. The first is Aphrahat, the Persian sage (died circa AD 345). Aphrahat believed that the dead "sleep" in their graves, although in Aphrahat's conception of this slumber, the righteous anticipate the moment of their resurrection while the wicked dread it.[58] At the resurrection, humans are reconstituted, judged, and then escorted to a location appropriate to their state. Those who are invited to heaven will find the following:

> The air of that region is pleasant and glorious, and
> its light shines out and is goodly and gladsome.
> Planted there are beautiful trees, whose fruits fail
> not, and whose leaves fall not. Their boughs are
> glorious, their perfume delightful and of their taste
> no soul shall grow weary forever. Spacious is the re-
> gion, nor is it limited; yet its inhabitants shall see its
> distance even as that which is near. There the inher-
> itance shall not be divided and no man shall say to
> his fellow: "This is mine and that is thine."[59]

Aphrahat also describes the righteous, indicating that they are free
from passions, have no sexual differences, and are restored to youthful
vigor.[60] The nature of resurrection and resurrected bodies was widely
debated among Christians. Ignatius of Antioch (died circa AD 110),
whose ideas about the descent of Christ we discussed earlier, was ad-
amant that Christ was resurrected so that he could eat and drink "like
one who is composed of flesh, although spiritually he was united with
the Father."[61] A similar resurrection of the flesh was considered necessary for humans because the soul was unable to suffer punishment
with a body.[62] But what about those who were not destined for punishment? Prominent pagan philosophers, such as the second-century
philosopher Celsus, were appalled by the resurrection of the flesh because, in their estimation, a soul would not wish to be clothed again
in a body that had suffered corruption.[63]

By the fourth century, debates about bodily resurrection became
more specific: if one's genitals are present and in working order in heav-
en, then "the victory over them—and our reward for this victory—can
continue for all eternity." Moreover, if genitalia were missing, "the virgin would then be equal to the prostitute," a serious problem in a world
that valued hierarchy.[64] In the end, Augustine's reasoning set the stage
for medieval thinking, and his thoughts were dominated by the imagery of a reassembled statue. Resurrection restored bodily material and
integrity, both blessed with eternal incorruption.[65]

Odes of Solomon is the second-century work of an unknown author and was composed for liturgical purposes. It also contains a beautiful poetic account of Christ's visit to the realm of the dead.

Aphrahat, the Persian sage, was born in modern Iran around AD 280. He was an early Syriac Christian monk and perhaps a bishop. His only extant work, *Demonstrations*, is a collection of twenty-three homilies, each on a different gospel topic.

Ephrem of Syria was born around AD 306. Ephrem is the most famous of the Syriac Fathers. Although he did write in prose, he is most famous for his lyric teaching hymns, which are filled with rich imagery taken from scripture, folk traditions, and various philosophies. Later sources suggest these texts were set to folk tunes and sung by all-women choirs accompanied by a lyre.

A second Syriac Christian of the fourth century, Ephrem of Syria (died AD 373 in Edessa), held many points in common with Aphrahat (see box 12.12). Ephrem's description of the transition to eternity is, however, even more vivid. At the last trumpet, the souls of the righteous will be led back to their bodies. The light from their souls will once again shine through their bodily eyes, their skin will acquire color, and any indications of age, injury, or infirmity will disappear.[66] According to Ephrem, the heavenly area surrounds this world like a halo,[67] while its gates open only for the risen righteous who will prosper in some very cooperative trees:

> Should you wish
> 　　to climb up a tree
> with its lower branches
> 　　it will provide steps before your feet,

▲ **FIGURE 12.6** Ephrem the Syrian, mosaic in Nea Moni of Chios, Greece, eleventh century. Later Byzantine art often focused on the earliest Church fathers as figures of remembrance and veneration. This image of Ephrem is produced in Nea Moni, a monastic church dedicated to the Virgin Mary about whom Ephrem wrote hymns and homilies. Photo: Wikimedia Commons

eager to make you recline
    in its bosom above,
on a couch of its upper branches. . . .

Who has ever beheld such a banquet
    In the very bosom of a tree,
With fruit of every savor
    Ranged for the hand to pluck. . . .
To rinse the hands there is dew,
    And leaves to dry them with after
    —a treasure story which lacks nothing
    Whose Lord is rich in all things.[68]

There are no seasons, so flowers bloom to continually perfume the air while fruits ripen for eating throughout the year.[69] At the center of the garden is Christ as the tree of life; all other trees render him homage as they bask in the light of his presence.[70]

Finally, Ephrem believed that heaven would have multiple stories, designed from the first as a reward for those who excelled, and that this design had been adumbrated in stories of Noah's ark (see box 12.13) and Moses's ascension of Mount Sinai:

> When He made this intricate design
>   He varied its beauties
> So that some levels
>   Were far more glorious than others.
> To the degree that one level
>   Is higher than another,
> So too is its glory
>   The more sublime.
> In this way He allots
>   The foothills to the most lowly,
> The slopes to those in between
>   And the height to the exalted
>
> When the just ascend its various levels
>   To receive their inheritance,
> With justice he raises up each one
>   To the degree that accords with his labors;
> Each is stopped at the level
>   Whereof he is worth,
> There being sufficient levels in Paradise for everyone:
>   The lowest for the repentant,
> The middle for the righteous.
>   The heights for those victorious,
> While the summit is reserved for God's presence.
>
> Noah made the animals live
>   In the lowest part of the Ark

> ### BOX 12.13 The Tripartite Pattern of the Ark
>
> "A window shalt thou make to the ark, and in a cubit shalt thou finish it above; and the door of the ark shalt thou set in the side thereof; *with* lower, second, and third *stories* shalt thou make it."
>
> (Genesis 6:16)

In the middle part
　　He lodged the birds
While Noah himself, like the Deity,
　　Resided on the upper deck.
On Mount Sinai it was the people
　　Who dwelt below,
The priests round about it,
　　And Aaron halfway up,
While Moses was on its heights,
　　And the Glorious One on the summit.

A symbol of the divisions
　　In that Garden of Life
Did Moses trace out in the Ark
　　And on Mount Sinai, too;
He depicted for us the types of Paradise
　　With all its arrangements:
Harmonious, fair and desirable
　　In all things—
In its height, its beauty,
　　Its fragrance, and its different species.
Here is the harbor of all riches
　　Whereby the Church is depicted.[71]

BOX 12.14   Celestial Society

"But they which shall be accounted worthy to obtain that world, and the resurrection from the dead . . . [cannot] die any more: *for they are equal unto the angels*; and are the children of God, being the children of the resurrection."

(Luke 20:35–36; emphasis added)

Although the poetry of the Syriac Fathers is beautiful, its geographical range was limited by language barriers and the doctrinal conflicts of the era. Latin Christianity followed Augustine, whose views were far more restrained. To him, the unmediated vision of God (see Revelation 22:4), which he called the beatific vision, was the state to which the righteous aspire because it is the final union with God, "the cause of the 'unspeakable joy'" in which "in a certain way, the human mind dies and becomes divine, and is inebriated with the riches of God's house."[72] It is, however, not to be imagined as a static existence, for as John wrote from Patmos: "His servants shall serve [worship] him" (Revelation 22:5) because that is what will come naturally.[73] The corrupted human nature would be healed and fully subject to God—sinning would be impossible. According to Augustine, humans will be the equals of angels (see box 12.14), and the two communities will participate in a single society (see Hebrews 12:22) marked by unbroken tranquility and perfect order (see Philippians 4:7). Therefore, the order of heaven in Augustine's view was social, and although there would be different levels of happiness and glory, the peace of the realized city of God would not be marred by discontent or envy.[74]

Conclusion

Interest in the fate of the dead was not a Christian invention. But early leaders and thinkers certainly stamped the endeavor with distinctive ideas that arose from the revelation of God in the person of Jesus and the new view of resurrection that his life and death engendered. Christ dominated their conceptions of life in the space between death and the general Resurrection by his participation in that realm. He could also be found in visions of hell and was at the center of heaven's perfected society. Indeed, no place is without Christ, and that is very good news—the gospel, in fact!

Notes

1. See Éric Rebillard, *Christians and Their Many Identities in Late Antiquity, North Africa, 200–450 CE* (Ithaca, NY: Cornell University Press, 2012), 5–6, 64.
2. See Rebillard, *Christians and Their Many Identities*, 79.
3. See Rebillard, *Christians and Their Many Identities*, 68–70.
4. Other passages that refer to this event, or may be so taken, are Matthew 12:40, Romans 10:7, and Ephesians 4:9. The success of Christ's proclamation is assumed from Matthew 27:52, in which it is reported that "many of the bodies of the saints which slept" arose and came out of their tombs after the Resurrection.
5. See Berard L. Marthaler, *The Creed* (Mystic, CT: Twenty-Third Publications, 1987), 168.
6. Martin F. Connell, "Descensus Christi Ad Inferos: Christ's Descent to the Dead," *Theological Studies* 62, no. 2 (2001): 264–65.
7. In citing the examples that follow, I am indebted to Jared Wicks, "Christ's Saving Descent to the Dead: Early Witnesses from Ignatius of Antioch to Origen," *Pro Ecclesia* 17, no. 3 (2008): 281–309. The reader will find here a good summary and detailed bibliographic access to many more texts that deal with the descent motif.
8. Ignatius of Antioch, "Letter to the Magnesians," in *The Epistles of Saint Clement of Rome and Saint Ignatius of Antioch*, trans. James A. Kleist (Westminster, MD: Newman Bookshop, 1946), 72.

9. Clement of Alexandria, *Stromateis* 6.6, in *Ante-Nicene Fathers* 2:490; emphasis added.

10. Clement of Alexandria, *Stromateis* 6.6, in *Ante-Nicene Fathers* 2:491.

11. Clement of Alexandria, *Stromateis* 2.9, in *Ante-Nicene Fathers* 2:357; Stromateis 6.6, in *Ante-Nicene Fathers* 2:491.

12. *Shepherd of Hermas, Similitudes* 9.16.2, in Carolyn Osiek, *Shepherd of Hermas: A Commentary* (Philadelphia: Fortress Press, 1999), 232. English translations of the *Shepherd of Hermas, Similitudes* are taken from this edition translated by Osiek.

13. *Shepherd of Hermas, Similitudes* 9.16.2.

14. *Shepherd of Hermas, Similitudes* 9.16.2.

15. See Clement of Alexandria, *Stromateis* 6.6, in *Ante-Nicene Fathers* 2:490.

16. Clement of Alexandria, *Stromateis* 6.6, in *Ante-Nicene Fathers* 2:490. See also *Stromateis* 29, *Ante-Nicene Fathers* 2:357.

17. J. N. D. Kelly, *Early Christian Creeds*, 3rd ed. (New York: Longman, 1972), 114; 28–90. This formulation is from the creed developed at the Fourth Council of Sirmium in AD 359. The first reference to Christ's descent in a creed came from this council; the Old Roman Creed simply stated that Christ died and was buried.

18. See Kelly, *Early Christian Creeds*, 383.

19. Bart D. Ehrman and Zlatko Pleše, *The Apocryphal Gospels: Texts and Translations* (New York: Oxford University Press, 2011), 481. Much about the context and transmission of the *Gospel of Nicodemus* is contested, but it is probably later than the middle of the fourth century. The text is not a response to, or otherwise linked with, the creed of Fourth Sirmium, but it does show that the combat motif was not limited to creeds and the work of educated elites. Its extraordinary influence in the Middle Ages can be judged by its translation into the medieval vernacular of nearly every European language. See Ehrman and Pleše, *The Apocryphal Gospels*, 422.

20. See Ehrman and Pleše, *The Apocryphal Gospels*, 483–85.

21. Augustine, *Eighty-Three Different Questions*, trans. David L. Mosher, vol. 70 in The Fathers of the Church: A New Translation series (Washington, DC: Catholic University of America Press, 1982), 76; written AD 388–395.

22. See Augustine, *Eighty-Three Different Questions*, 97.

23. Augustine, *Letters, Volume 3 (131–164)*, trans. Sister Wilfrid Parsons, vol. 20 in The Fathers of the Church: A New Translation (Washington, DC: Catholic University Press of America Press, 1953), 392; written in AD 414.

24. Ligori G. Müller, *The De Haeresibus of Saint Augustine: A Translation with an Introduction and Commentary* (Washington, DC: Catholic University of America Press, 1956), 115.

25. A. Trumbower, *Rescue for the Dead: The Posthumous Salvation of Non-Christians in Early Christianity* (Oxford: Oxford University Press, 2001), 133, 140.

26. See Jacques Le Goff, *The Birth of Purgatory,* trans. Arthur Goldhammer (Chicago, IL: University of Chicago Press, 1984), 7–11.

27. See Le Goff, *The Birth of Purgatory*, 43.

28. Augustine, *Enchridion* 29:110, in *Nicene and Post-Nicene Fathers* 2:423–24; emphasis added.

29. Augustine, *City of God* 21:27; *Nicene and Post-Nicene Fathers* 2:473–74.

30. See Le Goff, *Birth of Purgatory,* 81.

31. Augustine, *Commentary on the Lord's Sermon on the Mount*, trans. Denis J. Kavanagh, vol. 11 in The Fathers of the Church: A New Translation series (Washington, DC: Catholic University of America Press, 1951), 30, 48.

32. For a solid introduction on the topic, see Alan E. Bernstein, *The Formation of Hell: Death and Retribution in the Ancient and Early Christian Worlds* (Ithaca, NY: Cornell University Press, 1993).

33. See Homer, *Odyssey* 4, 11; Vergil, *Aeneid* 6; see also Meghan Henning, "Eternal Punishment as Paideia: The Ekphrasis of Hell in the *Apocalypse of Peter* and the *Apocalypse of Paul*," *Religious Studies Faculty Publications* 95 (2014): 4, https://ecommons.udayton.edu/rel_fac_pub/95.

34. See Henning, "Eternal Punishment as Paideia," 5–6.

35. Interested readers will wish to consult *Numen* 56, no. 2/3 (January 2009), which is an entire volume dedicated to hell. Jan Bremmer's "Christian Hell: From the *Apocalypse of Peter* to the *Apocalypse of Paul*" (289–325) and Danuta Shanzer's "Voices and Bodies: The Afterlife of the Unborn" (326–65) are both excellent.

36. See Henning, "Eternal Punishment as Paideia," 10–13.

37. See C. Detlef G. Müller, "Apocalypse of Peter" in *New Testament Apocrypha,* vol. 2, *Writings Relating to the Apostles; Apocalypses and Related Subjects*, ed. Wilhelm Schneemelcher and R. McL. Wilson (Louisville, KY: Westminster John Knox, 1992), 622. References to the *Apocalypse of Peter* are taken from this translation. The text is dated to about AD 135 by a reference to the Bar Kochba revolt, some seventy or so years after the traditional date of Peter's death in the Neronian persecution in Rome. It assumes an immediate judgment and transition to one's final state with no interim period.

38. *Apocalypse of Peter* 8, in Martha Himmelfarb, *The Apocalypse: A Brief History* (Walden, MA: Willey-Blackwell, 2010), 97.

39. See Henning, "Eternal Punishment as Paideia," 14.

40. See *Apocalypse of Peter* 9.

41. See *Apocalypse of Peter* 7.

42. See Hugo Duensing and Aurelio de Santos Otero, "Apocalypse of Paul," in *New Testament Apocrypha*, vol. 2, *Writings Relating to the Apostles; Apocalypses and Related Subjects*, ed. Wilhelm Schneemelcher and R. McL. Wilson (Louisville, KY: Westminster John Knox, 1992), 714.

43. See *Apocalypse of Paul* 34–36.

44. See *Apocalypse of Paul* 31.

45. See Henning, "Eternal Punishment as Paideia," 14–15.

46. See Jan N. Bremmer, "Descents to Hell and Ascents to Heaven in Apocalyptic Literature," in *The Oxford Handbook of Apocalyptic Literature*, ed. John J. Collins (New York: Oxford Press, 2014), 347–48.

47. See *Apocalypse of Paul* 39–40.

48. See Himmelfarb, *Apocalypse*, 100, 103.

49. *Apocalypse of Paul* 42–44.

50. See Duensing and Otero, "Apocalypse of Paul," 712.

51. See Augustine, *Of True Religion* 52.101.

52. See Brian E. Daley, *The Hope of the Early Church: A Handbook of Patristic Eschatology* (Grand Rapids, MI: Baker Academic, 1991), 148–49. This text is the single best monograph on the eschatology of the patristic era.

53. As quoted in Trumbower, *Rescue for the Dead*, 131.

54. Fergus J. King, "Revelation 21:1–22:5. An Early Christian Locus Amoenus?," *Biblical Theology Bulletin* 45, no. 3 (2015): 174.

55. See Ute Possekel, "Expectations of the End in Early Syriac Christianity," in *Apocalyptic Thought in Early Christianity*, ed. Robert J. Daly (Grand Rapids, MI: Baker Academic, 2009), 172–73.

56. *Doctrines of the Restoration: Sermons and Writings of Bruce R. McConkie*, ed. Mark L. McConkie (Salt Lake City: Bookcraft, 1989), 269; as cited in Scott H. Faulring, Kent P. Jackson, and Robert J. Matthews, eds., *Joseph Smith's New Translation of the Bible: Original Manuscripts* (Provo, UT: Religious Studies Center, Brigham Young University, 2004), 10. For more on the Joseph Smith Translation of 1 Corinthians 15:40 as a modern revelatory change that does not reflect Paul's original argument, see Jared T. Parker and Todd B. Parker, "An Analysis of the Joseph Smith Translation of 1 Corinthians 15:40," *Religious Educator* 19, no. 2 (2018): 83–117.

57. Ode 11:7–12, in Michael Lattke, *Odes of Solomon: A Commentary*, trans. Marianne Ehrhardt (Minneapolis, MN: Fortress Press, 2009), 150–51. I have used the translation of the Syriac rather than the Greek. The *Odes* are attributed to Solomon because of their use of wisdom themes and motifs.

58. See Aphrahat, *Demonstrations* 8.19.

59. Aphrahat, *Demonstrations* 22.12; in *Nicene and Post-Nicene Fathers* 2/13: 406.

60. See Aphrahat, *Demonstrations* 22.12.

61. Ignatius, *To the Smyrnaeans* 2–3.

62. See Mark Finney, *Resurrection, Hell and the Afterlife: Body and Soul in Antiquity, Judaism, and Early Christianity* (New York: Routledge, 2016), 150.

63. See Origen, *Against Celsus* 5.14.

64. Caroline Walker Bynum, *The Resurrection of the Body in Western Christianity, 200–1336* (New York: Columbia University Press, 1995), 90–91.

65. Bynum, *The Resurrection of the Body in Western Christianity*, 95.

66. Ephrem the Syrian, *Carmina Nisibena* 49.16.

67. Ephrem the Syrian, *Hymns* 1.8.

68. Ephrem the Syrian, *Hymns* 9.3–4, in *Hymns on Paradise*, trans. Sebastian Brock (Crestwood, NY: St. Vladmir's Seminary Press, 1990), 137.

69. Ephrem the Syrian, *Hymns* 10.2–4, 6–9; 9.16–17; 11.9–15.

70. Ephrem the Syrian, *Hymns* 3.2, 15.

71. Ephrem the Syrian, *Hymns* 2.10–13.

72. Daley, *Hope of the Early Church*, 146.

73. The Greek word here translated as "serve," is *latreuō*, which means either "to serve" or "to worship." In the NRSV, the phrase is translated as "his servants will worship him."

74. See Daley, *Hope of the Early Church*, 146–47. The two more significant celestial cities of the New Testament are found in Hebrews 12:22 and Revelation 21–22.

FACING THE END

The Second Coming of Jesus Christ and the Millennium

Nicholas J. Frederick

For the Lord himself shall descend from heaven with a shout, with the voice of the archangel, and with the trump of God: and the dead in Christ shall rise first: Then we which are alive and remain shall be caught up together with them in the clouds, to meet the Lord in the air: and so shall we ever be with the Lord. Wherefore comfort one another with these words.
—1 Thessalonians 4:16–18

T o be a Christian in the first century was to be consumed by the
anxiety of eschatology. Typically
understood as the study of the "end times" or "last days," eschatology
(a word that does not appear in the Bible but has become a critical
part of the theological study of the Bible and early Christian thought)
poses questions such as the following: When is Jesus returning? When
will the righteous be resurrected? What will the millennial earth look
like? How will God's judgment work for both the righteous and the
wicked?[1] Even a cursory reading of Paul's letters, as well as other New
Testament texts such as the Gospel of Mark or the book of Revelation,
reveals how intrigued many early Christian members of the Church
were by these questions and how desperately they sought answers (see
box 13.1). Yes, it was true that Jesus, the Messiah, had been crucified at
the hands of the Roman government, but he had also been resurrected, liberated from the bonds of death. He had appeared to hundreds
of his devoted followers (see 1 Corinthians 15:4–8) and had promised
he would return (see Matthew 24:27, 30; Acts 1:11). But when? How?
And how would the world change when he did return? This chapter
looks at how some early Christians understood and discussed the Second Coming, the Millennium, and the permanent establishment of
God's kingdom on the earth.[2]

The Jewish Eschatology of Christianity

Most of the first generation of converts to the movement that would
become known as "Christianity" originated within Judaism. This
was initially because of the fact that Jesus himself was a Jew, and he

ministered primarily to Jews, and so they were the first to hear his message. As such, these early converts brought with them their own Jewish preconceptions into their understanding and interpretation of the Christian message and mission. It matters that we understand this context, otherwise we might think that eschatology began with Jesus's Resurrection. But eschatological ideas were already prominent within the Judaism of Jesus's time, mostly in the writings of the Hebrew prophets. This belief in the idea that Jehovah had a grand destiny in mind for the house of Israel became particularly important following the destruction of the northern kingdom of Israel (722 BC) at the hands of the Assyrians and the conquest of the southern kingdom of Judah (586 BC) by the Babylonians. Those who lived on after these invasions envisioned a final, decisive "day of the Lord," when Jehovah would return, conquer the wicked, and vindicate Israel, establishing once and for all his kingdom on earth in perpetuity. Postexilic prophets such as Zechariah spoke of an era where old women and men could sit in the streets of Jerusalem with young girls and boys, enjoying a new era devoid of violence and oppression (see Zechariah 8:4–5). Isaiah predicted that Jehovah would create "new heavens and

◄ FIGURE 13.1 Relief from the wooden doors of the Church of Santa Sabina, Rome, carved around 432–440, depicting a scene that has been interpreted as either the Parousia (Christ's Second Coming) or his ascension. Christ appears in the skies, encircled by a jeweled crown, reaching out his hand and holding an unfurled scroll. To either side are the Greek letters alpha and omega (see Revelation 1:8), and in each corner are the four living creatures from Revelation 4:6–8. Below, the Virgin Mary with the Apostles Peter and Paul look toward heaven. Photo: Scala/Art Resource NY

a new earth," and specifically that he would "create Jerusalem a rejoic-ing, and her people a joy" (Isaiah 65:17–18). Ezekiel prophesied of a new temple from which waters would flow that would bring healing to the earth (see Ezekiel 47:8). According to the prophet Joel, the arrival of the "great and terrible day of the Lord" would be preceded by wonders in heaven and in the earth. Joel spoke of "blood, and fire, and pillars of smoke" and predicted that the "sun shall be turned into darkness, and the moon into blood" (Joel 2:30–31). For many Jews at the time of Jesus, wearied from centuries of persecution and yearn-ing for their redemption, divine vindication was a matter of *when* rather than *if*.[3] And many hoped that *when* would be soon.[4]

For those Jews who came to believe in Jesus, the question be-came how to reconcile their Jewish preconceptions about how the end of the world would occur with their newfound faith in Jesus as the Messiah. Did Jesus's Resurrection from the dead represent the fulfillment of the promised "day of the Lord?" Had Jehovah truly de-scended from heaven and brought the promised vindication? If so, why was Rome still in charge? Why did Israel's enemies go unpun-ished? Why did the earth seem to continue as if nothing important had actually occurred? Yes, Jehovah had *already* descended and estab-lished his kingdom on the earth, but that kingdom was somehow *not yet* fully realized, and many early Christians found themselves caught up in this tension between *already* and *not yet*.[5] In the early decades of Christianity, it was the task of authors such as Paul, Peter, and John

▲ **FIGURE 13.2**   Sixth-century mosaic depiction of a prophet of ancient Israel, Sant'Apollinare Nuovo, Ravenna, Italy. Early Christian eschatological hopes grew out of the prophesies of the Old Testament. Photo: Used with permission, courtesy of MAR—Art Museum of the City of Ravenna, Cidm Archive

to help situate the new world in which the Christians lived in a way that made sense of the lived experience of a political and social world in which nothing really seemed to have changed. And yet, for the faithful, the world had changed dramatically.

The Eschatology of the New Testament

In his letters, written approximately two decades after the Crucifixion, Paul attempted to describe what that new world order entailed. For Paul, Jesus's physical return to the earth was a certainty. He even describes to the Thessalonian church the order in which the Resurrection of humanity will occur: first, the dead will rise to join with Jesus, then those who are still alive will rise to meet him—a group which Paul seems to hope would include himself: "The dead in Christ will rise first. Then *we* who are alive, who are left, will be caught up in the clouds together with them to meet the Lord in the air" (1 Thessalonians 4:15–17 New Revised Standard Version; emphasis added).[6] In Thessalonica, the belief in the imminence of Jesus's Second Coming apparently had led to a fair amount of confusion, with some Christians perhaps quitting their jobs or radically altering their former way of life (see 2 Thessalonians 3:6–13). Paul reminds these Saints that, while the Second Coming will happen, two things have to happen first: a "rebellion" (Greek *apostasia*) and the revelation of a figure whom Paul calls "the man of sin" (2 Thessalonians 2:3). Yet, even here, Paul suggests that these things were "already at work" (2 Thessalonians 2:7).[7]

Jesus's physical return—sometimes termed his *Parousia* (see box 13.2)—to the earth will see the beginning of the end of this era as he delivers his kingdom to his father, subdues all the forces of evil, puts his enemies under his feet, and conquers death itself (see 1 Corinthians 15:24–26). For Paul, the temporary physical absence of Jesus from the earth is not cause for concern; God the Father has given his Spirit to those who believe, and those who live by the Spirit have a part in God's new kingdom (see Ephesians 1:13–14), one in which "there is neither Jew nor Greek, there is neither bond nor free, there

Parousia is a Greek word indicating "presence" or "arrival." Its Latin equivalent, *adventus*, was often used to signal the arrival of a Roman dignitary such as the emperor. In the New Testament, *parousia* appears twenty-four times, most often in Paul's epistles to refer both to the "coming" of Jesus (1 Thessalonians 4:15; 1 Corinthians 15:23) and to Paul's own arrival in a city (see 2 Corinthians 10:10; Philippians 2:12). Whether Paul intended to use the term in such a technical way is debated, but *parousia* has come to be used synonymously with *Second Coming* in New Testament eschatological scholarship.

is neither male nor female" (Galatians 3:28). Paul even includes, at the end of his first letter to the Corinthians, the short Aramaic phrase *marana-tha*, "Come, our Lord" (1 Corinthians 16:22).[8]

However, as Christianity reached the end of the first century and started into the second, the delay in Jesus's return was enough to cause doubt and anxiety in the minds of some Christians. The epistle canonized as 2 Peter records that there are "scoffers" who questioned the reality of Jesus's Second Coming. "Where," they ask, "is the promise of his coming? For since the fathers fell asleep, all things continue as they were from the beginning of the creation" (2 Peter 3:4). Peter's response is to remind his listeners that God does things on his own schedule, and just because the Second Coming has not happened as fast as some may have expected does not mean that God has somehow ignored his people. "The Lord," Peter writes, "is not slack concerning his promise, as some men count slackness" (2 Peter 3:9). Instead, any delay is only there so that God can give all who need it a fair chance to repent: God is "not willing that any should perish, but that all should come to repentance" (2 Peter 3:9). Peter

▲ FIGURE 13.3　Relief, carved lid of a sarcophagus (stone coffin), late third/early fourth century, depicting a scene of final judgment in which the Lord has separated sheep (on his right) from goats (on his left), as in the climactic final parable Jesus told at the conclusion of his apocalyptic sermon on the Mount of Olives (see Matthew 25:31–46). Photo: Metropolitan Museum of Art, New York City, metmuseum.org (public domain)

gently rebukes those Christians who insist on having a firmer grasp on God's eschatological timetable with the reminder that "the day of the Lord will come as a thief in the night" (2 Peter 3:10).

The book of Revelation provides the most explicit blueprint for how some early Christians may have envisioned the end of this world and the beginning of the next heavenly one.[9] Following a series of plagues, calamities, and destruction, when the world seems as if it has descended as low as it can go, Jesus triumphantly returns in a remarkable scene. Clothed in red and riding a white horse, Jesus, along with the heavenly armies, rides out of heaven and cleanses the world of all that pollutes it (see Revelation 19:11–16). Satan and his associates are quickly dispatched, and for the first and only time in the New Testament, mention is made of a period of "a thousand years" where the righteous will reign with Jesus while Satan remains sealed up in a bottomless pit (Revelation 20:2–3). Following that thousand-year period, Satan is loosed, and after one final battle (often referred to as "the battle of Gog and Magog"), Satan is cast forever into a "lake of fire and brimstone" to be "tormented day and night for ever and ever" (Revelation 20:8–10).[10]

▲ **FIGURE 13.4** Apse mosaic, San Vitale, Ravenna, Italy, sixth century, depicting the glorified Christ with plentiful imagery from the book of Revelation: Christ, clothed in purple as "King of Kings" (Revelation 17:14), sits enthroned on a blue orb above a green, paradisiacal setting, evoking the new heaven and new earth (see Revelation 21:1; Isaiah 65:17). Surrounded by a rainbow (Revelation 4:1–2) and flanked by angels and saints, Christ extends a crown of life (Revelation 2:10) and holds the scroll sealed with seven seals (Revelation 5:1–10). Photo: Mark D. Ellison

This mention of a thousand-year period of peace, what is typically referred to today as the Millennium, would come to dominate future eschatological discussions among Christians. (The term *millennium* comes from two Latin words: *mille*, meaning "thousand," and *annus*,

Early Latter-day Saint Millenarianism

The earliest members of The Church of Jesus Christ of Latter-day Saints lived in what Grant Underwood has termed a "millenarian world."[11] The expectation that Jesus would shortly return to the earth drove much of the Church's actions in the early 1830s, especially as it concerned purchasing and developing land in Jackson County, Missouri, the revealed site of the city of Zion (see Doctrine and Covenants 57:1–3). The Lord's promise to Joseph Smith that he would come quickly (see Doctrine and Covenants 33:18; 34:12; 35:37; 39:24; 41:4; 49:28; 54:10; 68:35) served to stoke the eschatological fire, as many anticipated the return of Jesus happening during their lifetime. However, just as with the Christians of the first century, the Latter-day Saints of the nineteeth century would not live to witness that return. Like the Christians of the second, third, and fourth centuries, Latter-day Saints of the twentieth and twenty-first centuries have had to grapple with the unresolved tension of eschatological hope and the perceived delay in Christ's coming. In studying early Christian eschatology, we glimpse how other groups of faithful believers adjusted to living in a world that did not end as expected: they set their sights on God's work in the present rather than focusing too much on the future.

meaning "year.") Over the next two thousand years, three different views on the millennium would develop, all of them reacting in some way to the anxiety of Jesus's prolonged absence. What was likely the earliest of the three has become known as premillennialism. It teaches that Jesus's Second Coming will occur prior to the Millennium, the thousand years of peace. This viewpoint is held by many Christians in the United States, including members of The Church of Jesus Christ of Latter-day Saints (see box 13.3). Simply put, this view holds that things get worse before they get better. A second theological position, postmillennialism (or progressive millennialism) teaches that Jesus's Second Coming will not happen until the end of the millennial thousand years of peace. This position, a more recent development, is held by more liberal-leaning Christians who see the current state of the world as generally positive and continually improving because of the preaching of the word of God and the increasing success of social reform movements.[12] A third position, amillennialism, is the idea that the thousand-year period mentioned in the book of Revelation should be interpreted symbolically rather than literally; this position will be discussed later in this chapter.[13]

Into the Second Century: A Period of Transition

The writings of Christians who emerged as pivotal voices in the post-apostolic era inherited Christian communities at odds with eschatology. How could Christians reconcile their belief in Jesus's present kingdom with the reality that the world around them really was not that different than it had been prior to Jesus's ministry? As we will see in this section, some Christians grew more and more disappointed as the years stretched into decades without God's eschatological promises being fulfilled. For these Christians a new ethos emerged, one that pivoted around living as Christians in a world no longer infused with eschatological hope. Other Christians took their frustrations with the delay of the Second Coming and Millennium in a different direction and instead sought ways to hurry God's timetable. Still others remained convinced that they were actually living in the eschatological age, that the kingdom of God was a spiritual one rather than a physical one. What remained certain, though, was that eschatological anxiety continued to be a major factor in the activities and beliefs of many Christians; just because Jesus may have delayed his return did not mean that Christians had forgotten the promise.[14]

Toward the middle of the second century, Christian thinkers began to try to find ways to make Christian ideas understandable and appealing to their non-Christian associates. One problem these

▲ **FIGURE 13.5** The heavenly Jerusalem, mosaic from the Church of Santa Maria Maggiore, Rome, fifth century. In the second century, Justin Martyr maintained the hope expressed in the book of Revelation that the end times would include the righteous living in peace in the heavenly Jerusalem—a radiant city with walls adorned with precious jewels and gemstones (Revelation 21:9–12). Photo: Wilpert, Die römischen Mosaiken und Malereien, Bd3 Tafeln Mosaiken (1916), Taf. 73 (public domain)

thinkers faced was the reality that more than a century had passed since the Crucifixion, yet Jesus had not returned, and the millennial kingdom remained unrealized. One of these thinkers, known as Justin Martyr (died before AD 167), believed that the entire course of history has pointed toward a return of Christ. The Second Coming, Justin argues, was only a short time away, a "great and terrible day" in which the fires of judgment will consume the whole world.[15] He writes that Christ "will appear in Jerusalem" and destroy all his enemies.[16] Justin does, however, sense that the delay in the Second Coming might be a frustration for some Christians, so he attempts to assuage them: "For the reason why God has delayed to do this [destroy the world], is his regard for the human race. For He foreknows that some are to be saved by repentance, some even that are perhaps not yet born."[17]

What is particularly intriguing about Justin's writings is his sense that it may be possible to be considered a Christian without believing that Jesus would actually return and establish his millennial kingdom on earth. He notes that while he "and others are right-minded Christians in all points and are assured that there will be a resurrection of the dead and a thousand years in Jerusalem, which will then be built, adorned, and enlarged," he readily admits that "many who belong to the pure and pious faith and are true Christians think otherwise."[18] Justin's words mark a turning point within the Christian church. Those who succeeded Justin would generally fall into one of two camps: some, like Irenaeus and Tertullian, would continue to discuss ideas such as Jesus's Second Coming and the Millennium as real events, foregrounding them as important Christian beliefs. Others, like Clement and Origen, would increasingly downplay eschatological ideas, discussing them in ways that effectively *spiritualized* them, thus finding an acceptable way to deal with a topic that was becoming more and more uncomfortable in light of their failed expectations for Jesus's return in his glory.[19]

Irenaeus, Tertullian, and the Anxiety of Eschatology

Irenaeus (circa AD 130–202) lived in Lyon, France, and was among the first Christian theologians to identify the crisis that the Christian church was facing at the end of the second century. One of the primary purposes of the Church from its inception had been evangelization, preaching the word of God to all the nations in hopes of converting as many as possible to Christianity. Even Justin, a convert himself, wrote in an attempt to make Christian theology more accessible to non-Christians. But Irenaeus realized that in focusing all its efforts on expansion and missionary work, the Church had neglected to consolidate internal questions of theology and Christology; now it was faced with a particularly thorny challenge—the decision over what constituted orthodoxy and what constituted heresy.[20] Irenaeus himself would take up this challenge in a lengthy five-volume work entitled *Against Heresies*, a largely polemical work aimed at particular groups and ideas that had arisen in the Christian church that Irenaeus felt represented a departure from the true faith of the Apostles.

Irenaeus devoted almost the entirety of book 5 of *Against Heresies* to questions of the Second Coming, the Resurrection, and the millennial kingdom. Like Justin, Irenaeus was a premillennialist and felt that he and others were living "in the last times."[21] He sensed that the Second Coming was not necessarily imminent, however, because certain preceding signs had not yet occurred, such as the division of the kingdom into ten and the coming of the anti-Christ.[22] When Jesus does return, he shall "come from heaven in the clouds, in the glory of the Father, sending [the anti-Christ] and those who follow him into the lake of fire; but bringing in for the righteous the times of the kingdom."[23] Irenaeus espoused a literal millennial kingdom on earth, writing that "when this present fashion of things passes away, and man has been renewed, and flourishes in an incorruptible state, so as to preclude the possibility of becoming old, then there shall be a new heaven and a new earth, in which the new man shall remain continually, always holding fresh converse with God."[24] In

▲ **FIGURE 13.6**   Christ returning on the clouds, mosaic, apse of the Church of Saints Cosmas and Damian, Rome, sixth–seventh centuries. This depiction expresses the expectations that Christ would return "on the clouds of heaven" (Matthew 24:30) and the saints on earth would be "caught up in the clouds" to meet Christ and the faithful host risen from death (1 Thessalonians 4:17). Photo: Art Resource

a rather provocative statement, Irenaeus goes further in describing the nature and purpose of this millennial kingdom: "The righteous shall reign in the earth, waxing stronger by the sight of the Lord: and through Him they shall become accustomed to partake in the glory of God the Father, and shall enjoy in the kingdom conversation and communion with the holy angels, and union with spiritual beings; and those whom the Lord shall find in the flesh, awaiting Him from heaven."[25] Finally, and quite importantly, Irenaeus explicitly rejects those "Christians" who would attempt to interpret the eschatological teachings of the Apostles allegorically: "If, however, any shall endeavor to allegorize prophecies of this kind, they shall not be found consistent with themselves in all points, and shall be confuted by the teaching of the very expressions."[26]

Irenaeus's fiery defense of literal eschatology would find support a generation later in the form of Tertullian of Carthage. Tertullian, who converted to Christianity in the AD 190s, left behind a massive library of writings. While he rarely, if ever, mentions the actual return of Jesus to the earth, he clearly viewed the events surrounding Jesus's return and the Millennium as actual, future events—ones that would become matters of life and death for some believers—thus aligning him with other premillennial thinkers such as Justin and Irenaeus.[27] The anti-Christ, Tertullian wrote, "is now close at hand and gasping for the blood . . . of Christians."[28] Tertullian's words here hint at the increased persecution Christians were facing, persecutions that likely brought to mind the prophecies of Jesus that Christians would be delivered up and killed (see Matthew 24:9) prior to his return. In fact, in Tertullian's own city of Carthage (in modern-day Tunisia), the twenty-two-year-old noble-woman Perpetua, who was newly married and had just given birth to her first child, was arrested, tortured, and then killed for entertainment in an arena because she refused to deny Christ.[29] "I cannot be called anything other than what I am, a Christian," Perpetua boldly declared.[30] And she was not the only one who suffered this fate. Saturus, Felicitas, and others were tortured and killed by her side. "So they were stripped naked, placed in nets and thus brought out into the arena." A crazed cow was set loose upon them. "First the heifer tossed Perpetua and she fell on her back. . . . Then she got up. And seeing that Felicitas had been crushed to the ground, she went over to her, gave her her hand, and lifted her up. Then the two stood side by side."[31] How could Christians not hope for a better world in the face of such torture and tragedy!

Perhaps Tertullian's most notable connection with early Christian eschatology was his association with the Montanists, a group of Christians who would challenge the role of text and tradition in the early Church.[32] Montanus emerged from Phrygia in the AD 160s and subsequently declared himself a prophet, claiming that he gave voice to the divine: "Man is like a lyre, and I flit about like a plectron [a pick]; man sleeps, and I awaken him; behold, it is the Lord who changes the hearts of men and gives men a heart."[33] Montanus was accompanied by two women, Maximilla and Prisc(ill)a, who spoke as prophetesses and who viewed themselves as key figures in the unfolding apocalypse.[34] Maximilla claimed that "after me there will no longer be a prophet, but the end," while Prisc(ill)a was reported to have had a dream where the location of the Second Coming was going to occur.[35] In an oracle attributed by later sources to Prisc(ill)a, she said: "Having assumed the form of a woman. . . . Christ came to me in a bright robe and put wisdom in me, and revealed to me that this place is holy, and that it is here that Jerusalem will descend from heaven."[36] The location of the "new Jerusalem" was the Phrygian town of Pepouza (in modern-day Turkey), and Montanus and his two female associates urged their adherents to follow strict ethical practices in preparation for the descent of Jerusalem from heaven.

Clement, Origen, and the Allegorization of Eschatology

As the second century ended, writers such as Irenaeus and Tertullian as well as movements such as Montanism suggested that beliefs in the imminent physical return of Jesus and the establishment of a millennial kingdom upon the earth were viable ideas. However, it is

▲ **FIGURE 13.7**   Christ being received into heaven, detail from the Munich Ascension Ivory, Bayerisches Nationalmuseum München, ca. AD 400. One of the earliest (if not the earliest) scenes of the Ascension in Christian art. Over the early Christian centuries, the idea of being received into heaven began to be given more emphasis than the idea of a divine kingdom on earth. Photo: Wikimedia Commons (public domain), cropped

likely that these views were becoming more and more the minority position. The fact remained that Jesus had not physically returned, and the Roman Empire appeared to be in little danger of being overthrown.[37] Christians began to find different ways to interpret Paul's eschatological ideas, searching for more of an allegorical application. One of these early Christians was Clement of Alexandria, who sought to make Christian ideas philosophically sound in his writings.[38] Clement's more rational Christianity had little need for a physical Second Coming of Jesus, believing that true salvation in this world primarily occurs through finding Christ spiritually and ultimately through an "assimilation with God."[39] The ideal life, Clement believed, was not one directed toward the end but the present—a life devoted to the eternal contemplation of God, "to gaze on God, face to face, with knowledge and comprehension."[40]

Clement's attempts to allegorize Christian doctrine found a worthy successor in Origen (circa AD 185–254), who also, like Clement, spent time in Alexandria and became, in the opinion of one writer, "the greatest genius the early church ever produced."[41] Like Clement, Origen believed that interpreting Christianity allegorically would reveal its key doctrines. Literal interpretations, Origen seemed to feel, acted as pedagogic devices to assist Christians who were not quite prepared for the theological depth of Christianity. As such, he criticized those theologians who interpreted the millennial description in the book of Revelation literally or, as he called it, in a "Jewish sense."[42] In fact, Origen found true liberation not from the return of Jesus to earth but from his own departure from it: "I must progress beyond this world, to be able to see what these 'tents' are, which the Lord has made."[43] With statements such as this, Origen "sketches out a picture of the eschatological contemplation of God as constant spiritual movement and growth."[44]

One of Origen's most remarkable ideas, *apokatastasis* (Greek for "restoration"), proved to be the ultimate rejection of a literal, physical eschatology.[45] For Origen, *apokatastasis* was a final restoration of all things, when the course of the entirety of human history would return to enjoy union with God, where "the end is always like the beginning."[46] In a sense, Origen was promoting a form of universal salvation, proposing that everyone receives a form of redemption: "All beings, who, from that single beginning, have been moved, each by their own motion, through various stages allotted them for their deserts, will ultimately be restored to unity with God through subjection to Christ."[47] Origen's eschatology, according to one writer, was "not a Platonized form of genuine Christian eschatology, but an alternative to eschatology, indeed an evasion of it."[48] The scope of Origen's thought stretched beyond the expectation of a physical kingdom of Jesus established on earth following the future return of Jesus Christ. Instead, Origen opined about the preexistence of souls and the possibility that Satan and his demons may, eventually, find some measure of salvation.[49]

For his contemporaries and successors, Origen's spiritualized eschatology "of resurrection, judgment and reward sounded dangerously close to the Platonist hope for an immortality simply of the soul, or to a Gnostic devaluation of the material cosmos."[50] Some Christian writers responded with fiery defenses of a literal, premillennial eschatology. Toward the middle of the third century, an Egyptian bishop named Nepos wrote a tract entitled *Against the Allegorists*, the purpose of which was apparently to defend a literal interpretation of the Second Coming and the Millennium.[51] Sextus Julius Africanus (AD 160–240), a learned Palestinian chronicler, adopted the eschatological notion (and one that has become popular today) of a seven-thousand-year period as the time allotted for human existence, with the last one thousand years apparently representing the millennium.[52]

Augustine and the Realization of Eschatology

The end of the fourth century would see the emergence of the pivotal theologian Augustine (AD 354–430), whose influence on the doctrine of Western Christianity can hardly be overstated. Augustine's monumental work, *The City of God*, convincingly argued that the battle between Jesus and Satan lay not in the future but in the past. It had been fought on a spiritual plane, and Jesus had already triumphed. The "city of God" and the "city of the world" would both continue on, and eventually Satan would be stripped of any power he held on earth, but the earth's history was not in any way moving toward a climactic moment where Jesus would victoriously appear and vanquish the wicked. Augustine's eschatological reworking allowed Christians to come to terms with a world that was crumbling around them. Alaric I, king of the Visigoths, would sack Rome in AD 410, but by locating the true work of God in heaven, Christians found a way to cope with their current circumstances on earth. After all, they had survived Roman persecution and now they had outlived Rome. Christ now reigns, Augustine argued, through the lives of faithful

▲ **FIGURE 13.8**   A city-gate sarcophagus (stone coffin, damaged), late fourth century, Ancona, Italy. Christ and his apostles are depicted on the front panel along with small figures of a man and woman kneeling at Christ's feet (representing the man for whom this sarcophagus was made and his wife, portrayed as believing Christians in the attitude of worship). The backdrop of city walls and city gates evoke the idea of the heavenly city, the new Jerusalem, the eternal abode of the faithful dead. Photo: Mark D. Ellison

Christians in whom an ethical imperative exists to continue the spiritual fight for the city of God.[53]

It was largely due to Augustine's ideas that much of the Western Christian world embraced the idea of amillennialism.[54] As discussed earlier, premillennialism teaches that Jesus will return to earth prior to the Millennium, and postmillennialism teaches that Jesus will return after the Millennium, but, thanks in large part to Augustine, the next thousand years of Christian history would find the Christian church largely leaning in an amillennial direction.[55] Augustine was heavily influenced by Clement of Alexandria and Origen and adopted their

▲ **FIGURE 13.9** Mosaic, Jesus as judge, dividing the sheep (the righteous) from the goats (the wicked; see Matthew 25:31–46). Photo: Wilpert, Die römischen Mosaiken und Malereien, Bd3 Tafeln Mosaiken (1916), Taf. 99.2 (public domain)

allegorical methodology, which impacted how he developed his own millennial perspective.[56] According to Augustine, Jesus will, at some future point, physically return to the earth, but that reign will not last for one thousand years. His reign will be short because the kingdom of God is already present on the earth in the form of the Church. Augustine argued that the one thousand years mentioned in Revelation 20 referred to the period between Jesus's first and second comings and represented the period of the Church. Jesus's Second Coming would serve to inaugurate a new period, where he will judge the wicked and reward the righteous and create a new heaven and a new earth.[57] The urgency for Jesus's Second Coming and the premillennial hope of the first- and second-century church was largely abandoned by the time the fourth century ended, the "already" finally outlasting the "not yet."

Few theological topics are as controversial as eschatology. Christian churches today still debate the reality of the Second Coming and

BOX 13.4   Latter-Day Saints and the Second Coming of Jesus Christ Today

Today, Latter day Saint leaders have made it clear that rather than concern ourselves with whether the Second Coming of Jesus Christ will happen in the immediate future, we should focus instead on preparing the world for his coming by "gathering Israel" through missionary work and temple work and by working toward creating Zion—a community where we can be united, live righteously, and eliminate poverty. This mindset aligns closely with the Book of Mormon, where the grand eschatological concern is explicitly the gathering of Israel through the spreading of the Book of Mormon. Rather than passively waiting for the world to change, we are tasked with actively assisting in the creation and building up of a better world here and now. Recently, President Russell M. Nelson has urged Latter-day Saints to "remember that the fulness of Christ's ministry lies in the future. The prophecies of His Second Coming have yet to be fulfilled. We are just building up to the climax of this last dispensation—when the Savior's Second Coming becomes a reality."[58]

the significance of the Millennium. While postmillennialism saw a resurgence in the United States following the events of the American Revolution and the Second Great Awakening, Joseph Smith and other of his contemporaries such as William Miller argued for a premillennial view of history and focused their efforts on preparing for an imminent return of Jesus to restore his kingdom once again. Toward the end of the twentieth century, readers anxious about the end of the millennium pored over texts such as Revelation 11 hoping for insights into the whether the "rapture" would occur pretribulation or posttribulation and who might find themselves "left behind." As members of The Church of Jesus Christ of Latter-day Saints, we embrace the doctrine that Jesus will personally return to the earth in all his glory and establish his kingdom here upon the earth, and we have begun gathering Israel together in anticipation of these events (see box 13.4). In this respect we face many of the same questions that Paul, Irenaeus, and other premillennialists have wrestled with. How much time do we have? How much should we be investing in a world that could cease to exist tomorrow? And how should we deal with the disappointment that often comes as the years go by and we begin to realize it may be a future generation who will see the Savior's return in the flesh? Of these questions, and the anxiety that comes with them, I find solace in Paul's departing words to the Corinthians: *Marana-tha*. "Come, our Lord."

Notes

1.   Those interested in learning more about eschatology, both in the Western Christian tradition as well as in other faith traditions, see *The Oxford Handbook of Eschatology*, ed. Jerry L. Walls (Oxford: Oxford University Press, 2008); *The Oxford Handbook of Millennialism*, ed. Catherine Wessinger (Oxford: Oxford University Press, 2011).

2.   According to Webster's, the English term *Second Coming* originated in the fifteenth century to describe the "time when Jesus Christ will return to judge humanity at the end of the world." *Merriam-Webster.com Dictionary*, s.v. "Second Coming," https://www.merriam-webster.com/dictionary/Second%20Coming. In the standard works of The Church of Jesus Christ of Latter-day Saints, the term *Second Coming* appears only in Doctrine & Covenants 34:6.

3.   For more on this topic, see Donald E. Gowan, *Eschatology in the Old Testament*, 2nd ed. (New York: T&T Clark International, 2000).

4.   See Psalms of Solomon 17; 1 Enoch 46:1–7; 48:2–10; 62:1–7. The Jews who dwelt at Qumran and authored the Dead Sea Scrolls appear to have anticipated both a *priestly* and a *lay* messiah (see the Rule of the Community scroll).

5. It is normal for scholars of the New Testament to talk about eschatology as tension between the "already" and the "not yet." G. K. Beale offers this helpful explanation: "The expression 'already-not yet' refers to two stages of the fulfillment of the latter days. It is 'already' because the latter days have dawned in Christ, but it is 'not yet' since the latter days have not consummately arrived. . . . Christians live between D-day and V-day. D-day was the first coming of Christ, when the opponent was defeated decisively; V-day is the final coming of Christ, when the adversary will finally and completely surrender." G. K. Beale, "The End Starts at the Beginning," in *Making All Things New: Inaugurated Eschatology for the Life of the Church*, ed. Benjamin L. Gladd and Matthew S. Harmon (Grand Rapids, MI: Baker Academic, 2016), 3–14.

6. Compare 1 Corinthians 7:29–31, where Paul's "already/not yet" eschatology is on full display. See discussion in Gordon D. Fee, *The First Epistle to the Corinthians,* rev. ed. (Grand Rapids, MI: Eerdmans, 2014), 376–78.

7. For a useful, balanced discussion of 2 Thessalonians 2:2–7, a passage with a long interpretive history in our own faith tradition, see Gene L. Green, *The Letters to the Thessalonians* (Grand Rapids, MI: Eerdmans, 2002), 304–18.

8. While "come, our Lord" is one possible reading of *marana-tha,* because of the uncertainty of how this phrase would have been pointed in the original Aramaic, there are other possible readings. According to one scholar, "the Aramaic *Maranatha* formula occurs only here in Scripture and has three possible renderings: (1) "Our Lord has come!" (a confession); (2) "Our Lord is coming!" or "Our Lord is now present!" (a confession); and (3) "Our Lord, come!" (an imperative petitioning the Parousia)." D. E. Garland, *1 Corinthians* (Grand Rapids, MI: Baker Academic, 200), 773.

9. In addition to the book of Revelation, 4 Ezra and 2 Baruch are further examples of apocalyptic texts that performed a similar function in helping readers navigate through tumultuous times.

10. These passages in Revelation 20 have come to have a rather significant impact on Latter-day Saint perspectives on the events of the end times, such as the Millennium, the battle of Gog and Magog, and the final fate of the earth. For a thorough discussion of how these events are portrayed in Revelation and how they may have been understood in the ancient world, see Craig R. Koester, *Revelation: A New Translation with Introduction and Commentary* (New Haven: Yale University Press, 2014), 769–91.

11. Grant Underwood, *The Millennial World of Early Mormonism* (Urbana, IL: University of Illinois Press, 1993).

12. Credit for systematizing the postmillennial perspective is often given to Daniel Whitby (1638–1726), an English Unitarian minister.

13. Most members of The Church of Jesus Christ of Latter-day Saints would identify comfortably with premillennialism, the millennial position held by many Americans: "In the United States, the most popular and prevalent of these three types of millennialists has been the premillennial view, a position held by conservative and fundamentalist evangelical Christians. Postmillennialism, a position held generally among liberal or progressive evangelicals, if at all has been far less popular." Jon R. Stone, "Nineteenth- and Twentieth-Century American Millennialisms," in *The Oxford Handbook on Millennialism*, ed. Catherine Wessinger (Oxford: Oxford University Press, 2011), 494.

14. For a fine survey of millennial ideas among early Christians, including writers outside the scope of this paper such as Ignatius or Hippolytus, see Charles E. Hill, *Regnum Caelorum: Patterns of Millennial Thought in Early Christianity*, 2nd ed. (Grand Rapids, MI: Eerdmans, 2001). Pages 1–20 are particularly helpful in establishing the key issues and controversies. Also useful is Martin Erdmann, *The Millennial Controversy in the Early Church* (Eugene, OR: Wipf and Stock, 2005).

15. See Justin, *Dialogue with Trypho* 28, 32, 40, 49. In this chapter, all quotations from early Christian authors, unless otherwise noted, come from Alexander Roberts, James Donaldson, Philip Schaff, Henry Wace, A. Cleveland Coxe, eds. *The Ante-Nicene Fathers*, 10 vols. (Peabody, MA: Hendrickson Publishers, Inc., 1996).

16. Justin, *Dialogue with Trypho* 85.

17. Justin, *1 Apology* 28.4. Regarding Justin's statement, Stephen O. Presley writes: "To begin with, one curious aspect of Justin's eschatology is the apparent lack of concern about the delay of the Lord's second coming. Justin never addresses the issue and even indicates that the Lord's delay may be part of a larger plan of redemption that includes even some not yet born." Presley, *Eschatology: Biblical, Historical, and Practical Approaches: A Volume in Honor of Craig A. Blaising*, ed. D. Jeffrey Bingham and Glenn R. Kreider (Grand Rapids, MI: Kregel Inc., 2016), 273.

18. Justin, *Dialogue with Trypho* 80.

19. I have in mind here those who might think that conversion to Christianity represented a spiritual "resurrection" of sorts, an idea that we encounter in some fashion in 1 Corinthians 2–4 and 2 Timothy 2:18 and which becomes popular among certain Gnostic groups. It should also be said that this type of allegorizing of scripture is by no means a negative practice—every group, including our own faith tradition, has ideas and teachings from scripture that they interpret literally and others that they see as allegorical. See, for example, various Latter-day Saint teachings on the nature of hell.

20. The topic of how orthodoxy and heresy were determined in the early centuries of Western Christianity remains a point of heated debate. The classic work on this topic remains Walter Bauer's *Orthodoxy and Heresy in Earliest Christianity* (1934; repr., Mifflintown, PA: Sigler Press, 1996). Bauer argued that the church that emerged victorious by the middle of the fifth century (a group of Christians now commonly referred to as the proto-orthodox church by Bart Ehrman and others, although even that term has not escaped criticism) was originally just one of many different groups of Christians, each with their own beliefs and ideas. Bauer's model of diversity followed by ecclesiastical consolidation remains convincing today, although scholars continue to debate the nuances of the conflict.

21. Irenaeus, *Against Heresies* 4.preface.4. Of the premillennial stance of Justin, Irenaeus, and Tertullian, Jonathan Menn notes that "much of this early millennialism, which was drawn largely from Jewish eschatological ideas, had a physical, sense-oriented quality in which the blessings of the Millennium were amplified versions of contemporary, earthly life." Menn, *Biblical Eschatology*, 2nd ed. (Eugene, OR: Wipf and Stock, 2018), 64. See also Irenaeus, *Against Heresies* 5.33.3.

22. According to *Against Heresies* 5.30.2, some signs, however, are already being fulfilled, such as individual apostasy and the popularity of the heretics.

23. Irenaeus, *Against Heresies* 5.30.4.

24. Irenaeus, *Against Heresies* 5.36.1. In addition, Irenaeus devotes large parts of *Against Heresies* 5.33 to direct quotes of Papias regarding the situation of the just during the Millennium. According to Eusebius, Papias (circa AD 60–130), the bishop of Hierapolis, was among the first to seriously promote the premillennial idea that Jesus would reign for a thousand years on earth. Eusebius, who did not hold the same eschatological view, was quite critical of Papias's literal interpretation of one thousand years and blamed him for Irenaeus's similar premillennial leanings. See Eusebius, *Ecclesiastical History* 3.39.11–13.

25. Irenaeus, *Against Heresies* 5.35.1; adapted.

26. Irenaeus, *Against Heresies* 5.35.1.

27. See, for example, Tertullian, *On Prayer* 5.1; Tertullian, *Apologeticum* 39.2.

28. Tertullian, *Flight in Persecution* 12.

29. Tertullian mentions Perpetua in his *On the Soul* 55.

30. *Martyrdom of Perpetua and Felicitas* 3, in *The Acts of the Christian Martyrs*, trans. Herbert Mursurillo (Oxford: Clarendon Press, 1972), 109. While it has been common in the past to interpret such tales of Christian persecution and martyrdom as historical fact, we should exercise caution in how much historicity we attribute to such stories. See discussion in Candida

Moss, *Ancient Christian Martyrdom: Diverse Practices, Theologies, and Tra-ditions* (New Haven: Yale University Press, 2012).

31.   *Martyrdom of Perpetua and Felicitas* 20, in *Acts of the Christians Martyrs*, 129.

32.   This association has given rise to much discussion as to whether Tertullian held eschatological ideas prior to his association with the Montanists or whether his eschatological ideas were indebted to the Montanists. For a thorough discussion of the evidence, see Christine Trevett, *Montanism: Gender, Authority and the New Prophecy* (Cambridge: Cambridge University Press, 2002), 66–76.

33.   Ronald E. Heine, *The Montanist Oracles and Testimonia* (Macon, GA: Mercer University Press, 1989), 3. See also Epiphanius, *Refutation of All Heresies* 48.11.

34.   The importance of these two prominent females within the Montanist movement continues to be debated. See Anne Jensen, *God's Self-Confident Daughters: Early Christianity and the Liberation of Women,* trans. O. C. Dean Jr. (Louisville, KY: Westminster John Knox Press, 1996), 133–77; Trevett, *Montanism*, 155–59.

35.   Heine, *Montanist Oracles*, 3. See also Eusebius, *Ecclesiastical History* 5.16.17.

36.   Heine, *Montanist Oracles*, 5. See also Epiphanius, *Refutation of All Heresies* 49.1. This statement may have been made by Quintilla, a later prophetess, rather than Priscilla. Epiphanius, the source for it, cannot remember which. Heine includes it with the "authentic" oracles. See discussion in Trevett, *Montanism*, 167–71.

37.   As Diarmaid MacCulloch writes, "Among the Montanists' contemporaries in the mainstream leadership, only Bishop Irenaeus of Lyons showed positive enthusiasm for a vision of the world's last days coming in his lifetime, and his views on this caused such embarrassment to the next generations of Christians that their original expression in Greek has entirely disappeared and even many of the manuscript copies of its Latin transition censor out its passages on this subject." MacCulloch, *Christianity: The First Three Thousand Years* (New York: Viking, 2009), 139.

38.   Clement of Alexandria has traditionally been understood to have been the student of Pantaenus, who is credited with originating the allegorical school of interpretation that became popular in Alexandria in the late second and third centuries. Clement, and later Origen, would promote allegorical interpretations of scripture, which would lead to a rejection of a literal one-thousand-year future physical kingdom in favor of the establishment of a present spiritual kingdom. A good summary of Clement as reader of scripture and philosophy is provided by Ann R. Meyer: "As both

a philosopher committed to ancient Greek thought and a convert to Christianity, Clement sought to reconcile Platonism with Christian theology. In doing so he was especially attentive to what he viewed as elements of Hellenic philosophy in the New Testament teachings of John's Gospel and the letters of Paul. In his writings, Clement defends Hellenic philosophy as a vehicle of truth within the Judeo-Christian tradition." Meyer, *Medieval Allegory and the Building of the New Jerusalem* (Rochester, NY: D. S. Brewer, 2003), 30.

39. Clement, *Stromata* 2.23.136. While Clement's writings tend to strike many of his readers as overly philosophical, Judith L. Kovacs writes: "While Clement makes significant use of Plato and the teachings of various schools of Hellenistic philosophy, he understands his own teaching as an exposition of the Bible, and his writings are full of quotations from and allusions to Scripture, and ideas based on it." Kovacs, "Clement as Scriptural Exegete: Overview and History of Research," in *Clement's Biblical Exegesis: Proceedings of the Second Colloquium on Clement of Alexandria*, ed. Veronika Cernuskova, Judith L. Kovacs, and Jana Platova (Leiden: Brill, 2017), 37.

40. Clement, *Stromata* 7.10.5.

41. John Anthony McGuckin, ed., *The Westminster Handbook to Origen* (Louisville, KY: Westminster John Knox Press, 2004), 25.

42. Origen, *First Principles* 2.11.2.

43. Origen, *Homilies on Numbers* 162.10–12.

44. Daley, *Hope of the Early Church*, 50.

45. For the argument that Origen was not necessarily the original developer of *apokatastasis*, see Ilaria L. E. Ramelli, *The Christian Doctrine of Apokatastasis: A Critical Assessment from the New Testament to Eriugena* (Leiden: Brill, 2013).

46. Origen, *First Principles* 1.6.2. Origen did not feel that every Christian was prepared for this teaching: "It should be noted at this point that Origen is very reluctant to teach the doctrine of *apokatastasis* to everyone, because it might provoke moral laxity. It should not be taught to those to whom the threat of eternal punishment is still useful, just as children profit from the threat of punishment, even if the parent eventually refrains from executing it. Origen sees the Church as a pedagogical institute that accommodates to each individual soul, teaching some, threatening others as still-irrational children, and applying remedial punishments for their sins." Bart Van Egmond, *Augustine's Early Thought on the Redemptive Function of Divine Judgement* (Oxford: Oxford University Press, 2018), 7–8.

47. Origen, *First Principles* 1.6.2.

48. R. P. C. Hanson, *A Study of the Sources and Significance of Origen's*

Interpretation of Scripture (Louisville, KY: Westminster John Knox Press, 2002), 354.

49. For Origen's views on the preexistence of souls, see *First Principles* 2.8; see also chapter 7 in this volume. The passage usually associated with the rehabilitation of Satan is *First Principles* 3.6.5. For the problems of interpreting this particular theological notion, see Mark J. Edwards, "The Fate of the Devil in Origen," *Ephemerides Theologicae Lovanienses* 86, no. 1 (2010): 163–70.

50. Brian Daley, "Eschatology in the Early Church Fathers," in *The Oxford Handbook of Eschatology*, ed. Jerry L. Walls (Oxford: Oxford University Press, 2008), 98.

51. Eusebius, *Ecclesiastical History* 7.24. The date of Nepos's work is unknown, but it is generally believed that he was writing in response to Origen. It was in response to Nepos that Dionysius of Alexandria wrote *On the Promises*, which "rebuked Bishop Nepos of Arsinoe sternly for millenarianist teaching, and he attempted the most thorough and perceptive piece of biblical criticism that has survived from the early church, to demonstrate that the book of Revelation could not have been written by the author of the fourth gospel." W. H. C. Frend, *The Rise of Christianity* (Philadelphia: Fortress Press, 1984), 383.

52. See Daley, *Hope of the Early Church*, 61. The idea that the earth would have six thousand years of existence before the seventh thousand-year period, the Millennium, is termed by some as "the sexta-septamillennial tradition." Texts such as Psalm 90:4, Jubilees 4:29–30, and 2 Peter 3:8 are often used to support it, and it was a viewpoint held by at least one prominent early Christian writer (see *The Epistle of Barnabas* 15). Of such an approach, Menn argues: "Even today, some people try to make eschatological predictions using the 'day=1000 years' idea. That entire approach is false. Peter's statement was not designed to prove that a day equals a thousand years, or that a thousand years equals a day. Peter's meaning simply is that God is not limited by our notions of time." Menn, *Biblical Eschatology*, 65n18.

53. The essays presented in *Augustine's "City of God": A Critical Guide*, ed. James Wetzel (Cambridge: Cambridge University Press, 2012), do a fine job of fleshing out the significance of this work within the history of Christian thought.

54. See Augustine, *The City of God* 20.7. "This view of the Endtime predominated in both the Roman Catholic and Orthodox branches of Christianity throughout the Middle Ages and into the modern era." W. Michael Ashcraft, "Progressive Millennialism," in *The Oxford Handbook of Millennialism*, ed. Catherine Wessinger (Oxford: Oxford University Press, 2011), 45.

55. "Amillennialism, the traditional Christian position from the time of St. Augustine to the Reformation, has been the least prevalent type of millennialism in America, held primarily by the Disciples of Christ and some of the Reformed churches." Jon R. Stone, "Nineteenth- and Twentieth-Century American Millennialisms," in *The Oxford Handbook on Millennialism*, ed. Catherine Wessinger (Oxford: Oxford University Press, 2011), 494. For those who want to dive deeper into the nuances that separate the three millennial positions, see Craig A. Blaising, Kenneth L. Gentry Jr., and Robert B. Strimple, *Three Views on the Millennium and Beyond* (Grand Rapids, MI: Zondervan, 1999).

56. This is not to say that Augustine invented or introduced amillennial thought into the Church. Strains of it already appear in the writings of those who preceded Augustine, including Origen and Clement. According to Charles E. Hill, "a solidly entrenched and conservative, non-chiliastic eschatology was present in the Church to rival chiliasm from beginning to end." Hill, *Regnum Caelorum*, 253.

57. See Augustine, *City of God* 20:7–16.

58. President Russell M. Nelson, "The Future of the Church: Preparing the World for the Savior's Second Coming," *Ensign*, April 2020, 7–11, https://media.ldscdn.org/pdf/magazines/liahona-april-2020/16719_2020-04-0006-the-future-of-the-church-eng.pdf.

✳ 14 ✳

AFTERWORD
Medieval Christians

Miranda Wilcox

Go ye therefore, and teach all nations, baptizing them in the name of the Father, and of the Son, of the Holy Ghost.

— Matthew 28:19

A ncient and medieval Christians followed Christ's command to preach the gospel of Christ across Europe, Africa, and Asia. Christian communities emerged from China to Ireland, from Ethiopia and India to Iceland and Poland.[1] The far-flung Christian communities developed regional traditions of worship and community influenced by local political, economic, and educational resources. This chapter cannot adequately capture the rich diversity and complexity of Christianity in the thousand-year period known as the Middle Ages between the fifth and fifteenth centuries. Instead, I illustrate medieval devotion to Christ with examples that will invite resonance with fellow Christians today.

This chapter features examples of medieval Christians making sense of Christ's Incarnation, ministry, Passion, and Resurrection in their daily lives and cultural idioms. These Christians lived across the spectrum of diverse modes of religious life (see fig. 14.1).[2] Clergy were ordained to perform sacraments or assist in their performance. Ascetics consecrated their lives to the service of God—for example, monastics retreated from secular and family life to live in organized religious communities, mendicants traveled providing pastoral care and serving the poor, and hermits and anchoresses prayed alone. The professed or professional religious—the clergy and ascetics—were distinguished by dress, hairstyle, and education; they became a distinct social class from the lay aristocracy and peasants with delegated duties and specialized skills. Laity were baptized Christians who were not ordained and did not live in organized religious communities; laity received sacraments from clergy and many practiced ascetic

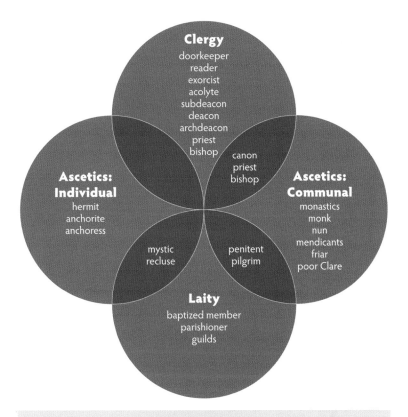

▲ FIGURE 14.1 Spectrum of Common Religious Roles in Medieval Western Europe

behaviors. Laity who undertook ascetic renunciations as penitents or who worked for ecclesiastic institutions blurred these boundaries.

Many medieval Christians devoted their lives to following Christ (see box 14.1). However, Christendom was not always aligned with Christ's way of peace. The atrocities of the Crusades, Inquisition, and persecution of Jews fueled by supersessionist zeal are, perhaps, better known than the medieval devotional practices I highlight in this chapter, yet these devotional practices remain potent examples for committed Christians today. Instead of perceiving medieval Christians as deluded by apostasy, we should revere them for keeping the light of

> **BOX 14.1   Why It Matters**
>
> We should revere medieval Christians for keeping the light of Christ alive. They spread Christianity across Africa, Asia, and Europe. They preserved and transmitted scripture. They developed rich traditions of worship and diverse modes of religious life. They devoted their lives to Jesus Christ.

Christ alive by enculturating Christianity across the world, preserving and transmitting scripture, and developing rich traditions of worship and diverse modes of religious life. They devoted their lives to Jesus Christ.[3]

Incarnation: Cultural Translation and Transformation

> *Unus enim Deus unus et mediator Dei et hominum homo Christus Iesus.*
>
> [For there is one God, and one mediator between God and men, the man Christ Jesus.]
>
> —1 Timothy 2:5

Making sense of the union of Christ's human and divine natures for Christians far afield from the Mediterranean womb of Christianity meant that communities needed to translate this mystery into their vernacular languages and into their cultural paradigms. Monastics initiated this work in medieval England. During the sixth and seventh centuries, Christian missionaries from (modern-day) Ireland, Italy, and France evangelized pagan Germanic peoples who had recently migrated to England. These missionaries founded monasteries where English men and women professed obedience to the community's rule of behavior to devote their full attention to religious life. In the early medieval period, monastics lived on land donated by wealthy laity in return for their intercessory prayers. Performing the scripture-based liturgy required literacy, so religious communities became centers of education, preserving and transmitting scriptural and cultural traditions.

One of the most prolific and learned scriptural exegetes of the early medieval period was a monk and priest named Bede (AD 673–735). In *The Ecclesiastical History of the English People*, which he finished in AD 731, Bede offers a rare biographic account about becoming a monk.

> When I was seven years of age I was, by the care of my kinsmen, put into the charge of the reverend Abbot Benedict and then of Ceolfrith, to be educated. From then on I have spent all of my life in this monastery, applying myself entirely to the study of the Scriptures; and, amid the observance of the discipline of the Rule and the daily task of singing in the church, it has always been my delight to learn or to teach or to write.[4]

The primary focus of Bede's life and that of his fellow monks at Wearmouth Jarrow in northeast England was "the study of the Bible and the integration of its lessons to Christian life."[5] His monastery produced the oldest surviving copy of the complete Vulgate, Jerome's fifth-century Latin translation of the Bible.[6] The manuscript also included a series of illustrations, including Christ in Majesty at the junction between the Old and New Testaments (see fig. 14.2). Bede's abbot intended to take the seventy-five-pound Bible, now known as the Codex Amiatinus, to the shrine of Peter the Apostle in Rome but died on the long journey.

Bede's vocation led him to translate and interpret Latin scriptures and theology for his people. One of Bede's favorite scriptures was 1 Timothy 2:5, which he frequently quoted in his homilies, or sermons, on the Gospels. He concluded one homily with this meditation on Christ's role as mediator between heaven and earth:

▲ FIGURE 14.2   Christ in Majesty in the Codex Amiatinus, written at Wearmouth-Jarrow before 716, Florence, Biblioteca Medicea Laurenziana, MS Amiatino 1, fol. 796v. Photo: Wikimedia (public domain)

> Surely there was a necessary sequence, that first the
> blood of the Christ had to be shed for the redemp-
> tion of the world; and through his resurrection and
> ascension there might be opened up to human be-
> ings the gate of the heavenly kingdom; and thus at
> last there might be sent those who would preach
> to all nations throughout the world the word of life
> and administer the sacraments of faith, by which
> they could be saved, and arrive at the joys of the
> heavenly fatherland, with the human being Jesus
> Christ, the very Mediator between God and human
> beings working with them, he who lives and reigns
> for ever and ever. Amen.[7]

For Bede, preachers were "the successors of the prophets and apostles" whose foremost duty was to share the Word made flesh by interpreting sacred scripture and administering saving sacraments.[8]
Bede understood that preaching the "word of life" may involve the
evangelization of non-Christian communities, as the English mission
did to the Saxons, but he also understood the value of pastoral care to
deepen the faith of baptized Christians. Pastoral care might involve
preaching about the scriptures, as Bede did in homilies, or translating Latin scriptures into English, as he was doing on his deathbed.
Pastoral care might also involve translating Christian doctrine into
familiar cultural media.

In his *Ecclesiastical History,* Bede related the story of Abbess Hild
and the cowherd Cædmon.[9] Hild was baptized at age fourteen with
the Northumbrian royal family and felt called to be a nun. In AD 675,
she founded a double monastery at Whitby where nuns, monks, and
agricultural workers lived. One night, Cædmon was asleep in the
stable when he was visited by a divine messenger who commanded
him to "Sing creation." Cædmon composed a hymn in Old English
praising God and shared it with members of the monastery the next
morning. Hild was eager to utilize Cædmon's divine gift to share
scripture stories in English; she invited Cædmon to become a monk.

Then, monks who could read the Bible in Latin taught Cædmon the scriptures, and he transformed them into Old English poems.

Other English artists, probably living in monasteries, were likewise inspired to create poetry and art depicting Christ in culturally familiar forms. For example, in the eighth century an eighteen-foot-high stone monument was sculpted in Ruthwell, now in Dumfriesshire, Scotland. It was decorated with twining vines inhabited with birds and panels depicting scenes from the life of Christ. One panel bordered by a Latin inscription evoking Luke 7:37–38 and John 12:3 depicts Christ holding a book while Mary Magdalene washes and dries his feet. Another panel is bordered by an Old English runic inscription quoting or alluding to the poem now titled "The Dream of the Rood," in which the Cross shares his eye-witness account of Christ's Crucifixion. The runic inscription and the poem describe Christ as a heroic prince hastening to leap upon the cross and die to save humanity from sin while the Cross stands tall despite its honor-bound duty to protect the Lord from harm (see fig. 14.3).[10]

In addition to depicting Christ as a heroic warrior freeing humanity from the bonds of the devil, the early English also named Christ a physician freeing humanity from the disease of sin. The early English understood the Hebrew root of the name *Jesus* in Matthew 1:21 to mean "healer," so they translated *Jesus* into *Hælend*, the Old English word "healer."[11] Ælfric (circa AD 955–1010), a monk at Cerne Abbey, wrote two collections of homilies in which he repeatedly explained that Christ heals his people from their sins. In a sermon about Jesus healing a man at the pool of Bethesda (see John 5:1–9), Ælfric elaborates how Christ heals the rupture between humanity and divinity:

> Thus the unhealthy laid inside that gate, but the almighty *hælend*, who descended to free mankind, is able to heal them in soul and body through his true gift. His name is *Hælend*, because he heals his people, just as the angel said about him before he was born: He heals his people from their sins.[12]

▲ FIGURE 14.3   Ruthwell Cross, detail from south side, monument in Dumfries and Galloway, Scotland. Photo: Doug Sim, 3 May 2009, CC-BY-SA-3.0

These few examples illustrate how medieval monastics translated their new faith into their cultural media and how Christianity transformed it—analogous to Christ's mediation between God and humanity in which he translates God to us in human form thereby transforming humanity.

Ministry: Following in the Footsteps of Christ and Religious Vocations

Sicut Filius hominis non venit ministrari sed ministrare.

[Even as the Son of man is not come to be ministered unto, but to minister.]

—Matthew 20:28

Medieval Christians felt called to imitate the life of Christ. They looked to Christ's ministry as recorded in the Bible for inspiration and discerned vocations to prayer, poverty, preaching, evangelizing, nursing, celibacy, pastoral care, contemplation, and other good works.

Between the eleventh and thirteenth centuries, many Christians desired to reform and revitalize their worship, and they sought models in the Acts of the Apostles (see Acts 2:42–47; 4:32–37). Some monastics experimented with new forms of ascetic life; they "tried to resurrect ancient ideals by reinvigorating communities or founding wholly new ones by attempting to return to the apostolic life, which meant a life of poverty, the communal sharing of goods, and, in some cases, itinerant preaching. Others imitated the eremitical model of the Egyptian and Syrian hermits of the desert. For still others, the canonical measure was another written document to be observed, now with the strictness and severity its author intended: the Benedictine Rule and the Rule of St. Augustine."[13] A great diversity of orders proliferated to meet the needs of Christians in different regions. Some orders focused on retreat from the world (Cistercians and Carthusians), and others focused on active engagement with the world (Dominicans and Franciscans).

The boundary between the professed religious and the laity began blurring with the emergence of communities of male and female lay penitents who integrated their charitable service and economic endeavors outside monastic boundaries.[14] Jacques de Vitry, a Parisian master, canon regular, and bishop, wrote a letter in AD 1216 describing men and women "undertaking an active, urban apostolate":

> Many people of both sexes, rich and worldly, have been fleeing the world, renouncing everything for Christ. They are called lesser brothers and lesser sisters.... These same [ones], moreover, live according to the form of the primitive church of whom it was written, "the multitude of believers was of one heart and one soul" [Acts 3:32]. By day they go into the cities and towns to benefit others through active work; but at night they return to their hermitage or solitary places where they are free to devote themselves to contemplation.[15]

Animated by the desire to imitate Christ's life through voluntary poverty, care of the poor and sick, and religious devotion, a number of informal penitent communities ministered to urban, commercial populations. Some of these groups include the Waldensians in northern Italy, the Humiliati in Lombardy, and the Beguines in the Low Countries.[16]

Francesco di Bernardone (AD 1181–1226) and Chiara Offreduccio (AD 1193–1253) are good examples of spiritual seekers who articulated new expressions of penitent living still practiced today.[17] Better known as Francis and Clare of Assisi, they renounced their wealthy families and devoted themselves to following Christ's footsteps by practicing physical asceticism, material poverty, and a nexus of spiritual values, including service, humility, and love. Francis described how encountering socially shunned lepers was a significant stage of his conversion from secular ambitions:

> The Lord gave me, Brother Francis, thus to begin
> doing penance in this way: for when I was in sin, it
> seemed too bitter for me to see lepers. And the Lord
> himself led me among them and *I showed mercy* [Sir-
> ach 35:4] to them. And when I left them, what had
> seemed bitter to me was turned into sweetness of
> soul and body. And afterward I delayed a little and
> left the world.[18]

This encounter with the marginalized shook his life and revealed his vocation "to follow the footprints of Christ and to fully embrace the logic of the Cross, which leads, here and now, to a reversal of values."[19]

Francis attracted followers, who he instructed to "live according to the pattern of the Holy Gospel."[20] Penance, peace, and mercy were hallmarks of the Franciscan lifestyle. Inspired by Francis, Clare devoted herself to penance and poverty. Other women joined her at San Damiano, including her mother and sisters, and they "formed an independent house of penitents, closely allied with the Lesser Brothers, following their own rule based on Francis' precepts."[21] *The Testament of St. Clare* begins:

> Among all the other gifts which we have received
> and continued to receive daily from our benefac-
> tor, *the Father of mercies* (2 Corinthians 1:3), and
> for which we must express the deepest thanks to
> our glorious God, our vocation is a great gift. Since
> it is the more perfect and greater, we should be so
> much more thankful to Him for it. For this reason
> the Apostle writes: "Acknowledge your calling"
> (1 Corinthians 1:26). The Son of God became for
> us *the Way* (cf. John 14:6) which our Blessed Father
> Francis, His true lover and imitator, has shown and
> taught us by word and example. Therefore, beloved
> Sisters, we must consider the immense gifts which
> God has bestowed on us, . . . not only after our con-
> version but also while we were still [living among]
> the vanities of the world.[22]

Clare's *Testament* "sounds all of the central themes of her and Francis's vision of religious life, including penitence, poverty, humility, love, and mutual charity that joins the sisters, and loving, service-oriented leadership."[23] The followers of Francis and Clare eventually organized into a family of formal religious orders. Single men became the Friars Minor or Lesser Brothers, single women became the Poor Ladies or Poor Clares, and the married couples became the Brothers and Sisters of Penance. Franciscans were and are committed to encounter Christ—particularly in his vulnerable humanity—in their active engagement with their poor, sick, and unbelieving neighbors. They are among many medieval Christians who felt called to develop a diverse range of religious vocations to minister as Jesus ministered.

Passion: Meditations and Visions of Christ

Mihi autem absit gloriari nisi in cruce Domini.

[Far be it from me to glory except in the cross of the Lord.]

—Galatians 6:14

Medieval Christians cultivated the faculty of imagination in meditative worship of Christ, and some were graced with visions of Christ. Popular devotional texts invited and guided readers to imagine scenes from the life of Christ in vivid and immediate detail, thus empowering meditators to "move from thoughts of Christ's humanity to those of his divinity" as they cultivated their capacity "to bridge material and spiritual knowing."[24] These devotional texts provided "intimate scripts" for the performances of feelings.[25] Contemplating Christ's suffering generated the affect of compunction, a state of penitential contrition, and "the rise of compassionate devotion to the suffering Christ."[26] Compassion for the Savior's suffering yielded compassion for human suffering.

There was a tradition of influential and widely read devotional guides often titled *Meditationes vitae Christi* (*Meditations of the Life of Christ*). One of the oldest surviving meditations in this tradition was composed between AD 1300 and AD 1325 by a Poor Clare from Pisa for her fellow nuns. There is evidence that this short Italian meditation was expanded into two longer Italian versions and a composite Latin edition, which was subsequently translated and adapted into all the major European vernaculars, including Middle English, French, German, Catalan, Swedish, and Irish.[27]

Building on the tradition of compassionate devotion developed by John of Fécamp, Anselm of Canterbury, Goscelin of St. Bertin, Bernard of Clairvaux, Aelred of Rievaulx, Francis of Assisi, and Bonaventure, the Poor Clare synthesized a method of cultivating an intimate relationship between the meditator and Christ. She advises the meditator,

> . . . so when you hear about any of the deeds and words of Lord Jesus, whether this is through the Gospels or through preaching or in another way, be sure to put them before your mind's eye and reflect on them, because it seems to me that in this way of meditating on the deeds of Lord Jesus Christ there will be greater sweetness and devotion than by other means. And the whole foundation for spiritual growth seems to me to come down to this: that always and everywhere you watch him with the eyes of your mind with devotion in everything that he does. Now how he is with his disciples, now when he walks with sinners, or when he sits or sleeps or wakes, or when he serves others, or when he heals the sick, or when he raises the dead and performs other miracles like this. Then consider all his deeds and manners. And contemplate his face with special care, if you are able to contemplate it, for this seems to me more difficult than anything else; but I believe that this will be for you the greatest experience of solace that you might have. And prepare yourself to receive him kindly, if he should come to you.[28]

The meditator is repeatedly guided to have compassion for Jesus's vulnerable body, as a poor refugee, bleeding in Gethsemane, tortured by Roman soldiers, and dying on the cross. Recognizing that Christ lovingly suffered pain for the meditator's salvation should wrench her heart: "O soul, have compassion for your Lord, who bore so much pain for you only for Love!"[29] At the moment of Jesus's death on the cross, the Poor Clare urges the meditator: "Therefore, o sinner, plant this tree, that is, the Passion of your Creator, in the middle of your heart, and remember that he suffered this most bitter death for you! And prepare yourself to follow him by the road of penitence and the denial of your own will."[30] It is impossible to remain indifferent in the face of God's profound gesture of love, and so the meditator reciprocates with love.

Meditating on the life of Christ inspired artists. Images, poems, and music explored Christ's transcendent vulnerability in his atoning sacrifice. Imagining Mary's joys and sorrows at her son's birth or death stimulated meditators' familiar experiences and tender emotions for mothers and children. This exercise was a particularly poignant avenue to stimulate contrition, which is "the first act of penance" that "is essentially a change of heart, a spiritual sorrow growing out of love for God and hatred for one's sin."[31] One of the most devastating Marian lyrics, "O all women that ever were born," melds the image of Mary cradling her dead son to a mother holding a baby dancing on her lap.

> Of all women that ever were born
> That bear children, abide and see
> How my son lies me before
> Upon my knee, taken from [the] tree.
> Your children you dance upon your knee
> With laughing, kissing, and merry cheer:
> Behold my child, behold now me,
> For now lies dead my dear son, dear.[32]

This fifteenth-century Middle English poem animates the figure of the Mother of Piety, the Pietà, which had become a popular devotional image that "enhanced the immanent sense of divine presence" in painting and sculpture in fourteenth-century Germany.[33] A beautiful

▲ FIGURE 14.4   The Virgin with the Dead Christ by the Master of Rimini, South Netherlands, ca. 1430: alabaster statue, London, England, Victoria and Albert Museum. Photo: StefenettiE, 13 January 2019, CC-BY-SA-4.0

alabaster sculpture of the Pietà was carved by the Master of Rimini (recently identified as Gilles de Backere) in southern Netherlands in the AD 1430s. Affective devotion created souls receptive to divine vision (see fig. 14.4).

Around AD 1430, a Carthusian monk at the Sheen Charterhouse produced *A Mirror to Devout People,* a companion text to the *Meditationes vitae Christi,* for a nun at the neighboring Birgittine Syon Abbey. In addition to harmonizing the Gospels, *A Mirror* drew on many sources, including Peter Comestor's *Historia scholastica,* Nicholas of Lyre's *Glossa ordinaria,* and revelations of women, including Catherine of Siena, Mechtild of Hackeborn, Elizabeth of Töss, and Birgitta of Sweden.[34] Their revelations and those of other mystics inspired attentive devotion.

Jesus appeared to medieval mystics personally, and they received him kindly. For example, Julian of Norwich prayed for "a bodily sight" and "knowledge of the bodily pains of our savior."[35] In May AD 1373 while severely ill, Julian experienced a series of sixteen showings during which she witnessed Christ's Passion and conversed with him. Over several decades she composed two accounts of "what she believes was revealed to her by God initially through her visions and through subsequent contemplative reflection."[36] By AD 1393 Julian had become an anchoress. She devoted her life to prayer and contemplation enclosed in a small dwelling attached to a church in Norwich where she advised people who came to her for spiritual guidance and comfort.

Julian begins *A Revelation in Love* with her vision of Christ's self-giving love manifest in his crucified face. She witnessed "the red blood trickling down from under the garland hot and afresh and right plenteously" and learned that the embodied suffering and death of Jesus is "the supreme revelation of the love of God."[37] After this painful vision, she "saw that He is to us everything that is good and comfortable for us. He is our clothing, that for love wrappeth us, halsyth (embraces) us, and becloseth us for tender love, that he may never leave us."[38] Christ's "homely loving" clothes humanity with intimate care and protection as God clothed Adam and Eve; Christ's work of salvation on the cross renews God's work of creation.[39]

Julian was surprised to learn that sin is a necessary part of mortal experience, not divine punishment or retribution. Christ assured her that "*Sin is behovely (necessary), but all shall be well, and all shall be well, and all manner of things shall be well.*"[40] Consequently, she learned that Christ's Atonement was not an economic transaction, for God "exacts no price from anyone, directly or vicariously, for nothing is owed."[41] Christ assured Julian, "*It is a joy, a bliss, an endless liking to me that ever I suffered passion for thee.*"[42] Julian reflected that "this is His thirst: a love longing to have us all together whole in Him to His bliss."[43]

Understanding "how Christ hath compassion on us for the cause of sin," expanded Julian's theology of human identity: "I saw that each kind [instinctive or natural] compassion that man hath on his even [fellow] Christian with charity, it is Christ in him."[44] Christ's self-emptying models the divine process of becoming for humanity. She related one poignant conversation when she heard God's tender encouragement amid her mortal misunderstanding, distraction, and vulnerability: "Tenderly our Lord God touches us, and blissfully calleth us saying in our soul: *Let be all thy love, my dearworthy child. Attend to me. I am enough to thee, and enjoy in thy Savior and in thy salvation.*"[45] Julian realized that she will not understand her own soul until she knows God who is "the maker to whom it is oned [at one with]. . . . For our soul sitteth in God in very rest, and our soul stands in God in very strength, and our soul is kindly rooted in God in endless love."[46] After decades of reflection about her visions, Julian realized that they manifest divine love, personally and universally.

> Thus was I learned that love was our Lord's meaning. And I saw full securely, in this and in all, that ere God made us, He loved us, which love was never slaked, no never shall. And in this love He hath done all his works, and in this love He hath made all things profitable to us. And in this love our life is everlasting.[47]

In these revelations and meditations, Julian of Norwich fashions herself as a Christian Everywoman who cultivates a personal relationship with Jesus.

Resurrection: Divine Proximity through Liturgy and Drama

> *Quid quaeritis viventem cum mortuis? Non est hic sed surrexit.*
>
> [Why seek ye the living among the dead? He is not here, but is risen.]
>
> —Luke 24:5–6

Medieval Christians elaborated and expanded the liturgy of ancient Christians to evoke proximity through ritual with God in this life and the life to come.[48] Liturgy structured the individual life cycle and communal calendar. Individuals mapped their lives by participating in salvific sacraments that included by AD 1200 the rites of initiation (Baptism and Confirmation), the Eucharist (Mass), the confession of sins (Penance), the ordination of priests, the anointing of the sick (Extreme Unction), and marriage unions (Matrimony). Special days commemorating Christ's life (including Christmas, Epiphany, Easter, Pentecost) and the lives of saints (exemplary Christians) were celebrated annually. Many clerical communities followed the Divine Office, a daily round of prayers, scripture reading, and hymn singing every few hours.

If "liturgy lay at the heart of medieval religion, the Mass lay at the heart of liturgy."[49] The clergy and congregation gathered to celebrate the "sacrament of the Lord's passion."[50] Archbishop Amalarius of Metz (circa AD 775–850) explained in *On the Liturgy*: "In the sacrament of the bread and wine, and also in my memory, Christ's passion is manifest. He himself said: 'However often you do these things, you will do them in my memory'—that is, however often you bless this bread and this chalice, you remember my birth as a man, and my passion and resurrection."[51] During the late medieval period, while priests officiated the Mass, the laity were instructed to kneel quietly in prayer, to change posture in response to key phrases, and to gaze on the priest's elevation of the Eucharist at the climax of the ceremony with arms raised in divine greeting. John Mirk, a late fourteenth-century canon, provided a prayer for this sacred moment in his *Instructions for Parish Priests*:

> Jesus, lord, welcome thou be,
> In form of bread as I thee see;
> Jesus! for thy holy name,
> Shield me today from sin and shame;
> Shrift and housel [confession and communion],
> lord, thou grant me both,
> Ere that I shall hence go,
> And very contrition of my sin,

That I, lord, never die therein;
And as thou were of a maid born,
Suffer me never to be forlorn,
But when that I shall hence wend,
Grant me the bliss without end. AMEN.[52]

The ceremony of the Mass included divine praise, reading of scripture, confession of sins, and intercession for the needs of living and dead; specific elements would vary according to the liturgical season, feast, or day of the week. Mass was "focused on the event that made all of them possible and meaningful, the consecration which renewed and gave access to the salvation of mankind on Calvary."[53]

By the late Middle Ages, the laity's reverence for this sacramental grace was manifest in their taking responsibility to fund, make, donate, and maintain the sacred environment and objects for the celebration of Mass in their parishes; "They provided the draperies in which they were covered, the images and ornaments and lights which encoded the dedication and functions of the altar and its worship."[54] Contributing to the upkeep of their parish church became a mark of lay piety; men and women were deeply involved in "churchkeeping" as they contributed their homemaking and artisanal skills and made pious bequests in their wills.[55]

Medieval festivals commemorating events in Christ's life were designed for clergy and laity to join together to act their faith with their bodies in liturgical ritual and to establish sympathetic connections with their biblical models.[56] In dramatic rituals, the participants became protagonists in Christian history. For example, during Holy Week, medieval Christians reenacted events of Christ's last week as recounted in the Gospels. They processed on Palm Sunday, washed each others' feet on Maundy Thursday, adored the cross on Good Friday, and opened the empty tomb on Easter morning. Medieval Christians realized that a performance is a mode of becoming that endures beyond the performance in the body and consciousness of the participant.[57]

One example of the dramatic elaboration of Easter Mass occurred in the late tenth century in Winchester. The *Regularis Concordia* drawn up by Bishop Æthelwold includes a dialogue sung antiphonally dramatizing the meeting of the three Marys (Mary Magdalene, Mary the mother of James, and Mary representing Salome) and two angels at Christ's empty tomb on Easter morning, as described in Luke 24:1–8. This Latin dialogue begins with the brother who plays the angel singing, "Whom do you seek?" and the brothers playing the Marys responding, "Jesus of Nazareth." The angels' pronouncement follows, "He is not here; He is risen, just as he had foretold. Go, announce that He has risen from the sepulcher."[58] The liturgical participants were charged, as were the Marys who came bringing spices to the tomb, with the responsibility to witness and announce Christ's Resurrection (see fig. 14.5).

The goal of liturgy—evoking divine presence—was expanded beyond churches to the civic arena when some cities in northern and eastern England organized drama festivals associated with religious holidays. City officials assigned guilds, professional confraternities, to perform a cycle of biblical pageants retelling salvation history from Creation to Doomsday. In York, around fifty mystery plays were performed on pageant wagons during the Feast of Corpus Christi. The guilds would stop their wagons at designated locations along the processional route through the city and perform their play for the townspeople gathered on the side of the road or watching from windows of houses along the route.

The York Resurrection plays highlight personal and political consequences of the Easter liturgy. In one play, scenes of the three Marys visiting Christ's empty tomb are juxtaposed with the realpolitik of Pilate persuading local leaders that Christ's death was legal. Two of the Marys depart to spread news of Christ's Resurrection while Mary Magdalene remains grieving at the tomb. The resurrected Christ tenderly asks Mary Magdalene, "Whom seekst thou this long day?" She does not recognize Jesus until he bares his wounds to her, and she exclaims: "My Lord Jesus, I know now thee."[59] Their dialogue manifests "that recognizing Christ comes from being recognized by him."[60] The

◄ **FIGURE 14.5** *Vistatio Sepulchri* in the Benedictional of St. Æthelwold, written by the scribe Godeman for St. Æthelwold, bishop of
Winchester from 963–984. London, British Library MS Additional
49598, fol. 51v. Photo: Used with permission, British Library

play ends with Mary rejoicing:

> All for joy me likes to sing,
> Mine heart is gladder than the glee,
> And all for joy of thy rising
> That suffered dead upon a tree.
> Of love now is thou crowned king,
> Is none so true living more free.
> Thy love passes all earthly thing,
> Lord, blessed must thou ever be.[61]

In the York Corpus Christi plays, "the dead come to life in the bodies
of the living. It's a description of resurrection—and of theater. . . . It
is a presencing of Christ in the community of the faithful."[62] Resurrection and community in Christ are envisioned and practiced in
devotional performance as well as sacramental ritual.

Conclusion

Hearing the voices of medieval Christians may have evoked a sense of
a kinship and gratitude. Their faith motivated them to transmit sacred
scriptures by hand and to preserve Christian worship, education, and
hospice amid the dynastic political turmoil of their kingdoms. Studying their creative devotion enriches mine. While not every aspect of
medieval Christianity is worthy of emulation, much may be admired.
The lives, work, and art of medieval Christians yield insights about
how Christianity transforms human culture, how ministering in the
Savior's way includes discerning spiritual vocation, how meditating on
Christ's life cultivates a personal relationship with him, and how enact-
ing the drama of salvation anticipates resurrection and communion.

Notes

1. See Diarmaid MacCulloch, *Christianity: The First Three Thousand Years* (New York: Penguin Books, 2009), 231–85. The examples in this chapter are drawn from Western Europe because that is the area I research and teach.

2. I borrow categories and definitions from Lisa Kaaren Bailey, *The Religious Worlds of the Laity in Late Antique Gaul* (London: Bloomsbury Academic, 2016), 1–52. See also Julia Barrow, *The Clergy in the Medieval World: Secular Clerics, Their Families and Careers in North-western Europe, c.800–c.1200* (Cambridge: Cambridge University Press, 2015), 35–52.

3. See Miranda Wilcox, "Narrating Religious Heritage: Apostasy and Restoration," *BYU Studies Quarterly* 60, no. 3 (2021): 213–28.

4. Bede, *Ecclesiastical History of the English People* 5.24, in *The Ecclesiastical History of the English People*, trans. Judith McClure and Robert Collins (Oxford: Oxford University Press, 1994), 293. English translations of *Ecclesiastical History* are taken from this edition translated by McClure and Collins.

5. George Hardin Brown, *A Companion to Bede* (Boydell & Brewer, 2009), 33.

6. See Codex Amiatinus (Florence: Biblioteca Medicea Laurenziana, MS Amiatino 1), https://www.bl.uk/collection-items/codex-amiatinus; Christopher de Hamel, *Meetings with Remarkable Manuscripts: Twelve Journeys into the Medieval World* (New York: Penguin Books, 2016), 54–95.

7. Bede, Homily 9, in *Homilies on the Gospels: Book Two, Lent to The Dedication of the Church*, trans. Lawrence T. Martin and David Hurst (Spencer, MA: Cistercian Publications, 1991), 86–87.

8. Brown, *A Companion to Bede*, 73.

9. Bede, *Ecclesiastical History* 4.24.

10. See "Dream of the Rood," in *Old English Poems of Christ and His Saints*, ed. and trans. Mary Clayton, Dumbarton Oaks Medieval Library (Cambridge, MA: Harvard University Press, 2013), 160–73; Éamonn Ó Carragáin, *Ritual and the Rood: Liturgical Images and the Old English Poems of the Dream of the Rood Tradition* (London: British Library; Toronto: University of

Toronto Press, 2005), xxvi–xxvii.

11. Damien Flemming, "*Jesus*, that is *hælend*: Hebrew Names and the Vernacular Savior in Anglo-Saxon England," *Journal of English and Germanic Philology* 112, no. 1 (2013): 26–47.

12. Ælfric, *Homilies of Ælfric: A Supplementary Collection*, ed. John C. Pope, vol. 359 in the Early English Text Society series (London: Oxford University Press, 1967), 234, lines 91–97; translated by Flemming, "*Jesus*, that is *hælend*," 44.

13. Kevin Madigan, *Medieval Christianity: A New History* (New Haven: Yale University Press, 2015), 148–49. See also Giles Constable, *The Reformation of the Twelfth Century* (Cambridge: Cambridge University Press, 1996).

14. See Walter Simons, *Cities of Ladies: Beguine Movements in the Medieval Low Countries, 1200–1565* (Philadelphia: University of Pennsylvania Press, 2001); Catherine M. Mooney, *Clare of Assisi and the Thirteenth-Century Church* (Philadelphia: University of Pennsylvania Press, 2016), 1–3.

15. Translated and quoted in Mooney, *Clare of Assisi*, 42–43; see also 36–48.

16. MacCulloch, *Christianity*, 396–412.

17. See André Vauchez, *Francis of Assisi: The Life and Afterlife of a Medieval Saint*, trans. Michael F. Cusato (New Haven: Yale University Press, 2021); Mooney, *Clare of Assisi*.

18. Francis of Assisi, *The Testament* 1–3, in *Francis of Assisi: Early Documents*, vol. 1, *The Saint*, ed. Regis J. Armstrong, J. A. Wayne Hellmann, and William J. Short (New York: New City Press, 1999), 124. English translations of *The Testament* are taken from this volume.

19. Vauchez, *Francis of Assisi*, 133.

20. Francis of Assisi, *The Testament* 14, 125.

21. Mooney, *Clare of Assisi*, 4.

22. *Francis and Clare: The Complete Works*, ed. and trans. Ignatius C. Brady and Regis J. Armstrong (New York: Paulist Press, 1982), 226-27. See Mooney, *Clare of Assisi*, 202-12.

23. Mooney, *Clare of Assisi*, 202.

24. Michelle Karnes, "Nicholas Love and Medieval Meditations on Christ," *Speculum* 82, no. 2 (2007): 388.

25. Sarah McNamer, *Affective Meditation and the Invention of Medieval Compassion* (Philadelphia: University of Pennsylvania, 2009), 12.

26. McNamer, *Affective Meditation*, 2.

27. See the preface and introduction in Sarah McNamer, trans., *Meditations on the Life of Christ: The Short Italian Text* (Notre Dame, IN: University of Notre Dame Press, 2018).

28. McNamer, *Meditations on the Life of Christ*, 81–83.

29. McNamer, *Meditations on the Life of Christ*, 113; see also 131.

30. McNamer, *Meditations on the Life of Christ*, 149.

31. Karen Saupe, ed., *Middle English Marian Lyrics*, TEAMS Middle English Texts Series (Kalamazoo, MI: Medieval Institute Publications, 1998), 12. For example, see McNamer, *Meditations on the Life of Christ*, 137: "Now imagine the sorrow that the mother of Lord Jesus must have felt seeing him so afflicted."

32. "Of alle women that ever were borne," in *Middle English Marian Lyrics*, no. 42, lines 1–8. The Middle English spelling has been modernized.

33. William Forsyth, *The Pietà in French Late Gothic Sculpture: Regional Varieties* (New York: Metropolitan Museum of Art, 1995), 17; see also 17–19.

34. Paul J. Patterson, "Translation Debates and Lay Accessibility in the *Meditationes Vitae Christi* and Middle English Lives of Christ," in *Illuminating Jesus in the Middle Ages*, edited by Jane Beal (Leiden: Brill, 2019), 319–23.

35. Julian of Norwich, *The Shewings of Julian of Norwich*, ed. Georgia Ronan Crampton, TEAMS Middle English Text Series (Kalamazoo, Michigan: Medieval Institute Publications, 1994), ch. 2, lines 48-49, p. 39. The Middle English spelling has been modernized.

36. Philip Sheldrake, *Julian of Norwich: "in God's Sight" Her Theology in Context* (Malden, MA: Wiley-Blackwell, 2018), 108.

37. Julian of Norwich, *Shewings*, ch. 4, lines 114–15, p. 42; Sheldrake, *Julian of Norwich*, 109.

38. Julian of Norwich, *Shewings*, ch. 5, lines 143–47, p. 43.

39. Sheldrake, *Julian of Norwich*, 104–17.

40. Julian of Norwich, *Shewings*, ch. 27, lines 937–38, p. 72. Italicized text indicates Christ's direct speech to Julian.

41. Denys Turner, *Julian of Norwich: Theologian* (New Haven: Yale University Press, 2011), 212–13.

42. Julian of Norwich, *Shewings*, ch. 31, lines 1049–50, p. 76.

43. Julian of Norwich, *Shewings*, ch. 31, lines 1038–39, p. 76.

44. Julian of Norwich, *Shewings*, ch. 28, lines 963–65, 978-80, p. 73.

45. Julian of Norwich, *Shewings*, ch. 36, lines 1236–37, p. 82.

46. Julian of Norwich, *Shewings*, ch. 56, lines 2290, 2298–99, p. 117.

47. Julian of Norwich, *Shewings*, ch. 86, lines 3407–11, p. 155.

48. See *Oxford Research Encyclopedias: Religion*, s.v. "Medieval Christian Liturgy," by Joanne M. Pierce, May 9, 2016, https://doi.org/10.1093/acrefore/9780199340378.013.84.

49. Eamon Duffy, *The Stripping of the Altars: Traditional Religion in England, 1400–1580* (New Haven: Yale University Press, 1992), 92; see also chapter 3, "The Mass."

50. Amalar of Metz, *On the Liturgy*, vol. 1, ed. and trans. Eric Knibbs, Dumbarton Oaks Medieval Library (Cambridge, MA: Harvard University Press, 2014), 5.

51. Amalar of Metz, *On the Liturgy*, vol. 2, 169–71. See 1 Corinthians 11:24–25.

52. John Mirk, *Instructions for Parish Priests*, ed. E. Peacock and F. J. Furnivall, vol. 31 in the Early English Books series (1868; repr., London, 1902), 9–10, lines 290–301. The Middle English spelling has been modernized.

53. Duffy, *Stripping of the Altars*, 119.

54. Duffy, *Stripping of the Altars*, 114, 132–35.

55. See Katherine L. French, *The People of the Parish: Community Life in a Late Medieval English Diocese* (Philadelphia: University of Pennsylvania Press, 2001); *The Good Women of the Parish: Gender and Religion After the Black Death* (Philadelphia: University of Pennsylvania Press, 2008).

56. See M. Bradford Bedingfield, *The Dramatic Liturgy of Anglo-Saxon England* (Woodbridge: Boydell Press, 2002), 1–11.

57. See Jill Stevenson, *Performance, Cognition, and Devotional Culture: Sensual Piety in Late Medieval York* (New York: Palgrave MacMillan, 2010), 2.

58. Thomas Symons, ed. and trans., *Regularis Concordia Anglicae nationis monachorum sanctimonialiumque: The Monastic Agreement of the Monks and Nuns of the English Nation* (New York: Oxford University Press, 1953), 50. See also Bedingfield, *Dramatic Liturgy*, 156–70.

59. "Christ's Appearance to Mary Magdalene," lines 26, 80, in *The York Plays*, ed. Richard Beadle (London: Edward Arnold, 1982), 356, 358. The Middle English spelling has been modernized.

60. Sarah Beckwith, *Signifying God: Social Relation and Symbolic Act in the York Corpus Christi Plays* (Chicago: University of Chicago Press, 2001), 85.

61. "Christ's Appearance to Mary Magdalene," lines 134–41, p. 359.

62. Beckwith, *Signifying God*, 72.

CONTRIBUTORS

DANIEL BECERRA is an Assistant Professor of Ancient Scripture at Brigham Young University in Provo, UT, and is a scholar of early Christianity. He holds secondary specialties in New Testament and in Greco-Roman philosophy. He received a PhD in religion (early Christianity) and an MA in religious studies from Duke University, a MTS in New Testament/early Christianity from Harvard Divinity School, and a BA in ancient Near Eastern studies from Brigham Young University. His primary research interests concern moral formation in Late Antiquity (ca. 2nd–7th centuries CE), particularly within Christian ascetic contexts. He also researches topics relating to theology and ethics in the Book of Mormon.

ARIEL BYBEE LAUGHTON is an independent historian and writer living in Houston, Texas. She holds a BA in History from Brigham Young University and both an MA and PhD in Religion from Duke University. Laughton has published research on women and gender in early Christianity, the rise of asceticism, historical theologies of atonement, and heresiology in Late Antiquity. She is currently writing about gender and dress ethics in the Book of Mormon.

JASON R. COMBS is an Assistant Professor of Ancient Scripture at Brigham Young University in Provo, UT. He holds a bachelor's degree in Near Eastern Studies from Brigham Young University, master's degrees in Biblical Studies from Yale Divinity School and in Classics from Columbia University, as well as a PhD in Religious Studies with an emphasis on the history of early Christianity from the University of North Carolina at Chapel Hill. Combs has published research for an academic audience as well as for a general Latter-day Saint audience on the literary and cultural contexts of canonical and apocryphal gospels, the textual transmission of gospels, and the history of visions and dreams.

MARK D. ELLISON is an Associate Professor of Ancient Scripture at Brigham Young University. He earned bachelor's and master's degrees from BYU, a master's degree in Religious Studies (Bible and Archaeology) from the University of South Florida, and a master's and PhD in Early Christianity and Early Christian Art from Vanderbilt University. His publications for academic audiences examine artifacts and texts in the exploration of early Christian socioreligious history, with particular interest in marriage, households, worship, and ritual. For Latter-day Saint audiences, he has published on aspects of religious belief and practice in the New Testament, Christian tradition, the Book of Mormon, and Latter-day Saint history.

NICHOLAS J. FREDERICK is an Associate Professor of Ancient Scripture at Brigham Young University in Provo, UT. He holds a bachelor's degree in Classics from Brigham Young University, a master's degree in Comparative Studies also from Brigham Young University, and a PhD in the History of Christianity with an emphasis in Mormon Studies from Claremont Graduate University. Frederick's research primarily revolves around the intertextual relationship between the Bible and Mormon scripture.

CATHERINE GINES TAYLOR is the Hugh W. Nibley Postdoctoral Fellow at the Neal A. Maxwell Institute for Religious Scholarship. She specializes in late antique Christian art history and iconography. Dr. Taylor holds graduate degrees in art history from the University of Manchester (PhD) and Brigham Young University (MA and BA). Her scholarship is focused on the interdisciplinary study of art, scripture, lay piety, Christian patronage, and patristic texts. More specifically, her research centers on images of women in early Christian contexts. Her monograph on the iconography of the Annunciation was published by Brill in 2018. Additionally, she edited *Material Culture and Women's Religious Experience in Antiquity*, published by Lexington Books, with Mark Ellison and Carolyn Osiek in 2021. Dr. Taylor's current research investigates the typologies of Wisdom on sarcophagi in late ancient Gaul and within comparative funerary contexts.

MATTHEW J. GREY is a Professor of Ancient Scripture and an affiliate faculty member of the ancient Near Eastern studies program at Brigham Young University. He has a BA in Near Eastern studies from Brigham Young University, an MA in archaeology and the history of antiquity from Andrews University, an MSt in Jewish studies from the University of Oxford, and a PhD in ancient Mediterranean religions (with an emphasis on archaeology and the history of ancient Judaism) from the University of North Carolina at Chapel Hill. His areas of research include the archaeology and social history of Roman Palestine, sacred space and ritual in ancient Judaism and early Christianity, and the experience of cultural minority groups (such as Judeans and Jesus followers) in the Roman world. Since 2011, he has also been an area supervisor over the synagogue excavations at the ancient Jewish village of Huqoq in Israel's Galilee region.

KRISTIAN S. HEAL is a scholar of early Syriac Christianity with interests in the reception of the Bible, homiletics, poetry, manuscripts, and the history and transmission of Syriac literature. He took a bachelor's degree in Jewish Studies from University College London, a master's degree in Syriac Studies from the University of Oxford, and a PhD in Theology from the University of Birmingham. He has published broadly on early Syriac literature and is the author or editor of six books. Kristian is currently a Research Fellow at the Neal A. Maxwell Institute for Religious Scholarship at Brigham Young University.

D. JILL KIRBY is an Associate Professor of Religious Studies at Edgewood College in Madison, WI. She holds a bachelor of science degree from the United States Military Academy at West Point, NY and master's degrees from the University of Arizona, in Tucson, and the University of Maryland, in College Park. She also taught physics at the United States Military Academy from 1991 to 1994 and retired from the U.S. Army in 1981. Kirby's specialties are in apocalyptic literature and the intersection of science and religion.

CECILIA M. PEEK is an Associate Professor of Classical Studies and the coordinator of the Ancient Near Eastern Studies program at Brigham Young University in Provo, UT. She holds a bachelor's degree in Classics from Brigham Young University, and a master's degree and PhD in Ancient History and Mediterranean Archaeology from the University of California, Berkeley. Peek has published on Hellenistic and Roman history, specifically on the career of Cleopatra VII. She has also published on New Testament topics for Latter-day Saint audiences.

GAYE STRATHEARN is a Professor of Ancient Scripture at Brigham Young University and currently serves as an associate dean in Religious Education. She holds a bachelor's degree in Physical Therapy from the University of Queensland, both bachelor's and master's degrees in Near Eastern Studies from Brigham Young University, and a PhD in Religion with an emphasis in New Testament and Christian Origins from Claremont Graduate University. Her research interests focus mainly on Biblical and early Christian topics for Latter-day Saint audiences. She is currently working on an edited volume on the Sabbath day.

THOMAS A. WAYMENT is a Professor of Classics in the Department of Comparative Arts and Letters at Brigham Young University in Provo, UT. He earned his PhD in New Testament Studies from the Claremont Graduate University (2000) and has taught at BYU for the past 20 years. His research focuses on the intersection of textual production and community formation with particular emphasis on the way communities create and adopt literary texts. Much of his work engages the dynamics of early Christian networks as evidenced through literary and documentary papyri. He has also focused on the scribal culture evidenced in the production of New Testament manuscripts.

MIRANDA WILCOX is an associate professor of English and holds a MMS and PhD in Medieval Studies from the University of Notre Dame. Her research focuses on early medieval religious culture in Western Europe, particularly the practices of professing faith and versifying scriptural narratives. She also writes about Latter-day Saint historical consciousness and identity formation. She co-edits the Living Faith book series published by the Maxwell Institute for Religious Scholarship.

✳ INDEX ✳

deacons, 98–100, 105, 111–12, 151–52, 154, 168, 454, 507
 See also women, deacons
death, 216, 253, 255, 267, 270, 347, 352
 after (*see* afterlife)
 caring for (the dead), 401–3
 Fall, as consequence of, 277–78, 314, 334, 355
 eternal progress, as step in, 384–87, 446
 as reality, 398–400, 424–25
 work for (the dead), 396–97, 401–4, 407, 410–11, 417–25
degrees of glory. *See* afterlife
Didache, 198, 201, 218, 343, 347
Deification. *See* God (Godhead; Deity), becoming like
docetism, 293–94, 300
Doctrine and Covenants, 10, 12, 79, 228
 See also SCRIPTURE INDEX
domus ecclesiae. See sacred space
Dura Europos, Syria, 156–57, 213–14, 216

E

Easter Sunday, 34, 36, 53, 214, 524–25
Eastern Orthodox, 179, 210, 226, 313
Eastern Roman Empire, 120, 381
Eden. *See* Garden of Eden
Edessa, Syria, 33, 41, 458
Egeria (active ca. AD 381–384), 32–37, 40–41, 58, 176, 198, 207, 214
elders, 100, 111–14, 154, 157, 160, 454
 See also presbyter
Elijah, 12–13
England, 4, 508–509, 525
Ephrem the Syrian (ca. AD 306–373), 205, 211–12, 460–63
Epiphany. *See* Holy Week

Epistle of Barnabas, 343, 364, 501
Epistles of Clement. See Clement of Rome
eschatology, 347, 418, 472–77, 482, 493–95
 as allegory, 488–91
 as literal, 485–88
 of New Testament, 477–82
eternal life. *See* afterlife
Eucharist, 37, 113–14, 116, 152, 154, 156, 168, 172–79, 214, 221–33, 346–47, 523
Euodia (first century AD), 103
Eusebius of Caesarea (ca. AD 260–339), 3–5, 17–18, 65, 159, 175–76, 191, 240, 498
Eutyches (ca. AD 378–454), 307–10, 325
Evagrius of Pontus (ca. AD 345–399), 126, 382
Eve, 215, 217, 251
 depictions of, 258, 261, 276, 314, 346, 348, 440
 Fall of (*see* Fall of Adam and Eve)

F

faith, 27, 68, 143, 158, 172, 197, 199, 208–9, 211–14, 219, 232, 239, 252, 334, 340, 347, 358, 377, 379, 401, 407, 413–14, 420, 422, 441, 524, 527
Faith, Rule of. *See* Rule of Faith
Fall of Adam and Eve, 48, 217, 253–63, 267–71, 275–80, 358, 378, 380
family, 101, 108, 112, 116, 121–22, 126, 129, 143, 145, 148–49, 153, 158, 160, 179, 274, 370, 380, 400–1, 404, 410–11, 420, 425, 448, 506
 See also husbands and fathers; wives and mothers; children (sons and daughters)

New Testament (*continued*)

   eschatology (*see* eschatology, New Testament, of,)

   as historical source, 198

   limits of, 373, 456

   readership of, 152

   as scripture, 343, 347, 352, 373, 417

   women, accounts of, 100–7, 111

   See also SCRIPTURE INDEX

Nicene Council. *See* Councils, Nicaea (first)

Nicene Creed, 299, 301–5

   See also Councils

Niceno-Constantinopolitan Creed, 301, 303–4, 307, 309, 312, 319–20

   See also Councils

Nympha (first century AD), 107, 129, 152

O

Oaks, Dallin H. (Latter-day Saint leader), 10, 128–29, 356

obedience, 31, 34, 120, 259, 345, 352, 357–58, 400

Odes of Solomon, 456–58, 460

offerings

   dead, on behalf of, 404, 410,

   sacrifice, 177, 347, 354

   as tithes, 121, 169

offices of the Church, 30, 97–138, 154, 175–6

   See also apostles; deacons; elders; bishops; presbyter; women

Old Testament, 40–43, 52, 77, 80, 142, 226, 250–51, 292, 335, 337, 340, 352

   See also SCRIPTURE INDEX

Olympias (ca. AD 361–408), 127

ordinances (sacraments), 233–234

   See also baptism; confirmation;

Eucharist; marriage

orders (religious), 514, 516–17

organization of the Church. *See* offices of the Church; church (early/ancient), leadership structure of

Origen of Alexandria (ca. AD 385–254), 93, 252, 316, 351, 378, 382

   and allegorization of eschatology, 490–491

   on eternal progression, 384–86

   on humanity and the fall, 264–74

   and scriptural interpretation, 46–51, 82–83

   See also preexistence

original sin. *See* Augustine, original sin

P

paganism, 31, 83, 100, 298, 315, 339, 400–1, 508

Pantaenus (died ca. AD 200), 83, 499

papacy, 6, 9

Papias, bishop of Hierapolis (ca. AD 60–130), 498

Parentalia, 404, 420

Parousia, 477–79

   See also Jesus Christ, Second Coming of

Passover, 52–55, 223, 352

Paul (Saul of Tarsus, first century AD)

   on apostasy, 6

   on baptism, 214–15, 420–21

   and canon, 68–69

   and gender roles, 110, 121

   on Godhead, 292

   on grace, 330–35, 358–59

   and preaching, 27–29

   and purgatory 446–47

   on resurrection, 417–18, 449, 457

   on the Second Coming, 477–78

patristics, 9, 19

SCRIPTURE INDEX

OLD TESTAMENT

BOOK OF MORMON

DOCTRINE AND COVENANTS

124:38–41, 14, 180
124:39–42, 228
128:15, 228, 397
128:16, 228
128:17, 16, 21, 228
128:18, 14, 228

128:20, 12
128:21, 12
130:22, 79, 318
137:5, 12
137:9–10, 221
138:18, 342

138:20–22, 447
138:23, 342
138:25–34, 447
138:35, 447
138:50–52, 447
138:53–56, 273

PEARL OF GREAT PRICE

Moses
2:27, 256
3:5, 273
4:1–4, 273
5:16–25, 255
6:51, 273
7:18, 10

Abraham
3:22–26, 273, 312

Joseph Smith–History
1:17, 13
1:19, 11
1:38–39, 16

Articles of Faith
1:1, 293
1:6, 101
1:7, 293